Regulating a Thousand Cuts

GLOBAL LAW AND POLICY SOLUTIONS TO CUMULATIVE ENVIRONMENTAL PROBLEMS

REBECCA L. NELSON
University of Melbourne

CAMBRIDGE
UNIVERSITY PRESS

CAMBRIDGE
UNIVERSITY PRESS

Shaftesbury Road, Cambridge CB2 8EA, United Kingdom

One Liberty Plaza, 20th Floor, New York, NY 10006, USA

477 Williamstown Road, Port Melbourne, VIC 3207, Australia

314–321, 3rd Floor, Plot 3, Splendor Forum, Jasola District Centre, New Delhi – 110025, India

103 Penang Road, #05–06/07, Visioncrest Commercial, Singapore 238467

Cambridge University Press is part of Cambridge University Press & Assessment, a department of the University of Cambridge.

We share the University's mission to contribute to society through the pursuit of education, learning and research at the highest international levels of excellence.

www.cambridge.org
Information on this title: www.cambridge.org/9781316515105

DOI: 10.1017/9781009091930

First published 2025

Cover image: Recycle / LockieCurrie / E+ / Getty Images

A catalogue record for this publication is available from the British Library

Library of Congress Cataloging-in-Publication Data
NAMES: Nelson, Rebecca (Law teacher) author
TITLE: Regulating a thousand cuts : global law and policy solutions to cumulative environmental problems / Rebecca Nelson, University of Melbourne.
DESCRIPTION: Cambridge, United Kingdom ; New York, NY : Cambridge University Press, 2025. | Includes bibliographical references and index.
IDENTIFIERS: LCCN 2025011597 (print) | LCCN 2025011598 (ebook) | ISBN 9781316515105 hardback | ISBN 9781009095952 paperback | ISBN 9781009091930 epub
SUBJECTS: LCSH: Environmental impact analysis–Law and legislation | Environmental law, International | Environmental protection
CLASSIFICATION: LCC K3585 .N45 2025 (print) | LCC K3585 (ebook) | DDC 344.04/6–dc23/eng/20250318
LC record available at https://lccn.loc.gov/2025011597
LC ebook record available at https://lccn.loc.gov/2025011598

ISBN 978-1-316-51510-5 Hardback

To my family

Contents

Figures

Tables

Preface

Almost fifteen years ago, I was a doctoral student zigzagging some 3,000 miles across the western United States in a campervan, husband and three-month-old daughter in tow, interviewing water agency officials about groundwater law. The idea for this book was first inspired by their observations. The comment that I heard again and again went along the lines of "It's the cumulative impacts of groundwater pumping that are a big deal for us. Gosh, it would be good to have a better approach to that." It was not just the frequency of that comment that was striking, or the fact that I went on to hear the very same thing from officials in Australia, too. It was the reverberations of that same problem across very different environmental contexts. Cumulative impacts were a major concern for biodiversity, for climate change, for human health – for so many things that we value about our environment. Not only would it be useful to many different environmental settings to have a better way to deal with cumulative impacts but the wisdom collected across those settings could also surely help inform initiatives in other places and contexts.

Cumulative impacts are sneaky. Many diverse small harms aggregate with large ones, often over a long period of time, and in our legal blind spots – or in spots of willful blindness. To best address cumulative environmental problems, then, the design of laws and other formal rules needs to respond to why it is difficult to address these problems (what makes them sneaky?), while being alert to weaknesses in typical laws.

Accumulations of harm or risk also lie at the center of concerns about disproportionate impacts on populations who have fewer resources to deal with them, from Canada's First Nations fighting against cumulative impacts to caribou, to the aggregate climate vulnerabilities that affect coastal populations in South Asia. Dealing with cumulative environmental problems then is not just a question of what we care about, but who we care about, and our responsibilities to each other.

*

If I could construct this book in a three-dimensional shape, I would make it a series of bridges crossing boundaries between disciplines, jurisdictions, and parts of our natural world. Powering that construction would be the conviction that despite the massive and intractable environmental problems that we face, lawyers who want to address those problems can benefit immensely from gazing across these boundaries.

Crossing disciplinary boundaries is a deeply held objective for me. It sprouted as I studied for my undergraduate degrees in law and environmental engineering at the University of Melbourne. It grew when I practiced as an environmental and resources lawyer in a private firm and in a government agency, working with scientists and engineers across diverse environmental areas. Stanford Law School's social science–infused vision of law and the interdisciplinary Stanford Woods Institute for the Environment nurtured those aspirations further when I was a master's and JSD (Doctor of the Science of Law) student.

But the seed of those boundary-spanning aspirations formed much earlier, in practicing cultural boundary-crossing as the child of parents from a small southern Italian village and a small Midwestern US town, myself growing up in a large Australian city. Love of languages, from the Italian of home to the French, Chinese, Latin, and German of school and university certainly also contributed. These cultural and linguistic backgrounds have also informed and benefited the case studies of this book.

Professionally, in the almost twenty years since I finished my first law degree, I have reveled in working in diverse contexts, gaining diverse perspectives, working with agencies and nonprofits where I work closely with those of different disciplinary views and traditions – from ecologists to Indigenous knowledge-holders to economists. I have had most of these experiences in Western countries as a non-Indigenous person. Where I have worked in the context of lower-income countries, I have done so from a position of privilege. That much of my practical and scholarly experience has been in Western contexts with a rule of law tradition doubtless shapes the perspectives I share in this book, which stem from the belief that law is not (or not merely) performative; it is an essential tool that can make a difference.

Acknowledgments

Though it seems to buck the orthodox trend of sequencing in acknowledgments, there is no group of people more important to thank than my family. It is not easy to reduce to words on a flat page their support, inspiration, and love. There is also no font that captures it – I know, I've looked.

*

I owe many colleagues many thanks for the discussions and "aha" moments that have informed my thinking on the subject matter of this book. Parallel with this book, I have worked on other projects that have helped inform this work. For that, I thank Debra Perrone, L. M. Shirley, Rod Marsh, Pete Dupen, Martine Maron, Dru Marsh, Debbie Medaris, and Rebecca Spindler. Federica Cittadino, Elisabeth Alber, Philippa England, Revel Pointon, Debra Perrone, and Nícola Ulibarrí have lent expert insights into their jurisdictional contexts in a way that was invaluable for the case studies.

I am also grateful for the thoughts of attendees of seminars and conferences at which I have presented portions of this book, including attendees of the Melbourne Law School's Faculty Research Seminar Series, the Frontiers in Environmental Law Colloquium, the Environment Institute of Australia and New Zealand Annual Conference, the Engineers Australia Hydrology and Water Resources Symposium, the International Union for the Conservation of Nature Academy of Environmental Law Colloquium, the Australian Land Conservation Alliance Conference, the Sant'Anna Legal Studies Program, the Eurac Research Institute for Comparative Federalism, the International Society of Public Law Annual Conference, and the Law and Society Association of Australia and New Zealand.

I am enormously fortunate to be part of an institution that attracts postgraduate law students from around the world. Over the years, too many to name have generously shared their knowledge of their home countries' laws with me, especially the students of my Water Law and Natural Resources Management class and my PhD advisees, who are respected judges, practicing lawyers, and policy practitioners in their respective jurisdictions. I heartily thank the students who have directly undertaken research assistance for this book – Jack Brookes, Isaac Gillespie-Hortop, Timothy Gilling, José Manuel Cortes Leighton, Selina Li, Malavika Hosahally Narayana, L. M. Shirley, Lucas Volfneuk, Alli Whitmore, Nuria Yu, Joseph Zivny, and the Melbourne Law School Academic Research Service for the coordinating assistance and expert eyes of Louise Ellis and Kirsty Wilson – for these excellent contributions. Without their work, it would have been difficult to achieve the geographic representation of laws to which the book aspires. Portions of Chapter 3 derive from an article coauthored with L. M. Shirley, "The Transformational Potential of Cumulative Environmental Effects Concepts as 'Spotlight' and 'Lighthouse' in National and International Laws" (2023) 12(1) *Transnational Environmental Law* 150–174. Portions of the discussions on coordination in Chapters 2 and 7 derive from a published book chapter, Rebecca L. Nelson, "Victims and Villains: Cities and the Environment on the Constitutional Stage" in Erika Arban (ed), *Cities in Federal Constitutional Theory* (Oxford University Press, 2022) 161–179. Thanks also to Amanda Belton, Mar Quiroga, and Sama Hosseini for their expert assistance with figures; and to my word-processing wizards, Olivia, Leo and Silvia Nelson Smith.

Special thanks to my amazing feedback group of Stanford alumnae, especially A. R. Siders, Nícola Ulibarrí, and Amanda Cravens, for their weekly injections of interdisciplinary wisdom (A. R. Siders, Cassandra M. Brooks, Amanda E. Cravens, Rebecca L. Nelson, Dan R. Reineman and Nicola Ulibarri, "How to Beat Isolation? Academic Feedback Groups Fit the Bill, and Promote Growth as Scholars and Humans" (2020) 582 *Nature* 597–598).

Wonderful colleagues have generously given their thoughts on parts of this work and who I have not already mentioned – thank you Bruce Lindsay, John Howe, and Christine Parker. And even though we didn't have the chance to talk about the book, I am grateful for the years of wisdom, wit, and confidence-instilling mentorship of the late Professor Sandy Clark AM.

I gratefully acknowledge funding for this work received from the Australian Research Council (#DE180101154), the University of Melbourne, the Melbourne Law School, and the Institute for Comparative Federalism at Eurac Research, which generously hosted my research visit in South Tyrol as the 2020 Federal Scholar in Residence.

Finally, I acknowledge that this book is a product of living, learning, and working on the unceded traditional lands of the Wurundjeri People of the Kulin Nation, and I pay my respects to Elders past, present, and emerging.

Table of Treaties and Legislation

TREATIES

1972

Convention Concerning the Protection of the World Cultural and Natural Heritage, November 16, 1972, Paris, in force December 17, 1975, 1037 U.N.T.S. 151

1979

Convention on the Conservation of European Wildlife and Natural Habitats, September 19, 1979, Bern, in force June 6, 1982, E.T.S. 104

1982

United Nations Convention on the Law of the Sea, December 10, 1982, in force November 16, 1994, 1833 U.N.T.S. 396

1991

Convention on Environmental Impact Assessment in a Transboundary Context, February 25, 1991, Espoo, in force September 10, 1997, 1989 U.N.T.S. 309

Protocol on Environmental Protection to the Antarctic Treaty, October 4, 1991, Madrid, in force January 14, 1998, 30 I.L.M. 1461

Convention of the Protection of the Alps (Alpine Convention), November 7, 1991, Salzburg, in force March 6, 1995, [1996] OJ L61/32

1992

Convention on the Protection of the Marine Environment of the Baltic Sea Area April 9, 1992, Helsinki, in force January 17, 2000, 2099 U.N.T.S. 195

United Nations Framework Convention on Climate Change, May 9, 1992, New York, in force March 21, 1994, 1771 U.N.T.S. 107

Convention on Biological Diversity, June 5, 1992, Rio de Janeiro, in force December 29, 1993, 1760 U.N.T.S. 79

1994

Protocol on the Implementation of the 1991 Alpine Convention in the Field of Mountain Farming, December 20, 1994, Chambéry, in force December 18, 2002, [2006] OJ L 271/63

Protocol on the Implementation of the Alpine Convention of 1991 Relating to Nature Protection and Landscape Conservation, December 20, 1994, Chambéry, in force December 18, 2002

1998

Convention on Access to Information, Public Participation in Decision-Making and Access to Justice in Environmental Matters Aarhus, June 25, 1998, in force October 30, 2001, 2161 U.N.T.S. 447

2002

Black Sea Biodiversity and Landscape Conservation Protocol to the Convention on the Protection of the Black Sea against Pollution June 14, 2002, Sofia, in force June 20, 2011

2015

Paris Agreement under the United Nations Framework Convention on Climate Change, December 12, 2015, in force November 4, 2016, 3156 U.N.T.S. 79

2018

Regional Agreement on Access to Information, Public Participation, and Justice in Environmental Matters in Latin America and the Caribbean March 4, 2018, Escazú, in force April 22, 2021

REGIONAL: EUROPEAN (PARLT, COUNCIL OF EUROPE)

Consolidated version of the Treaty on the Functioning of the European Union [2016] OJ C202/1

Council Directive 92/43/EEC of May 21, 1992, conservation of natural habitats and of wild fauna and flora [1992] OJ L206/7, as amended

Council of Europe Landscape Convention, October 20, 2000, Florence, in force March 1, 2004, E.T.S. 176

Directive 2001/42/EC of the European Parliament and of the Council of June 27, 2001, on the assessment of the effects of certain plans and programmes on the environment [2001] OJ L197/30, as amended

Directive 2008/56/EC of the European Parliament and of the Council of June 17, 2008, establishing a framework for community action in the field of marine environmental policy [2008] OJ L164/19

Directive 2009/147/EC of the European Parliament and of the Council of November 30, 2009, on the conservation of wild birds [2010] OJ L20/7, as amended

Directive 2011/92/EU of the European Parliament and of the Council of December 13, 2011, on the assessment of the effects of certain public and private projects on the environment [2012] OJ L26/1, as amended

Directive 2014/52/EU of the European Parliament and Council of April 16, 2014, amending Directive 2011/92/EU on the assessment of the effects of certain public and private projects on the environment [2014] OJ L124/1

Directive 2018/2001 of the European Parliament and of the Council of December 11, 2018, on the promotion of the use of energy from renewable sources [2018] OJ L328/82, as amended

Regulation 1367/2006 of the European Parliament and of the Council of September 6, 2006, on the application of the provisions of the Aarhus Convention on Access to Information, Public Participation in Decision-making and Access to Justice in Environmental Matters to Community institutions and bodies [2006] OJ L264/13

Regulation (EU) 1151/2012 of the European Parliament and of the Council of November 21, 2012 on quality schemes for agricultural products and foodstuffs [2012] OJ 343/1 (now repealed)

Regulation 2021/2115 of the European Parliament and of the Council of December 2, 2021, establishing rules on support for strategic plans to be drawn up by Member States under the common agricultural policy (CAP Strategic Plans) and financed by the European Agricultural Guarantee

Fund (EAGF) and by the European Agricultural Fund for Rural Development (EAFRD) and repealing Regulations (EU) No 1305/2013 and (EU) No 1307/2013 [2021] OJ L435/1, as amended

Regulation (EU) 2023/1984 of the European Parliament and of the Council of September 13, 2023, on the deployment of alternative fuels infrastructure [2023] OJ L234/1

Regulation (EU) 2024/1143 of the European Parliament and of the Council of 11 April 2024 on geographical indications for wine, spirit drinks and agricultural products, as well as traditional specialities guaranteed and optional quality terms for agricultural products, amending Regulations (EU) No 1308/2013, (EU) 2019/787 and (EU) 2019/1753 and repealing Regulation (EU) No 1151/2012 [2024] OJ L 2024/1143

Regulation (EU) 2024/1991 of the European Parliament and of the Council of June 24, 2024, on nature restoration and amending Regulation (EU) 2022/869 [2024] OJ L 2024/1991

INDIVIDUAL COUNTRIES

Angola

Decreto Presidencial n. 117/20 Regulamento Geral de Avaliação de Impacte Ambiental e do Procedimento de Licenciamento Ambiental [Presidential Decree No. 117/20 General Regulation for Environmental Impact Assessment and Environmental Licensing Procedure] 2020

Australia

Commonwealth

Basin Plan 2012

Carbon Credits (Carbon Farming Initiative) Act 2011

Clean Energy Finance Corporation Act 2012

Environment Protection and Biodiversity Conservation Act 1999

Environment Protection and Biodiversity Conservation Amendment Act 2013

Great Barrier Reef Marine Park Act 1975

Great Barrier Reef Marine Park Regulations 2019

Great Barrier Reef Marine Park Zoning Plan 2003

National Greenhouse and Energy Reporting Act 2007

Nature Repair Act 2023
Northern Australia Infrastructure Facility Act 2016
Regional Investment Corporation Act 2018
Water Act 2007
Water Regulations 2008

Intergovernmental
Great Barrier Reef Intergovernmental Agreement 1979, Commonwealth of Australia and the State of Queensland
Great Barrier Reef Intergovernmental Agreement 2009, Commonwealth of Australia and the State of Queensland
Murray-Darling Basin Agreement, set out in Water Act 2007 (Australia) Sch 1

Queensland
Environmental Offsets Act 2014
Environmental Protection Act 1994
Environmental Protection Regulation 2019
Great Barrier Reef Protection Amendment Act 2009
Human Rights Act 2019
Land Act 1994
Planning Act 2016
Planning Regulation 2017
Mineral Resources Act 1989
State Development and Public Works Organisation Act 1971
Vegetation Management Act 1999
Vegetation Management (Regrowth Clearing Moratorium) Act 2009
Water Act 2000

South Australia
Planning, Development and Infrastructure Act 2016
Wilderness Protection Act 1992

Victoria
Commissioner for Environmental Sustainability Act 2003
Environment Protection Act 2017
Water Act 1989
Yarra River Protection (Wilip-gin Birrarung murron) Act 2017

Western Australia
Rights in Water and Irrigation Act 1914

Bhutan

Constitution of the Kingdom of Bhutan 2008

Brazil

Decreto n° 11.367, de 1° de janeiro de 2023 [Presidential Decree No. 11,637 of January 1, 2023]

Canada

Nisga'a Nation Harvest Agreement between Canada, British Columbia and the Nisga'a Nation, in force May 11, 2000
Canadian Environmental Protection Act 1999
Fishery (General) Regulations, SOR/93-53
Impact Assessment Act 2019

Chile

Ley sobre Bases Generales del Medio Ambiente, Ley No. 19300 [Law on the General Bases of the Environment, Law No. 19300], 1994, as amended
Código de Aguas [Water Code], Decreto con Fuerza de Ley [Decree with the Force of Law] No. 1122, 1981, as amended

China

Air Pollution Control (Vehicle Design Standards) (Emission) Regulations 1992, Cap. 311 sub. leg. J, as amended (Hong Kong SAR)

Germany

Grundgesetz für die Bundesrepublik Deutschland [Basic Law for the Federal Republic of Germany] (Constitution) 1949, as amended

Greece

Νόμος Αριθ. 4014 (2011) Περιβαλλοντική αδειοδότηση έργων και δραστηριοτήτων, ρύθμιση αυθαιρέτων σε συνάρτηση με τη δημιουργία περιβαλλοντικού ισοζυγίου και άλλες διατάξεις της αρμοδιότητας του Υπουργείου Περιβάλλοντος [Law No. 4014 (2011) on Environmental Licensing of Works and Activities, Regulation of Illegal Constructions in Connection with Environmental Stability and Other Provisions Falling Under the Competence of the Ministry of Environment], as amended

India

National

Air (Prevention and Control of Pollution) Act 1981, as amended
Biological Diversity Act 2002
Biological Diversity (Amendment) Act 2023
Biological Diversity Rules 2024

Andhra Pradesh

Andhra Pradesh Water, Land and Trees Act 2002

Indonesia

Peraturan Pemerintah Republik Indonesia nomor 22 tahun 2021 tentang Penyelenggaraan Perlindungan Dan Pengelolaan Lingkungan Hidup [Government Regulation no. 22 of 2021 on Environmental Protection, Organization and Management]

Italy

National

Costituzione della Repubblica Italiana [Constitution of the Italian Republic] 1947, as amended

Legge 28 febbraio 2024, n. 24, Disposizioni per il riconoscimento della figura dell'agricoltore custode dell'ambiente e del territorio e per l'istituzione della Giornata nazionale dell'agricoltura [Law on provisions for the recognition of the figure of the farmer as custodian of the environment and the territory and for the establishment of the National Agriculture Day]

Legge 6 ottobre 2017, n. 158, Misure per il sostegno e la valorizzazione dei piccoli comuni, nonchè disposizioni per la riqualificazione e il recupero dei centri storici dei medesimi comuni [Law on measures for the support and enhancement of small municipalities, as well as provisions for the redevelopment and recovery of the historic centers of the same municipalities], as amended

Legge 28 dicembre 2015, n. 221, Disposizioni in materia ambientale per promuovere misure di green economy e per il contenimento dell'uso eccessivo di risorse naturali [Law on environmental provisions to promote green economy measures and to contain the excessive use of natural resources], as amended

Legge 6 Dicembre 1991, n. 394, Legge quadro sulle aree protette [Framework law on protected areas], as amended

Legge 3 dicembre 1971, n. 1102, Nuove norme per lo sviluppo della montagna [Law on new rules for mountain development], as amended

Decreto Legislativo 3 aprile 2006, n. 152, Norme in materia ambientale [Legislative Decree on rules on environmental matters]

Decreto Ministeriale 26 luglio 2017, n. 57167, Disposizioni nazionali per l'attuazione del regolamento (UE) n. 1151/2012 e del regolamento delegato (UE) n. 665/2014 sulle condizioni di utilizzo dell'indicazione facoltativa di qualita' «prodotto di montagna» [Ministerial Decree 57167 on national provisions for the implementation of Regulation (EU) No. 1151/2012 and Delegated Regulation (EU) No. 665/2014 on the conditions of use of the optional quality indication "mountain product"], as amended

Decreto Ministeriale 3 settembre 2002, Linee guida per la gestione dei siti Natura 2000 [Ministerial decree on guidelines for the management of Natura 2000 sites]

Decreto del Presidente della Repubblica 8 settembre 1997, n. 357, Regolamento recante attuazione della direttiva 92/43/CEE relativa alla conservazione degli habitat natuali e seminaturali, nonchè della flora e della fauna selvatiche [Presidential Decree on regulations implementing Directive 92/43/EEC on the conservation of natural and semi-natural habitats and of wild fauna and flora], as amended

Decreto del Presidente della Repubblica 31 agosto 1972, n. 670, Approvazione del testo unico delle leggi costituzionali concernenti lo statuto speciale per il Trentino-Alto Adige [Presidential decree on the approval of the consolidated text of the constitutional laws concerning the special statute for Trentino-Alto Adige], as amended

Decreto Legislativo 22 gennaio 2004, n. 42, Codice dei beni culturali e del paesaggio, ai sensi dell'articolo 10 della legge 6 luglio 2002, n. 137 [Legislative decree on cultural heritage and landscape code, pursuant to article 10 of law n. 137 of July 6, 2002] (Italy)

South Tyrol

Legge provinciale 10 luglio 2018, n. 9, Territorio e paesaggio [Provincial law on territory and landscape], as amended

Legge Provinciale 13 ottobre 2017, n. 17, Valutazione ambientale per piani, programmi e progetti [Provincial law on environmental assessment for plans, programs and projects], as amended

Legge Provinciale 12 maggio 2010, n. 6, Legge di tutela della natura e altre disposizioni [Provincial law on nature conservation and other provisions], as amended

Legge Provinciale 28 novembre 2001, n. 17, Legge sui masi chiusi [Provincial law on closed farms], as amended

Legge provinciale 14 dicembre 1998, n. 11, Disposizioni relative all'incentivazione in agricoltura [Provincial law relating to incentives in agriculture], as amended

Legge Provinciale 18 luglio 2023, n. 13, Gestione coordinata dei siti ed elementi oggetto di riconoscimenti UNESCO in provincia di Bolzano [Provincial law on coordinated management of UNESCO-recognized sites and elements in the province of Bolzano]

Japan

土壌汚染対策法 [Soil Contamination Countermeasures Act] 2002

Kenya

Climate Change Act 2016, as amended (Cap. 387A)

Climate Change (Carbon Markets) Regulations 2024

Environmental Management and Co-ordination Act 1999, as amended (Cap. 387)

Kiribati

Phoenix Islands Protected Area Conservation Trust Act 2009, as amended

Korea (Republic of Korea)

환경영향평가법 [Environmental Impact Assessment Act] 2011, as amended

기후위기 대응을 위한 탄소중립·녹색성장 기본법 [Framework Act on Carbon Neutrality and Green Growth for Coping with Climate Crisis] 2021, as amended

Kyrgyzstan

Инструкция о порядке проведения оценки воздействия намечаемой деятельности на окружающую среду (ОВОС) в Кыргызской Республике [Instruction on Environmental Impact Assessment] 1997

Laos

Decree on Environmental Impact Assessment No. 112/PM 2010
Decree on Environmental Impact Assessment No. 329 of 2022

Malawi

Water Resources Act 2013

Maldives

Environment Protection and Preservation Act of Maldives 1993

Marshall Islands

Environmental Impact Assessment Regulations 1994

Micronesia (Federated States of Micronesia)

Environmental Impact Assessment Regulations 1989

Namibia

Environmental Investment Fund Act 2001
Nature Conservation Amendment Act 1996

Panama

Decreto N°. 123, Reglamento del Proceso de Evaluaci ón de Impacto Ambiental [Decree No. 123 – Regulations on the Process of Environmental Impact Assessment] 2009

Papua New Guinea

Environment Act 2000, as amended
Fisheries Management Act 1998

Peru

Political Constitution of Peru 1993, rev. 2009
Decreto Supremo N° 019-2009-MINAM [Decree No 019-2009-MINAM]

Solomon Islands

Environment Act 1998

South Africa

Constitution of the Republic of South Africa, 1996
Environment Impact Assessment Regulations 2014
National Environmental Management Act 1998
Water Services Act 1997

Sweden

Miljöbalk [Environmental Code] 1998

Tanzania

Wildlife Conservation Act 2009, as revised 2022

Tuvalu

Climate Change Resilience Act 2019

Uganda

National Environment Act 2019

United Kingdom

Oil and Gas Authority (Offshore Petroleum) (Disclosure of Protected Material after Specified Period) Regulations 2018

United States of America

Federal

Boundary Waters Canoe Area Wilderness Act, Public Law 95-495 (92 Stat. 1649) 1978

United States Code

Title 15 § 2601 et seq (Toxic Substances Control Act)

Title 16 § 1531 et seq (Endangered Species Act)

Title 33 § 1251 et seq (Clean Water Act)

Title 42 § 300f et seq (Safe Drinking Water Act)

Title 42 § 4321 et seq (National Environmental Policy Act)

Title 42 § 9601 et seq (Comprehensive Environmental Response, Compensation and Liability Act)

Code of Federal Regulations

Title 33 Pt. 330 (Nationwide Permit Program Regulations)

Title 40 § 122.28 (National Pollutant Discharge Elimination System)

Title 40 § 1500 et seq (National Environmental Policy Act Regulations)

Title 50 § 402 (Endangered Species Act Interagency Cooperation Regulations)

State

ARIZONA

Arizona Revised Statutes, § 45-439

CALIFORNIA

Code of Regulations

23 §§ 340-358.4 (Groundwater Management)

Fresno County Code of Ordinances

Ch. 14.04 (Well Regulations)

Ch. 14.09 (Mandatory Public Water Connection Regulations within the Malaga County Water District)
Ch. 14.12 (Mandatory Sewer Connection Regulations)
Government Code
§§ 65000–66301 (Planning and Zoning Law)
Health & Safety Code
§§ 116270–116755 (Safe Drinking Water Act)
§§ 116680–116684 (Water Systems Consolidation Act)
§§ 116765–116772 (Safe and Affordable Drinking Water Fund Act)
§§ 39710–39723 (Greenhouse Gas Reduction Fund Investment Plan and Communities Revitalization Act)
Public Resources Code
Div. 13 (California Environmental Quality Act)
§ 71110 (environmental justice programs)
Water Code
Pt. 2.75, Div. 6 (A.B. 3030)
§ 106 (highest uses of water)
§ 106.3 (Human Right to Water Act)
§§ 10530–10550 (Integrated Regional Water Management Planning Act)
§§ 10610–10657 (Urban Water Management Planning Act)
§§ 10720–10738 (Sustainable Groundwater Management Act)
§§ 10780–10783 (Groundwater Quality Monitoring Act)
§§ 10800–10853 (Agricultural Water Management Planning Act)
§§ 10920–10936 (Groundwater Monitoring Program Act)
Div. 7, Ch. 4 (Porter-Cologne Water Quality Control Act)
§§ 13475–13485 (State Water Pollution Control Revolving Fund Act)
§§ 13486–13489 (Water and Wastewater Loan and Grant Program)
§§ 79500–79591 (Water Security, Clean Drinking Water, Coastal and Beach Protection Act)

MONTANA

Montana Code Annotated
§ 85-2-360
§ 85-20-401 (US National Park Service-Montana Compact)

NEBRASKA

Laws 1975 (LB 577)
Nebraska Revised Statutes § 46-714

NEW JERSEY

New Jersey Administrative Code § 7:1C-9.2

NEW YORK

New York City Administrative Code § 24-163

OREGON

Oregon Administrative Rules, Ch. 690, Div. 9

Oregon Revised Statutes § 390.835

TEXAS

Administrative Code, Title 30 § 293.23

Water Code, Title 2, Subtitle E §§ 36.108, 36.1084, 36.3011

UTAH

Utah Code, Title 73 § 5-15

WASHINGTON

Revised Code of Washington §§ 90.94.030(3)(h), 90.94.040(3)

Vanuatu

Waste Management Regulations Order 2018

1

Introducing Cumulative Environmental Impacts as a Central Problem for Law

Environmental and natural resources laws across the world confront a common problem: the need to deal with the "thousand cuts"[1] of interacting harms to ecosystems and people caused by multiple contributors over space and time. These environmental problems are not the Bhopals or Love Canals, the Mariana Dams or the Deepwater Horizons that make the front pages of newspapers: horrific, but singular and legally relatively straightforward problems. Our thorniest legal environmental issues are the large-scale, insidious, often slow-motion environmental tragedies that have many authors – large and small – cumulative environmental problems. Climate change, biodiversity loss, and urban air pollution are just some of these often intractable and seemingly diverse problems.

We often have plenty of laws directed to these problems, yet still they remain. Stubborn, intractable, often devastating. How can this be? This book analyzes why these types of environmental problems are so difficult to manage, reaching into many fields of research beyond the silo of law[2] to seek insights for designing rules to address cumulative environmental problems. Not even the most heroically optimistic of lawyers would argue that rules alone can fix these problems. But they can do better.

[1] This well-known metaphor has also found its way into formal legal contexts, e.g., in European biodiversity law; see *Sweetman v. Pleanala* [2012] EUECJ C-258/11, Opinion of AG Sharpston, [67].

[2] Mathias Siems, "Bringing in Foreign Ideas: The Quest for 'Better Law' in Implicit Comparative Law" in Nicholas H. D. Foster, Maria Federica Moscati and Michael Palmer (eds), *Interdisciplinary Study and Comparative Law* (Wildy, Simmonds & Hill 2016) 186–208, 208.

1.1 DEFINING AND DESCRIBING CUMULATIVE ENVIRONMENTAL HARMS

Cumulative environmental problems are neither new nor unusual. They occur the world over, through time, at different scales: a city, the world, the body of a single living thing, and much in between. In late nineteenth-century London, cumulative harm appeared in the form of over 2 million tons of manure excreted by the estimated 200,000 horses used for transport in the city, and their smells, dust, and disease.[3] The advent of motorized vehicles addressed that cumulative problem, but created a new one, as air pollution from ever-increasing vehicles stunted the lung growth of children.[4] Over a century later, in 2019, London introduced an "ultra-low emissions zone" that imposes steep charges on all but the cleanest of vehicles to reduce cumulative pollution from road transport.[5] Air quality has improved dramatically.[6]

We see cumulative harm globally. Our biodiversity is threatened by the cumulative effects of land use change, direct overexploitation, pollution, atmospheric warming, and invasive species.[7] So profound is human influence on the environment globally that its "magnitude, variety and longevity" arguably constitutes a new geological epoch, the Anthropocene.[8]

We see cumulative harm in the body of a single animal. When Lulu the killer whale died in 2016 in a fishing net off the coast of Scotland, she was one of the most contaminated animals ever found. Shockingly high levels of toxic polychlorinated biphenyls (PCBs) had accumulated in her body, at more than 100 times the levels known to harm the health of cetaceans.[9]

At their deceptively simplest, cumulative environmental problems might be understood as "aggregate effects caused by many actions." Environmental

[3] Peter Atkins, "The 'Charmed Circle'" in Peter Atkins (ed), *Animal Cities: Beastly Urban Histories* (Routledge 2012) 53–76, 66, 76.

[4] Royal College of Physicians, *Every Breath We Take: The Lifelong Impact of Air Pollution* (2016) 7, www.rcp.ac.uk/improving-care/resources/every-breath-we-take-the-lifelong-impact-of-air-pollution/.

[5] Ibid.

[6] Mayor of London, *Air Quality in London 2016–2024* (Greater London Authority 2024) 5–6.

[7] See generally Peter Stoett and others, "Biodiversity" in Paul Ekins, Joyeeta Gupta and Pierre Boileau (eds), *Global Environment Outlook 6: Healthy Planet, Healthy People* (United Nations Environment Programme 2019) 141–173, 148. See also Corey J. A. Bradshaw and others, "Underestimating the Challenges of Avoiding a Ghastly Future" (2021) 1:615419 *Frontiers in Conservation Science* 1–10.

[8] Simon L. Lewis and Mark A. Maslin, "Defining the Anthropocene" (2015) 519(7542) *Nature* 171, 171.

[9] Rebecca Morelle, "'Shocking' Levels of PCB Chemicals in UK Killer Whale Lulu" (BBC News, May 2, 2017) www.bbc.com/news/science-environment-39738582.

impact assessment laws offer more nuanced definitions and typologies of cumulative environmental effects.[10] An influential definition is "the impact on the environment which results from the incremental impact of [an] action when added to other past, present, and reasonably foreseeable future actions regardless of what agency ... or person undertakes such other actions."[11]

This book focuses on what might be considered the most difficult kinds of cumulative environmental problems: problems caused by relatively large numbers of diverse actors, which cause biophysical effects that aggregate in complex and unpredictable ways over relatively long periods of time, at spatial scales that extend across the boundaries of jurisdictions and legal regimes that often deal with narrow elements of the environment, such as biodiversity or water pollution.[12]

Such problems interact with our legal systems in different ways. At one end of the spectrum are the complex interactions between multiple larger projects that are often highly regulated. In northern Canada, the Bathurst herd of migratory tundra caribou, which are culturally and economically significant to First Nations, is declining. The causes are diverse: changes to their habitat caused by multiple diamond mines, roads, and other industrial development and exploration activities across their range.[13] At the other end of the spectrum lie the aggregate impacts of numerous small, typically unregulated activities, such as the impacts on human health of indoor air pollution from household cooking, motor vehicle air pollution, and poor access to healthy food, combined with heat waves exacerbated by climate change.[14]

Although scientists often examine the cumulative nature of many important environmental harms, there is comparatively little legal work on cumulative environmental problems as a type of problem faced around the world. Legal scholars more commonly analyze a particular problem in a particular legal jurisdiction – say, plastic waste in international law,[15]

[10] For a review of these, see Peter N. Duinker and others, "Scientific Dimensions of Cumulative Effects Assessment: Toward Improvements in Guidance for Practice" (2013) 21 *Environmental Reviews* 40–52, 43.

[11] Ibid, 42.

[12] As explained further later, this definition has some similarities with earlier work, e.g., J. B. Ruhl and James Salzman, "Climate Change, Dead Zones, and Massive Problems in the Administrative State: A Guide for Whittling Away" (2010) 98 *California Law Review* 59–120.

[13] See generally Anne Gunn, Don Russell and Lorne Greig, "Insights into Integrating Cumulative Effects and Collaborative Co-Management for Migratory Tundra Caribou Herds in the Northwest Territories, Canada" (2014) 19(4) *Ecology and Society* 4.

[14] Tord Kjellstrom and others, "Urban Environmental Health Hazards and Health Equity" (2007) 84 *Journal of Urban Health* 86–97, 90–91.

[15] E.g., Joan M. Bondareff, Maggie Carey and Carleen Lyden-Kluss, "Plastics in the Ocean: The Environmental Plague of Our Time" (2017) 22 *Roger Williams University Law Review* 383;

greenhouse gas pollution in Australia,[16] or soil contamination in China.[17] This book starts to fill that gap.

1.2 RULES AND THE CUMULATIVE IMPACT MINDSET OF THIS BOOK

The core objective of this book is to demonstrate how formal rules can be used to protect things we care about from the cumulative threats they face. I present a framework for assessing how laws can do this by performing four key interacting functions – conceptualization, information, regulatory intervention, and coordination – the CIRCle Framework of legal functions (Figure 1.1).

Environment-related legal literature is replete with examples of legal regimes in which one of these functions is missing, weak, or unlinked to another function. Emerging rights of nature can lack clarity in relation to what, precisely, is protected, perhaps until a court decision,[18] or may define an element of nature too narrowly to facilitate considering cumulative impacts[19] (unclear or weak *conceptualization*). Environmental harm from agriculture often occurs under exemptions from legal requirements so vast they have been termed an "anti-law" of the environment[20] (a lack of comprehensiveness in *intervention*). Laws and policies make only limited use of available scientific tools for evaluating cumulative impacts in sensitive marine systems[21] (a regulatory weakness related to *information*). Climate adaptation initiatives like buying out properties in risk-prone areas may overlook local contexts and

Luisa Cortat Simonetti Goncalves and Michael Gerbert Faure, "International Law Instruments to Address the Plastic Soup" (2019) 43 *William & Mary Environmental Law and Policy Review* 871–948.

16 E.g., Jacqueline Peel, "The *Living Wonders* Case: A Backwards Step in Australian Climate Litigation on Coal Mines" (2024) 36 *Journal of Environmental Law* 125–132.

17 E.g., Takashi Itakura, "Current Issues with the Regulatory Framework for Managing Soil Contamination in China" (2015) 18 *Asia Pacific Journal of Environmental Law* 119–146.

18 Ruth Barcan, "The Campaign for Legal Personhood for the Great Barrier Reef: Finding Political and Pedagogical Value in a Spectacular Failure of Care" (2020) 3 *Environment and Planning E: Nature and Space* 810–832, 823–824; Mihnea Tănăsescu and others, "Rights of Nature and Rivers in Ecuador's Constitutional Court" (2024) *The International Journal of Human Rights* 1–23, 10–11.

19 Rebecca Nelson, "Sick City Streams: New Approaches to Legal Treatments" (2020) 43 *Melbourne University Law Review* 748–821, 768–770.

20 J. B. Ruhl, "Farms, Their Environmental Harms, and Environmental Law" (2000) 27 *Ecology Law Quarterly* 263–349, 293–327.

21 Christian Simeoni and others, "Evaluating the Combined Effect of Climate and Anthropogenic Stressors on Marine Coastal Ecosystems: Insights from a Systematic Review of Cumulative Impact Assessment Approaches" (2023) 861:160687 *Science of The Total Environment* 1–18, 15.

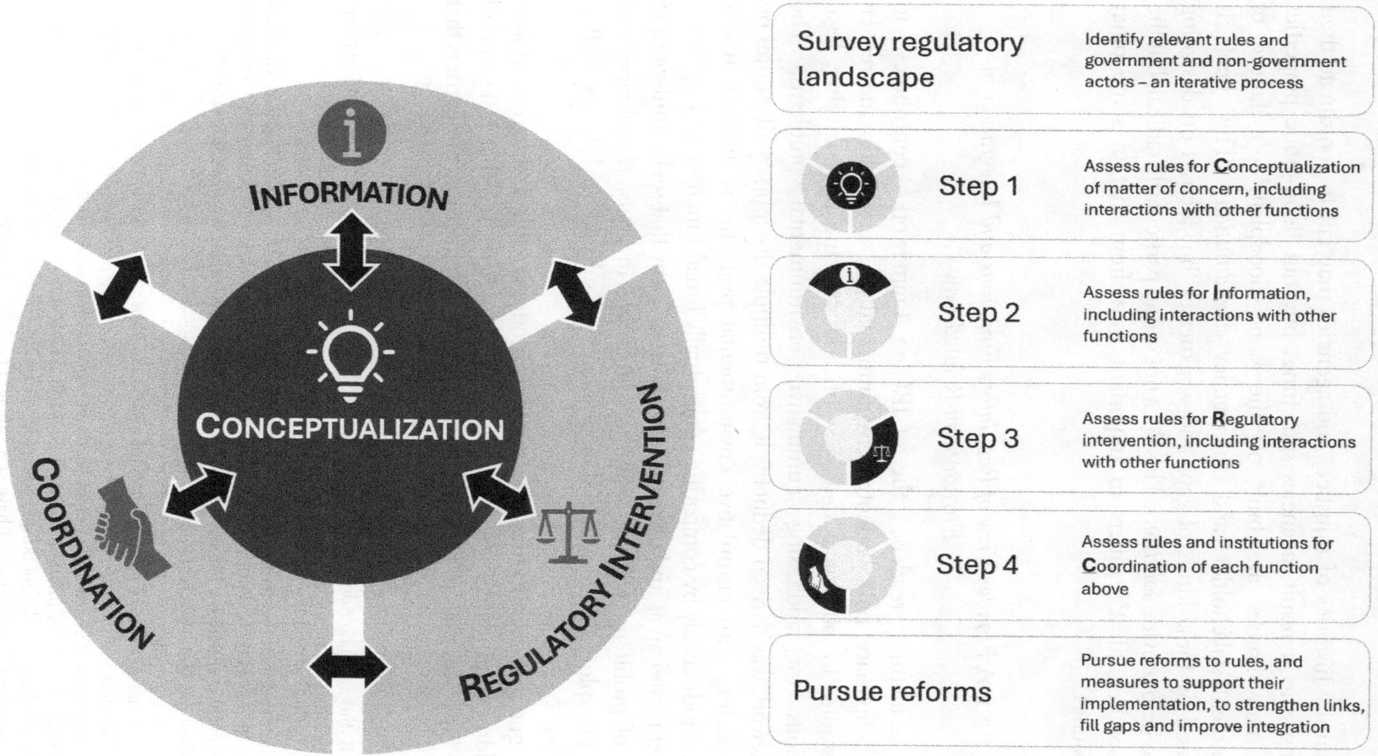

FIGURE 1.1 Applying the CIRCle Framework for assessing rules relevant to cumulative environmental problems

community histories of injustice, and agencies may fail to coordinate their responses; as a result, agencies sometimes buy out flood-prone properties while new houses are built on the same floodplain[22] (a failure of government–stakeholder and interagency *coordination*). This book is informed by these kinds of gaps and weaknesses, but focuses on designing laws to help provide *solutions*. This does not sound particularly radical, but the mindset behind it[23] differs in important ways from that of some other approaches.

1.2.1 *A Broader View of Regulatory Functions and Integration in Environment-Related Law*

For academic readers, the CIRCle Framework contributes to interdisciplinary, policy-oriented environmental law scholarship and regulatory studies by offering a new view of, and structure for analyzing, legal functions for addressing cumulative environmental problems. The Framework was derived deductively from multiple disciplinary literatures on why dealing with cumulative environmental problems is difficult. It was refined inductively by comparing conceptually broad functions of laws across subject matter areas and diverse jurisdictions in a way that seeks similarities in *types* of problems, without assuming similarities in goals. It embraces and seeks to explore differences in how problems are solved,[24] as I discuss further later on.[25]

I argue that each Framework function is indispensable to a regime of laws to address cumulative environmental problems. A regime that lacks one of these functions does not respond, as completely as it might, to the barriers that

[22] A. R. Siders, "The Administrator's Dilemma: Closing the Gap between Climate Adaptation Justice in Theory and Practice" (2022) 137 *Environmental Science and Policy* 280–289, 286–287.

[23] Others first used this terminology in the context of scientific EIA: A. John Sinclair, Meinhard Doelle and Peter N. Duinker, "Looking Up, Down, and Sideways: Reconceiving Cumulative Effects Assessment as a Mindset" (2017) 62 *Environmental Impact Assessment Review* 183–194.

[24] I adopt this approach, recognizing past criticism of functionalism in comparative law based on assuming similar goals and approaches to solutions: e.g., Naomi Creutzfeldt, Agnieszka Kubal and Fernanda Pirie, "Introduction: Exploring the Comparative in Socio-Legal Studies" (2016) 12 *International Journal of Law in Context* 377–389, 378–379; Oliver Brand, "Conceptual Comparisons: Towards a Coherent Methodology of Comparative Legal Studies" (2006) 32 *Brooklyn Journal of International Law* 405–466, 414–415, 418–419. Conceptualization as a CIRCle Framework function, for example, allows for comparing across cumulative environmental problems that have very different goals (see Chapter 4).

[25] See Section 2.4 of Chapter 2.

we know stand in the way of addressing cumulative environmental harm.[26] These CIRCle Framework functions must be integrated – linked to each other – as later chapters explain. This argument notes, as a starting point, the established concepts in policy design of consistency (mutually reinforcing tools for intervention), coherence (logical coexistence of policy goals), and congruence (mutually supportive goals and instruments for intervention).[27] Alongside these concepts, the CIRCle Framework emphasizes the need for mutually supportive integration of *functions* – conceptualization, information, regulatory intervention, and coordination – among the elements of a legal regime for dealing with a cumulative environmental problem. I describe these mutually supportive links as simply "regulatory integration" or "integrated" regulatory functions[28] and describe these links in more detail specific to each function in subsequent chapters.[29]

These arguments adopt a mindset about what law can do, and in fact does, that is broader than is sometimes offered through policy design literature or legal literature.[30] For example, when these literatures deal with "policy mixes," or "instrument mixes," as is central to the issue of cumulative impacts, they tend to focus on mechanisms for changing behavior,[31] that is, intervention, and links to policy goals in a general sense. Important typologies of difficult problems, which have also informed this work, tend to focus on what

26 See Chapter 2 for a discussion of why it is difficult to address cumulative environmental problems.

27 Michael Howlett and Jeremy Rayner, "Coherence, Congruence and Consistency in Policy Mixes" in Michael Howlett and Ishani Mukherjee (eds), *Routledge Handbook of Policy Design* (Routledge 2018) 389–403, 393–394.

28 This term also has useful echoes in the environmental management literature on "integrated catchment management," which, like cumulative environmental problems more generally, focuses on integrating different kinds of impacts on a watershed: see, e.g., Rebecca Nelson, "Challenges to Improved Integrated Management of the Murray-Darling Basin" in Barry Hart and others (eds), *Murray-Darling Basin, Australia: Its Future Management* (Elsevier 2021) 339–361.

29 These links are summarized in Figure 4.2 (focus on conceptualization), Figure 5.2 (focus on information), Figure 6.1 (focus on regulatory intervention), and Figure 7.2 (focus on coordination).

30 Many other scholars have also focused on the individual functions in focus here, as discussed in Chapters 4 to 7.

31 E.g., Heleen L. P. Mees and others, "A Method for the Deliberate and Deliberative Selection of Policy Instrument Mixes for Climate Change Adaptation" (2014) 19(2) *Ecology and Society* 1–15; Vilis Brukas and Ola Sallnäs, "Forest Management Plan as a Policy Instrument: Carrot, Stick or Sermon?" (2012) 29 *Land Use Policy* 605–613, 606; Christopher Hood, "Intellectual Obsolescence and Intellectual Makeovers: Reflections on the Tools of Government after Two Decades" (2007) 20 *Governance* 127–144, 139.

to do and who should do it, for example, through collaboration.[32] In the context of cumulative environmental problems, the CIRCle Framework suggests that law must do more to overcome barriers to effective solutions by delivering and linking a broader set of functions. Legal mechanisms can, and should, help us clarify what is important, gather and share information that we need to protect it or restore it, take action, and coordinate government actors and stakeholder groups to do these things, in an integrated way.

1.2.2 *Learning across Disciplines, Legal Contexts, and Jurisdictions*

This book is intended to span boundaries in different ways. Perhaps the longest spans lie between law and the many disciplines that help answer the question: Why is it difficult to deal with cumulative environmental problems?[33] The answers both point to the value of formal rules, and to psychological, technical, political, and many other challenges that rule designers should consider.

Just as important are the bridges between areas of law and their physical contexts. Much, though by no means all, legal scholarship focuses on a single body of law. Scholarly silos often separate, say, land use planning law from water law from endangered species law. By contrast, each chapter here spans multiple legal areas using the "bridge" of a CIRCle Framework function. Since each of these legal areas faces challenges in regulating cumulative problems, they have developed, unsurprisingly, different approaches to undertaking the same broad function. This variety provides tremendous scope for lesson learning.

Finally, this book responds to calls for learning across jurisdictions to improve responses to cumulative effects and environmental law and policy more generally.[34] This occurs in two ways. The first is the numerous examples

[32] E.g., Ruhl and Salzman, "Climate Change," 79–92 (typology of "massive problems"); Benjamin Cashore and Steven Bernstein, "Bringing the Environment Back In: Overcoming the Tragedy of the Diffusion of the Commons Metaphor" (2022) 43(3) *Perspectives on Politics* 478–501 (typology of problems based on sustainability concepts with distinct moral underpinnings and prescriptions for approaches to solutions); Brian W. Head, *Wicked Problems in Public Policy: Understanding and Responding to Complex Challenges* (Palgrave Macmillan 2022) 102–105 (collaborative approaches for environmental policy). For further discussion, see Chapter 2.

[33] See generally Chapter 2.

[34] E.g., Jonathan B. Wiener, "Learning to Manage the Multirisk World" (2020) 40 *Risk Analysis* 2137–2143, 2140; Robert E. Lutz, "The Laws of Environmental Management: A Comparative Study" (1976) 24(3) *American Journal of Comparative Law* 447, 448–449; Elizabeth Fisher and others, "Maturity and Methodology: Starting a Debate about Environmental Law Scholarship" (2009) 21 *Journal of Environmental Law* 213–250, 242–243; Raul Pacheco-Vega,

that appear in each chapter that deals with a CIRCle Framework function, drawn from 73 jurisdictions across 55 countries. The objective is not to recommend any example or to screen for examples using "best practice" criteria – if such a thing is even possible to determine across such a variety of contexts. Rather, these are illustrative examples[35] drawn from searches of scholarly and gray literatures, including yearbooks of legal developments around the world, legal inventories produced by international organizations, and digests of global laws for practitioners.[36] Diversity was the key objective in selecting these illustrative examples: diverse jurisdictions in terms of legal tradition and degree of industrialization; diverse environment-related issues that are important in the relevant jurisdiction; and diverse approaches to undertaking a CIRCle Framework function. The second way that the book spans jurisdictions is through three major case studies, introduced later in this chapter.

This boundary-spanning research approach builds on my past research using large-scale, multi-jurisdictional,[37] cross-sectoral,[38] and cross-disciplinary

"Environmental Regulation, Governance, and Policy Instruments, 20 Years after the Stick, Carrot, and Sermon Typology" (2020) 22 *Journal of Environmental Policy and Planning* 620–635, 631.

35 Jack S. Levy, "Case Studies: Types, Designs, and Logics of Inference" (2008) 25 *Conflict Management and Peace Science* 1–18, 6–7 ("they aim to give the reader a 'feel' for a theoretical argument by providing a concrete example of its application, or to demonstrate the empirical relevance of a theoretical proposition").

36 E.g., *Oxford Yearbook of International Environmental Law* (Maria Gavouneli and Timo Koivurova eds, first published 1990); IUCN, The Biodiversity Consultancy and Durrell Institute of Conservation and Ecology, Global Inventory of Biodiversity Offset Policies, https://portals.iucn.org/offsetpolicy; Chambers and Partners, Environmental Law 2023, https://practiceguides.chambers.com/practice-guides/environmental-law-2023.

37 E.g., Rebecca Nelson and L. M. Shirley, "The Latent Potential of Cumulative Effects Concepts in National and International Environmental Impact Assessment Regimes" (2023) 12(1) *Transnational Environmental Law* 150–174; Rebecca Nelson, "Paying Back the River: A First Analysis of Western Groundwater Offset Rules and Lessons for Other Natural Resources" (2015) 34 *Stanford Environmental Law Journal* 129–194; Rebecca Nelson, "Allocations and Legal Trends in the 21st Century" in Josselin Rouillard and others (eds), *Water Resources Allocation and Agriculture: Transitioning from Open to Regulated Access* (IWA 2022) 25–36.

38 E.g., Rebecca Nelson, "Breaking Backs and Boiling Frogs: Warnings from a Dialogue between Federal Water Law and Environmental Law" (2019) 42 *University of New South Wales Law Journal* 1179–1214; Rebecca Nelson, "Victims and Villains: Cities and the Environment on the Constitutional Stage" in Erika Arban (ed), *Cities in Federal Constitutional Theory* (OUP 2022) 161–179; Rebecca Nelson, Lee Godden and Bruce Lindsay, *A Pathway to Cultural Flows in Australia* (National Native Title Council 2018) www.mdba.gov.au/sites/default/files/publications/a-pathway-to-cultural-flows-in-australia_1.pdf.

methods.[39] It also draws from my experience working across government, nonprofit, and private sectors in interdisciplinary environments.

Aiming for breadth and boundary spanning necessarily trades off the ability to draw deep conclusions about any one area of law, jurisdiction, or cumulative problem context. I leave for future work the many productive avenues of inquiry that arise and offer the CIRCle Framework as a potential structure for analysis.

1.2.3 *Regulatory Functions as Ingredients with Sample Menus*

The CIRCle Framework describes and prescribes broad legal functions, noting that it would be impossible to make detailed prescriptions that would suit diverse problems and legal contexts around the globe. Regardless of whether you or your jurisdiction embraces command-and-control regulation, cap-and-trade mechanisms for property rights or earth jurisprudence; whether you work on microplastic pollution or landscape-scale biodiversity conservation, these regulatory concepts and contexts require a structure, a menu with the right ingredients. Those ingredients are the CIRCle Framework functions. They are intended to be assembled into different dishes to suit different contexts.

To continue the metaphor, this book does not recommend a set menu: If CIRCle Framework functions are the ingredients, then the many examples that illustrate each Framework function are a sample international buffet. But a caution is also warranted: Law in practice may differ from law on paper. The appropriateness of an approach illustrated by an example should be considered in light of the local context and regulatory culture. The fact that an example is included also does not mean it is implemented effectively – each example is necessarily presented in an abstracted way, outside its social context. The examples merely show that an approach is possible, and, as a matter of regulatory design, deals with an important need in responding to cumulative environmental problems. While I have tried to ensure that each example is used in practice, it lies to future work to empirically evaluate these mechanisms, and how they link to others, in their real-world contexts.

[39] E.g., Nelson, "Sick City Streams"; Rebecca Nelson, "Regulating Hidden Risks to Conservation Lands in Resource Rich Areas" (2021) 40 *University of Queensland Law Journal* 491–530; Nicola Ulibarri and others, "Assessing the Feasibility of Managed Aquifer Recharge in California" (2021) 57:e2020WR029292 *Water Resources Research* 1–18.

1.2.4 A *Starting Focus on What We Care About*

As I discuss in more detail later in this book,[40] the core and first analytical step of the CIRCle Framework is being clear about the thing we care about, which I call the "matter of concern" (Figure 1.1, Step 1). Only after we are clear about exactly what it is that we want to protect or restore can we assess how threats and legal mechanisms affect that thing.

Importantly, I do not argue that laws should focus on any specific matter of concern. A legal system might reflect concern about a species, a cultural landscape, a disadvantaged community, a river, an airshed, and many other things that matter. All of these things, and many others, can benefit from a cumulative impacts approach that centers on that thing, and understanding and dealing with impacts to it.

Starting with what we care about can be distinguished from focusing at once on specific categories or sizes of impacts. That is, a cumulative impacts mindset urges approaching a problem without any assumptions about targets for regulation, say, large corporations or particular industries. Rather, the aim is to understand the kinds of actions – all of them that may aggregate to become significant – that may affect the matter of concern. This encompasses impacts that are both large and small, and that are caused by "background" effects (say, the spread of an introduced species) and past human activities that have ongoing effects, as well as current and proposed human impacts. Small actions, as well as large ones, can aggregate to become significant. This does not necessarily mean limiting those small actions, or blaming those who undertake them. But recognizing these impacts is important, as is considering acceptable ways to intervene where they accumulate to cause significant unacceptable harm.[41]

1.2.5 *Optimism*

In its orientation and its findings, this book is optimistic. Yes, cumulative environmental problems can seem massive and intractable. But if a central failing of environmental law, on paper or in practice, is not taking account of cumulative environmental effects, existing laws also have "untapped potential . . . to address environmental change" and provide "a more expedient approach to addressing environmental change than waiting for full-scale

[40] See generally Chapter 4 (Conceptualization as a CIRCle Framework function).

[41] See Chapter 6 (Regulatory intervention as a CIRCle Framework function).

environmental law reform."[42] This book confirms this untapped potential in the context of cumulative environmental problems. Many areas of law can deal with cumulative environmental effects[43] – they are just too seldom structured and refined to do so.

In aiming to demonstrate how we might harness this untapped potential to deal with cumulative effects, I take a wide, panoramic view of relevant laws in terms of geography and subject matter. Using diverse illustrative examples from across the world not only demonstrates that different jurisdictions and areas of law face similar challenges; I hope that it also points to the potential for crafting solutions in one area of law by gaining inspiration from another (how might wildlife conservation law learn from approaches used to address cumulative air pollution?; how might rules for water resources benefit from approaches used in landscape planning?).

It is also a cause for optimism that the illustrative examples that appear in this book are so geographically diverse – and they are just a subset of what might have been included. The CIRCle Framework functions are not the exclusive preserve of any one legal tradition, nor expressed through a single rigid approach, nor found only in industrialized countries. Far from it. We see them around the world, in different forms, in place as we speak. This is important, because it expands the potential to identify precedents and lessons that speak to regulatory designers more broadly than might otherwise be the case – while recognizing that in some situations laws will require transformational change.

1.3 SCOPE OF RELEVANT RULES

If the core objective of this book is to advance a framework for evaluating formal rules that respond to cumulative environmental problems, a key question is the scope of those rules. This is worth clarifying carefully, given that different terminology is used in different places.[44] I include rules that are legally binding, including legislation adopted by a national or subnational parliament or congress or local government; regulations adopted by executive agencies; and, to a lesser degree, policy that is officially adopted by an agency of government or an institution, which might not be directly legally binding. This includes, for example, guidance on assessing cumulative impacts under environmental

[42] Ahjond Garmestani and others, "Untapped Capacity for Resilience in Environmental Law" (2019) 116 *Proceedings of the National Academy of Sciences* 19899–19904, 19899.

[43] See Chapter 3 (Regulatory Landscape).

[44] E.g., Nir Kosti, David Levi-Faur and Guy Mor, "Legislation and Regulation: Three Analytical Distinctions" (2019) 7 *The Theory and Practice of Legislation* 169–178.

impact assessment laws, or formal state guidance to local agencies on formulating statutory plans that consider cumulative effects.[45] In some jurisdictions, citizens may propose formal rules.[46] The common characteristic is that the state plays a role, though non-state actors may also feature under coordination arrangements. Indeed, I argue that cumulative environmental problems require state action because of their inherent qualities.[47]

The landscape of formal rules that undertake CIRCle Framework functions is wide – it includes those as diverse as constitutional environmental rights, natural resources management regimes, and the environmental impact assessment context that is most commonly associated with considering cumulative effects.[48] It includes formal rules that some associate with alternatives to state action, rather than state action itself, for example, rules that structure environmental markets, statutory conditions on the exercise of private property rights, and formal but voluntary rules for corporate environmental disclosures.

This work shares a well-known common feature of policy design scholarship in that it focuses on the "good side" of designing rules that are intended to achieve an aim, rather than examining how they might be misused.[49] It also does not focus significantly on rules that are not aimed at dealing with a problem, but that might indirectly undercut it. Such rules, like political campaign financing laws or international trade rules, are of great importance and potentially high indirect influence, but belong to a wider scope than can be addressed by this work.[50] Similarly, indirectly supportive rules, say, international technical capacity-building funds for environmental matters, lie beyond the present scope of this book.

1.4 HOW TO USE THIS BOOK

1.4.1 *Structure and Features*

This book serves multidisciplinary scholarly and professional audiences. It assumes a basic familiarity with modern environmental problems, such as climate change

45 See, e.g., discussion of a policy on cumulative impacts in the context of the Great Barrier Reef (Chapter 9) and state guidance on stakeholder engagement and addressing impacts to drinking water supplies in the context of local groundwater sustainability plans in California (Chapter 8).

46 E.g., Political Constitution of Peru 1993, rev. 2009, art. 2(20); Maeve P. Carey, *Petitions for Rulemaking: An Overview* (Congressional Research Service 2020) 9–10.

47 See Chapter 2.

48 See Chapter 3 (Regulatory Landscape).

49 Giliberto Capano and Michael Howlett, "The Knowns and Unknowns of Policy Instrument Analysis: Policy Tools and the Current Research Agenda on Policy Mixes" (2020) 10:2158244019900568 SAGE *Open* 1–13, 8.

50 See also discussion at Section 3.2.4.

and biodiversity loss, but does not assume familiarity with any particular jurisdiction. It is written to facilitate reading chapters independently and also sequentially. The last chapter serves as a "quick guide" to the book and translates key findings into a process for analyzing rules, summarized in Figure 1.1.

Chapters 2 and 3 adopt a theoretical posture. Chapter 2 explores multiple disciplinary insights on why cumulative environmental harms involve particularly pronounced challenges for human recognition, understanding, acceptance, and action. I argue that many of these challenges are difficult or impossible to address without the kind of well-considered, structured, and coordinated measures for which formal rules provide. Chapter 2 then advances a four-part functional framework for evaluating laws that are intended to deal with cumulative environmental problems: the CIRCle Framework (conceptualization, information, regulatory intervention, and coordination). The Framework advances the argument that law must perform and link four key functions to deliver an effective legal response to cumulative effects: clearly conceiving what and who matter (the "matter of concern"); producing, sharing, and allocating responsibility for information relevant to cumulative effects on the matter of concern; intervening in response to, or in anticipation of, unacceptable cumulative effects; and coordinating across and between levels of government, and with nongovernment entities to do these things. The design of legal mechanisms to carry out these functions should anticipate and seek to head off important challenges revealed by other disciplines. Chapter 3 lays the foundations for applying this Framework by sketching the landscape of areas of law that can help deal with cumulative environmental problems.

Chapters 4 to 7 take a "law on paper" position, undertaking a high-level analysis of how different legal approaches across environment-related laws in diverse jurisdictions can address cumulative environmental effects through each CIRCle Framework function. Each of these "function" chapters is structured first, to explain the nature of the function, its role in the CIRCle Framework and its links with other functions; second, to call attention to how that function might vary among environment-related laws in important ways; and third, to set out key, crosscutting design features that are important to delivering the function regardless of this variation. These design features are illustrated in tables that show, non-exhaustively, some important types of diversity in approaches adopted by laws around the world.

Chapters 8 to 10 take a "law in context" approach, examining three case studies of cumulative environment problems. Each case study chapter explores selected CIRCle Framework functions in their complex, real-world regulatory context. Whereas the chapters preceding these deal with individual mechanisms, the case studies explore how multiple mechanisms come together. Finally, Chapter 11 "zooms out" to offer guidance for applying the CIRCle Framework in a local context, synthesizing the book's key messages along the way.

1.4.2 *Legal Scholars, Regulatory Practitioners, Law Reformers, and Nonlawyers*

The book will be of general interest to law and policy scholars working in environmental and natural resources fields, who seek to identify gaps, weaknesses, and conflicts in existing systems of rules and to improve those rules. A wider legal scholarly audience with intersecting interests may be interested in particular chapters, for example, those working on law, technology, and information (Chapter 5, Information), and those working on constitutional law, federalism, and environmental governance (Chapter 7, Coordination).

Other readers will be motivated by practical purposes. Some regularly work with rules for dealing with cumulative harms, implementing systems, and making decisions to assess and address cumulative environmental effects. They may work as administrators in government environmental and natural resources agencies. They may also work in international and nongovernment contexts, as policymakers in development banks and engineers working in large engineering corporations that undertake environmental impact assessments for major projects. These readers will be interested in ways to improve the structure or implementation of relevant rules, as described in Chapters 4 to 7. These chapters will also interest those who seek to reform the rules or influence how they apply in a particular instance, such as nongovernmental organizations (NGOs), actors in social movements, and informed citizen-activists.

For nonacademics and nonlawyers, Chapters 2 (multidisciplinary insights and the CIRCle Framework) and 11 (summary and guidance) form the best starting points. These chapters adopt a more general style than the chapters that dive more deeply into law, and can act as a pathfinder for the more detailed legal chapters. Nonlegal and legal practitioners alike may also be interested in a case study aligned to their field of work in terms of subject matter or area of law (see Table 1.1).

1.5 INTRODUCTION TO MAJOR CASE STUDIES

1.5.1 *Purpose and Selection*

The case studies presented in Chapters 8–10 are illustrative.[51] They were selected to draw out cumulative environmental problems that are diverse, challenging, and highly developed with respect to particular CIRCle Framework functions. Each case study focuses on a geographically constrained place and examines how multiple laws interact to deal with

[51] Levy, "Case Studies: Types, Designs, and Logics of Inference," 6–7.

TABLE 1.1 *Key characteristics of case studies*

Case study	Groundwater depletion and environmental justice in California's Central Valley, US	Biodiversity of the Great Barrier Reef, Australia	Alpine grasslands as biocultural landscapes, Italy
Legal landscape for addressing cumulative environmental problem (bolded text indicates **major focus**)	**Water resources management plans**, safe drinking water, pollution, environmental impact assessment (EIA), land use law	EIA and **strategic assessment**; pollution law; land management standards; greenhouse gas emissions cap; carbon offsets; restoration subsidies	Constitutional protections for landscapes; landscape plans; EIA; protected species and **conservation areas**; farm subsidies; food product certification; farm inheritance law; public acquisition
Levels of governance	State and local laws	International conventions, federal and state laws	International conventions, laws at the European Union, national, provincial and local levels
Matter of concern and impacts in focus	Preventing aggregate withdrawal of water for farms and large cities reducing access to groundwater for vulnerable communities reliant on household or small community wells	Preventing decline in health of the World Heritage Great Barrier Reef due to polluted runoff from catchments and greenhouse gas emissions causing climate change, focusing on catchment grazing and coal mines	Maintaining and restoring biodiverse and culturally valuable Alpine grasslands, countering abandonment of traditional extensive grazing practices and small-scale development
CIRCle Framework functions in focus	Conceptualization and its links to the other functions	Information Intervention Links between intervention and information	Coordination Intervention Links between coordination and intervention

cumulative effects in that place. This shows how the complexity of dealing with cumulative effects derives, in part, from the fact that separate legal regimes often regulate distinct types of effects.

Research for each case study involved analyzing documentary sources related to law, policy, and the environmental context. This was supplemented by discussions with numerous local contacts familiar with the case study across government, NGOs, and academia.

Cumulative environmental problems are so common that there is no shortage of legal and factual contexts to investigate. Given this abundance of options, and the fact that this is the first monograph to concentrate on the legal aspects of regulating cumulative environmental problems, diversity was an important factor guiding the selection of case studies.

A first dimension of diversity is the key legal mechanisms that form the major focus of each case study: statutory natural resources planning, strategic environmental assessment law, and habitat protection, respectively. This approach shows that different legal mechanisms can address cumulative effects, but it also prevents directly comparing how a single type of mechanism is implemented in different contexts. These are illustrative, rather than comparative, case studies. Other elements of diversity are levels of governance (local, state/provincial, national, and transnational); jurisdictions (the United States, Australia, and Italy/Europe: Figure 1.2); natural resources (freshwater, marine, and mountain grassland), and types of concerns (resource sustainability, biodiversity, and biocultural values) (see Table 1.1).

The case studies build on past research approaches[52] and time spent physically working in each jurisdiction on issues relevant to each case study (in Australia, for most of my career as a lawyer, government adviser, and scholar; in California, for my graduate training; and in South Tyrol as a scholar in residence at the Eurac Research Institute for Comparative Federalism).

The cases do have some common dimensions. In each, the matter of concern is well-known and sometimes iconic. This acknowledged importance means that disputes tend to focus on the best way to protect or restore the matter of concern, rather than whether to do so. This maximizes the likelihood of developing – and here, illustrating – sophisticated regulatory responses. Each case study occurs in a relatively large, industrialized, high-income jurisdiction with complex and well-developed environment-related laws. This helps illustrate the challenges of integrating functions across areas of law. But it means that the case studies may not address additional issues that

[52] See Section 1.2.2.

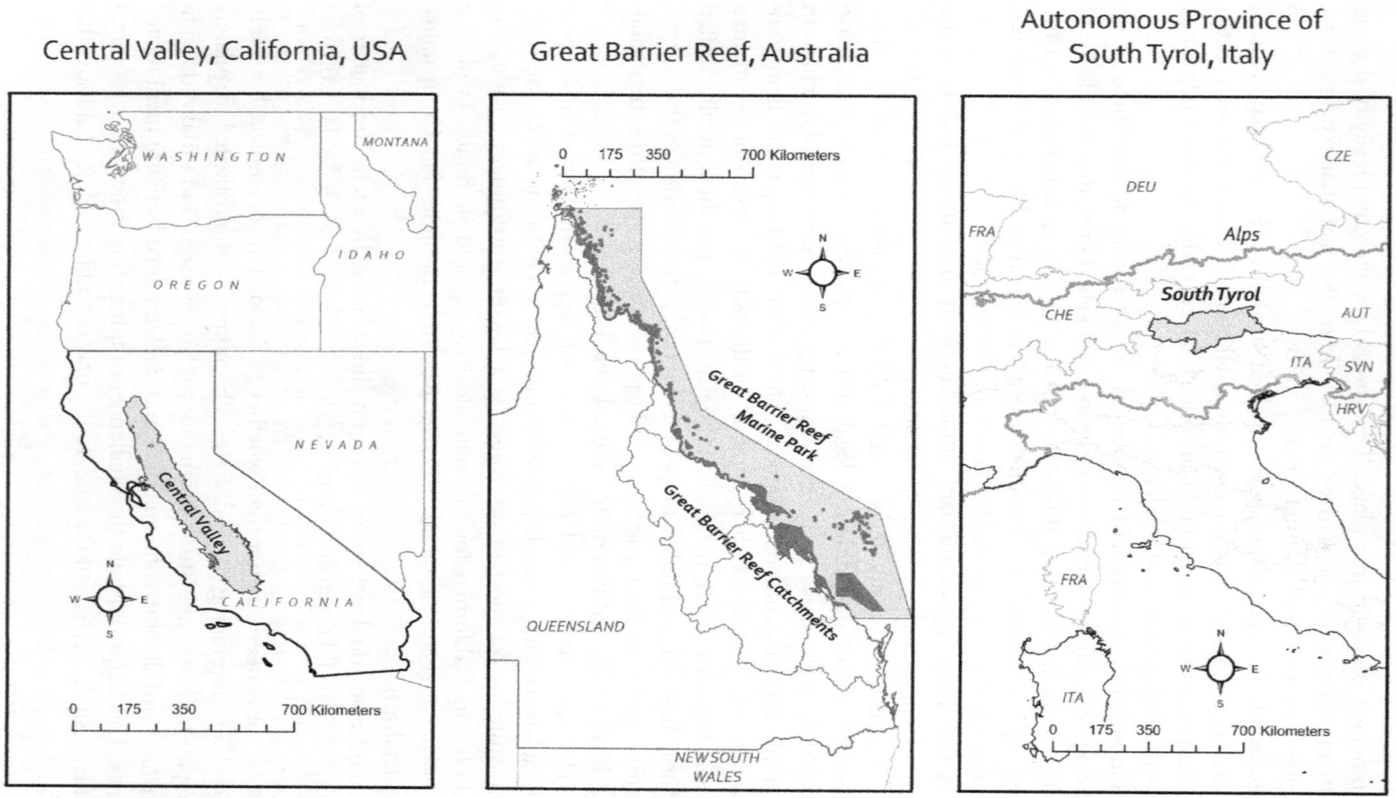

FIGURE 1.2 Major case study locations

may arise in advancing and integrating the CIRCle Framework functions in a smaller or lower-income jurisdiction, for example, a small island or large state in the Global South. These additional issues are difficult to generalize. On one hand, if there are relatively fewer government actors and fewer or less entrenched legal silos, coordination and integrating functions may be easier. On the other hand, challenges are likely where foundational environment-related laws are developing, government resourcing is heavily constrained, and contributors to cumulative impacts have lower capacity to explore ways to reduce harm. Importantly though, the selection of major case studies does not suggest that lower-income jurisdictions lack innovative legal approaches to CIRCle Framework functions: This innovation emerges clearly from the many illustrative examples used across the chapters on each Framework function (Chapters 4–7).

1.5.2 *Introducing the Case Studies*

The three case studies work sequentially through the key CIRCle Framework functions, building from a focus on conceptualization and how it links to other functions (California's Central Valley), to considering connections between information and regulatory intervention (Australia's Great Barrier Reef), and regulatory intervention and coordination (Italy's Alpine grasslands) (Table 1.1). The case studies ask diverse questions: How can the idea of environmental justice, as a cumulative impact concept, be operationalized through statutory groundwater plans? How can rules influence distant and diverse, cumulatively significant threats to a coral reef? How can the cumulative effects of human activities, and the abandonment of activities, be influenced to protect "cultural landscapes" and their habitats that inherently require human action to maintain their conditions? Here, I briefly introduce the case studies in an abstract-like, citation-free form as a prelude to fuller discussion in later chapters.

1.5.2.1 Groundwater Planning and Environmental Justice in the Central Valley of California

California's Central Valley is one of the world's thirty-seven "mega aquifers": very large reservoirs of underground water that generally span political boundaries and, together, account for most of the world's groundwater resources. The region has one of the world's most notoriously overused groundwater resources, and its aquifer is the most intensely depleted in the United States. It supports one of the most world's most productive agricultural regions and a growing population, including many disadvantaged communities. Some such communities lack a municipal government and public water systems, and so these communities access drinking water from domestic wells, many of which have dried up during recent droughts. But regulating cumulative withdrawals to protect groundwater levels and access to drinking water has proven challenging.

No federal or state agency regulates groundwater withdrawals in California in a general sense. A strong traditional preference for "local control" of groundwater inhibited comprehensive state-level monitoring and regulation of groundwater until the twenty-first century. When state legislation finally appeared, it was prompted in part by a major drought and its effects on the Central Valley. California introduced statewide monitoring legislation, identified groundwater basins that were "critically overdrafted," and ultimately passed the 2014 Sustainable Groundwater Management Act. The Act requires self-nominated local "groundwater sustainability agencies" to manage groundwater to achieve sustainable groundwater conditions.

This case study uses the Sustainable Groundwater Management Act as a springboard for introducing the CIRCle Framework in a real-world context, focusing on how it provides for conceptualizing what and who matter in groundwater management, and how these decisions connect with functions for information, regulatory intervention, and coordination. California laws and policies spotlight the question of "who matters" through the concept of environmental justice. This inherently cumulative concept speaks to the unfair aggregation of environmental and socioeconomic stressors on subpopulations. This case study shows how groundwater depletion, access to drinking water, and environmental justice collide in local groundwater sustainability plans, and how an integrated response depends on good information, diverse interventions, and multilevel interactions.

1.5.2.2 Strategic Assessment and Biodiversity of the Great Barrier Reef

Australia's Great Barrier Reef ("Reef") is the world's largest coral reef ecosystem. It was inscribed on the list of World Heritage in 1981 on the basis of being of exceptional natural beauty, an outstanding example of earth's history, representing significant ongoing ecological and biological processes, and providing important natural habitat for in situ conservation of biodiversity. The Reef faces cumulative threats from diverse activities – developments such as ports and shipping, global climate change, coastal development, regional catchment runoff from agriculture, urban development, clearing of native vegetation, and extractive activities. Dealing with these stressors is fraught with controversy, particularly related to agriculture, associated regional land clearing, and extractive activities. These activities are economically valuable but contribute directly to water quality problems for the Reef and to global climate change, which in turn affects the Reef.

Concerned at these threats, in 2012 the World Heritage Committee requested that Australia complete a strategic environmental assessment for the Reef, which the Committee would scrutinize to ensure that it properly addressed cumulative impacts. Though strategic assessments are often considered tools for producing information at a point in time, the resulting joint federal- and state-level strategic assessments for the Reef also influenced ongoing information arrangements. The assessments also anticipated and led to contentious changes in regulatory interventions in relation to water quality. However, they were decidedly silent on climate change mitigation, focusing instead, half-heartedly, on adaptation.

Focusing on the contrasting impacts of cattle grazing and coal mining, this case study examines how the strategic assessments have supported two key regulatory functions of the CIRCle Framework for managing cumulative impacts: information and regulatory intervention. It shows that regulatory strategic assessment can provide for entrenching and integrating ongoing information collection and can directly influence diverse regulatory interventions to address cumulative impacts. At the same time, the Reef context reveals ongoing regulatory challenges in making comprehensive links between the intersecting problems of water quality and climate change.

1.5.2.3 Alpine Grasslands as Biocultural Landscapes in South Tyrol, Italy

Traditional pastoral practices have maintained Alpine grasslands over thousands of years, and Alpine biodiversity and local cultural heritage now depend on these practices. Across the Alps, biocultural grassland landscapes face diverse threats. Some herders abandon pastures and meadows as traditional, labor-intensive agricultural methods become uneconomic. In other cases, grasslands give way to intensive agriculture and developments such as infrastructure for urban expansion, tourism accommodation, and renewable energy projects. That is, harmful effects of nonuse, as well as new uses, accumulate to threaten Alpine grasslands. This type of cumulative environmental problem has analogs in other places where elements of the environment require active management. Nonuse challenges a typical legal focus on prohibiting or restricting activities to prevent environmental harm rather than encouraging or compelling action.

Harms to Alpine grasslands are not distributed uniformly: The Autonomous Province of Bolzano/Bozen-South Tyrol ("South Tyrol"), Italy, experiences some of the lowest rates of land abandonment and high rates of grassland retention. This relative success occurs in the context of complex regulatory arrangements. Interventions engage interlinked laws for nature, impact assessment, agriculture, landscape, and governance. Each of these areas comprises laws at the international, European Union (EU), national, provincial, and municipal levels.

This case study investigates how a diverse set of regulatory interventions, many focused on incentives, provides for maintaining and restoring grasslands in South Tyrol. It reveals how diverse forms of coordination – links between areas of laws, coordinating institutions, and dispute resolution processes – facilitate implementation in a context of deep multilevel governance.

1.6 CONCLUSION

By bringing together experience across diverse geographic places and legal areas and presenting a new framework for analysis, this book aims to spur greater regulatory engagement with cumulative environmental problems. The case studies presented in this book, and its illustrative examples, scratch the surface of the almost infinite combinations of threats and legal responses that arise in cumulative environmental problems. They highlight some of the challenges that regulatory designers face in addressing these problems and show how laws that undertake the CIRCle Framework functions – conceptualization, information, regulatory intervention, and coordination – can help.

The great diversity of legal mechanisms presented in this book suggests that there is significant scope for empirical research to delve deeper in relation to single case studies, as well as undertake comparative investigations across key variables in the mechanisms for individual CIRCle Framework functions, for example, comparing institution-based and rules-based legal mechanisms for coordination. It would also be useful to explore how the different mechanisms, and their evolution, sustain responses to cumulative environmental problems over time, as cumulative environmental problems change – questions that require deeper study of implementation experience. Another question that this book raises for further investigation is how best to combine coordination mechanisms for different Framework functions, and the extent to which different functions may benefit from different approaches in disparate contexts.

So many thinkers, and so much knowledge across diverse disciplines, can help us to deal with cumulative environmental problems. Rules can be responsive to this knowledge. Rules for key CIRCle Framework functions can be designed to counter the human cognitive quirks, dizzying complexity, ethical ambiguity, and other spanners in the works of social responsiveness that produce inaction and incomplete action when faced with cumulative environmental problems. Not only *can* they do it, but around the world, they actually *do* do it across many areas of law. Probably not perfectly, and not without difficulty – but in a way that gives us fertile ground for learning lessons to apply across diverse problems, to act to protect what matters.

2

Why Cumulative Environmental Problems Are Difficult and Implications for Law

Introducing the CIRCle Framework

2.1 INTRODUCTION

To design effective regulation for cumulative environmental problems, we need to understand why it is challenging to deal with them. We can then design a regulatory regime to anticipate and head off these challenges as much as possible. We can also avoid incorporating regulatory features that might entrench or exacerbate these challenges. While laws cannot single-handedly solve cumulative environmental problems, the core premise of this book is that across a wide range of legal areas related to the environment,[1] rules can supply guiding structures to support governments and others to do so.

As outlined in Chapter 1, key features of cumulative environmental problems are that they (1) are caused by many *heterogeneous actors*, undertaking (2) *diverse activities*; (3) involve *scientific complexity and unpredictability* of the resulting effects, which (4) aggregate over a *long period of time*; and (5) *engage multiple regulatory regimes* that may each deal separately with single issues (such as biodiversity or water pollution). This chapter collects insights from diverse disciplinary and interdisciplinary literatures – cognitive science, complex systems, public administration and policy analysis, science and technology studies, ethics, economics, management of common pool resources, and environmental management – to illuminate the key challenges associated with these features.[2] Synthesizing these challenges produces a

[1] See Chapter 3 for a discussion of potentially relevant areas of law.

[2] The chapter does not address disciplinary insights into cumulative effects that lack one or more important characteristics of cumulative environmental problems as defined earlier. For example, compound/multi-hazard planning deals with the aggregation of risks that accumulate over a shorter time period than is in focus here.

"CIRCle Framework" of four key functions that are needed, and that formal rules can deliver, to support action to address cumulative environmental problems: conceptualization, information, regulatory intervention, and coordination. Section 2.2 discusses the difficulties that lead to each Framework function in turn. Section 2.3 synthesizes why these difficulties make formal rules desirable, and the design features they indicate, and presents the CIRCle Framework that results from the preceding analysis.

First, a quick word about method. Since the terminology associated with cumulative effects (here used interchangeably with "cumulative impacts") varies between disciplines, and relevant knowledge is widely dispersed, finding it is not straightforward. The research for this chapter focused on the five features of cumulative environmental problems set out earlier, as well as the general idea of cumulative impacts or effects and related types of problems, for example, "wicked" and "super wicked" problems, "intractable policy problems," and collective action problems. These ideas engage vast literatures, far beyond what a single chapter could explore in depth. So, rather than delving deeply, this chapter focuses on key principles and research findings that are most relevant to considering how law could and should address cumulative environmental problems. To this end, references in this chapter skew toward review and synthesis articles and articles that deal with multiple jurisdictions, with original research articles cited mainly for illustrative purposes or because they are seminal contributions. Much other research, and many other disciplines, are relevant and helpful but fall outside the scope of this chapter and are reserved for future work refining the CIRCle Framework. The focus here is distilling implications for law from other disciplines; additional discussion and contributions from legal and regulatory scholarship are discussed in later chapters that each focus on a single CIRCle Framework function.

2.2 WHY IS DEALING WITH CUMULATIVE EFFECTS SO HARD? INSIGHTS FROM OUTSIDE LAW

2.2.1 *Conceptualizing the Matter of Concern Threatened by Cumulative Environmental Harm*

We begin by asking the simplest questions related to a cumulative environmental problem: cumulative effects *on what, or whom*? In other words, what do we care about, what is the "matter of concern" to be protected from cumulative environmental harm, or restored, and what do acceptable conditions for it look like? Answering even these initial questions is beset by challenges.

Laws in different jurisdictions legitimately protect diverse things related to the environment – here termed the “matter of concern.” This may be, for example, a natural resource like water as the foundation of a human right, the preservation of “wilderness,” a particular species, or the relationship between an Indigenous group and a place. Across this diversity, insights from environmental impact assessment (“EIA”) literature, cognitive science, economics, political science, and ethics suggest that clearly articulating important dimensions of a matter of concern – conceptualizing it – is not straightforward. Ambiguity, subjectivity, different values held by different actors, and the multiple possible dimensions of a matter of concern all pose challenges. Conceptualization, in turn, affects what information is needed to assess and respond to the problem, which actors are identified as potentially causing harm, and which actors and regulatory regimes are and should be engaged in dealing with the problem.

2.2.1.1 Conceptualizing Key Dimensions of a Matter of Concern: The Roles of Values, Science, and Transparency

EIA literature demonstrates the centrality and also the challenging complexity of conceptualization in terms of the multiple dimensions that are relevant and the subjectivity of decisions about these dimensions, whether decisions occur inside or outside an EIA context. EIA scholars, practitioners, and detailed technical guidelines on EIA generally agree that cumulative effects assessment involves first selecting environmental components as the focus for assessment, defining their boundaries, and defining the baseline conditions against which effects are considered to determine whether they are significant or unacceptable.[3]

These are important insights into the many dimensions of conceptualization that are also relevant outside EIA, but they make selecting these dimensions seem like a purely technical exercise. In reality, these are normative questions involving subjective decisions: Science can guide, but not decide.[4] Different interest groups will have different views, with variation across institutional, cultural and political settings.[5] In relation to thresholds of acceptable change to a matter of concern, policy analysis scholars note that even with

[3] E.g., F. Chris Jones, “Cumulative Effects Assessment: Theoretical Underpinnings and Big Problems” (2016) 24 *Environmental Reviews* 187–204, 191; Larry Canter, *Cumulative Effects Assessment and Management: Principles, Processes and Practices* (EIA Press 2015) 25–77.

[4] Jones, “Cumulative Effects Assessment,” 196, 198.

[5] Cary Coglianese and Shana M. Starobin, “Social Science and the Analysis of Environmental Policy” (2020) 37 *Review of Policy Research* 578–604, 581.

fulsome scientific information, deciding "how safe is safe" in relation to pollution depends on normative values and diverse criteria, from economic efficiency to equity.[6] The conflict management literature shows that clarity and transparency about what matters is necessary to understand, recognize, and, if possible, accommodate the different interests involved.[7]

Conceptualizing what we care about raises fundamental questions about links between people and the environment. Variants of EIA have arisen that expressly recognize these links. These variants include cultural impact assessment, health impact assessment, human rights impact assessment, and socio-economic impact assessment.[8] Conceptualizing a matter of concern as having economic value can also engage other concepts and regimes, such as natural capital and environmental economic accounting.[9]

Links between people and the environment are consequential because the amount of change to a matter of concern that is deemed unacceptable will depend on why it matters and who plays a role in deciding. The amount and type of acceptable change to a desert oasis, for example, may well be different if it constitutes cultural heritage, as opposed to habitat for an endangered fish.

Equally challenging, complexity science shows that environmental systems are dynamic, whereas much environmental law assumes stationarity.[10] This underscores the normative nature of deciding a threshold of unacceptable change, because there is no "natural" equilibrium.[11] In practice, however, time can feature strongly in selecting threshold conditions of acceptable change, and this can have important implications. If conditions of the matter of concern have changed significantly, choosing a temporally earlier set of

6 Ibid 585–588.

7 Lisa V. Bardwell, "Problem-Framing: A Perspective on Environmental Problem-Solving" (1991) 15 *Environmental Management* 603–612, 607–608 (giving an example of two children fighting over an orange; without determining their interests in the orange, an intervening parent halved the orange, then one child ate the pulp and discarded the skin, and the other did the reverse).

8 See generally Riki Therivel and Graham Wood (eds), *Methods of Environmental and Social Impact Assessment* (Routledge 2018).

9 See, e.g., William E. Rees, "Cumulative Environmental Assessment and Global Change" (1995) 15 *Environmental Impact Assessment Review* 295–309; Murray Patterson, Garry McDonald and Derrylea Hardy, "Is There More in Common Than We Think? Convergence of Ecological Footprinting, Emergy Analysis, Life Cycle Assessment and Other Methods of Environmental Accounting" (2017) 362 *Ecological Modelling* 19–36.

10 Robin Kundis Craig, "Stationarity Is Dead – Long Live Transformation: Five Principles for Climate Change Adaptation Law" (2010) 34 *Harvard Environmental Law Review* 9–73, 37–38.

11 See note 64 and accompanying text.

conditions as the threshold of acceptability will make contemporary conditions appear more degraded.

Articulating spatial boundaries is also a key part of conceptualization, and also not straightforward. EIA practitioners recommend that spatial boundaries for assessment and potential intervention reflect the scale of the matter of concern that receives impacts.[12] This might be, for example, the spatial distribution of a species, a local community, a transboundary water resource, or the global climate. But there are also trade-offs to consider. Cognitively, if "[p]resented at too large a scale, the problem seems unapproachable and overwhelming; if too small, it is easily dismissed," whereas a middle way can allow for "small wins."[13] Many criteria may apply to selecting a spatial scale: the complexity and time associated with analysis, the number of actors involved, the scalar fit with legal frameworks, economic relevance, and so on.[14]

Ultimately, the subjective nature of these decisions creates a need for transparency. Conceptualizing spatial boundaries, for example, requires transparently considering the implications of different spatial options and trade-offs between options,[15] given that there may be no natural or objective way to conceptualize them.[16] More generally, transparency about the rationale for conceptualizing the matter of concern in a particular way also helps to untangle problems of incoherence, discussed next. Transparency of decisions about what and who matter intersects with issues of information necessary to support environmental democracy and accountability, discussed more fully later.[17]

2.2.1.2 Coherence, Changing Values, and the Need for Coordination in Conceptualizing a Matter of Concern

Because conceptualizing cumulative environmental problems involves multiple dimensions, multiple actors, and decisions over potentially long time periods, the way a matter of concern is conceptualized may differ

[12] Riki Therivel and Bill Ross, "Cumulative Effects Assessment: Does Scale Matter?" (2007) 27 *Environmental Impact Assessment Review* 365–385, 366.

[13] Bardwell, "Problem-Framing," 609.

[14] Sonja A. M. Karstens, Pieter W. G. Bots and Jill H. Slinger, "Spatial Boundary Choice and the Views of Different Actors" (2007) 27 *Environmental Impact Assessment Review* 386–407, 401.

[15] Ibid 406.

[16] C. J. Walters, *Adaptive Management of Renewable Resources* (Macmillan 1986) 14, 34–38.

[17] See Chapter 5. Note that, as discussed in Section 1.2.4, I do not argue that laws should focus on any specific matter of concern. This book focuses on how formal rules can respond to cumulative change to a matter of concern, rather than on processes for deciding what matters.

problematically between actors and through time unless it is formalized. Policy design literature refers to conflicting goals as lacking "coherence,"[18] a term that I adopt here. For example, even within a single watershed, different governments and stakeholders may agree that "drought" is a problem, but have in mind different types of impacts and care about different human and natural systems that may be affected.[19] Similarly, in the EIA context, practitioners can define the core components of a system differently, including whether sociocultural dimensions of biophysical impacts are even considered.[20]

Incoherent conceptualizations are problematic because they can lead to different methodologies and conclusions about changing conditions and can obstruct effective responses to cumulative environmental problems. At minimum, incoherent conceptualizations can make it "impossible to see the elephant for all of its parts,"[21] reducing the comparability and usefulness of assessments if their insights cannot be aggregated with others. Incomparable assessments can compound challenges of insufficient data availability for responding to cumulative environmental problems (discussed later in the chapter), given that understanding cumulative effects fundamentally means aggregating the effects of multiple activities. If goals are uncertain or ambiguous, this also reduces the success of cooperative interventions to avoid environmental harm.[22]

Avoiding inadvertent incoherence in conceptualization requires "frame reflection" and construction of a shared narrative that either resolves or can accommodate different value preferences.[23] This requires some form of interaction between relevant actors, which here is termed coordination, discussed further later on.[24]

18 Michael Howlett and Jeremy Rayner, "Coherence, Congruence and Consistency in Policy Mixes" in Michael Howlett and Ishani Mukherjee (eds), *Routledge Handbook of Policy Design* (Routledge 2018) 389–403, 394.

19 See generally Amanda E. Cravens and others, "Integrating Ecological Impacts: Perspectives on Drought in the Upper Missouri Headwaters, Montana, United States" (2021) 13 *Weather, Climate, and Society* 363–376.

20 Emma E. Hodgson, Benjamin S. Halpern and Timothy E. Essington, "Moving Beyond Silos in Cumulative Effects Assessment" (2019) 7:211 *Frontiers in Ecology and Evolution* 1–8, 3, 6. See also Peter N. Duinker and others, "Scientific Dimensions of Cumulative Effects Assessment: Toward Improvements in Guidance for Practice" (2013) 21 *Environmental Reviews* 40–52, 42–3; Jones, "Cumulative Effects Assessment," 196.

21 Hodgson, Halpern and Essington, "Moving Beyond Silos," 1, 3, 6.

22 Ben R. Newell and others, "The Psychology of Environmental Decisions" (2014) 39 *Annual Review of Environment and Resources* 443–467, 458.

23 Brian W. Head and John Alford, "Wicked Problems" (2015) 47 *Administration and Society* 711–739, 723.

24 See Section 2.2.4.

Coordination is also required where a conceptualization of what and who matter needs to change due to social or environmental change. Contemporary societies seek to protect many things that were not protected even fifty years ago.[25] Environmental stressors like climate change may require triage or "directed adaptation" for ecosystems.[26] Such intentional change requires coordination to review objectives that form part of a conceptualization with stakeholders as part of an adaptive management approach.[27]

2.2.2 *Informing Decisions by Understanding Conditions of Matters of Concern, Threats, and Interventions*

Considering cumulative effects requires collecting, sharing, and analyzing information about the matter of concern and its current conditions, which activities have affected it and are likely to affect it, and whether those effects would push conditions to become unacceptable. This is easy to say, and more difficult to do.

2.2.2.1 Information Needed to Perceive Incremental Change, Data Shortages, and the Need for Coordination

Cumulative environmental harm can involve slowly shifting environmental conditions that are difficult to discern, even for experienced experts.[28] This "shifting baseline syndrome" means younger generations may be unaware of past conditions (a sociological phenomenon) and individuals may forget their past experience (a psychological phenomenon).[29] A lack of environmental data, reduced interaction with the natural world, and reduced knowledge of the natural environment also make it difficult to perceive cumulative environmental harm.[30] By contrast, perceiving individually large, sudden-onset

25 Benjamin J. Richardson, *Time and Environmental Law: Telling Nature's Time* (CUP 2017) 98–107.

26 Gregor W. Schuurman and others, "Navigating Ecological Transformation: Resist-Accept-Direct as a Path to a New Resource Management Paradigm" (2022) 72 *BioScience* 16–29, 20–22.

27 Larry Canter and Samuel F. Atkinson, "Adaptive Management with Integrated Decision Making: An Emerging Tool for Cumulative Effects Management" (2010) 28 *Impact Assessment and Project Appraisal* 287–297, 290–291, 292–293.

28 See generally S. K. Papworth and others, "Evidence for Shifting Baseline Syndrome in Conservation" (2009) 2(2) *Conservation Letters* 93–100.

29 See generally ibid; Masashi Soga and Kevin J. Gaston, "Shifting Baseline Syndrome: Causes, Consequences, and Implications" (2018) 16 *Frontiers in Ecology and the Environment* 222–230.

30 Soga and Gaston, "Shifting Baseline Syndrome," 224–225.

environmental changes is relatively easy. Empirically, shifting baseline syndrome has been identified in diverse natural resources and geographic contexts, including in relation to fishers in Indonesia, Mexico, and Tanzania; water availability in Alaska; and wildlife in Bolivia.[31]

Shifting baselines are problematic because they can lead to "increased tolerance for progressive environmental degradation."[32] At the extreme, change that occurs beyond human perception is beyond human control – it does not even arise as an issue for regulatory intervention.[33]

Perceiving and understanding accumulating harm requires aggregating comparable (interoperable) data about conditions of the matter of concern through time. But long-term data collection can be a low political priority, and aggregating information from multiple sources encounters challenges with comparability. As a result, data availability is often a problem for assessing cumulative effects.[34] In practice, different agencies of the same government may collect data differently such that it is not interoperable, agencies may lack a mechanism for obtaining data collected by private actors (even research institutions), and no single institution may have the mandate to assemble and interpret the data.[35]

Conversely, coordinating the data-related activities (e.g., collecting, sharing, analyzing) of multiple actors can reduce unnecessary duplication and cost,[36] making the most of available resources. Environmental management and

[31] Ibid 223.

[32] Papworth and others, "Evidence for Shifting Baseline Syndrome," 95; Soga and Gaston, "Shifting Baseline Syndrome," 222, 225.

[33] Rebecca Nelson, "Breaking Backs and Boiling Frogs: Warnings from a Dialogue between Federal Water Law and Environmental Law" (2019) 42 *University of New South Wales Law Journal* 1179–1214, 1203.

[34] Rebecca Nelson, "Water Data and the Legitimacy Deficit: A Regulatory Review and Nationwide Survey of Challenges Considering Cumulative Environmental Effects of Coal and Coal Seam Gas Developments" (2019) 23 *Australasian Journal of Water Resources* 24–34, 29–30; Bram Noble, Jialang Liu and Paul Hackett, "The Contribution of Project Environmental Assessment to Assessing and Managing Cumulative Effects: Individually and Collectively Insignificant?" (2017) 59 *Environmental Management* 531–545, 540; Zhao Ma, Dennis R. Becker and Michael A. Kilgore, "Barriers to and Opportunities for Effective Cumulative Impact Assessment within State-Level Environmental Review Frameworks in the United States" (2012) 55 *Journal of Environmental Planning and Management* 961–978, 964–965.

[35] François Bregha, "Institutional Barriers to Environmental Information" (1992) 20 *Environmental Monitoring and Assessment* 191–200, 192–193.

[36] Rachel Eberhard, Nathan Johnston and Jo-Anne Everingham, "A Collaborative Approach to Address the Cumulative Impacts of Mine-Water Discharge: Negotiating a Cross-Sectoral Waterway Partnership in the Bowen Basin, Australia" (2013) 38 *Resources Policy* 678–687, 683 (describing 100 duplicated monitoring points discovered through collaboration).

assessment literature emphasizes the importance of coordinating to form a shared understanding of an environmental problem and to share related information,[37] and highlights the need for better intergovernmental coordination in assessing cumulative impacts.[38]

2.2.2.2 Costs and Resistance to Data Collection and Sharing

Collecting data about matters of concern and threats to them may involve high costs. This is especially true where a resource is hidden, as in the case of groundwater, or difficult to reach, as for ocean biodiversity. Cumulative impact assessments require significant time, expertise, and cost,[39] in part, driven by the need for significant data gathering. It can also be more expensive to comprehensively monitor many individually small activities, which may constitute cumulatively significant threats, than a few large ones. Cuts to monitoring budgets, sometimes driven by a short-term focus and misperceptions of wastefulness, can create discontinuities that compromise the value of the data,[40] and make it difficult or impossible to assess incremental change (trends) over time.[41]

Lower-cost monitoring methods can include citizen science, hybrid government–citizen science programs, or high-tech automated initiatives.[42] Crowdsourcing data in a way that involves stakeholders may also increase understanding of a problem, but faces challenges in relation to ethics, data quality, data ownership/sharing, and, potentially, exploitation of unremunerated

[37] E.g., Jens Newig and Oliver Fritsch, "Environmental Governance: Participatory, Multi-Level – and Effective?" (2009) 19 *Environmental Policy and Governance* 197–214, 209.

[38] Zhao Ma, Dennis R. Becker and Michael A. Kilgore, "Assessing Cumulative Impacts within State Environmental Review Frameworks in the United States" (2009) 29 *Environmental Impact Assessment Review* 390–398, 392, 397.

[39] Ma, Becker and Kilgore, "Barriers to and Opportunities for Effective Cumulative Impact Assessment," 971 (noting that the evidence on whether this is greater than for EIA without cumulative impact assessment is equivocal).

[40] Eric Biber, "The Problem of Environmental Monitoring" (2011) 83 *University of Colorado Law Review* 1–82, 23–26, 39–41.

[41] E.g., Michael P. Schaubs, Ground Water Levels in the Lost Creek Designated Ground Water Basin (Colorado Division of Water Resources, Department of Natural Resources, 2010) 2, https://dnrweblink.state.co.us/dwr/0/edoc/2753828/DWR_2753828.pdf?searchid=9c553d8a-080a-4fa7-865f-63c663345acd.

[42] See generally M. Hino, E. Benami and N. Brooks, "Machine Learning for Environmental Monitoring" (2018) 1 *Nature Sustainability* 583–588; Susanne Becken and others, "A Hybrid Is Born: Integrating Collective Sensing, Citizen Science and Professional Monitoring of the Environment" (2019) 52 *Ecological Informatics* 35–45.

citizen scientists.[43] Attention to standards for data quality, accessibility, and sharing, and methods for rewarding contributions could help deal with these challenges.[44]

High-tech monitoring methods also raise their own legal issues related to privacy, safety, evidentiary value, and other concerns.[45] Using technology to monitor individually small activities that are potentially cumulatively significant can encounter resistance because of an assumption that their impacts represent "a drop in the ocean" that does not warrant monitoring. Sometimes monitoring is perceived to threaten individual or community privacy, as in community hostility to wildlife monitoring using camera traps in Nepal[46] and drones in Tanzania.[47] Monitoring technology has sometimes legitimized military interventions, such that it can produce an atmosphere of fear.[48]

Participatory approaches to deploying monitoring technology may help address community concerns.[49] Indeed, some argue that with the right safeguards and awareness of "red flags," technology can empower local populations, and environmental monitoring is increasingly participatory in practice.[50] Technology can empower those who experience cumulative impacts to advocate for regulatory intervention, from Indigenous paraecologists in Ecuador advocating for "rights of nature"[51] to community groups in

43 See generally Kathryn A. Lee, Jonathan R. Lee and Patrick Bell, "A Review of Citizen Science within the Earth Sciences: Potential Benefits and Obstacles" (2020) 131 *Proceedings of the Geologists' Association* 605–617.

44 Ibid 613.

45 See generally Chris Sandbrook, "The Social Implications of Using Drones for Biodiversity Conservation" (2015) 44(Suppl 4) *Ambio* 636–647; Jesús Jiménez López and Margarita Mulero-Pázmány, "Drones for Conservation in Protected Areas: Present and Future" (2019) 3 *Drones* 10, 17; Chris Sandbrook, Rogelio Luque-Lora and William M. Adams, "Human Bycatch: Conservation Surveillance and the Social Implications of Camera Traps" (2018) 16 *Conservation and Society* 493–504.

46 See generally Yashaswi Shrestha and Renaud Lapeyre, "Modern Wildlife Monitoring Technologies: Conservationists versus Communities? A Case Study: The Terai-Arc Landscape, Nepal" (2018) 16 *Conservation and Society* 91–101.

47 Sandbrook, "The Social Implications of Using Drones for Biodiversity Conservation," 640.

48 Naomi Millner, "As the Drone Flies: Configuring a Vertical Politics of Contestation within Forest Conservation" (2020) 80:102163 *Political Geography* 1–13, 2–3.

49 See generally Shrestha and Lapeyre, "Modern Wildlife Monitoring Technologies," 99. Participatory approaches are discussed later as a form of coordination: see Chapter 7.

50 Nathan Young and others, "Ethical Ecosurveillance: Mitigating the Potential Impacts on Humans of Widespread Environmental Monitoring" (2022) 4 *People and Nature* 830–840, 834–838.

51 M. R. Peck and others, "The Conflict between Rights of Nature and Mining in Ecuador: Implications of the Los Cedros Cloud Forest Case for Biodiversity Conservation" (2024) 6 *People and Nature* 1096–1115, 1108–1110.

Guatemala using drones in participatory forest monitoring to support community claims against transnational businesses,[52] to citizen science surveillance programs for invasive species that use low-cost smartphones, image recognition, and machine learning.[53] Ultimately, any blanket rejection of technology deserves reexamination in light of cumulative environmental problems and the significant benefits technology offers communities in facilitating the collection of information. Without it, cumulative environmental problems may build, unperceived and unaddressed.

Responding to cumulative environmental problems requires not just collecting, but also sharing and aggregating interoperable data associated with multiple and potentially numerous activities to give useful insights into a cumulative problem.[54] Data for understanding cumulative environmental problems, then, should be "FAIR" – findable, accessible, interoperable (as discussed earlier), and reusable.[55]

Yet, both governments and commercial entities may experience disincentives to sharing information. Regulated entities may also resist sharing information due to concerns that it is commercially sensitive and could give away an advantage to their competitors.[56] Arguments about trade secrets or intellectual property can be prominent in the case of new technology, for example, allegedly environmentally harmful fluids used in hydraulic fracturing,[57] and resource analyses that have commercial value, like in oil and gas.[58] Governments may resist sharing data, preferring to adopt a "what we don't know won't hurt us" attitude, or want to avoid public alarm.[59] Some environmental data may be classified as a state secret (as is soil pollution data in

[52] Millner, "As the Drone Flies: Configuring a Vertical Politics of Contestation within Forest Conservation," 12.

[53] Petr Pyšek and others, "Scientists' Warning on Invasive Alien Species" (2020) 95 *Biological Reviews* 1511–1534, 1522–1524.

[54] A. John Sinclair, Meinhard Doelle and Peter N. Duinker, "Looking up, Down, and Sideways: Reconceiving Cumulative Effects Assessment as a Mindset" (2017) 62 *Environmental Impact Assessment Review* 183–194, 192.

[55] Mark D. Wilkinson and others, "The FAIR Guiding Principles for Scientific Data Management and Stewardship" (2016) 3:160018 *Scientific Data* 1–9; Hodgson, Halpern and Essington, "Moving Beyond Silos," 3.

[56] Nelson, "Water Data," 30.

[57] See generally Keith B. Hall, "Hydraulic Fracturing: Trade Secrets and the Mandatory Disclosure of Fracturing Water Composition" (2012–2013) 49 *Idaho Law Review* 399–435.

[58] See generally Abbe E. L. Brown, "The Future of Intellectual Property" in Daniel J. Gervais (ed), *Rights to Do, Rights to Prevent, and an Intersected Approach? Lessons from Intellectual Property, Information Control and Oil and Gas* (Edward Elgar 2021) 105–127.

[59] Bregha, "Institutional Barriers to Environmental Information," 194–195.

China).[60] Other reasons include wanting to avoid "arming" opponents to a politically preferred project,[61] or protecting corrupt government officials who benefit from environmental harms.[62]

Finally, to usefully address cumulative environmental problems, data must also be contextualized by reference to specific matters of concern and their thresholds, rather than numerical values about abstracted environmental conditions. For example, reporting aggregate volumes of withdrawals from a river system, without more, says little about cumulative impacts in terms of stress relative to ecological thresholds and acceptable change. A small aggregate volume might be ecologically insignificant if withdrawn from a large river system, or catastrophic if withdrawn from a small stream in an arid zone. Context matters, but contextualizing data requires analysis, which, as described next, takes work and can be complex.

2.2.2.3 Complexity, Dynamism, Modeling, and Uncertainty

Complexity scholars show that predicting how potentially large numbers of activities will interact and aggregate to affect something is complex, involving deep uncertainty, feedback loops, emergent behavior, complex interactions, and nonlinear responses.[63] External drivers such as climate change and global economic shifts can combine with internal local-scale drivers like interactions between species to produce continuous change.[64]

This has several important implications. The psychological difficulty of constructing accurate mental models of dynamic systems[65] means formal scientific modeling is often needed to understand a complex system and its possible futures. Such models can require substantial data and computing capabilities,[66]

[60] Takashi Itakura, "Current Issues with the Regulatory Framework for Managing Soil Contamination in China" (2015) 18 *Asia Pacific Journal of Environmental Law* 119–146, 128–130.

[61] Bregha, "Institutional Barriers to Environmental Information," 195.

[62] Crispin Andrews, "Wildlife Monitoring: Should UAV Drones Be Banned?" (July 14, 2014) (discussing corruption in the context of illegal export of elephant tusks and rhinoceros horns), https://eandt.theiet.org/content/articles/2014/07/wildlife-monitoring-should-uav-drones-be-banned/.

[63] See generally Lael Parrott and Wayne S. Meyer, "Future Landscapes: Managing within Complexity" (2012) 10 *Frontiers in Ecology and the Environment* 382–389.

[64] Ibid 384.

[65] Newell and others, "The Psychology of Environmental Decisions," 450.

[66] Emma E. Hodgson and Benjamin S. Halpern, "Investigating Cumulative Effects across Ecological Scales" (2018) 33 *Conservation Biology* 22–32, 27–28.

and require significant time, expertise, and cost to undertake,[67] as well as multiple disciplines.[68] This is not a new issue. In the 1960s, Colorado lawyers noted the "dramatic possibilities" for efficiently managing large numbers of groundwater withdrawals of "utiliz[ing] the services of a computer," noting with evident envy that Nevada had such a device.[69] With improving computing capabilities, the feasibility of cumulative analysis methods further increases.[70]

Even with sophisticated models, it may be necessary to use significant simplifications and assumptions,[71] and significant uncertainty may be unavoidable due to nonlinearities and indirect effects.[72] Accordingly, information about predicted futures may best be presented as scenarios or "envelopes" rather than precise predictions,[73] and there is a need for ongoing adaptive management to counter uncertainties associated with cumulative effects.[74]

In other words, information about cumulative impacts is often complex and unavoidably uncertain. Uncertain information tends to discourage individuals from voluntarily adopting pro-environmental behavior, undermines cooperative solutions to a problem,[75] and heightens risks that information will not be used to take action.[76] Empirical research suggests that EIA, an important context for cumulative effects analysis, does not necessarily have a significant effect on decision-making.[77] Other risks to high-quality data and analysis for informing decision-making include cost cutting, regulatory capture,

67 Ma, Becker and Kilgore, "Barriers to and Opportunities for Effective Cumulative Impact Assessment," 971.

68 Hodgson and Halpern, "Investigating Cumulative Effects across Ecological Scales," 29.

69 Raphael J. Moses and George Vranesh, "Colorado's New Ground Water Laws" (1966) 38 *University of Colorado Law Review* 295–310, 303.

70 Hodgson and Halpern, "Investigating Cumulative Effects across Ecological Scales," 28.

71 Ibid 27.

72 Hodgson, Halpern and Essington, "Moving Beyond Silos," 1, 4.

73 Parrott and Meyer, "Future Landscapes," 387.

74 See generally Canter and Atkinson, "Adaptive Management with Integrated Decision Making."

75 Newell and others, "The Psychology of Environmental Decisions," 454, 458. See also Section 2.2.3.1.

76 Ben Orlove and others, "Climate Decision-Making" (2020) 45 *Annual Review of Environment and Resources* 271–303, 286; National Research Council, *Using Science as Evidence in Public Policy* (National Academies Press 2012) 14–15.

77 Urmila Jha-Thakur and Thomas B. Fischer, "25 Years of the UK EIA System: Strengths, Weaknesses, Opportunities and Threats" (2016) 61 *Environmental Impact Assessment Review* 19–26, 21; Ivar Lyhne and others, "Theorising EIA Effectiveness: A Contribution Based on the Danish System" (2017) 62 *Environmental Impact Assessment Review* 240–249, 243; John J. Loomis and Maurício Dziedzic, "Evaluating EIA Systems' Effectiveness: A State of the Art" (2018) 68 *Environmental Impact Assessment Review* 29–37, 31–32.

manipulation by proponents, and political pressure,[78] all of which underscores the importance of transparency.

Research on "actionable" or usable science suggests at least a partial antidote to this disconnect between information and action: Decision-makers are more likely to use information that is credible (scientifically adequate), salient (relevant to decision-makers' needs), and legitimate (fair, unbiased, and respectful of stakeholders).[79] These characteristics can develop through processes to "co-produce" knowledge[80] by meaningfully involving stakeholders in genuine deliberation and social learning, as opposed to one-way consultation.[81] This poses a challenge for cumulative environmental harms, however, which involve many actors. Though not impossible,[82] initiating and maintaining the involvement of many stakeholders in iterative scientific work can be expensive, time-consuming, and complex.[83] That is, it requires attention to coordination about information, discussed further later.[84]

For completeness, it is also important to note that complex, multilayered policy settings can produce a need to collect information about the regulatory landscape itself to determine gaps and weaknesses. Even understanding which interventions are available to address diverse threatening activities, and who the relevant regulators are, may be a significant task. But it is critical to evaluating whether existing mechanisms are adequate to deal with threats, or whether change is needed.[85]

78 Erin O'Donnell and Rebecca Nelson, "Shield Science for Robust Decisions" (2020) 3 *Nature Sustainability* 675–676, 675.

79 For a seminal article on this issue, see David W. Cash and others, "Knowledge Systems for Sustainable Development" (2003) 100 *Proceedings of the National Academy of Sciences* 8086–8091. See also Laurenz Langer, Janice Tripney and David Gough, *The Science of Using Science: Researching the Use of Research Evidence in Decision-Making* (University College London 2016) 27.

80 Orlove and others, "Climate Decision-Making," 17; see generally Aparna Bamzai-Dodson and others, "Engaging with Stakeholders to Produce Actionable Science: A Framework and Guidance" (2021) 13(4) *Weather, Climate, and Society* 1027–1041.

81 See generally Amanda E. Cravens and Nicole M. Ardoin, "Negotiating Credibility and Legitimacy in the Shadow of an Authoritative Data Source" (2016) 21:30 *Ecology and Society* 1–14; Nicola Ulibarri, "Collaborative Model Development Increases Trust in and Use of Scientific Information in Environmental Decision-Making" (2018) 82 *Environmental Science and Policy* 136–142.

82 Cravens and Ardoin, "Negotiating Credibility," 10.

83 Bamzai-Dodson and others, "Engaging with Stakeholders," 1030–1031 (the "inform" or "loading dock" approach).

84 See Section 2.2.4.

85 The case studies presented in Chapters 8 to 10 demonstrate approaches to collecting information about regulatory landscapes relevant to specific cumulative environmental problems.

2.2.3 *Intervening to Protect a Matter of Concern from Cumulative Harm*

Even if contributors to cumulative harm, and relevant decision-makers, meaningfully consider information about this harm, it is not a foregone conclusion that they will act to address it. Political factors and a sense of futility can discourage action. Allocating responsibilities to act among many heterogeneous contributors to harm can be ethically ambiguous. Adaptive intervention, needed to deal with uncertainty, strikes diverse challenges. This section addresses each of these issues in turn. Additional issues that arise from legal structures themselves – like the legal silos that produce fragmented, unconnected decision-making, and the cost of interventions – are addressed later in this book.[86]

2.2.3.1 Risk Perception, Futility, and Short-Termism as Barriers to Action

Although they may aggregate to cause serious harm (and putting aside the issue of shifting baselines), individually minor actions are often simply considered less serious than more dramatic single harms, which discourages action to address cumulative harms. People tend to perceive the risks of "acute hazards," that is, individual "high-energy events, which are usually of a short duration, such as cyclones and floods" differently to chronic hazards or "quiet crises," that is, "insidious and/or pervasive [hazards], commonly being of low energy and occurring over [longer] periods."[87] The latter often simply seem less important.[88] Cognitively, appreciating the aggregate risk of minor activities needs to overcome automatic assessments that a small impact caused by a familiar activity is not a threat, and relies on judging the effect of aggregating something – a type of thinking that tends not to be done well automatically.[89] Media reporting can reinforce these cognitive tendencies. While reporters flock to catastrophic environmental accidents (e.g., a supertanker oil spill), individually less dramatic cumulative effects receive little attention (e.g., the cumulatively greater amount of oil discharged annually by ships cleaning their ballast tanks).[90]

[86] See Chapter 6, Section 6.5.3.
[87] Melissa Haw, Chris Cocklin and David Mercer, "A Pinch of Salt: Landowner Perception and Adjustment to the Salinity Hazard in Victoria, Australia" (2000) 16 *Journal of Rural Studies* 155–169, 157.
[88] Ibid 166.
[89] Daniel Kahneman, *Thinking, Fast and Slow* (Penguin Books 2012) 93.
[90] Bregha, "Institutional Barriers to Environmental Information," 196.

A distinct cognitive challenge arises in cases of slowly accumulating harm that will only manifest relatively far in the future. People tend to have "cognitive myopia" and discount future consequences excessively in favor of immediate rewards or avoidance of immediate costs.[91] Indeed, policy responses that "discount the future irrationally" are considered a key feature of problems that are "super wicked."[92]

Even where an actor perceives that their activity, even though relatively minor, causes cumulative harm, a sense of futility ("changing my activity would make no difference") may discourage them from changing course.[93] Countering this sense of futility is possible with structured effort. It might involve, for example, communicating an ethical duty of collective action[94] or emphasizing the symbolic benefits of acting, like "freedom and independence from foreign oil" in the case of adopting lower emission cars.[95]

Decision-making structures that emphasize the short term may reinforce the effects of cognitive myopia and feelings of futility. Decision-makers in democratic political institutions tend to focus on short electoral cycles, though short-termism also varies among nations.[96] Short-term electoral cycles discourage intervention to deal with slowly accumulating threats that impose short-term costs on constituents[97] to create spatially and temporally diffuse benefits. This can affect things such as considering climate change scenarios and long-term planned activities like timber harvesting. Countering short-termism might involve mechanisms to "'lock[] in' long-term preferences" to avoid returning to short-term considerations as time progresses;[98] shortening the

[91] Elke U. Weber, "Breaking Cognitive Barriers to a Sustainable Future" (2017) 1:0013 *Nature Human Behaviour* 1–2, 1.

[92] Kelly Levin and others,"Overcoming the Tragedy of Super Wicked Problems: Constraining Our Future Selves to Ameliorate Global Climate Change" (2012) 45 *Policy Sciences* 123–152, 128.

[93] Daniel Sperling and Deborah Gordon, *Two Billion Cars: Driving Towards Sustainability* (OUP 2009) 171–172.

[94] See generally Jonathan Crowe, "'It Makes No Difference What We Do': Climate Change and the Ethics of Collective Action" (2021) 40 *University of Queensland Law Journal* 477–490.

[95] Sperling and Gordon, *Two Billion Cars*, 171–172.

[96] Hal E. Hershfield, H. Min Bang and Elke U. Weber, "National Differences in Environmental Concern and Performance Are Predicted by Country Age" (2014) 25 *Psychological Science* 152–160; Johanna Peetz and Michael J. A. Wohl, "Perceiving Time through Group-Based Glasses: Collective Temporal Orientation" (2019) 58 *British Journal of Social Psychology* 609–629, 615.

[97] Sari Graben and Eric Biber, "Presidents, Parliaments, and Legal Change: Quantifying the Effect of Political Systems in Comparative Environmental Law" (2017) 35 *Virginia Environmental Law Journal* 357–419, 410.

[98] Levin and others, "Overcoming the Tragedy of Super Wicked Problems," 128.

perceived temporal distance by describing the cumulative problem as urgent;[99] or expressly considering the interests of future generations.[100]

2.2.3.2 Allocating Responsibility for Action, Ethical Ambiguity, and the Role of Coordination

Effectively intervening to respond to cumulative environmental harm requires comprehensively considering activities that create harm and determining whether and how to allocate responsibility for preventing or responding to harm among multiple, and potentially many, contributors. There is no single "right" answer. Risk-based cost-benefit analyses and different ethical frameworks, for example, may produce different approaches.[101] Risk analysts suggest assessing "the relative importance of each nth risk effect, the potential improvement from addressing it and the costs (including delay) of doing so."[102] Even this apparently simple approach, however, is more difficult than it seems where there is uncertainty about whether a change will lead to an improvement in the matter of concern – and cumulative impacts can involve multiple sources and kinds of uncertainty associated with multiple interacting risks, leading to compounding uncertainty.[103]

To attribute responsibility to someone who contributes to harm, ethicists tend to rely on some combination of causation, coercion (i.e., whether an actor could have acted in a different way), knowledge of consequences, intentionality, and appreciation of the moral implications of the action.[104] These factors can all be problematic for cumulative impacts, especially for individually minor impacts. Causation may be difficult to predict or prove due to complex interacting effects, and the causes of a problem may include "background" natural causes and harms with uncertain origins. Individually, small effects may not be controllable in a meaningful way (e.g., using water for basic household needs or harming the environment to undertake basic economic development) or where reducing harm requires resources that someone lacks. Complex, nonlinear systems may mean a contributor does not appreciate or intend the consequences of their

[99] Orlove and others, "Climate Decision-Making," 15.

[100] See, e.g., Iñigo González-Ricoy and Axel Gosseries (eds), *Institutions for Future Generations* (OUP 2016).

[101] Jonathan B. Wiener, "Learning to Manage the Multirisk World" (2020) 40 *Risk Analysis* 2137–2143, 2139.

[102] Ibid 2140.

[103] See generally James Rising and others, "The Missing Risks of Climate Change" (2022) 610 *Nature* 643–651.

[104] Kelly G. Shaver, *The Attribution of Blame: Causality, Responsibility and Blameworthiness* (Springer 1985) 70; see also Philip Pettit, "Responsibility Incorporated" (2007) 117 *Ethics* 171–201.

action. Cumulative environmental problems can involve the "distributed moral actions" of many individuals, where an individual action is "either not morally charged at all or below a threshold of moral relevance."[105] Though the cumulative impact is morally bad, no individual intended it, so intentionality means that no one can be held responsible.[106]

An alternative "ethics without intentionality" would attribute responsibility for the entire environmental harm to each contributor to that harm in proportion to their ability "to avoid the negative outcome," regardless of their intention, provided the contributors know that they will be held responsible, and are able to learn from, and modify, their behavior.[107] An alternative, potentially more controversial (in Western cultures) ethic of collective responsibility would address cumulative harms by making an agent or non-agential set of actors responsible for distributed morally negative actions.[108]

Public administration scholars suggest a different solution to allocating responsibility: participatory and collaborative governance (a type of coordination; see later on) makes stakeholders more likely to accept the output of a decision-making process and comply with it if their legitimate representatives are involved, especially where this occurs early, transparently, is based on clear and understandable information, and does not exclude important groups.[109] In addition, introducing regulation to address cumulative environmental problems itself is considered ethically relatively unproblematic if one accepts that regulation is justifiable if it deters unwanted behavior.[110]

2.2.3.3 Adapting Interventions, Fairness, Path Dependence, and "Single Action Bias"

To cope with their inherent uncertainty, scholars have long prescribed adaptive management (relevantly here, adaptive interventions) for problems caused by

[105] Luciano Floridi, "Faultless Responsibility: On the Nature and Allocation of Moral Responsibility for Distributed Moral Actions" (2016) 374:20160112 *Philosophical Transactions of the Royal Society A: Mathematical, Physical and Engineering Sciences* 1–13, note 11.

[106] Ibid 4.

[107] Ibid 11.

[108] For a review of the variety of ways this is conceptualized in the philosophical literature, see generally Säde Hormio, "Collective Responsibility for Climate Change" (2023) 14:e830 *WIREs Climate Change* 1–14.

[109] Jens Newig and others, "The Environmental Performance of Participatory and Collaborative Governance: A Framework of Causal Mechanisms" (2018) 46 *Policy Studies Journal* 269–297, 291.

[110] Pettit, "Responsibility Incorporated," 175–176.

diverse and dispersed sources that interact in complex ways,[111] with the exception of problems involving "extreme existential risks" that are too rare and devastating to learn from.[112] However, this is confounded by ethical, economic, and psychological barriers to adapting the duties imposed on contributors to harm. Jurisdictions that seek to improve their laws to better deal with cumulative environmental problems are also adapting those laws and will strike similar barriers.

Countering adaptation, fairness can be perceived as requiring finality of decisions, certainty, and respect for settled expectations.[113] If new information or ideas about what matters or the effectiveness of existing interventions produces new responsibilities or restrictions, and possibly new costs, this can be perceived as unfair and support political obstruction on this basis. On the other hand, shared decision-making (i.e., coordination), transparency, and forms of popular accountability and conflict resolution can help increase legitimacy.[114]

Other factors can also make it difficult to adapt interventions. Path dependence means that past choices constrain future change due to experience, sunk costs, and vested interests.[115] Adaptive management requires iterative decision-making, but "single action bias" means that psychologically, decision-makers feel less worried after they take an initial action, even where "a portfolio of protective actions might have been advisable."[116] Risk aversion in decision-makers and other bureaucratic factors within and between government agencies further discourage adaptive management.[117]

2.2.4 *Coordinating among Governments and with Stakeholders*

The foregoing discussion has already alluded to the critical role of interactions between governments and stakeholders – those affected by and contributing to

[111] E.g., Walters, *Adaptive Management*, 333–354; Jones, "Cumulative Effects Assessment," 192, 196; Canter and Atkinson, "Adaptive Management with Integrated Decision Making"; J. B. Ruhl, "Regulation by Adaptive Management – Is It Possible?" (2005–2006) 7 *Minnesota Journal of Law Science and Technology* 21–57, 22–23.

[112] Wiener, "Learning to Manage the Multirisk World," 2140.

[113] Jonathan H. Adler, "Dynamic Environmentalism and Adaptive Management: Legal Obstacles and Opportunities" (2015) 11 *Journal of Law Economics and Policy* 133–162, 154.

[114] Robin Kundis Craig and others, "Balancing Stability and Flexibility in Adaptive Governance: An Analysis of Tools Available in U.S. Environmental Law" (2017) 22(2):3 *Ecology and Society* 1–15, 7.

[115] Daniel Rosenbloom, James Meadowcroft and Benjamin Cashore, "Stability and Climate Policy? Harnessing Insights on Path Dependence, Policy Feedback, and Transition Pathways" (2019) 50 *Energy Research and Social Science* 168–178, 170–171.

[116] Elke U. Weber, "Experience-Based and Description-Based Perceptions of Long-Term Risk: Why Global Warming Does Not Scare Us (Yet)" (2006) 77 *Climatic Change* 103–120, 116.

[117] Walters, *Adaptive Management*, 23, 30–32.

a cumulative environmental problem – and between governments engaged in a cumulative environmental problem. I use the generic term "coordination" to describe this interaction, intending it to flexibly embrace interactions of various types, from willing partnerships to dispute resolution among antagonists. Chapter 7 expands on this to cover links between laws that may not involve the direct interaction of actors; hence, I do not use the overarching term "collaboration," used in some other fields. This section expands on these rationales for coordination and explores barriers to coordination that stem from the inherent nature of cumulative environmental problems.

2.2.4.1 Coordination Is Needed to Respond to Cumulative Environmental Problems

As discussed earlier, the need for coordination arises in relation to conceptualizing the matter of concern because it involves value-rich decisions that often inherently affect people as part of the matter of concern and because coordination is needed to avoid incoherence in subjective decisions about what and who matter. The need for coordination with stakeholders and governments arises in relation to information because they hold knowledge and data that are important to understand the problem, because monitoring small activities can raise concerns that coordination can address, and because involving them creates opportunities for deliberation and learning that can make decisions more likely to be accepted. And the need for coordination arises in relation to intervention to address and head off ethical quandaries, enhance the legitimacy of decisions, and deal with the lack of a clear way to allocate and adapt responsibilities to act to address cumulative harms.

Coordination is also required for wider reasons related to these functions. Theories in the fields of public policy, public administration, and economics that analyze the distribution of regulatory authority in space show that environmental regulatory authority is often layered, overlapping, controversial, and dynamic between levels of government.[118] This means that intergovernmental coordination is required for sustainable management in general.[119]

Even where relevant regulatory competencies are not formally shared, cumulative environmental problems involve "unavoidable interdependencies" – they

[118] It is beyond the scope of this chapter to review the theories and numerous analytical concepts developed by the relevant disciplines in detail. For a useful review, see: Philipp Trein, Iris Meyer and Martino Maggetti, "The Integration and Coordination of Public Policies: A Systematic Comparative Review" (2019) 21 *Journal of Comparative Policy Analysis: Research and Practice* 332–349.

[119] E.g., Levin and others, "Overcoming the Tragedy of Super Wicked Problems," 127–128.

concern multiple levels of government simultaneously[120] as well as multiple actors at a single level. This produces a need for coordination. Government actors may be relevant to addressing a cumulative environmental problem because they perform a function that relates to an activity or impact that creates a harm or a benefit to a matter of concern. The cumulative harm may also extend horizontally or vertically across the geographic jurisdiction of multiple governments or governing arrangements, for example, air pollution extending across local, subnational, or national boundaries.

Multilevel governance scholars note that "cumulative outcomes of local phenomena create global problems" and "serious global trends," such as proliferating infrastructure, pollution, and resource use and their environmental effects.[121] They argue that cumulative effects counsel higher-level governance "to enhance understanding of a problem" and access scientific information; but, in addition, ensuring finer-grained local understanding of a problem and using legitimate, trusted, and effective local "problem-solving institutions" requires lower-level governance.[122] In other words, coordination between levels can harness "problem solving synergy" between "the unique governance capacities of local and national actors."[123]

Conversely, failing to coordinate carries risks: Overlapping regulatory actors may take different approaches to conceptualization, information, and intervention that are mutually undermining or, at minimum, fail to take advantage of potential synergies.[124] Without attention, concurrent regulatory competencies

[120] Johanna Schnabel, *Managing Interdependencies in Federal Systems: Intergovernmental Councils and the Making of Public Policy* (Palgrave Macmillan 2020) 1.

[121] Joyeeta Gupta and Claudia Pahl-Wostl, "Global Water Governance in the Context of Global and Multilevel Governance – Its Need, Form, and Challenges" (2013) 18 *Ecology and Society* 1–10, 1, 3.

[122] Ibid 57; Newig and others, "Environmental Performance," 290–291; Krister P. Andersson and Elinor Ostrom, "Analyzing Decentralized Resource Regimes from a Polycentric Perspective" (2008) 41 *Policy Sciences* 71–93, 76.

[123] Erin Ryan, "Environmental Federalism's Tug of War Within" in Kalyani Robbins (ed), *The Law and Policy of Environmental Federalism: A Comparative Analysis* (Edward Elgar 2015) 355–418, 362–363.

[124] Florian Kern and Michael Howlett, "Implementing Transition Management as Policy Reforms: A Case Study of the Dutch Energy Sector" (2009) 42 *Policy Sciences* 391–408, 401, 403; Karoline S. Rogge and Kristin Reichardt, "Policy Mixes for Sustainability Transitions: An Extended Concept and Framework for Analysis" (2016) 45 *Research Policy* 1620–1635, 1626; Marie Byskov Lindberg, Jochen Markard and Allan Dahl Andersen, "Policies, Actors and Sustainability Transition Pathways: A Study of the EU's Energy Policy Mix" (2019) 48:103668 *Research Policy* 1–15, 10; Anders Branth Pedersen, Helle Ørsted Nielsen and Carsten Daugbjerg, "Environmental Policy Mixes and Target Group Heterogeneity: Analysing Danish Farmers' Responses to the Pesticide Taxes" (2020) 22 *Journal of Environmental Policy and Planning* 608–619, 616.

may result in there being no, or no effective, regulation in important respects. This may occur where one level of government comes to expect that another will act, and ceases its own environmental protection action, posing potential problems where the other level's regulation contains important omissions.[125]

Sometimes, however, duplication and redundancy provide insurance against agency capture and greater opportunity for policy experimentation and interest group input as a valuable check and balance in a politically controversial area, and a facilitator of innovation.[126] Indeed, environmental issues may be so complex, interconnected, and disrespectful of territorial boundaries that it would be impossible and undesirable to eliminate duplication.[127]

The passage of time itself produces the need for coordination, since policy layering and drift over time can create incoherent goals between agencies and levels of government.[128] Allocations of legislative authority over the environment, and the degree to which this authority is exercised by different levels, can also change due to constitutional amendment, shifting judicial interpretation, or negotiation.[129]

The insidious nature of cumulative environmental problems and accompanying risks for maintaining political salience of the problem suggest that there may also be "side benefits" from involving more regulatory actors in

[125] Sara Dillon, "The Mirage of EC Environmental Federalism in a Reluctant Member State Jurisdiction" (1999) 8 *NYU Environmental Law Journal* 1–73, 13–15.

[126] Robyn Hollander, "Rethinking Overlap and Duplication – Federalism and Environmental Assessment in Australia" (2010) 40 *Publius* 136–170, 137, 139, 153–156; Gupta and Pahl-Wostl, "Global Water Governance," 55; Andersson and Ostrom, "Analyzing Decentralized Resource Regimes from a Polycentric Perspective," 76; Erin Ryan, "Negotiating Environmental Federalism: Dynamic Federalism as a Strategy for Good Governance" (2017) *Wisconsin Law Review* 17–39, 37; Barbara A. Cosens and Craig A. Stow, "Resilience and Water Governance: Addressing Fragmentation and Uncertainty in Water Allocation and Water Quality Law" in A. S. Garmestani and C. R. Allen (eds), *Social-Ecological Resilience and Law* (Columbia University Press 2014) 142–175, 156–157; Florian Brossette, Claudia Bieling and Marianne Penker, "Adapting Common Resource Management to Under-use Contexts: The Case of Common Pasture Organizations in the Black Forest Biosphere Reserve" (2022) 16 *International Journal of the Commons* 29–46, 38.

[127] Hollander, "Rethinking Overlap," 151–153.

[128] Kern and Howlett, "Implementing Transition Management," 395–397; Michael Howlett, Ishani Mukherjee and Jeremy Rayner, "Understanding Policy Designs over Time: Layering, Stretching, Patching and Packaging" in Michael Howlett and Ishani Mukherjee (eds), *Routledge Handbook of Policy Design* (Taylor & Francis 2018) 136–144, 137–138.

[129] Lee Godden and Jacqueline Peel, *Environmental Law: Scientific, Policy and Regulatory Dimensions* (OUP 2010) 127; Roderic O'Gorman, "Environmental Constitutionalism: A Comparative Study" (2017) 6 *Transnational Environmental Law* 435–462, 437; Ryan, "Negotiating Environmental Federalism," 37. Section 7.2.1 describes this issue in more detail.

coordinated efforts, as "norm sustainers."[130] If short-term political factors do not favor continued attention to a cumulative environmental problem by one regulatory actor, others may sustain attention to it. Peer pressure, including from a politically independent actor, may persuade a recalcitrant actor to act[131] and one actor may step in to compensate for another's inaction.[132] Within a single national jurisdiction, this might mean involving more levels of government or involving other bodies that can act as quasi-regulators (a type of coordination). It might also mean allowing more regulators or others to intervene. Empirically, greater coordination between policy officers and political actors can also encourage action to deal with cumulative harms.[133]

2.2.4.2 Barriers to Coordination

Despite this need for coordination, the characteristics of cumulative environmental problems suggest coordination is unlikely to emerge organically among contributors to a problem, nor among the multiple agencies and levels of government relevant to addressing it. I take these in turn.

Cumulative environmental problems lack characteristics that make collective action likely, and have characteristics that discourage collaboration. Common pool resources research has shown that stable self-governance through collective action emerges where the "user group" and boundaries of a resource are clearly defined, monitoring is undertaken in a way that is accountable to resource users, and where most individuals affected by operational rules can participate in modifying them.[134] This tends to suggest a resource that is relatively small, local scale, and managed by a relatively homogeneous user group.[135] Collaborative governance literature suggests that dense networks of linked organizations create social capital, relatively balanced power relations, and relationships of trust, which, among other factors,

[130] See generally Sharmila L. Murthy, "States and Cities as 'Norm Sustainers'" (2019) 37 *Virginia Environmental Law Journal* 1–51.

[131] See, e.g., Chapter 9 (Great Barrier Reef), Section 9.3.1.

[132] Todd S. Aagaard, "Regulatory Overlap, Overlapping Legal Fields, and Statutory Discontinuities" (2011) 29 *Virginia Environmental Law Journal* 237–303, 292–294.

[133] Elena Bondarouk, Duncan Liefferink and Ellen Mastenbroek, "Politics or Management? Analysing Differences in Local Implementation Performance of the EU Ambient Air Quality Directive" (2020) 40 *Journal of Public Policy* 449–472, 467.

[134] Frank Van Laerhoven, Michael Schoon and Sergio Villamayor-Tomas, "Celebrating the 30th Anniversary of Ostrom's Governing the Commons: Traditions and Trends in the Study of the Commons, Revisited" (2020) 14 *International Journal of the Commons* 208–224, 219 (citing Ostrom's design principles).

[135] Noting that there is increasing interest in larger-scale studies of common pool resources: ibid, 221.

promote the initiation of collaboration, whereas uncertainty and a lack of incentives (like a law requiring collaboration), discourage it.[136] By contrast, cumulative environmental problems involve larger scales and diverse contributors who do not necessarily or naturally share the same goals.[137] The problem may even escape the "physical control or even the knowledge of community-based resource management."[138] Heterogeneity among stakeholders can increase distrust, making coordination difficult.[139] The importance of formal rules increases with "larger, more complex, and more prolonged" problems[140] – all characteristics of cumulative environmental problems.

Formalizing supportive frameworks for coordination involving stakeholders secures the opportunity for ongoing, iterative engagement.[141] Indeed, the idea that cumulative environmental problems engage the shared responsibility of multiple actors and the need for a collaborative response between government, different industry sectors, and Indigenous Peoples appears in diverse principles, policies, and guides for cumulative effects assessment.[142]

Effective coordination between different agencies and levels of government to deal with a cumulative environmental problem is similarly unlikely to

[136] Kirk Emerson and Tina Nabatchi, "Initiating Collaborative Governance: The System Context, Drivers, and Regime Formation" in Kirk Emerson and Tina Nabatchi (eds), *Collaborative Governance Regimes* (Georgetown University Press 2015) 39–56, 42–49.

[137] Carol M. Rose, "Ostrom and the Lawyers: The Impact of Governing the Commons on the American Legal Academy" (2011) 5 *International Journal of the Commons* 28, 36–37.

[138] Ibid 37.

[139] Arvind Lakshmisha and Andreas Thiel, "Legitimacy, Shared Understanding and Exchange of Resources: Co-Managing Lakes Along an Urban–Rural Gradient in Greater Bengaluru Metropolitan Region, India" (2023) 71 *Environmental Management* 523–537, 534.

[140] Tanya Heikkila and others, "Collaboration Dynamics: Principled Engagement, Shared Motivation, and the Capacity for Joint Action" in Kirk Emerson and Tina Nabatchi (eds), *Collaborative Governance Regimes* (Georgetown University Press 2015) 57–80.

[141] Ibid 58–64 ("principled engagement" requiring iteration through phases of discovery, definition, determinations, and deliberation).

[142] E.g., Canadian Council of Ministers of the Environment, "Canada-Wide Definitions and Principles for Cumulative Effects" (2014) 1, https://ccme.ca/en/res/cedefinitionsandprinciples1.0e.pdf; "Navigating the Implementation Impasse: Enabling Interagency Collaboration on Cumulative Effects" (July 2019) Aotearoa Cumulative Effects (ACE) Framework, 8, www.sustainableseaschallenge.co.nz/tools-and-resources/ace-framework/; Department of Planning and Environment (NSW), "Cumulative Impact Assessment Guidelines for State Significant Projects" (October 2022) 13, www.planning.nsw.gov.au/sites/default/files/2023-03/cumulative-impact-assessment-guidelines-for-ssp.pdf; Pablo Cardinale, Lorne Greig and Patricia Miller, "Good Practice Handbook: Cumulative Impact Assessment and Management: Guidance for the Private Sector in Emerging Markets" (International Finance Corporation, 2013) 48, www.ifc.org/wps/wcm/connect/topics_ext_content/ifc_external_corporate_site/sustainability-at-ifc/publications/publications_handbook_cumulativeimpactassessment.

emerge by itself. Cumulative environmental problems likely lack important features that promote governmental coordination. These features include leaders who perceive that their interests are served by incurring the "high … transaction costs of initiating a collaborative effort," a starting appreciation of the salience of the issue among all participants,[143] and a shared set of "policy-core beliefs," such as common "policy-related values and perceptions about whose welfare counts, the relative authority of governments and markets, the proper roles of the general public, elected officials, civil servants, experts, and the relative seriousness and causes of policy problems."[144] Regulators tend to focus on single risks due to "mission-driven agencies, sometimes with narrow legal authority; fragmented institutions, with separate specialized domains … and the omitted voices of those affected."[145]

While cooperative networks can help better understand the nature of problems and identify and facilitate implementing solutions,[146] voluntary collaboration is unlikely to arise under conditions where parties have conflicting interests, lack trust and mutual commitment,[147] or even knowledge of who all the relevant parties are. The nature of cumulative environmental problems makes it more likely that these conditions will occur, partly because of the numbers of government actors involved and the difficulty of even forming relationships in the first place. In addition, where information is power, agencies at a single level of government or between levels of government may "hoard" it.[148] Collaborative governance also presents the challenge of sustaining participation through time,[149] which is particularly important where impacts accumulate incrementally. Indeed, the "turbulence" of the public sector can make it hard to sustain collaborative approaches,[150] and the

[143] Kirk Emerson, Tina Nabatchi and Stephen Balogh, "An Integrative Framework for Collaborative Governance" (2012) 22 *Journal of Public Administration Research and Theory* 1–29, 9.

[144] John C. Calanni and others, "Explaining Coordination in Collaborative Partnerships and Clarifying the Scope of the Belief Homophily Hypothesis" (2014) 25 *Journal of Public Administration Research and Theory* 901–927, 904, citing Paul A. Sabatier and Hank C. Jenkins-Smith, "The Advocacy Coalition Framework: An Assessment" in Paul A. Sabatier (ed), *Theories of the Policy Process* (Westview, 1999) 117.

[145] Wiener, "Learning to Manage the Multirisk World," 2139.

[146] Head and Alford, "Wicked Problems," 725–728 (citations omitted).

[147] Ibid 727–728.

[148] B. Guy Peters, "Information and Governing: Cybernetic Models of Governance" in David Levi-Faur (ed), *The Oxford Handbook of Governance* (OUP 2012) 113–128, 123.

[149] Neil Gunningham and Cameron Holley, "Next-Generation Environmental Regulation: Law, Regulation, and Governance" (2016) 12 *Annual Review of Law and Social Science* 273–293, 284.

[150] Head and Alford, "Wicked Problems," 728.

sheer difficulty and resource intensity of collaboration in this setting leads some scholars to urge public managers: "don't do it unless you have to."[151]

2.3 SYNTHESIS: THE NEED FOR RULES AND DESIGN FEATURES

Collectively, the many disciplinary insights outlined earlier both demonstrate the desirability of a rule-based (regulatory) approach to cumulative environmental problems and inform the design of rules to deal with these problems. This aligns with calls for stronger legal approaches in the cumulative effects assessment literature,[152] and points to key functions that those rules should support. In relation to coordination in multilevel natural resources contexts, resilience theorists similarly argue that governance should involve explicit written legal requirements, frequent information sharing, adequate local resources, harmonized methods and regulations, and formal structures that build on existing informal networks.[153]

Table 2.1 summarizes the key challenges indicated by the earlier discussion, and how they suggest that rules would be beneficial, as well as the key design features to which they point. These form a starting point for the discussions that each of the CIRCle Framework function chapters (Chapters 4 to 7) continues, developing and illustrating desirable design features.

2.4 THE CIRCLE FRAMEWORK OF REGULATORY FUNCTIONS

The earlier discussion has produced four deductively derived functions for laws to undertake to help address the inherent difficulties posed by cumulative environmental problems. Focusing on legal functions is an established way to analyze and compare laws across diverse jurisdictions and legal subject matters.[154] It also aligns with existing scholarship that seeks to understand

[151] Chris Huxham and Siv Vangen, *Managing to Collaborate: The Theory and Practice of Collaborative Advantage* (Routledge 2013) 13.

[152] E.g., Hodgson, Halpern and Essington, "Moving Beyond Silos," 3; Noble, Liu and Hackett, "The Contribution of Project Environmental Assessment," 544; Therivel and Ross, "Cumulative Effects Assessment: Does Scale Matter?," 372.

[153] Cosens and Stow, "Resilience and Water Governance," 161–162.

[154] Catherine Valcke and Matthew Grelette, "Three Functions of Function in Comparative Legal Studies" in Maurice Adams and Dirk Heirbaut (eds), *The Method and Culture of Comparative Law: Essays in Honour of Mark Van Hoecke* (Hart 2014) 99; Elizabeth Fisher and others, "Maturity and Methodology: Starting a Debate about Environmental Law Scholarship" (2009) 21 *Journal of Environmental Law* 213–250, 242–243 (calling for the development of such comparative approaches). See also Section 1.2.1, note 25 and accompanying text.

TABLE 2.1 *Challenges to addressing cumulative environmental problems and implications for regulatory responses*

Why is it hard to address cumulative environmental harms?	Formal rules can help because they can…	Rules should be designed to…
Function 1: Conceptualization		
Adequately articulating what we care about protecting from cumulative harm is complex: It has multiple dimensions (e.g., the place of people in the matter of concern, spatial boundaries, the influence of time on acceptable conditions, and the limits of acceptable change) and involves subjective, value-rich decisions – there is no objectively correct answer	Ensure the required dimensions of conceptualization are articulated, and that this occurs in a transparent way	Facilitate clearly and transparently conceptualizing the matter of concern
Incoherently conceptualizing a matter of concern between regulatory actors can obstruct effective responses to cumulative environmental problems, but intentional adaptive change in a conceptualization may be needed over time	Encourage coherence in how a matter of concern is conceptualized through time and between actors	Provide for coordination between actors relevant to conceptualization, including coordination to adapt a conceptualization
Function 2: Information		
Perceiving gradual change to a matter of concern without data is difficult, and risks shifting baselines	Require information collection to avoid shifting baselines	Provide for long-term, ongoing collection of comparable data about the matter of concern
Collecting data about matters of concern and numerous threats can be costly and collecting and sharing it can encounter commercial, community and political resistance	Apply data collection and sharing incentives or mandates, with appropriate safeguards, to counter disincentives	Provide for comprehensive data about threats that may be cumulatively significant; address cost and other concerns about collecting, sharing and analyzing data in a structured way

Why is it hard to address cumulative environmental harms?	Formal rules can help because they can…	Rules should be designed to…
With many actors involved, data are unlikely to be collected in a way that makes them comparable and interoperable, nor shared and aggregated to reveal aggregate harm, without formalized arrangements	Facilitate interoperability and aggregation through "FAIR" data collection standards and allocation of responsibility for aggregation/analysis	
Predicting future cumulative conditions may make models desirable and uncertainty unavoidable; uncertainty discourages take-up of information and can allow for inappropriate manipulation of models	Require relevant contributors to harm and decision-makers to engage with complexity and uncertainty in a transparent way	Provide for coordination between relevant actors regarding information and models
Function 3: Intervention		
Risk perception, a sense of futility and short-termism can obstruct individual and decision-maker responses to individually minor and slowly accumulating harms	Supply incentives or mandates to address threats	Address threats comprehensively, including individually minor but collectively significant threats
It can be unclear and ethically ambiguous how to allocate responsibility to act among many actors, including those that cause individually minor impacts and lack relevant information or resources	Supply elements that are ethically required for intervention, such as information about causation and consequences of actions, or resources, e.g., through incentives	
Complex, uncertain problems require adaptive management of interventions, but adaptation strikes challenges related to fairness, path dependence and "single action bias"	Structure decision points for adaptation	Expressly address fairness concerns

(*continued*)

TABLE 2.1 (*continued*)

Why is it hard to address cumulative environmental harms?	Formal rules can help because they can…	Rules should be designed to…
Function 4: Coordination of conceptualization, information, and intervention		
Coordination between government and stakeholders is needed to respond to cumulative environmental problems in relation to each foregoing function, but heterogeneity of stakeholders can create distrust and sustaining interaction can be challenging	Supply institutionalized structures for coordination involving diverse stakeholders and governments	In undertaking conceptualization, information and intervention, establish and maintain links among governments and stakeholders; and provide for resolving disputes
Coordination between governments is needed to avoid mutually undermining approaches, duplication, and policy gaps, but is unlikely to arise organically or be easy to sustain	Support the initiation and maintenance of coordination between governments	

multilevel governance by reference to regulatory functions.[155] Focusing on functions also facilitates connecting with disciplines and areas of practice that tend to focus on particular functions, say, information in the case of ecology and coordination in the case of multilevel governance scholarship.

Summarizing, then, the "CIRCle" Framework (Figure 2.1) comprises four key legal functions that encompass, respectively, formal mechanisms to support:

(1) Clearly and coherently **conceptualizing** the matter of concern that is the focus of protection or restoration, including the threshold conditions beyond which effects are unacceptable;

[155] Alejandro E. Camacho and Robert L. Glicksman, "Designing Regulation across Organizations: Assessing the Functions and Dimensions of Governance" (2021) 15(S1) *Regulation and Governance* S102–S122, S106.

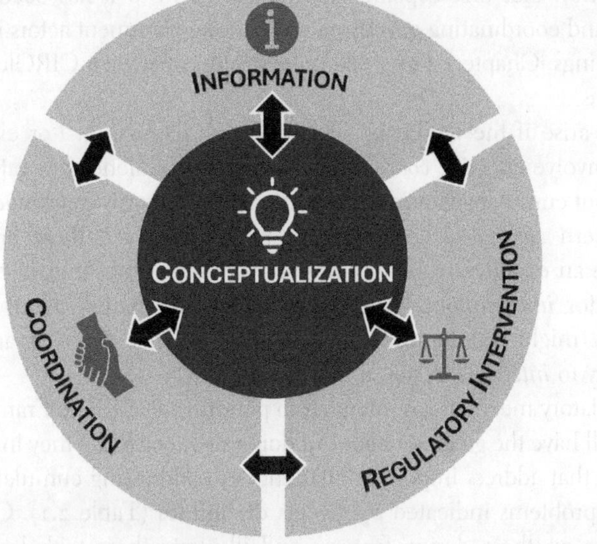

FIGURE 2.1 The CIRCle Framework: Integrated legal functions for responding to cumulative environmental problems

(2) Collecting, sharing, aggregating, and analyzing **information** about past and present environmental conditions, threats and expected future environmental conditions, taking into account the effects of multiple diverse activities and interpreting the acceptability of their cumulative effects, and the adequacy of interventions to deal with threats;

(3) **Intervening** to influence the behavior of contributors to cumulative harm to prevent or remedy unacceptable effects, or harness direct state action to do so; and

(4) **Coordinating each of the foregoing functions** between and across levels of government, and with nongovernment actors, including to resolve disputes.

Legal mechanisms that support these functions might be distributed among different individual laws, so it is necessary to think of the set of relevant laws – here termed the legal "landscape" for responding to cumulative environmental problems – as a whole. Chapter 3 sketches a wide range of areas of law that may be relevant to a cumulative environmental problem.

The CIRCle Framework recognizes that these functions interact with each other (Table 2.1; arrows, Figure 2.1) – they are *integrated*. The way that a matter of concern is conceptualized should translate into arrangements for collecting and sharing information about it, intervening in response to information that unacceptable cumulative harm to it has occurred or may occur, and coordinating government and nongovernment actors in relation to these things. Chapters 4 to 7 elaborate on links between CIRCle Framework functions.

Risks arise if the landscape of laws omits a function. For example, laws might involve effective *coordination* between jurisdictions to gather *information* about cumulative harms to a clearly and coherently *conceptualized* matter of concern against clearly defined threats. However, these laws may not produce an effective regulatory response if they do not integrate with mechanisms for *intervention*. Having aggregated information about a matter of concern might fail to protect it from cumulative harm if agencies lack authority to *intervene* to stop undesirable harm.

Regulatory mechanisms intended to perform the CIRCle Framework functions will have the greatest chance of doing so effectively if they include design features that address important challenges to addressing cumulative environmental problems indicated by diverse disciplines (Table 2.1). Chapters 4–7 elaborate on these design features and illustrate them with legal examples from around the globe.

Challenges related to introducing, implementing, and enforcing laws are highly jurisdiction-specific, reflecting varying conditions related to political structure and function,[156] funding, and surrounding legal structures to mention a few. Since this makes generalizing legal solutions to these challenges difficult, if not impossible, discussion of functions proceeds by way of diverse examples to illustrate individual functions, and discussion of combinations of mechanisms through case studies (Chapters 8–10).[157]

Finally, a caution and a disclaimer. While formal rules have a unique and important role to play, they are unlikely to be the whole solution to cumulative environmental problems, not least because introducing, implementing, and enforcing them is rarely straightforward, trouble-free, and comprehensive. Cumulative environmental problems are so difficult that many strategies are likely to be necessary to address them.[158] Focusing on formal rules is also not to discount the importance of nonregulatory actors and the actions of regulatory actors that are not expressly foreseen by legal rules. But formal rules are inescapably part of the picture of addressing cumulative environmental problems – not only as part of the solution but because, without good design, rules

[156] Graben and Biber, "Presidents, Parliaments, and Legal Change," 368, 401–404, 406–407.

[157] For an explanation of the approach to selecting illustrative examples and major case studies, see Section 1.2.3.

[158] Robert N. Stavins, "The Problem of the Commons: Still Unsettled after 100 Years" (2011) 101 *The American Economic Review* 81–108, 102.

may also be part of the problem. Regulations have the potential to reinforce some of the challenges described here, for example, where rules in different places conceptualize shared environmental problems in an incoherent way or provide for interventions that counteract one another. Unless regulatory systems are established with cumulative effects in mind, they may inadvertently facilitate cumulative harm.

3

Law and Cumulative Environmental Problems

A Landscape for Analysis

3.1 INTRODUCTION

A broad landscape of laws can help deliver the CIRCle Framework functions of conceptualization, information, regulatory intervention, and coordination, which this book argues are vital to address cumulative environmental problems.[1] This chapter provides a bird's eye view of this landscape, not aiming to be comprehensive, but to point to some major topographical features, as it were. I argue that rather than just a zoomed-in view of environmental impact assessment ("EIA") – the original Western legal context for developing the terminology of cumulative effects – a broad range of laws and policies can and must deal with cumulative environmental problems.[2] Assessing how existing laws deal with any given cumulative environmental problem also requires navigating this much broader regulatory landscape.

Section 3.2 sketches the broad landscape of key domestic legal areas that can help address cumulative environmental problems – the scene for much of the book's later discussion of legal mechanisms. Section 3.3 provides a brief supplementary discussion of international legal mechanisms. Each of the four chapters that follows explores a CIRCle Framework function using illustrative mechanisms from around the world and across many legal areas. Since so many areas of law influence cumulative environmental problems, Section 3.4 presents a simple "compass" for navigating this landscape. This helps to orient

[1] See Chapter 2 for the derivation of the CIRCle Framework of regulatory functions for regulating cumulative environmental problems.

[2] Legal rules and concepts can also impede legal responses to these problems. The main focus here, though, is how laws intentionally seek to address cumulative environmental problems.

and structure an inquiry into a cumulative environmental problem. It also alerts regulatory designers to the typical advantages and disadvantages of different areas of law in delivering the CIRCle Framework functions of conceptualization, information, regulatory intervention, and coordination.

3.2 THE DOMESTIC LEGAL LANDSCAPE

Though we might think of EIA as the source of cumulative impact-related laws, to start building a more panoramic view of laws relevant to cumulative environmental problems, I take several steps back. I start by examining how traditional and customary laws may help address cumulative impacts, before considering the role of EIA, including strategic environmental assessment ("SEA") law. Widening our gaze, I then discuss how cumulative impacts appear in broader environmental and natural resources laws, and in public law more generally. Finally, I briefly consider the role of international law and the policies of international organizations (particularly development banks) in dealing with cumulative environmental impacts.

3.2.1 *The Traditional and Customary Law Canvas of Cumulative Effects Concepts*

Discussions of cumulative impacts and the law commonly not only center on EIA but also start there. But traditional and First Nations' environment-related laws are both a chronologically more accurate starting point and, in many cases, a source of law of continuing importance. For brevity, I use the term "traditional laws" to embrace the laws of Indigenous and other traditional peoples.

A substantial legal literature urges involving Indigenous and traditional peoples in environment-related laws, but traditional laws themselves warrant attention in the context of cumulative environmental problems. Indeed, traditional laws may speak to all four CIRCle Framework functions, influencing:

- the conceptualization of what we should restore or protect from cumulative harm, including special places, practices, and relationships between people and their environments, which traditional laws may link in unique ways;[3]

[3] See Section 4.2.2 for a discussion about links between people and the environment in law.

- sources of information and appropriate ways of accessing information relevant to predicting or measuring environmental harms, drawing on traditional knowledges;[4]
- legal obligations to protect against and remedy cumulative environmental harm, for example, by engaging obligations related to cultural rights;[5] and
- coordination, for example, by engaging potentially affected Indigenous and traditional peoples as important partners, with whom other governments coordinate in undertaking these functions.[6]

Take the Nguni principle of *ubuntu* in southern Africa,[7] which has been described as "both the African principle of transcendence for the individual, and the law of the social bond."[8] The individual is seen as "intertwined with others from the beginning of life":[9] "[w]e come into the world obligated to others, and in turn these others are obligated to us, to the individual."[10] *Ubuntu* also implies responsibility to past and future generations,[11] and a commitment to democratically building a "shared representation of reality."[12] Such values and practices of interdependence are clearly relevant to conceptualizing linked human communities affected by cumulative harm, and to allocating responsibilities in a way that is more collective than individualistic.

Traditional laws appear in or influence contemporary formal laws in several ways that address cumulative environmental problems. "Pluralist" laws may directly reflect concepts from traditional laws that are relevant to cumulative impacts, including through recognizing Indigenous rights or customary law and reflecting Indigenous values in international environmental law

[4] See Section 5.3.1.

[5] See, e.g., Table 4.2, row 3.

[6] See, e.g. Section 4.1.2.

[7] For a critical review of scholarly consideration of *ubuntu*, see generally Ephraim Taurai Gwaravanda, "*Ubuntu* Environmental Ethics: Conceptions and Misconceptions" in Munamato Chemhuru (ed), *African Environmental Ethics: A Critical Reader* (Springer Nature 2019) 79, 79–92. Gwaravanda counsels against a generalized approach to *ubuntu* environmental ethics in favour of recognizing diverse related versions.

[8] Drucilla Cornell and Nyoko Muvangua, "Introduction: The Re-Cognition of uBuntu" in Drucilla Cornell and Nyoko Muvangua (eds), *Ubuntu and the Law: African Ideals and Postapartheid Jurisprudence* (Fordham University Press 2011) 1–28, 3.

[9] Ibid 8.

[10] Ibid 3.

[11] Aïda C. Terblanché-Greeff, "Ubuntu and Environmental Ethics: The West Can Learn from Africa when Faced with Climate Change" in Munamato Chemhuru (ed), *African Environmental Ethics: A Critical Reader* (Springer Nature 2019) 93–109, 99.

[12] Cornell and Muvangua, "Introduction: The Re-Cognition of uBuntu", 8.

regimes.[13] In this vein, *ubuntu* is recognized as a justiciable constitutional principle central to South African constitutional rights.[14] Less directly, traditional laws may influence the implementation of contemporary formal law and policy, including by Indigenous and traditional peoples participating in processes for implementing laws and policies under formal coordination mechanisms.[15] Just as importantly, in introducing new regulatory approaches to deal with cumulative impacts, regulatory designers should carefully consider how any proposal would interact with traditional and customary laws and avoid any potential adverse effects on customary rights.[16]

3.2.2 *EIA, SEA, and Western Scientific Cumulative Effects Concepts*

All-embracing versus narrow and selective, the contrast between some traditional laws and project-level EIA law could not be greater. Project-level EIA originated in the United States National Environmental Policy Act of 1969,[17] then spread to various US states, with other countries following suit in the 1970s and 1980s.[18] EIA is now globally ubiquitous.[19]

Globally, most national EIA laws include a cumulative impacts provision.[20] These provisions occur in the laws of all major legal traditions: common law (as in Canada, United Kingdom), civil law (as in France, Italy), Islamic law (as in Saudi Arabia, Mauritania), and mixed systems

[13] Benjamin J. Richardson, *The Ties That Bind: Indigenous Peoples and Environmental Governance* (Osgood Hall Law School of York University 2008) 25–27; Hilmer J. Bosch, Joyeeta Gupta and Hebe Verrest, "A Water Property Right Inventory of 60 Countries" (2021) 30 *Review of European, Comparative and International Environmental Law* 263–274, 265–267.

[14] Cornell and Muvangua, "Introduction: The Re-Cognition of uBuntu", 7–8, 10.

[15] E.g., Chapter 2, n 142 (cumulative impacts guidance context); Table 7.4, row 3 (water planning context).

[16] See generally Barbara van Koppen, "Water Allocation, Customary Practice and the Right to Water: Rethinking the Regulatory Model" in Malcolm Langford and Anna F. S. Russell (eds), *The Human Right to Water: Theory, Practice and Prospects* (CUP 2017) 57–83, 73.

[17] Neil Craik, *The International Law of Environmental Impact Assessment: Process, Substance and Integration* (CUP 2008) 23; Tseming Yang, "The Emergence of the Environmental Impact Assessment Duty as a Global Legal Norm and General Principle of Law" (2018) 70 *Hastings Law Journal* 525–572, 530.

[18] Craik, *International Law of EIA*, 23–24.

[19] Neil Craik, "The Assessment of Environmental Impact" in Emma Lees and Jorge E. Viñuales (eds), *The Oxford Handbook of Comparative Environmental Law* (OUP 2019) 876–899, 895–896.

[20] Rebecca Nelson and L. M. Shirley, "The Latent Potential of Cumulative Effects Concepts in National and International Environmental Impact Assessment Regimes" (2023) 12 *Transnational Environmental Law* 150–174, 160–161.

(as in Malta, Zimbabwe); they occur less frequently in Asia and Australasia at the national level.[21]

The EIA process involves several stages, including "screening" a project to determine the need for environmental assessment; "scoping" to determine key elements of the environment expected to be impacted, relevant baseline conditions and alternatives to the project; substantive prediction and evaluation of impacts of the project (environmental assessment); public participation; the final decision; and follow-up.[22] EIA laws often define cumulative impacts and require them to be considered at several of these stages. A representative definition of cumulative effects – from the many that exist in EIA law – is effects "that result from additive effects caused by other past, present, or reasonably foreseeable actions together with the plan, programme, or project itself and synergistic effects (in combination) which arise from the interaction between effects of a development plan, programme or project, on different components of the environment."[23]

The concept of cumulative impact performs different roles in the EIA processes envisioned by different legislative schemes. First, cumulative impacts may be a screening criterion, which must be considered to determine whether a project requires any form of environmental assessment at all. For example, EIA may be required if a project falls into a named category (like a power plant) or is likely to create cumulative impacts.[24] An alternative formulation is to require EIA for a development proposal that is likely to "significantly" affect the environment, which requires considering, among other things, "the potential for cumulative environmental impacts."[25] As a screening criterion, cumulative impacts provisions theoretically may be highly influential: They expand the use of EIA outside its usual bounds if they trigger EIA requirements for activities of a category or scale that is usually exempt.

21 Ibid.

22 Riki Therivel and Graham Wood, "Introduction" in Riki Therivel and Graham Wood (eds), *Methods of Environmental and Social Impact Assessment* (Routledge 2018) 1–19; United Nations Environment Programme (UNEP), "Environmental Impact Assessment Training Resource Manual" (2002) 100, https://wedocs.unep.org/handle/20.500.11822/26503.

23 Martin Broderick, Bridget Durning and Luis E. Sánchez, "Cumulative Effects" in Riki Therivel and Graham Wood (eds), *Methods of Environmental and Social Impact Assessment* (4th edn, Routledge 2017) 649–678, 650.

24 See Table 6.3, row 1.

25 Environmental Impact Assessment Regulations 1994 (Marshall Islands), art. 4(vi) "significant effect". For a distinct but related approach, see Environmental Impact Assessment Regulations 1989 (Federated States of Micronesia), arts. 1.3(a) (definition of cumulative impact), (b) (definition of effects includes cumulative impacts), 4.1 (comprehensive EIA required in event of likely significant cumulative impacts).

For projects that require EIA, cumulative impacts influence a second role, scoping, by affecting the type of environmental assessment required. For example, if the project "generates cumulative and/or indirect and/or synergistic effects," this may trigger a requirement to carry out an environmental impact study involving deeper analysis.[26] It may also "upgrade" the assessment type required to a more publicly contestable form of assessment.

The third, and most obvious, role of the concept of cumulative impacts is that of cumulative impact assessment (CIA): influencing the substantive content of the environmental assessment. This is expressed in diverse ways in different statutes: the assessment must, or may (variously) require a description of the "cumulative impacts" of the proposed project;[27] the "cumulative and synergistic" consequences of the project;[28] or the "cumulative and synergistic impacts and the induced risks" of the project.[29] Theoretically speaking, this is the stage at which the deepest inquiry into cumulative impacts would be expected.

Finally, cumulative effects may be included in an EIA law's definition of environmental harm,[30] impact,[31] or effect.[32] This has potentially further-reaching application not only to all stages of EIA but also the post-EIA process. For example, where a proponent must monitor a project's ongoing impacts, this could require analysis to understand these impacts in light of the cumulative impacts of other projects. This highlights the challenges associated with findable, accessible, interoperable, and reusable data, discussed earlier,[33] to facilitate this continuing analysis.

EIA that includes CIA differs from "regular" EIA in important ways. Firstly, it involves, at least to some extent, identifying other actors and actions in the past, present, and reasonably foreseeable future that impact the same element

26 Decreto N° 123, Reglamento del Proceso de Evaluaci ón de Impacto Ambiental [Decree No. 123 – Regulations on the Process of Environmental Impact Assessment] 2009 (Panama) arts. 18, 24.

27 Environment Impact Assessment Regulations (South Africa) 2014 app 1 cl 3(1)(j)(i); Environmental Impact Assessment Act (Republic of Korea) 2011 (as amended to 2019) art. 4(5); Decreto Presidencial n. 117/20 Regulamento Geral de Avaliação de Impacte Ambiental e do Procedimento de Licenciamento Ambiental [Presidential Decree No. 117/20 General Regulation for Environmental Impact Assessment and Environmental Licensing Procedure (Angola) art. 10(1)(e), replacing Decreto no 51/04 Sobre a Avaliação de Impacto Ambiental [Decree No. 51/04 on Environmental Impact Assessment] 2020 (Angola)).

28 Инструкция о порядке проведения оценки воздействия намечаемой деятельности на окружающую среду (ОВОС) в Кыргызской Республике [Instruction on Environmental Impact Assessment] 1997.

29 Decreto Supremo N° 019-2009-MINAM [Decree No 019-2009-MINAM] (Peru) 2009 annex IV cl 5(b).

30 Environment Act 2000 (Papua New Guinea) , as amended, s 2 "environmental harm" (a)(ii).

31 Environment Act 1998 (Solomon Islands) s 2 "impact" (d).

32 Miljöbalk [Environmental Code] 1998 (Sweden) ch 6 s 2.

33 See Sections 2.2.2 and 5.3.3.

of the environment. By contrast, regular EIA does not disaggregate actions; instead, it tends to consider the overall effects of those actions as environmental "context" or "existing circumstances."[34] Thus, CIA highlights not only the metaphorical "thousand cuts" but also who wields (and has wielded, and will wield) a sword. Secondly, considering other actors in space and time expands CIA-inclusive EIA's spatial and temporal boundaries relative to regular EIA.[35] CIA also alters EIA investigations by considering whether "individually minor effects will be collectively significant,"[36] illuminating relatively small, potentially unregulated effects that regular EIA may otherwise disregard. Finally, CIA also emphasizes nonlinear responses, such as impacts that become amplified or exponentially greater due to other development activities and natural background changes in environmental conditions.[37] By contrast, "traditional" EIA tends to conceptualize a single source of impact in isolation,[38] potentially underrepresenting to decision-makers and the public the true extent of likely environmental harm. Considering cumulative impacts exposes the true extent of a project's potential harm and, by revealing the full suite of contributors to the harm, also exposes more options for reducing aggregate environmental damage.[39]

Nelson and Shirley have argued elsewhere that these differences potentially produce two distinct benefits. They provide better technical information for a decision-maker by casting new light on the impacts of the proposed project in the context of other projects in the same environment. CIA also spotlights decisions about what matters, thereby inviting deliberation and exposing differences for contestation in a transparent way.[40]

Rather than EIA, which focuses on a single project, SEA law is often argued to be the more appropriate way to assess and manage cumulative impacts.[41]

34 Rebecca Nelson, "Breaking Backs and Boiling Frogs: Warnings from a Dialogue between Federal Water Law and Environmental Law" (2019) 42 *University of New South Wales Law Journal* 1179–1214, 1199.

35 F. Chris Jones, "Cumulative Effects Assessment: Theoretical Underpinnings and Big Problems" (2016) 24 *Environmental Reviews* 187–204, 195.

36 Ibid 189.

37 Cheryl K. Contant and Lyna L. Wiggins, "Defining and Analyzing Cumulative Environmental Impacts" (1991) 11 *Environmental Impact Assessment Review* 297–309, 299–303.

38 Bruce Pardy, "In Search of the Holy Grail of Environmental Law: A Rule to Solve the Problem" (2005) 1 *McGill International Journal of Sustainable Development Law and Policy* 29–58, 38.

39 Nelson, "Breaking Backs," 1211.

40 Nelson and Shirley, "Latent Potential," 157–159.

41 Morten Bidstrup, Lone Kørnøv and Maria Rosário Partidário, "Cumulative Effects in Strategic Environmental Assessment: The Influence of Plan Boundaries" (2016) 57 *Environmental Impact Assessment Review* 151–158, 151 (citing numerous studies that make this argument).

It enables a more proactive, strategic consideration of cumulative impacts over a longer term in a way that can analyze potential future scenarios resulting from different policy choices at a larger geographic scale and with greater opportunity for collaboration.[42] However, compared to EIA, SEA and its cousin, regional plans,[43] are used comparatively rarely.[44] Perhaps more troubling is the criticism that SEA sometimes seems to have little influence on decision-making.[45] The Great Barrier Reef case study explores this issue a decade after the Reef SEA, suggesting that, at least in that context, the SEA had a significant influence on interventions related to water quality.[46] Increasing interest in using SEA to structure the renewable energy transition highlights the importance of a pathway to increasing the impact of SEA.[47]

3.2.3 *Natural Resources, Pollution, Conservation, and Other Environment-Related Laws*

Many environmental threats simply do not trigger project-level EIA or SEA requirements. As a result, even if cumulative impacts requirements under these laws were formulated ideally in law on paper and implemented well in practice, they could not adequately address the real-world cumulative impacts on matters of concern to which those assessments were directed. This highlights the desirability of understanding and improving how cumulative impact considerations appear in broader areas of environment-related law, not as an "add-on," but as an integral part of these laws. While EIA and SEA laws are typically procedural in nature, geared toward producing information to inform

42 Jones, "Cumulative Effects Assessment," 194–197.

43 See, e.g., Bram Noble and Kelechi Nwanekezie, "Conceptualizing Strategic Environmental Assessment: Principles, Approaches and Research Directions" (2017) 62 *Environmental Impact Assessment Review* 165–173, 166, 169; S. Simon Marsden, "Strategic Environmental Assessment of Australian Offshore Oil and Gas Development: Ecologically Sustainable Development or Deregulation?" (2016) 33 *Environment and Planning Law Journal* 21–30, 23.

44 Mary Peters and Manu Kumar, "Strategic Environmental Assessment: Experience, Status and Directions" (2012) 21(2) *European Energy and Environmental Law Review* 92–98, 93; Monica Fundingsland Tetlow and Marie Hanusch, "Strategic Environmental Assessment: The State of the Art" (2012) 30(1) *Impact Assessment and Project Appraisal* 15–24, 17 (referring to sixty countries having adopted SEA, though with no "exact overview" and a lack of clarity about whether this refers to adoption in law as opposed to policy).

45 E.g., see generally Víctor Lobos and Maria Partidario, "Theory versus Practice in Strategic Environmental Assessment (SEA)" (2014) 48 *Environmental Impact Assessment Review* 34–46, esp. at 40.

46 See Chapter 10.

47 See generally Kelechi Nwanekezie, Bram Noble and Greg Poelzer, "Transitions-Based Strategic Environmental Assessment" (2021) 91:106643 *Environmental Impact Assessment Review* 1–10.

decisions about large projects rather than changing interventions, environment-related laws in other areas provide for a broader range of functions in relation to a broader range of activities.

Take natural resources planning and management laws in domains such as water, forestry, fisheries, and hunting rights. These laws are natural legal venues for responding to cumulative impacts,[48] albeit on a single issue, because they provide scope to consider many individual impacts over a region covered by a plan. Perhaps the legal intervention that most clearly expresses the concept of cumulative impacts is a limit placed on resource extraction such as a cumulative total volume of water that may be withdrawn from a river.[49] These types of interventions may be accompanied by mechanisms to conceptualize precisely what should be protected and provide information and coordination relating to it, as shown by the many examples used later in this book.[50]

Rather than focusing on the aggregate effects of taking resources away from an environment, pollution law provides a further context for considering cumulative impacts by focusing on the aggregate effects of putting pollution into an environment. Mechanisms to limit aggregate pollution, like a "total maximum daily load" that limits the granting of pollution discharge licenses[51] are long-established. They now have newer legal siblings specifically designed to address cumulative impacts, such as risk-based "general environmental duties" that apply to all activities, regardless of size.[52] Like natural resources laws, many pollution laws have a narrow focus on individual "silos" of activities or impacts; this invites us to investigate how legal mechanisms can span these silos to consider cumulative impacts – a key question to which later chapters return.[53]

Laws that establish areas protected for conservation purposes may also include cumulative impact concepts, but in a way that recalibrates the focus to the "matter of concern" to be protected or restored, rather than the type of activity or impact that causes harm. The Great Barrier Reef case study demonstrates complex legal arrangements to protect a marine park, with a focus on cumulative impacts to the area from both marine and land-based

48 Peter N. Duinker and Lorne A. Greig, "The Impotence of Cumulative Effects Assessment in Canada: Ailments and Ideas for Redeployment" (2006) 37 *Environmental Management* 153–161, 158.

49 E.g., Nelson, "Breaking Backs," 1209–1210.

50 See Chapter 4 (Conceptualization), Chapter 5 (Information), and Chapter 7 (Coordination).

51 33 U.S.C. § 1313(d).

52 Table 6.3, row 2.

53 See Section 6.5.1 (Connected decision-making) and Section 10.4.2.2 (Coordination as mutually reinforcing links between laws in a policy mix).

sources.[54] The South Tyrol case study focuses on incentive-based interventions to promote ecologically valuable grazing on Alpine grasslands, with a focus on those designated as valuable habitat under European legal instruments.[55] Numerous examples throughout the book illustrate how conservation laws address cumulative harm to things as diverse as the geysers of Yellowstone National Park in the United States, to wildlife on communal land in Tanzania, to the Kiribati Phoenix Islands Protected Area.[56] Emerging nature restoration laws, and, to some extent, rights of nature laws, focus on reversing a legacy of cumulative degradation to places and ecosystems.[57]

Coastal zone and marine spatial planning and land use planning, beyond protected areas, advance cumulative impact concepts by adopting a regional-scale view and covering multiple sources and types of impact. Coastal zone and marine spatial planning are well-established contexts for managing cumulative impacts.[58] Unlike EIA law, land use planning has the advantage of influencing many categories of development of many sizes in a region, rather than being restricted to large projects. However, both land use planning and EIA law scrutinize only new developments or changes in land use, rather than the ongoing impacts of existing uses. Nonetheless, land use laws provide scope for expressing cumulative impact concerns at the intersection of people and the environment. This is epitomized in the cumulative view of environmental justice – the accumulation of environmental and socioeconomic burdens – which is considered under land use and other areas of law in California, discussed further in the Central Valley case study.[59]

Later chapters of this book reveal a rich array of other environment-related legal mechanisms that contribute an important function to help deal with a cumulative environmental problem, whether or not they make explicit or implicit reference to cumulative impacts. Demonstrating this diversity, they include laws to incentivize traditional agricultural practices, limit the carbon embodied in buildings, manage traffic to reduce ambient air pollution, and publicize corporate reports on greenhouse gas emissions, among many others.

54 See Chapter 9.

55 See Chapter 10.

56 Table 7.2, row 4; Table 6.3, row 3; Table 7.3, row 4.

57 E.g., Regulation (EU) 2024/1991 of the European Parliament and of the Council of June 24, 2024, on nature restoration and amending Regulation (EU) 2022/869, OJ L 2024/1991, July 29, 2024; Nature Repair Act 2023 (Australia); Table 4.2, row 5.

58 E.g., see generally Elizabeth Macpherson and others, "Designing Law and Policy for the Health and Resilience of Marine and Coastal Ecosystems – Lessons from (and for) Aotearoa New Zealand" (2023) 54 *Ocean Development and International Law* 200–252.

59 See Section 8.3.2.2.

3.2.4 *Cumulative Environmental Problems in Broader Public Law Settings*

Some legal scholars point to the narrowness of even these broader environmental and natural resources laws. These scholars warn of environmental risks posed by "concatenations of political, economic and cultural threats,"[60] and urge us to question more fundamental structures and practices of our society, and the laws that support them. Larger drivers of environmental change may link to legal arrangements that indirectly drive cumulative harm. For example, domestic advertising and other laws drive unsustainable food systems in a way that is difficult to address using isolated policy tools rather than more holistic interventions that address broader social, commercial, and political dimensions of the problem.[61] This view points to the potential for harnessing even broader public laws to deal with cumulative impacts, beyond specific environment-related statutes.

While a specific cumulative environmental problem will dictate which of these broader areas of law are most relevant in a way that is difficult to generalize or discuss here in detail, it is worth noting the general potential of constitutional laws. Constitutions provide for environmental values in diverse ways. Some provisions have potential to address cumulative harm by seeking to secure outcomes (e.g., a "healthy environment," secured by an enforceable right). Other, "contrajudicative" provisions provide for outputs, such as requiring legislation about an environmental matter in the case of a constitutional directive provision, which does not specify the outcome required[62] but nonetheless provides scope for action to address cumulative harms.

Enforceable constitutional human rights to a healthy environment form a relatively prominent vehicle for considering cumulative impacts that limit the right. The South African *Fuel Retailers* case connected, on one hand, an EIA-based statutory requirement to consider the cumulative impacts of a development on "the environment, socio-economic conditions and cultural heritage" with, on the other hand, the precautionary principle and South Africa's constitutional environmental right.[63] The decision-maker was found not to

[60] James R. May and Erin Daly, *Global Environmental Constitutionalism* (CUP 2013) 6.

[61] See generally Tanita Northcott and others, "Ecological Regulation for Healthy and Sustainable Food Systems: Responding to the Global Rise of Ultra-Processed Foods" (2023) 40 *Agriculture and Human Values* 1333–1358.

[62] See generally Lael K. Weis, "Environmental Constitutionalism: Aspiration or Transformation?" (2018) 16 *International Journal of Constitutional Law* 836–870.

[63] Fuel Retailers Association of Southern Africa v Director-General: Environmental Management, Department of Agriculture, Conservation and Environment, Mpumalanga Province and Others (Constitutional Court) (2007) 6 SA 4, [72]–[82].

have considered the cumulative effects of the "proliferation of filling stations" on the relevant aquifer, nor the cumulative socioeconomic impacts on existing filling stations, as it was required to do.[64]

More recently, in the German Constitutional Court, claimants in the *Neubauer* case successfully argued that Germany's failure to introduce a greenhouse gas emissions cap required by the Paris Agreement violated constitutional freedoms, which were informed by a directive provision that the state "shall protect the natural foundations of life and animals by legislation."[65] The Court found that future generations would bear a greater burden on account of the depletion of the available CO_2 budget (a cumulative concept) in a way that was not constitutionally justified. More timely transition to climate neutrality was required.[66]

Meanwhile, constitutional coordination provisions that provide for multiple levels of government to coordinate actions are important to cumulative environmental problems: These problems often engage multiple levels of government,[67] and coordinating functions is vital to an effective response.[68] The South Tyrol case study shows how a mosaic of legislative powers granted to national and provincial governments contribute to protecting Alpine grasslands, with associated coordination arrangements that deliver the constitutional principle of "loyal cooperation."[69]

3.3 THE INTERNATIONAL LEGAL LANDSCAPE

This book focuses mainly on domestic legal systems and contexts for regulatory design, but connections between national and international contexts are an important part of this picture. Indeed, international and supranational laws, norms, or institutions arise in each of the case studies. These range from the internationally informed human right to water in California, to the World Heritage status of the Great Barrier Reef, to the tangle of supranational and international law that influences Alpine grasslands in South Tyrol. For

64 *Fuel Retailers*, [99].

65 Grundgesetz für die Bundesrepublik Deutschland [Basic Law for the Federal Republic of Germany] 1949, as amended, art. 20a; *Bundesverfassungsgericht*, Order of the First Senate of March 24, 2021 – 1 BvR 2656/18.

66 For a discussion of the case, see Agnes Hellner and Yaffa Epstein, "Allocation of Institutional Responsibility for Climate Change Mitigation: Judicial Application of Constitutional Environmental Provisions in the European Climate Cases Arctic Oil, Neubauer, and L'affaire Du Siècle" (2023) 35 *Journal of Environmental Law* 207–227, 216–220.

67 See further Chapter 7, Section 7.2.

68 Section 2.2.4.

69 Section 10.4.2.3.

completeness, this section sets out a brief analysis of the ways in which international legal arrangements deal expressly with cumulative environmental impacts, focusing on treaties and multilateral development bank policies.

3.3.1 *International Law*

EIA law began its migration from the domestic to the international realm in the 1970s,[70] developing early international statements on EIA.[71] The most broadly ratified EIA treaty, the Convention on Environmental Impact Assessment in a Transboundary Context (Espoo Convention),[72] is silent on whether its project-level EIA obligations extend to cumulative impacts. The Convention appears to assume that national laws will supply EIA procedures,[73] and includes cumulative impact concepts only in the context of SEA, rather than EIA.[74]

Other multilateral environmental agreements (MEAs) refer expressly to cumulative impacts in one of two ways. The first type applies to projects generally, mirroring national EIA laws. Notably, the Regional Agreement on Access to Information, Public Participation and Justice in Environmental Matters in Latin America and the Caribbean (Escazú Agreement)[75] requires parties to make public "a description of the main environmental impacts of the project or activity and, as appropriate, the cumulative environmental impact."[76] By contrast, the geographically wider 1998 Convention on Access to Information, Public Participation in Decision-making and Access to Justice in Environmental Matters (Aarhus Convention)[77] does not expressly mention cumulative impacts, though related guidance does do so in a cursory way.[78]

[70] Craik, *International Law of EIA*, 90–91.

[71] An early iteration of international EIA policy was principle 17 of the Rio Declaration on Environment and Development (Rio Declaration), Rio de Janeiro (Brazil), June 3–14, 1992, UN Doc. A/CONF.151/26/Rev.1 (Vol. 1), June 14, 1992.

[72] Espoo, February 25, 1991, in force September 10, 1997.

[73] Ibid preamble, art. 1(v), (vi).

[74] G. Sander, "International Legal Obligations for Environmental Impact Assessment and Strategic Environmental Assessment in the Arctic Ocean" (2016) 31(1) *The International Journal of Marine and Coastal Law* 88–119, 98–99; R. L. Johnstone, "Evaluating Espoo: What Protection Does the Espoo Convention Offer the Arctic Marine Environment?" (2013) 5(1) *The Yearbook of Polar Law Online* 337–57, 350–351.

[75] Escazú, March 4, 2018, in force April 22, 2021.

[76] Article 7 (17)(b).

[77] Aarhus, June 25, 1998, in force October 30, 2001.

[78] Findings and recommendations with regard to communication ACCC/C/2008/31 concerning compliance by Germany, Aarhus Convention Compliance Committee, ECE/MP.PP/C.1/2014/8, 2014, [40], [61].

A second type of MEA containing cumulative impact provisions applies to specific regional environments or contexts, such as marine, coastal, and mountain environments.[79] The geographic limitation of these MEAs is arguably a strength: Like terrestrial and marine spatial planning at the domestic level, focusing on a mountain range or sea aligns with scientific aspirations that CIA occur at an ecologically relevant regional scale,[80] and may capture the extent of a distinct environment that experiences adverse effects. MEAs that expressly use cumulative impact concepts do so in different ways. Some require or suggest[81] that cumulative impacts be considered as a component of substantive environmental assessment.[82] Others use cumulative impact concepts to categorize areas for protection and propose activities for control.[83] As a further alternative, cumulative impacts expressly may be relevant to a duty to consult and cooperate with other Parties about activities.[84]

Finally, as the case studies later in this book illustrate, MEAs may provide for regulatory functions that help to address cumulative environmental problems even where their texts do not expressly mention cumulative impacts. A request from a Committee under the World Heritage Convention triggered an influential SEA of the Great Barrier Reef, which focused on cumulative impacts;[85] meanwhile, the Paris Agreement's climate target influenced Australia's statutory targets years after the SEA, which largely ignored climate mitigation despite the Reef's extreme vulnerability to climate change.[86] The Alpine Convention, a regional MEA, and several biodiversity-focused treaties are an important part of the picture of mechanisms that interventions that promote traditional grazing practices that support Alpine grasslands in South Tyrol, Italy.[87] Guidance documents produced by treaty bodies may also expressly call attention to

79 Nelson and Shirley, "Latent Potential," 21–22.

80 Jones, "Cumulative Effects Assessment," 194–195 (especially note 35), 197.

81 Convention on the Protection of the Marine Environment of the Baltic Sea Area, Helsinki, Finland (Helsinki Convention), April 9, 1992, in force January 17, 2000, art. 7(3).

82 The Black Sea Biodiversity and Landscape Conservation Protocol to the Convention on the Protection of the Black Sea against Pollution (Black Sea Protocol), Sofia (Bulgaria), June 14, 2002, in force June 20, 2011, art. 6.

83 Protocol on Environmental Protection to the Antarctic Treaty, Madrid, October 4, 1991, in force January 14, 1998, annex I art. 2(1)(b), annex V art. 4(2)(a).

84 Ibid art. 6 (1)(d).

85 Convention Concerning the Protection of the World Cultural and Natural Heritage, November 16, 1972, Paris, in force December 17, 1975, 1037 U.N.T.S. 151; see Section 9.3.1.

86 Paris Agreement under the United Nations Framework Convention on Climate Change, December 12, 2015, in force November 4, 2016, 3156 U.N.T.S. 79; see Table 9.1.

87 See Table 10.1.

cumulative impacts even where the treaties themselves do not.[88] Like domestic laws, then, we see that international laws can focus on a matter of concern, impacts, and activities in a way that contributes to addressing cumulative environmental problems – not to speak of other treaties outside environmental regimes that indirectly influence cumulative harm.[89]

Beyond treaties, customary international law presents limitations for adopting cumulative impact concepts, at least for project-level environmental assessment. Forming consistent state practice[90] on including CIA in EIA and demonstrating accompanying *opinio juris* appear challenging. It is difficult to attribute state motivation to international obligation, and state practice requires action beyond treaty obligations[91] and technically excludes EIA undertaken by non-state entities.[92] In any case, the wealth of treaties that impose EIA obligations reduce the importance of a stand-alone customary obligation.[93]

3.3.2 *Multilateral Development Banks*

Policies of multilateral development banks ("banks") present a further context for considering international responses to cumulative environmental problems. Bank operational policies are not binding in the same way as national legislation and ratified MEAs, but these policies must be followed in the execution of individual funded development projects,[94] for example, assessing the environmental impact of constructing a hydroelectric dam. Operational policies use the concept of cumulative impacts in varied ways, sometimes without definitions.[95] Some policies suggest that EIA ought to

88 E.g., see generally Sarah Court and others, *Guidance and Toolkit for Impact Assessments in a World Heritage Context* (UNESCO 2022).

89 See generally Margaret A. Young, "Fragmentation" in Lavanya Rajamani and Jacqueline Peel (eds), *The Oxford Handbook of International Environmental Law* (OUP, 2021) 86–101.

90 Michael Wood and Omri Sender, "Customary International Law," in Anne Peters and Rüdiger Wolfrum (eds), *Max Planck Encyclopedia of Public International Law* (OUP, 2025) [8]–[28].

91 Craik, *International Law of EIA*, 124–125.

92 Ibid 125.

93 Ibid.

94 World Bank, "The World Bank Environmental and Social Framework" (2017) ix, www.worldbank.org/en/projects-operations/environmental-and-social-framework.

95 "Environmental and Safeguards Compliance Policy" (Banco Interamericano de Desarrollo/Inter-American Development Bank 2006) s B.3 pt 4.17; "Safeguard Policy Statement" (Asian Development Bank 2009) Policy Paper app 1 s D pt 1(4); "Environmental and Social Safeguards Policy" (Council of Europe Development Bank 2016) para 43.

consider cumulative impacts;[96] others also link cumulative impacts to screening and scoping.[97]

The significance of these policies extends beyond individual projects; bank operational policies can also evolve into norms that influence or even bind third parties, such as investors, far beyond the parameters of discrete lending agreements.[98] For example, bank policies on cumulative impacts may be referenced in EIA documents for major projects in countries that are not borrowers, as has occurred for port developments on Australia's Great Barrier Reef.[99]

3.4 A COMPASS FOR THE REGULATORY LANDSCAPE

This chapter has argued that a great variety of laws can help address cumulative environmental problems. Indeed, realistically, no one type of law could single-handedly address the incremental, creeping degradation of environments that we care about. At the same time, ongoing degradation suggests that there are problems with how laws take up this challenge on paper or in practice – or both.

To diagnose gaps, weaknesses, and strengths, we need to cast a regulatory eye across a panoramic landscape of laws. We can orient ourselves by asking a simple question: What is the core purpose of this area of law, what is its focus? Reflecting on key differences in legal focus helps to structure an analysis across this landscape, as illustrated by the case study analyses. A law's focus also raises hypotheses for regulatory designers to consider about its advantages, disadvantages, and predispositions in relation to the CIRCle Framework functions of conceptualization, information, regulatory intervention, and coordination.

We can distinguish between laws that focus on a matter of concern (like a protected conservation area law or an endangered species law), from those that

96 "Environmental and Safeguards Compliance Policy," s B.5 pt 4.19; "The World Bank Environmental and Social Framework," 18, 23; "Safeguard Policy Statement," para 50, app 1 s D pt 1 para 4.

97 E.g. "Environmental and Social Policy" (European Bank for Reconstruction and Development, 2024) 15, 34.

98 Galit A. Sarfaty, "The World Bank and the Internalization of Indigenous Rights Norms" (2005) 114 Yale Law Journal 1791, 1792–1793, 1800–1801; Ihsan Ugur Delikanli, Todor Dimitrov and Roena Agolli, *Multilateral Development Banks: Governance and Finance* (Springer 2018) 114.

99 Advisian Worley Parsons Group, *Abbot Point Growth Gateway Project Environmental Impact Statement – Volume 2 Main Report* (August 17, 2015) 454 (citing International Finance Corporation definition of cumulative impacts), www.statedevelopment.qld.gov.au/__data/assets/pdf_file/0019/33544/abbot-pt-eis-vol-02-main-report.pdf.

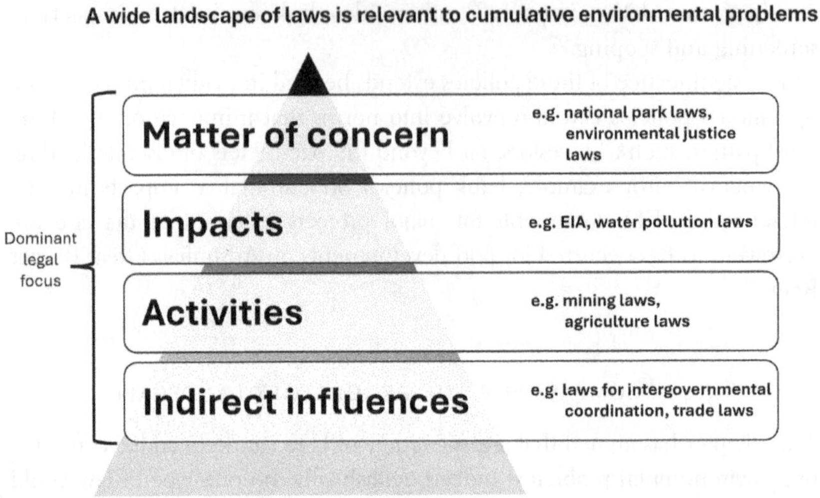

FIGURE 3.1 Laws relevant to regulating cumulative environmental problems

focus on specific kinds of activities (like mining, or farming) or impacts (like many EIA laws, pollution or natural resources laws), from those that have indirect influence, for example, by dealing with crosscutting institutional or coordination issues (as in allocating legislative powers over the environment among different levels of government, with associated rules for resolving disputes)[100] (Figure 3.1). These general distinctions are applied in each case study presented later in this book[101] as a way to chart an analytical course through many relevant laws, noting that in some cases a law may span these categories.

Determining the focus of a particular law can also point to potential areas of weakness that deserve the attention of regulatory designers. A law that focuses on a matter of concern may have strong mechanisms for conceptualization, but pay less attention to other CIRCle Framework functions. A law that focuses on coordination generally between levels of government (an indirect influence) may not provide much clarity about the regulatory functions that need coordination in an environmental context; and other like issues. The design of specific impact-focused laws, like those dealing with greenhouse gas emissions, may need more express attention to how they connect to laws that

[100] It would also be possible to draw this "indirect influence" category much wider, to include, for example, political campaign financing laws and other laws that influence the political power exercised by entities that undertake relevant activities, though doing so lies beyond this scope of the present work.

[101] See Section 8.3, Table 9.1, and Table 10.1.

deal with other types of impact than will be the case for project-focused laws, which inherently consider multiple impacts of a single project. This is the classic problem of legal "silos" obstructing connected decision-making, to which the chapter on regulatory intervention returns, and the Great Barrier Reef case study explores.[102]

3.5 CONCLUSION

This chapter has argued that a great variety of laws can usefully contribute to addressing cumulative environmental problems. These laws include the EIA and SEA laws that attract the attention of the literature that discusses cumulative impacts most prominently. But far broader laws are also relevant, including traditional and customary laws, natural resources allocation laws, laws for protected areas and species, terrestrial and marine planning, and broader public laws. International law and policy can also be an important part of this picture.

The regulatory landscape sketched here includes laws that have diverse core purposes and typical approaches. Regulatory designers might usefully consider these differences in their jurisdiction, and how they might present advantages and disadvantages in delivering CIRCle Framework functions.

Each cumulative environmental problem will engage a unique set of laws from across this broad regulatory landscape. Evaluating how these laws deal with a problem involves first finding them, then considering them together, including how different regulatory functions interact, and the degree to which they are integrated. The case study chapters illustrate this to examine different sets of functions using diverse collections of laws across all of the categories discussed here. Chapter 8 tackles groundwater sustainability in California, examining how conceptualization interacts with the other CIRCle Framework functions through a natural resources planning law. Chapter 9 focuses on the ecological health of the Great Barrier Reef in Australia, examining how SEA links information and regulatory intervention across diverse laws for protecting the Reef, addressing carbon and water pollution, and managing development activities. Finally, Chapter 10 explores how intervention and coordination – across multiple vertical levels of government, using laws that span nature protection, impact assessment, agriculture, landscape, and governance – protect biocultural landscapes in South Tyrol, Italy.

[102] See Sections 6.5.1 and 9.5.4.

4

Conceptualization

Laws for Defining What Matters, Who Matters, and What Unacceptable Harm Means

Links with Other Chapters

- Chapter 1 explains how examples used in this chapter were chosen.
- Chapter 2 synthesizes key challenges related to conceptualization and introduces the CIRCle Framework of regulatory functions to address cumulative environmental problems.
- Chapter 3 sketches the landscape of laws that may respond to cumulative environmental problems, including those that focus on a matter of concern (the conceptualization of which is the core of this chapter).
- Chapter 5 ("Information") discusses rules for collecting and analyzing data and information that link with conceptualization.
- Chapter 6 ("Regulatory intervention") discusses how rules can influence behavior to ensure that cumulative harm to the matter of concern stays within acceptable limits.
- Chapter 7 ("Coordination") covers coordinating between and among agencies and levels of government, nongovernment, and quasi-government entities, including to inform conceptualization.
- Each case study (Chapters 8–10) focuses on specific CIRCle Framework functions. Chapter 8 examines conceptualization in detail using the context of groundwater management and environmental justice in California, and explains how conceptualization links to the CIRCle Framework functions of information, regulatory intervention, and coordination.

4.1 CONCEPTUALIZATION AS A REGULATORY FUNCTION

At the heart of a regulatory regime to address a cumulative environmental problem[1] is the thing that matters, and that is threatened by cumulative impacts, such as water quality, or biodiversity, or a sacred site. This is the "matter of concern," the subject matter for protection or restoration. The first function of rules for addressing a cumulative environmental problem is articulating in law what matters, or providing a process for doing so. I use the term "matter of concern" for brevity and because it is intentionally neutral: This book does not suggest that environment-related laws should adopt any particular matter of concern. Indeed, matters of concern may vary widely, corresponding to the wide range of laws that are capable of regulating cumulative impacts – from environmental impact assessment ("EIA") law, to natural resources laws dealing with fisheries, water allocation, and forestry, to land use planning and endangered species and beyond.[2] A matter of concern may be a part of the nonhuman environment described without an express link to humans (e.g., water quality, a national park, or a species); or a part of the nonhuman environment expressed in a way that directly links either with humans in general (e.g., ecosystem services, or cultural landscapes) or with a specific human community that is affected by changes in the environment (e.g., children, Indigenous Peoples, or disadvantaged communities).

The main argument of this chapter is that while matters of concern vary, legal mechanisms can better address cumulative harm to them if they conceptualize the matter of concern in a way that addresses challenges inherent in cumulative environmental problems,[3] using rules that have specific features. This involves more than simply stating a goal or writing a definition into a rule – it is a challenging, multidimensional task that engages with questions of values – hence "conceptualization." As discussed earlier in this book, the multiple dimensions that need to be clarified to respond to cumulative harm, the subjective, value-rich nature of decisions about these dimensions, and the demonstrable risks of incoherent decisions about these matters are all notable challenges. They point to the need for rules to provide structure, transparency, and some degree of stability for conceptualization.

Conceptualization is part of a broader framework of interlinking functions that form the "CIRCle Framework" – conceptualization, information,

[1] For the full definition of cumulative environmental problems used in this book, see Section 1.1.

[2] See Chapter 3 (Landscape for Analysis).

[3] See Section 2.2.1.

regulatory intervention, coordination – for formal rules, broadly defined,[4] to respond to cumulative environmental problems. Formal rules are the focus of the CIRCle Framework and of this book, while also acknowledging that informal practices and nonlegal factors (e.g., courage of leaders) have an important role to play that rules cannot replace.

A foundational premise of this chapter is that it is important for rules to distinguish deciding the thing that matters and thresholds at which its conditions would become unacceptable (conceptualization), from understanding the current conditions of the matter of concern and what threatens it (which relates to information), from deciding what do about those threats (a decision about intervention), from coordinating among government and nongovernment entities to do these things. These are interlinked and potentially contested – but, importantly, separate – functions in the CIRCle Framework.

Conceptualization has links to well-established constructs and principles. Emphasizing conceptualization aligns with the scientific focus on clearly defined "valued environmental components" in cumulative impact analysis[5] – though the intention here is to address broader legal contexts beyond EIA.[6] By contrast, "problem framing" in the policy analysis literature refers to unpacking what actors do to persuade decision-makers and others about a problem and its importance, drawing simultaneously on values, narratives about cause and effect, the difference between observed and desired conditions, and preferred solutions.[7] However, the purpose of the CIRCle Framework differs from the goals of scientific cumulative impact analysis and policy analysis: Here, the goal is to design rules to guide decision-making. The function of conceptualization, then, takes that part of "problem framing" that defines what is important to protect or restore, and what protection or restoration means. Conceptualization relates more closely to policy aims, objectives, and targets in policy design,[8] but is here elaborated in a way that is specific to cumulative environmental problems and formal rules.

After setting out the place of conceptualization in the CIRCle Framework, Section 4.2 explores how variation in the matter of concern can affect how

[4] See Section 1.3 for a discussion of the scope of rules adopted in this book.

[5] Peter N. Duinker and others, "Scientific Dimensions of Cumulative Effects Assessment: Toward Improvements in Guidance for Practice" (2013) 21 *Environmental Reviews* 40–52, 43; see also Sections 1.2.4 and 2.2.1.

[6] For an overview of the landscape of laws that can be useful in dealing with a cumulative environmental problem, see Chapter 3.

[7] Brian W. Head, *Wicked Problems in Public Policy: Understanding and Responding to Complex Challenges* (Palgrave Macmillan 2022) 8–12.

[8] Michael Howlett, *Designing Public Policies: Principles and Instruments* (2nd edn, Routledge 2019) 44–45.

difficult it is to clearly conceptualize it. This alerts rule designers to issues that deserve special attention in their context. Using the findings of Chapter 2 as a foundation,[9] and drawing on illustrative legal examples from around the world, Section 4.3 advances four categories of design features that help conceptualize a matter of concern fully, clearly, and transparently, by specifying, or providing a process for specifying its key dimensions: key environmental and human elements of the matter of concern ("what matters" and "who matters"); the spatial boundaries of the matter of concern; the limit of conditions to it that are acceptable, and their relationship to time, or the conditions that are sought, in the case of something that needs restoring; and adapting each of these things when required. Chapter 8 then provides deeper insights about conceptualization in a case study of concerns about groundwater and environmental justice in California's Central Valley.

4.1.1 *What Is Conceptualization?*

As used in this book, conceptualization refers to how legal mechanisms define what and who matter for protection from cumulative threats, noting that processes for resolving conflicts about conceptualization among governments and with stakeholders are discussed separately, through the function of coordination.[10] Mechanically, legal mechanisms may undertake conceptualization through statutes or regulations or indirectly through policies or processes for which they provide. This should be distinguished from deciding what matters on a case-by-case basis, as developments arise that might affect something that matters. That approach does not provide for stability or certainty, and invites shifting baselines.[11]

As suggested by the cross-disciplinary insights in Chapter 2, legal mechanisms can support conceptualizing a matter of concern by providing clarity and transparency about its important dimensions: its environmental and, if relevant, social dimensions ("what" and "who" matters); its spatial boundaries; important thresholds that describe the limits of acceptable conditions, which may have a temporal element; and providing for adapting these things (Figure 4.1). Section 4.3 takes up these dimensions as design features for conceptualization, providing illustrative examples of legal approaches to specifying them.

A conceptualization that is clear in these ways reduces ambiguity and uncertainty about what matters. Without clarity about elements that matter

9 See Section 2.2.1.

10 See Chapter 7 on Coordination.

11 See Section 2.2.2.1.

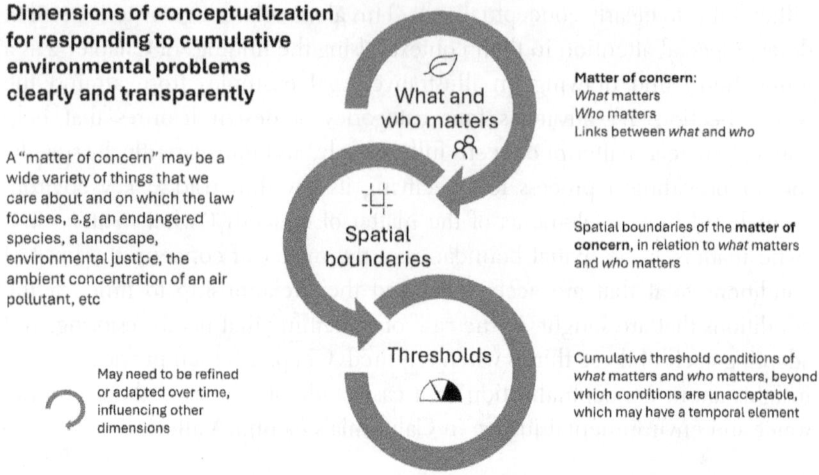

FIGURE 4.1 Clearly and transparently conceptualizing a matter of concern to facilitate responding to cumulative environmental harm requires identifying its key elements and the spatial boundaries and cumulative threshold conditions that correspond to those elements in a way that facilitates adaptation over time

and thresholds, it is difficult to know what to monitor to understand the extent of cumulative change and when to intervene to control cumulative change. Clarity about a matter of concern allows policymakers, public servants, and others to consider the ways in which different rules might be unaligned and make it difficult for the law to achieve its objects. For example, interventions might be directed at subtly different things. The California groundwater case study in Chapter 8 illustrates this, showing how different laws aimed at protecting groundwater actually take different views of what and who matter.

While the need for clarity may seem self-evident, in practice, a failure to clearly identify important dimensions of a matter of concern "sometimes obscures policy debate and the capacity for evaluation [and] contributes to poor practice … at both the level of particular impacts and across landscapes or jurisdictions."[12] Consider the ambiguity and contestation surrounding well-established (and still ambiguous) terms such as "resilience" or conceptualizations of elements of the environment as legal persons, which has garnered popular support but may lack clarity in relation to rights and duties and spatial delimitation.[13] Regulatory clarity

[12] Martine Maron and others, "The Many Meanings of No Net Loss in Environmental Policy" (2018) 1 *Nature Sustainability* 19–27, 19.

[13] Ruth Barcan, "The Campaign for Legal Personhood for the Great Barrier Reef: Finding Political and Pedagogical Value in a Spectacular Failure of Care" (2020) 3 *Environment and Planning E: Nature and Space* 810–832, 822–824; Erin O'Donnell, "Rivers as Living Beings: Rights in Law, but No Rights to Water?" (2020) 29 *Griffith Law Review* 643–668, 655–656.

about what matters and important thresholds also helps head off key difficulties in dealing with cumulative environmental problems, such as baseline shift and policy drift.[14]

Transparency requires articulating the values underlying why something matters. This can influence the dimensions of conceptualization (such as thresholds or spatial boundaries) and other CIRCle Framework functions, like publicly justifying plans for a future intervention even if it is not immediately possible; or clarifying whether a specific type of intervention is appropriate. For example, if an area of natural heritage is protected because it is unique, this would probably rule out a regulatory strategy that allows offsetting harm to the unique thing by creating a benefit somewhere else.[15] Transparency also helps identify parties relevant to coordination (e.g., involving a bird protection association where an area is conserved as habitat for birds). Formal rules can be useful for transparency because they are often accompanied by publicly available elaborations of what is intended by a rule, for example, through committee debates, explanatory memoranda, and management plans or policies.

As noted in Chapter 2, having rules that clearly and transparently conceptualize a matter of concern does not imply that this conceptualization should be set in stone. It may need to change with time, for example, with significant changes in social values. Contemporary environmental law seeks to protect many things that were not protected even fifty years ago.[16] Environmental stressors like climate change may require triage or "directed adaptation."[17] Therefore, legal mechanisms to support conceptualization should also include processes for transparently modifying how a matter of concern is conceptualized.

4.1.2 *Conceptualization as an Integrated Regulatory Function in the CIRCle Framework*

Conceptualization of the matter of concern is the basis for functions related to information, regulatory intervention, and coordination. This section explains how these functions work together to contain cumulative change to the matter of concern within acceptable limits (Figure 4.2, buliding on Figure 2.1, which depicts basic links between regulatory functions).

[14] See Section 2.2.1.

[15] See Section 6.2 for a discussion of offsetting as a regulatory strategy for intervention.

[16] Benjamin J. Richardson, *Time and Environmental Law: Telling Nature's Time* (CUP 2017) 98–107.

[17] Gregor W. Schuurman and others, "Navigating Ecological Transformation: Resist-Accept-Direct as a Path to a New Resource Management Paradigm" (2022) 72 *BioScience* 16–29, 20–22.

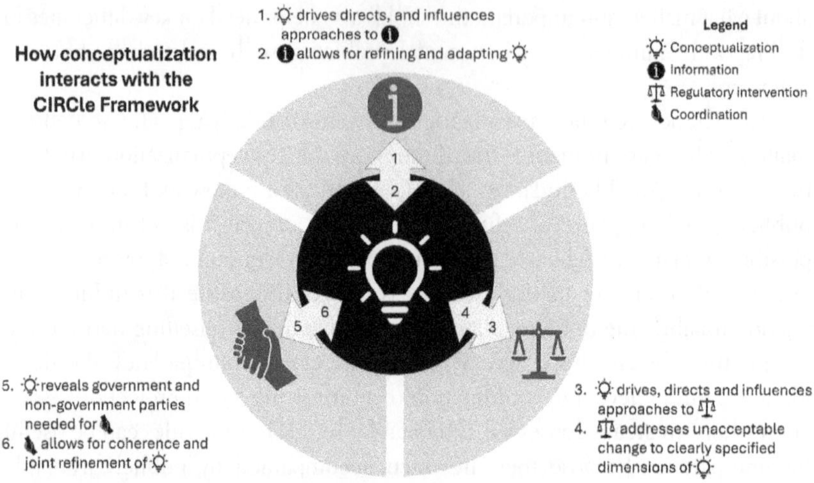

FIGURE 4.2 Integration of legal mechanisms for conceptualization with other CIRCle Framework functions, each necessary for regulating cumulative environmental problems

Clearly and transparently conceptualizing a matter of concern drives efforts to collect information about its conditions and to prevent unacceptable change to it by intervening. The way a matter of concern is conceptualized will indirectly influence and may even rule out some approaches to gathering information and intervening. A "reductionist" natural capital accounting approach to information or intervention, for example, would seem poorly aligned with a conceptualization that rests on holistic concepts of ecological integrity.[18] What is perceived as a threat – and therefore a candidate for intervention – will vary based on how the matter of concern is conceptualized.[19] If pesticide concentrations in irrigation water is a matter of concern but nitrates are not, regulatory intervention would consider farmers that use excess pesticides but not those who produce excess nitrates.

Clear conceptualizations also facilitate identifying regulatory actors with responsibility for the matter of concern for the purpose of coordinating approaches. This includes, for example, actors whose responsibilities are determined by the spatial boundaries of a matter of concern (e.g., within the

[18] See Section 4.1.1.

[19] Guido Plassmann, "Nature Protection in the Alps – Which Motivation?" in Guido Plassmann and others (eds), *Alpine Nature 2030: Creating [Ecological] Connectivity for Generations to Come* (Federal Ministry for the Environment, Nature Conservation, Building and Nuclear Safety (Germany) 2016) 17–24 ("the definition of threats may vary according to which concept of natural environment we are employing"), 21.

territory of a province or city) or its legal designation (e.g., the listing of a species as endangered).[20]

A key variable for conceptualization is the degree to which it includes people.[21] This has flow-on effects for approaches to coordination. In settler jurisdictions, for example, some matters of concern will inherently require the central involvement of Indigenous Peoples – not just as an exercise in respecting and including Indigenous knowledges as information (though that is also important)[22] but to help legal articulations of what matters reflect Indigenous views in a way that is inseparable from the involvement of Indigenous Peoples and their local contexts.[23] An environmental justice lens that highlights cumulative impacts on disadvantaged communities also points to involving those communities in responding to impacts as a matter of procedural justice.[24] The implication of this relationship between conceptualization and coordination is not merely expanding the circle of nongovernment actors involved in conceptualization: Enabling their meaningful involvement may require dedicated resources.[25] Clearly conceptualizing a matter of concern is also necessary (but not sufficient[26]) to address risks of different regulatory actors adopting different and incoherent conceptualizations of what and who matter. Coordination makes it possible to act, taking a coherent, or at least not mutually undermining, view of what matters.

Conversely, other regulatory functions in the CIRCle Framework influence how a matter of concern is conceptualized. Legal mechanisms for information may lead to adapting a conceptualization by producing information about the current conditions of the matter of concern or current or likely impacts to it. For example, better understanding how a species or ecosystem responds to stressors – say, a coral species being more sensitive to high marine temperatures than previously known – may lead to a desire to protect or promote different, more heat-tolerant coral species.[27] Understanding that water wells used by a

[20] See also Coordination, Section 7.2.2.

[21] See Section 4.2.2.

[22] See Chapter 5 (Information), Table 5.2 and accompanying text.

[23] Mihnea Tănăsescu and others, "Rights of Nature and Rivers in Ecuador's Constitutional Court" (2024) *The International Journal of Human Rights* 1–23, 15 (in relation to "variegated Indigenous traditions" in the context of contextualizing rights of nature in Ecuador).

[24] Gordon Walker, *Environmental Justice: Concepts, Evidence and Politics* (Routledge 2012) 47–50 (discussing impacts in general).

[25] E.g. Section 8.4.2.2.

[26] See Chapter 7 on Coordination for processes for resolving conflict among governments and stakeholders in relation to the other CIRCle Framework functions: conceptualization, information and regulatory intervention.

[27] See Section 9.5.3 (Reef Restoration and Adaptation Program).

groundwater-reliant disadvantaged community are going dry because others are overpumping the aquifer may prompt incorporating groundwater sustainability issues into conceptualizations of environmental justice, or vice versa.[28] Equally, by facilitating new interactions between agencies, levels of government, or nongovernment actors, legal mechanisms for coordination may lead to refining how a matter of concern is conceptualized.

4.2 DIFFERENT APPROACHES TO WHAT AND WHO MATTER

A matter of concern can take many forms. This is unsurprising: Different nations, cultures, and communities value different things. Even taking a single thing that we care about, there are multiple ways to conceptualize it as a matter of concern, each of which expresses different values and none of which is universally or objectively "correct." "Clean water," for example, might be expressed as a river that is swimmable, a municipal water supply that meets detailed drinking water standards, or lake water that is so clear that it attracts tourists for its aesthetic value. Some matters of concern have characteristics that make it more challenging (but no less important) to articulate the dimensions of a conceptualization that help deal with cumulative impacts (Figure 4.1). Other matters of concern inherently adopt a cumulative impacts mindset.

This part explores two ways in which a matter of concern can vary and present challenges: the degree to which the matter of concern is reductionist or multidimensional and the degree to which it includes human communities (summarized in quadrants in Table 4.1). Multidimensional and human-linked matters of concern are entirely legitimate but can pose special challenges because they are prone to ambiguity and specifying thresholds may be difficult – issues to which regulatory designers ought to be especially attuned. Ultimately, no quadrant is universally "right." Rather, it is clarity and transparency that are important so that rules can protect what matters. Exploring the diversity of matters of concern also supports the earlier argument that a wider range of laws is relevant for controlling cumulative effects than is typically conceived to be so.[29]

4.2.1 *From Reductionist to Multidimensional Matters of Concern*

Environment-related laws traditionally break up pieces of the nonhuman environment into smaller parts, say, individual species or pollutants – an approach termed atomism or reductionism.[30] Some contemporary

[28] See generally Chapter 8.

[29] See generally Chapter 3 (Landscape for Analysis).

[30] Klaus Bosselmann, "Losing the Forest for the Trees: Environmental Reductionism in the Law" (2010) 2 *Sustainability* 2424–2448, 2430, 2432.

TABLE 4.1 *Varying matters of concern and implications for the challenges of conceptualization: illustrative examples*

Elements of concern	Reductionist	Multidimensional
Only nonhuman environment[a]	Viability of individual species Ambient concentration of a pollutant	Ecological integrity Biodiversity
Linked human and environmental elements	Access to urban green space Cultural right to hunt a specific species	Environmental justice Landscape

Greater potential for ambiguity, and need for attention to clarity
Greater challenge to specify cumulative threshold conditions

[a] Note that a focus on the nonhuman environment may be motivated by human needs, e.g., sensitivity to air pollutants.

environmental legal scholars criticize a reductionist approach to environmental protection or praise a more holistic or integrated view of what we ought to care about through law. They point to broader matters of concern like the connectedness between people and places, or planetary boundaries, as better reflecting ecological reality or spotlighting unaddressed harms.[31]

The distinction between reductionist and multidimensional matters of concern highlights risks that make clarity especially critical for regulatory designers. Multidimensional matters of concern may increase ambiguity and therefore the potential for interpreting the matter of concern in different ways, as well as increasing the difficulty of specifying an acceptable threshold of change. This, in turn, risks producing information-gathering measures, interventions, and coordination that undermine or do not support each other. The meaning of fine particulate (PM2.5) air pollution (which causes illness with both short- and long-term exposure)[32] is clear. By contrast, a law may seek to protect "air quality," without more detail and without a process for elaborating which components matter. This gives decision-makers significant discretion to

[31] E.g. Christine Parker and Fiona Haines, "An Ecological Approach to Regulatory Studies?" (2018) 45 *Journal of Law and Society* 136–155; Elizabeth Macpherson and others, "Designing Law and Policy for the Health and Resilience of Marine and Coastal Ecosystems – Lessons from (and for) Aotearoa New Zealand" (2023) 54 *Ocean Development and International Law* 200–252.

[32] Ioannis Manisalidis and others, "Environmental and Health Impacts of Air Pollution: A Review" (2020) 8:14 *Frontiers in Public Health* 1–13, 5–6.

decide precisely what matters in a way that may depart from what was intended, privilege "loud voices," or lead to different interpretations in different places or through time, failing to guard against inadvertent cumulative harm.

Lack of clarity is a pronounced problem for cumulative impact analysis under project-level EIA laws. These laws tend to be vague about what matters (e.g., "resources, ecosystems and human communities" in the United States[33]). This, in turn, means that different analysts may interpret what matters differently, either inadvertently or strategically, making it difficult to gain a clear view of cumulative impacts on something affected by multiple projects.[34] To reduce the potential for ambiguity and incoherence in regulating cumulative harms, broadly specified matters of concern benefit from more detailed definitions, policies, and regulatory processes for understanding what and who matters in a local context.[35]

Whether a matter of concern has a reductionist or multidimensional nature also has important implications for other regulatory functions in the CIRCle Framework. A reductionist matter of concern produces a narrower scope of activities that can be understood as contributing to cumulative environmental harm. If the ambient concentration of PM2.5 is the matter of concern, only activities that increase PM2.5 – such as power plants, vehicles, and wood stoves – are potential contributors to cumulative harm. If "air quality" is what matters, without further detail, then additional activities, say, activities that contribute to ozone, contribute to cumulative harm. This has flow-on effects for collecting information about potentially threatening activities, designing diverse interventions required to deal with more diverse threats, and considering the actors relevant to coordination.

4.2.2 *From Separation to Links between Human and Environmental Elements*

Diverse legal concepts link humans and their environment. Traditionally, Western law conceives of humans as separate from the other-than-human environment (for brevity, "environment").[36] Western law has tended to link the two through constructs like property and narrowly specified rights, like

33 Council on Environmental Quality (U.S.), *Considering Cumulative Effects under the National Environmental Policy Act* (1997) 23.

34 See Section 2.2.1.2, Note 20.

35 This is discussed as a design feature later, and further in the context of groundwater in California (Chapter 8).

36 Bosselmann, "Losing the Forest for the Trees: Environmental Reductionism," 2430–2431.

water rights or a right to access a beach. Conversely, some Indigenous laws emphasize interconnectedness and "consider[] reductionist worldviews to be fundamentally flawed."[37] There is much in between. Legal concepts of landscape and heritage recognize and value the way humans shape an environment, from outstanding landscapes to those that are ordinary or ecologically degraded.[38] Some recent concepts recognize the value of the environment to humans in a utilitarian way. In this category, we see ecosystem services, environmental accounting, and natural capital conceived at different scales, from individual parcels of land to the whole globe.[39]

Other legal concepts focus on the way that damaging the environment hurts people, or their rights. Environmental justice may be interpreted as ensuring that no subpopulation experiences disproportionate environmental burden.[40] "Solastalgia" captures the emotional pain felt by human individuals experiencing environmental loss.[41] Environmental rights focus on human dependence on the environment. This occurs through some rights of nature approaches[42] and rights to a healthy environment.[43] Similarly, the human-centered principle of intergenerational equity may be interpreted as requiring "assessment of the cumulative impacts of proposed activities on the environment."[44] Impact assessment also increasingly addresses how changes to the

37 Martuwarra RiverOfLife and others, "Recognizing the Martuwarra's First Law Right to Life as a Living Ancestral Being" (2020) 9 *Transnational Environmental Law* 541–568, 547 (regarding First Nations Peoples in Western Australia). See also Macpherson and others, "Designing Law and Policy for the Health and Resilience of Marine and Coastal Ecosystems," 238 (regarding relatedness of Māori and oceans).

38 E.g., Council of Europe Landscape Convention, October 20, 2000, Florence, in force March 1, 2004, E.T.S. 176, arts. 1, 2. See Chapter 10 for further discussion of this Convention in the context of Alpine grasslands.

39 See generally J. B. Ruhl and James Salzman, "A Global Assessment of the Law and Policy of Ecosystem Services" (2020) 39 *University of Queensland Law Journal* 503–523. See also note 49.

40 See generally Jon A. Mueller and Taylor Lilley, "Forty Years of Environmental Justice: Where Is the Justice?" (2022) 25 *Richmond Public Interest Law Review* 75–125.

41 See generally Lindsay P. Galway and others, "Mapping the Solastalgia Literature: A Scoping Review Study" (2019) 16 *International Journal of Environmental Research and Public Health* 1–16.

42 Erin O'Donnell, Cristy Clark and Rachel Killean, "Rights and Relationality: A Review of the Role of Law in the Human/Water Relationship" (2024) 17 *Water Alternatives* 207–238, 219–221. See pp. 221–224 for a discussion of water relationality more generally.

43 See generally John H. Knox and Ramin Pejan (eds), *The Human Right to a Healthy Environment* (CUP 2018).

44 *Gray v The Minister for Planning & Ors* [2006] NSWLEC 720, [122] (Pain J), cited by *New Acland Coal Pty Ltd v Ashman & Ors and Chief Executive, Department of Environment and Heritage* [2017] QLC 24, [1309] (Smith J).

nonhuman biophysical environment affect humans through visual, cultural, health, human rights, and socioeconomic impacts.[45]

Like multidimensional matters of concern, human–environment "linked" matters of concern can be ambiguous and increase the potential for different interpretations of what the matter of concern actually is. This risk requires special attention. A central and difficult question is: *Which* humans matter, and form part of the matter of concern? There is often no objective definition of a "community."[46] In the context of environmental justice, for example, foundational questions remain about the identity of the "community of justice": at the extremes, international and intergenerational, or local and intragenerational.[47] Chapter 8 demonstrates how choices about which communities matter can influence acceptable thresholds of harm (conceptualization) and feasible mitigation measures (intervention). Sometimes including human communities even introduces fundamental ambiguity about whether an effect is positive or negative. A cultural practice, say, Alpine grazing, may itself be what matters, or it might adversely affect a nonhuman part of the environment that matters, like forests that would expand in the absence of grazing (as discussed in Chapter 10).

Thresholds can also be more difficult to specify for human–environment linked matters. Take distributional environmental justice: It is difficult to quantify a threshold total environmental burden that is "too much," and legal approaches tend to express the threshold in a relative sense, as a "disproportionate" burden. The difficult question remains, though: disproportionate compared to the burden experienced by whom and where? Some kinds of harm to people involve a degree of subjectivity that also involves ambiguity, such as noise pollution or negative impacts on the aesthetic quality of an environment. The potential for greater ambiguity in human–environment linked matters suggests the need for even more attention to specifying the matter of concern in a detailed way, (or a process for specifying it) to avoid manipulation or inadvertently allowing unacceptable cumulative effects.

A matter of concern that links human and environmental elements has important implications for other regulatory functions in the CIRCle Framework. Effects on coordination have already been mentioned.[48] Human links may influence the type of effects and activities that are considered harmful and are candidates for intervention. On the face of it, recognizing a human dimension to a matter of concern expands the types of

45 See generally Riki Therivel and Graham Wood (eds), *Methods of Environmental and Social Impact Assessment* (Routledge 2018).

46 A. R. Siders, "The Administrator's Dilemma: Closing the Gap between Climate Adaptation Justice in Theory and Practice" (2022) 137 *Environmental Science and Policy* 280–289, 284.

47 Walker, *Environmental Justice*, 42–43.

48 See Section 4.1.2.

impacts that are cognizable as harm if humans rely on something that most or all nonhuman biota do not (e.g., deep groundwater).

While these concepts highlight some risks for well-chosen regulatory features to mitigate, some matters of concern, advantageously, have an inherently cumulative character. Environmental accounting and natural capital are inherently about aggregation.[49] Distributive environmental justice considers the cumulative burden of a range of different sources of pollution or other environmental harm on communities, often those that also suffer demographic disadvantage or social vulnerability or difference.[50] These burdens may be specified in some detail, as demonstrated by government efforts to quantify and map environmental (in)justice.[51] This inherently cumulative character provides a useful structure for appreciating and keeping track of the slow accumulation of individually minor harms.

4.3 CROSSCUTTING DESIGN FEATURES

Despite the great variation in conceptualizing matters of concern discussed above, Chapter 2 identified common challenges. This section now turns to regulatory design features that cut across different approaches to conceptualization, drawing illustrative regulatory examples from across the world.

4.3.1 *Specifying What and Who Matter*

To regulate cumulative adverse effects, we need to understand what constitutes harm to a matter of concern. This requires clarity about what the matter of concern is, or who they are, or both, including how human and environmental elements are linked.[52] Knowing this, we can determine whether a change from one state to another is harmful,[53] which informs other regulatory functions.

In practice, some rules specify a matter of concern broadly, perhaps for reasons of political compromise or to maximize administrative discretion, and rely on the courts to figure out or constrain what they mean.[54] This is slow,

49 See Section 2.2.1.1, Note 9.

50 Walker, *Environmental Justice*, 2–3 (setting out the range of social and environmental dimensions evident in the literature).

51 See generally Charles Lee, "A Game Changer in the Making: Lessons from States Advancing Environmental Justice through Mapping and Cumulative Impact Strategies" (2020) 50 *Environmental Law Reporter* 10203–10215. See also Section 8.3.2.2.

52 See Section 4.2.2.

53 Albert C. Lin, "Unifying Role of Harm in Environmental Law" (2006) (3) *Wisconsin Law Review* 897–986, 980–981.

54 E.g., Macpherson and others, "Designing Law and Policy for the Health and Resilience of Marine and Coastal Ecosystems," 220.

less democratic than available alternatives, inefficient (as bureaucracies guess at a meaning before a court clarifies things), and uncertain. Incoherence can emerge if different bureaucracies or courts come to different conclusions. It is far preferable for rules to clarify the matter of concern – or provide for a process to do this – so that other regulatory functions can support it. Clear rules do not necessarily need to be specified in highly technical scientific terms (see Table 4.2), they just require an absence of ambiguity from the perspective of those in the local context.

It may not always be possible or desirable for rule makers to specify the matter of concern in precise terms at the time a rule is drafted. Perhaps not enough is known about public values or scientific information, or perhaps specifying what matters requires negotiation between government and non-government entities. In such cases, rules can provide for processes, including coordination,[55] to clarify what and who matters. Table 4.2 sets out illustrative examples of approaches to regulatory design that facilitate clearly specifying the matter of concern even where further work is required.

4.3.2 *Specifying Boundaries of Matters of Concern*

Clearly specifying the spatial boundaries of the matter of concern is an important dimension of conceptualization to address cumulative impacts[56] (time is also important, and is most relevant to thresholds and adaptation[57]). The boundaries of environmental resources often do not match jurisdictional or administrative boundaries,[58] and clarity about the boundaries of the matter of concern indicates which jurisdictions, regulators, and potentially traditional rights holders[59] are relevant in regulating cumulative harm. Comparing the boundaries of the matter of concern and jurisdictional boundaries may also

55 See generally Chapter 7 (Coordination).

56 This is well established in the project-level cumulative impact analysis context. See, e.g., F. Chris Jones, "Cumulative Effects Assessment: Theoretical Underpinnings and Big Problems" (2016) 24 *Environmental Reviews* 187–204, 199, 201; see generally Riki Therivel and Bill Ross, "Cumulative Effects Assessment: Does Scale Matter?" (2007) 27 *Environmental Impact Assessment Review* 365–385. Chapter 7 refers to this as a regulatory offsetting strategy for intervention.

57 See Section 4.3.3.2, and Rebecca Nelson, "Big Time: An Empirical Analysis of Regulating the Cumulative Environmental Effects of Coal Seam Gas Extraction under Australian Federal Environmental Law" (2019) 36 *Environmental and Planning Law Journal* 531–551, 533–536.

58 See generally Graeme S. Cumming, David H. M. Cumming and Charles L. Redman, "Scale Mismatches in Social-Ecological Systems: Causes, Consequences, and Solutions" (2006) 11:14 *Ecology and Society* 1–20.

59 E.g., Macpherson and others, "Designing Law and Policy for the Health and Resilience of Marine and Coastal Ecosystems," 233–234.

TABLE 4.2 *Mechanisms for clearly specifying a matter of concern, including in a precautionary way*

Legal mechanism	Illustrative example
Rule directly specifies elements of matter of concern	Islamic religious law provides for *Himas* (protected areas), which are centuries-old, community-managed areas of public resources traditionally designated by an imam for activities such as beekeeping, grass harvesting, or grazing.[a] Himas exist in diverse nations, including Indonesia, Iraq, Lebanon, Saudi Arabia, and Zanzibar, and are reflected in formal state laws to varying degrees.[b] Himas in Lebanon are being reestablished with high social acceptance through municipal laws and ministerial decrees.[c]
Rule specifies broad elements of a matter of concern, to be detailed by a local plan	In the California groundwater case study (Chapter 8), state legislation conceptualizes "what matters" in groundwater sustainability by reference to six specified sustainability indicators, which are elaborated by local plans to suit local contexts.[d]
Rule specifies analytical process to clarify dimensions of the matter of concern	Impact assessment for a designated project in Canada must take into account "changes to the environment or to health, social or economic conditions" that it is likely to cause, including cumulative effects.[e] Formal cumulative assessment policy guides the identification of "valued components," the matters of concern that are the subject of the assessment.[f] Specific guidance applies to assessing cumulative impacts on the rights of Indigenous Peoples, which involves evaluating "whether the present ability of the community to exercise rights has been diminished due to factors such as cumulative adverse effects and historical or current interferences with traditional practices."[g]
Rule specifies matter of concern in a precautionary way, to be confirmed	The water laws of the US state of Nebraska include a focus on groundwater pumping depleting river flows in systems that are hydrologically connected. A state agency may make a preliminary designation that an area is fully appropriated (a precautionary indication that hydrologically connected resources in an area are a matter of concern requiring intervention). This

(*continued*)

TABLE 4.2 (*continued*)

Legal mechanism	Illustrative example
	leads to default rules while investigations are ongoing. A final determination follows. Even where the final determination reverses the preliminary one, special rules are put in place for at least four years as a further precautionary measure.[h]
Rule broadly expresses matter of concern, clarified through court-ordered directives	The Constitutional Court of Ecuador found that a provincial government had breached the Aquepi River's legal right to ecological flows by authorizing an irrigation project, and ordered "directives for conceptualizing and measuring [rights of nature] violations in water-related ecosystems," thereby setting "concrete standards" and "giving specific content" to rights of nature norms.[i]

[a] See generally Hala Kilani, Assaad Serhal and Othman Llewlyn, *Al-Hima: A Way of Life* (IUCN 2007) 1–6.
[b] Rianne C. ten Veen, "Hima as a Protected Area – Opportunities and Challenges in the 21st Century" in Radhika Borde and others (eds), *Religion and Nature Conservation: Global Case Studies* (Routledge 2022) 215–224, 218–220.
[c] Kilani, Serhal and Llewlyn, *Al-Hima*, 9–11.
[d] See Section 8.4.2.4.
[e] Impact Assessment Act 2019 (Canada) art. 22(1)(a).
[f] Government of Canada, "Policy Framework for Assessing Cumulative Effects under the Impact Assessment Act" (*Government of Canada*, 2023) www.canada.ca/en/impact-assessment-agency/services/policy-guidance/practitioners-guide-impact-assessment-act/policy-framework-assessing-cumulative-effects-under-impact-assessment-act.html, archived at https://perma.cc/EUU2-44PM. Note that reforms to this guidance were anticipated at the time of writing.
[g] Government of Canada, "Policy Context: Assessment of Potential Impacts on the Rights of Indigenous Peoples" (*Government of Canada*, 2020) www.canada.ca/en/impact-assessment-agency/services/policy-guidance/practitioners-guide-impact-assessment-act/assessment-potential-impacts-rights-indigenous-peoples.html, archived at https://perma.cc/DC9Q-75G8. Note that reforms to this guidance were anticipated at the time of writing.
[h] Nebraska Revised Statutes § 46-714.
[i] Craig M. Kauffman and Pamela L. Martin, "How Ecuador's Courts Are Giving Form and Force to Rights of Nature Norms" (2023) 12 *Transnational Environmental Law* 366–395, 383.

illuminate problematic spatial gaps in regulatory responsibility, where harms can accumulate free of formal rules.

Boundaries are also important because they can influence available approaches to intervention. For example, if the concept of "favorable conservation status" of a species under the EU Habitats Directive refers to species present in a nation, rather than in Europe as a whole (i.e., same species, but different boundaries for the matter of concern), a nation may not be permitted to undertake positive action elsewhere to excuse harm in its own territory.[60]

Setting boundaries may be controversial and require extensive processes for information gathering, coordination, and trust-building among government and nongovernment bodies.[61] For human-linked matters of concern, it is not immediately clear, for example, which boundaries correspond to concerns about environmental justice and more complex ideas of spatiality may be needed.[62] For some environmental matters of concern, the relevant space is complex, being both lateral and vertical, as for groundwater, airspace, and oceans.

Concerns about the cost and other burdens of delineating legal boundaries arise in diverse contexts, from registers of communal land in the Philippines[63] to groundwater protection zones in France.[64] In such cases, laws may usefully set out a process for delineation, rather than doing it directly. The Great Barrier Reef Marine Park, discussed in the case study in Chapter 9, was formally proclaimed in 1983 under a 1975 law[65] that initially only referred to a roughly described "Great Barrier Reef Region."[66] A statutory body then arranged surveying and studies to establish boundaries. Spatially defined zones under subsequent statutory plans provided for conceptualizing different matters of concern across the Reef.[67] The legislation also intentionally made it more difficult to de-establish marine park areas by requiring each House of

60 Hendrik Schoukens, "Legal Considerations in Operationalizing Eco-Restoration in the European Union: A Sisyphean Task or Unlocking Existing Potential?" in Afshin Akhtar-Khavari and Benjamin J. Richardson (eds), *Ecological Restoration Law: Concepts and Case Studies* (Routledge 2019) 167–191, 176.

61 E.g., see Amanda E. Cravens and Nicole M. Ardoin, "Negotiating Credibility and Legitimacy in the Shadow of an Authoritative Data Source" (2016) 21:30 *Ecology and Society* 1–14; Section 8.4.2.1 regarding groundwater basin boundaries.

62 See generally Gordon Walker, "Beyond Distribution and Proximity: Exploring the Multiple Spatialities of Environmental Justice" (2009) 41 *Antipode* 614–636, 618–622 (in relation to distributional issues).

63 E.g. John Price, "The Status of Title to Land in Representative Jurisdictions of Asia and the Pacific" in Piyush Tiwari, Grant B. Stillman and Naoyuki Yoshino (eds), *Equitable Land Use for Asian Infrastructure* (Asian Development Bank Institute 2020) 107–128, 113.

64 Kelly L. Warner and others, "Interactions of Water Quality and Integrated Groundwater Management: Examples from the United States and Europe" in Anthony J. Jakeman and others (eds), *Integrated Groundwater Management: Concepts, Approaches and Challenges* (Springer 2016) 347–376, 358–360.

65 Great Barrier Reef Marine Park Act 1975, Act No. 85 of 1975 (Australia) ss 30–31; Commonwealth of Australia Gazette S195, August 31, 1983, 1–3.

66 Great Barrier Reef Marine Park Act 1975, Act No. 85 of 1975 (Australia) s 3(1), Schedule.

67 See generally Great Barrier Reef Marine Park Zoning Plan 2003 (Australia).

the national Parliament to pass a resolution to do so.[68] This raises the issue of adaptability, which is addressed further later on.[69] Table 4.3 illustrates diverse approaches to specifying spatial boundaries in conceptualizing a matter of concern.

4.3.3 *Specifying Cumulative Threshold Conditions of Matters of Concern*

It is not enough to be clear about what we want to protect from cumulative harm. We also need to know what protection means: the state or conditions of the matter of concern, beyond which additional impacts would be unacceptable, in relation to the elements that matter.[70] I term this set of conditions at the limit of acceptability "cumulative threshold conditions." "Threshold" indicates that one side is acceptable, while the other side is not. This is distinct from an ecological threshold, as discussed later on. Transparency about how thresholds are selected is also important to expose the role of values[71] (and whose values) and to guide any subsequent consideration of adapting a threshold by exposing the rationale for the threshold conditions as originally set.

4.3.3.1 Cumulative Thresholds versus Intervention and Information

The CIRCle Framework helps distinguish between conceptualizing the matter of concern, and intervention, being the decision about what to do to prevent the matter of concern being unacceptably affected. Logically, and tautologically, the *only* way to prevent an unacceptable change to the conditions of something that we care about is to be clear about the limits of conditions that are acceptable (conceptualization). Clarifying limits must come before, and is distinct from, ensuring that we act on an impact that would cause aggregate conditions to become unacceptable (intervention).[72] It is also related to, but distinct from, scientific ecological thresholds that describe the point at which there is a sudden shift in conditions in response to

68 Great Barrier Reef Marine Park Act 1975, Act No. 85 of 1975 (Australia) s 31(4).

69 See Section 4.3.4.

70 See Section 4.3.1.

71 David P. Lawrence, "Impact Significance Determination – Back to Basics" (2007) 27 *Environmental Impact Assessment Review* 755–769, 762.

72 Cathryn Clarke Murray and others, "The Insignificance of Thresholds in Environmental Impact Assessment: An Illustrative Case Study in Canada" (2018) 61 *Environmental Management* 1062–1071, 1063 ("a clear delineation between acceptable and unacceptable levels of impact; a decision point at which action must be taken to prevent unacceptable negative outcomes").

TABLE 4.3 *Mechanisms for specifying boundaries of a matter of concern*

Legal mechanism	Illustrative example
Rule that directly specifies precise boundaries	The boundary of the Boundary Waters Canoe Area Wilderness Area appears as a map reference in US legislation, which also (controversially) sets out spatial zones in which activities such as logging, snowmobiling, and mining are restricted.[a] These designations act as a link to related legislation in the state of Minnesota.[b]
Regulatory process used to specify boundaries	In Bangladesh, air pollution rules provide for declaring a "degraded airshed" in areas that exceed threshold values; priority areas for designation have "unique natural, historical and cultural significance."[c] Designation leads to a regulatory action plan.
	Matters of concern under South Korea's carbon neutrality legislation include socially disadvantaged groups. As well as legislating a focus on social groups vulnerable to climate change using a "climate justice" principle,[d] the law provides for designating "special districts for a just transition," in which specified measures are to be implemented to resolve socioeconomic imbalances that result from a green transition.[e]
Public register that specifies spatial boundaries	Chile's water law, which emphasizes water markets, provides for a register of water rights (Catastro Publico de Aguas). The details recorded for each water right include the right holder, source of water, spatial location of extraction, and relevant water user organization.[f]
Rule-based policy process to identify spatial area relevant for cumulative impacts	Policy on cumulative impact assessment under US environmental impact assessment legislation provides guidance on selecting geographic areas for analysis based on different types of valued resources.[g]

[a] Boundary Waters Canoe Area Wilderness Act, Pub. L. No. 95-495, 92 Stat. 1649 (1978) ss 3, 4, 10.

[b] See generally John Helland, "Chronology of Historical Actions for Boundary Waters Canoe Area Wilderness within Minnesota's Superior National Forest" (*Minnesota House of Representatives Research Department*, 2004) www.house.mn.gov/hrd/pubs/bwcawild.pdf, archived at https://perma.cc/RC53-NGAA.

[c] Mohammad Mostafa Hosain and Mohammad Ershadul Karim, "Bangladesh" (2022) 33 *Yearbook of International Environmental Law* 184–190, 187.

[d] Framework Act on Carbon Neutrality and Green Growth for Coping with Climate Crisis (기후위기 대응을 위한 탄소중립 · 녹색성장 기본법) (Republic of Korea), Act No. 18469, September 24 2021, amended by Act No. 20514, October 22 2024, art. 2(12) (definition of climate justice), 3(4) (principle of climate justice), 4(6) (obligations re climate justice).

[e] Ibid art. 48.

[f] Código de Aguas [Water Code], Decreto con Fuerza de Ley [Decree with the Force of Law] No. 1122, 1981, as amended (Chile) Title VIII art. 119.

[g] Council on Environmental Quality (U.S.), *Considering Cumulative Effects*, 12–16.

impacts (information). A water quality example of cumulative harm illustrates this: A cumulative threshold condition might quantify and transparently justify a desired level of water clarity in a lake threatened by nutrients and sediment in catchment runoff (conceptualization).[73] That is separate from predicting the impacts, such as the contribution of nutrients, climatic conditions, and so on, that would cause loss of water clarity to different degrees (information).

Scholars have long worried about thresholds, especially in impact assessment laws[74] that provide for assessing whether a proposed action would have a "significant impact" and laws that require "no net loss" of biodiversity, without clarifying "no net loss compared to what?"[75] "Significant impact" or "net loss" to a matter of concern triggers intervention, like not approving or requiring changes to a project. Commentators have characterized determinations of significance as value-dependent, imprecise, and context-dependent.[76]

Significance determinations also have another problem: They can conflate the functions of conceptualization and intervention. Conceptualization focuses on what and who matter and defines overall aggregate conditions of the matter of concern that are unacceptable, without being distracted by any particular proposed project. If actual or predicted conditions exceed cumulative threshold conditions – however this occurs, whether by 1 project or 1,000 projects or a cyclone or a heat wave – then, by definition, conditions are unacceptable and intervention is needed. The kind of intervention that should follow, its strictness, the burdens it entails, who must undertake it and when – these are different questions, discussed later in detail.[77] The important thing here is that the rules clearly define what constitutes unacceptable conditions, raising the question of what to do if they are predicted, rather than sweeping unacceptable conditions under the regulatory rug by providing a path for saying that a predicted impact is not "significant." This just invites shifting baselines and masks unacceptable cumulative impacts. Rules should clearly identify what we want to protect, provide for a threshold, and safeguard it from being warped by the influence of considering any particular proposed activity. In the EIA context, this could mean better linking EIA laws with other types of

73 E.g., as has occurred in relation to Lake Tahoe, California: Rebecca Nelson, "Regulating Nonpoint Source Pollution in the US: A Regulatory Theory Approach to Lessons and Research Paths for Australia" (2010) 35 *University of Western Australia Law Review* 340, 357–359. See also US Environmental Protection Agency, Lake Tahoe Water Quality Improvement Programs (n.d.) www.epa.gov/lake-tahoe/lake-tahoe-water-quality-improvement-programs, last accessed March 18, 2025, archived at https://perma.cc/KG2L-TAR2.

74 See generally Lawrence, "Impact Significance Determination."

75 See generally Maron and others, "The Many Meanings of No Net Loss."

76 Lawrence, "Impact Significance Determination," 759–761.

77 See Chapter 6.

laws that are better suited to determining thresholds for matters of concern, or processes under EIA laws for triggering or informing strategic assessments to determine thresholds.[78]

Some ways of specifying thresholds exacerbate the risk of shifting baselines and unplanned cumulative harm. It is risky to describe cumulative threshold conditions using current authorizations or levels of development. For example, a law might provide for assessing a project's significance by comparing predicted impacts to pre-project "baseline" conditions.[79] This comparison relates to a trigger for intervention – it does not clearly conceptualize the environmental elements that matter. A baseline of preexisting conditions is irrelevant if that does not reflect what society wants in terms of improving conditions (in the case of a restoration goal), or if the matter of concern could undergo significant cumulative change from baseline conditions and still be acceptable.

In addition, current conditions or current authorizations do not accurately indicate the impacts that current activities will cause to a matter of concern, so taking these approaches to thresholds risks overlooking unacceptable harms. Authorizations may have been granted but not activated fully or at all (e.g., years between infrastructure approvals and construction and impacts commencing). Further time lags can separate activities starting and impacts manifesting (e.g., pumping from groundwater wells reducing groundwater levels at distant locations over decades or longer[80]).

Other laws might set a "regulatory limit" based on an assumed "ecological threshold," which predicts the impacts of disturbance. Such a threshold seeks to identify when an ecosystem, for example, would enter an entirely different state.[81] Again, a regulatory limit speaks to intervention, not necessarily conceptualization that expresses a threshold of acceptable conditions; and ecological thresholds are information, not conceptualization: "no matter how precise and accurate, [ecological thresholds] represent information, not objectives...."[82]

The discussion thus far has generally framed cumulative threshold conditions in the context of linked interventions to limit harm – ensuring that conditions do not fall below an acceptable level – but cumulative threshold

78 This is one form of "tiering," discussed further in Section 6.5.1.

79 E.g., Murray and others, "The Insignificance of Thresholds," 1063.

80 Anthony J. Jakeman and others, "Integrated Groundwater Management: An Overview of Concepts and Challenges" in Anthony J. Jakeman and others (eds), *Integrated Groundwater Management: Concepts, Approaches and Challenges* (Springer 2016) 3–20, 11. For a discussion of the impacts of this for regulating cumulative effects, see generally Nelson, "Big Time."

81 Chris J. Johnson, "Identifying Ecological Thresholds for Regulating Human Activity: Effective Conservation or Wishful Thinking?" (2013) 168 *Biological Conservation* 57–65, 59–60.

82 Ibid 62.

conditions are also important in the context of restoration goals. A restoration threshold says that current conditions are not acceptable and need to improve to meet the threshold. This requires interventions both to improve conditions and limit further harm. If current conditions are unacceptable, any further harm requires intervention – indeed, further harm negates others' investments in restoration. Along these lines, Möckel argues that if a conservation objective under the EU Habitats Directive is to restore favorable conservation status, and a proposed development would cause an adverse effect and thus "substantial delays to this process . . . this then has a significant adverse impact on the conservation objective."[83]

Cumulative threshold conditions that express restoration goals would address cumulative impact problems noted around the world. Controls on project-level cumulative impacts on reindeer herded by Indigenous Sámi in northern Sweden are criticized for "never deliver[ing] anything better than what existed before an industrial project was proposed... There are no planning processes in place that would allow for proactive improvements in reindeer pastures or other ways to develop reindeer herding according to their own aspirations."[84] A clear restoration threshold would do these things. In Canada, Murray and others point to the "scorched earth" justification of project proponents who argue that a project would have an insignificant impact where pre-project conditions are already below acceptable conditions.[85] By contrast, case law in California has noted that "the greater the existing environmental problems are, the lower the threshold should be for treating a project's contribution to cumulative impacts as significant."[86] A clear, rule-based restoration threshold – the threshold above which conditions will become acceptable – would help avoid this.

4.3.3.2 Specifying Thresholds

Clearer cumulative threshold conditions are not impossible, and in fact appear in legal contexts outside EIA in diverse ways using different terms and underlying ideas (Table 4.4). Some reflect visions of the past,[87] the

[83] Stefan Möckel, "The Assessment of Significant Effects on the Integrity of 'Natura 2000' Sites under Article 6(2) and 6(3) of the Habitats Directive" (2017) 23 *Nature Conservation* 57–85, 63.

[84] Carl Österlin and Kaisa Raitio, "Fragmented Landscapes and Planscapes – The Double Pressure of Increasing Natural Resource Exploitation on Indigenous Sámi Lands in Northern Sweden" (2020) 9 *Resources* 1–27, 21.

[85] Murray and others, "The Insignificance of Thresholds," 1066–1067.

[86] *Communities for a Better Environment v. California Resources Agency*, 103 Cal.App.4th 98 at 120, 126 Cal. Rptr. 2d 441 at 457 (2002) (now disapproved of by later cases for other reasons).

[87] This approach has been criticized, e.g., in the biodiversity context, as discussed later.

TABLE 4.4 *Mechanisms for formulating cumulative threshold conditions for a matter of concern, and the role of time*

Legal mechanism	Illustrative example
Threshold conditions that refer to the past	Wilderness legislation in South Australia expressly seeks to achieve conditions in wilderness areas as they were "before European colonisation" and to protect them "from the effects of modern technology and exotic [species]."[a]
Threshold conditions that refer to the time of designation	Under the EU Habitats Directive, a favorable conservation status for a relevant habitat or species must remain stable, so that it regains its original state after a disturbance, and an unfavorable conservation status must not deteriorate further.[b] Temporally, ecological characteristics must not deteriorate "below their level at the time of designation" of a site.[c]
Threshold conditions that refer to a limited future decline	The Paris Agreement focuses on global average temperature as the matter of concern, and sets its goal by reference to a departure from preindustrial levels: "[h]olding the increase in the global average temperature to well below 2°C above pre-industrial levels and pursuing efforts to limit the temperature increase to 1.5°C above pre-industrial levels."[d]
Threshold conditions that refer to present distributive issues	The 2023 Environmental Justice Rules in New Jersey, US, focus on "overburdened communities" defined by income, minority status, and English proficiency;[e] a frequently updated online tool maps them.[f] Applicants for certain facility types must submit environmental justice impact statements demonstrating the facility will "avoid a disproportionate impact that would occur by creating adverse cumulative stressors in the overburdened community as a result of the facility's contribution."[g]
Atemporal threshold conditions	India's Central Pollution Control Board sets National Ambient Air Quality Standards, quantitative limits on air pollutants to protect public health, vegetation, and property.[h] Bhutan's Constitution requires that a minimum of 60 percent of its total land be maintained under forest cover.[i] Its national Climate Change Policy is to remain carbon neutral, in part by conserving its forests.[j]

(*continued*)

TABLE 4.4 (*continued*)

Legal mechanism	Illustrative example
Regulatory process for setting threshold conditions for elements of matter of concern	California's sustainable groundwater management planning process seeks to achieve "sustainability" within twenty years.[k] Local agencies must plan to avoid "undesirable results," being "significant and unreasonable effects" in six areas (e.g., chronic lowering of groundwater levels, water quality degradation), for which they must quantify goals.[l]

[a] Wilderness Protection Act 1992 (South Australia) ss 7(1)(d), 12(2)(b).
[b] Möckel, "The Assessment of Significant Effects on the Integrity of 'Natura 2000'," 61.
[c] European Commission and Directorate-General for Environment, *Managing Natura 2000 Sites – The Provisions of Article 6 of the "Habitats" Directive 92/43/EEC* (Publications Office 2019) 29.
[d] Paris Agreement under the United Nations Framework Convention on Climate Change, December 12, 2015, in force November 4, 2016, 3156 U.N.T.S. 79, art. 2(1)(a).
[e] New Jersey Administrative Code § 7:1C-1.5 "overburdened community".
[f] New Jersey Department of Environmental Protection, "Environmental Justice Rules Frequently Asked Questions" (2023) 10 https://dep.nj.gov/wp-content/uploads/ej/docs/ej-rule-frequently-asked-questions.pdf, archived at https://perma.cc/S5DJ-223Z; New Jersey Department of Environmental Protection, "Environmental Justice Law" (n.d.) https://dep.nj.gov/ej/law/, last accessed March 18, 2025, archived at https://perma.cc/V3WJ-5YE3.
[g] New Jersey Admin. Code § 7:1C-3.2(a)(9).
[h] Air (Prevention and Control of Pollution) Act 1981, as amended (India) s 16(2)(h); Central Pollution Control Board (India), National Ambient Air Quality Status and Trends 2019 (2020) 3, annex 2.
[i] Constitution of The Kingdom of Bhutan 2008, art. 5(3).
[j] National Environment Commission (Bhutan), *Climate Change Policy of the Kingdom of Bhutan* (2020) 5–6 www.nec.gov.bt/publications/climate-change, archived at https://perma.cc/KZ9K-JEVP.
[k] California Water Code § 10727.2(b)(1).
[l] 23 California Code Regs. §§ 354.22–354.30. See also Chapter 8 case study.

present, or even a future in which there has been some limited degradation. Some seek to preserve a "pristine" set of conditions because those conditions are inherently valued, such as "wilderness" conditions or a "heritage" landscape. At the other end of the spectrum, some laws adopt restoration objectives, which inherently seek to reverse cumulative damage and "challenge the scourge of shifting baselines."[88] Time can also feature in thresholds in a different way, as the achievement of conditions by a particular point in time.[89] An alternative, atemporal approach is to describe threshold conditions by

[88] Benjamin J. Richardson, "Timescales of Ecological Restoration" in Afshin Akhtar-Khavari and Benjamin J. Richardson (eds), *Ecological Restoration Law: Concepts and Case Studies* (Routledge 2019) 50–71, 52, 54.

[89] See Table 4.4, last row related to the sustainability goal of California's groundwater law.

reference to specific utilitarian environmental benefits that the law seeks to secure.

However they are expressed, detailed cumulative threshold conditions make it easier for different decision-makers to approach protection coherently, reducing the potential for inadvertent cumulative impacts. In some cases, quantified thresholds will be appropriate, and can relate to diverse matters of concern, for example, maximum air pollutant concentrations[90] or place-based cultural health indices developed by and for Indigenous Peoples from Aotearoa/New Zealand to the Marshall Islands and Nepal.[91] Quantification can helpfully reduce the discretion that can make decision-makers vulnerable to inappropriate influence from powerful interest groups associated with proposed projects.[92] But for emerging matters of concern and those that are considered indivisible, quantification may not be possible or desirable.[93]

Cumulative environmental problems inherently involve numerous and diverse contributors to harm, and multiple regulatory actors, so setting cumulative threshold conditions benefits from participatory, collective, and collaborative coordination.[94] Who is involved may affect both what and how threshold conditions are specified. Consensus may not always be possible, but, as discussed later in this book, rules for coordination can create conditions for fruitful interchange and dispute resolution in often politicized debates.[95] Under past Canadian EIA legislation, setting thresholds appears rarely to have been collaborative or reflected the values of affected communities,[96] but EIA policy now requires considering Indigenous community–defined thresholds in assessing whether impacts of a designated project are acceptable.[97]

4.3.4 *Adapting Conceptualizations*

Finally, and for completeness, the ways that rules conceptualize what matters for the purpose of regulating cumulative environmental harm may need to

90 Murray and others, "The Insignificance of Thresholds," 1063.

91 See generally Te Kīpa Kēpa Brian Morgan and others, "Towards Best-Practice Inclusion of Cultural Indicators in Decision Making by Indigenous Peoples" (2021) 17 *AlterNative: An International Journal of Indigenous Peoples* 202–214, especially table 1.

92 Eric Biber and Josh Eagle, "When Does Legal Flexibility Work in Environmental Law?" (2016) 42 *Ecology Law Quarterly* 787–840, 790.

93 Murray and others, "The Insignificance of Thresholds," 1063.

94 Ibid 1068–1069; Lawrence, "Impact Significance Determination," 762.

95 See Section 7.3.2 for more detailed discussion of coordination related to conceptualization.

96 Murray and others, "The Insignificance of Thresholds," 1065, 1068–1069 (based on ten EISs from 2010 to 2014 in British Columbia, Canada).

97 Government of Canada, "Policy Context: Assessment of Potential Impacts on the Rights of Indigenous Peoples."

change with time, especially in the context of climate change. This need for adaptation is not unique to regulating cumulative environmental problems; extensive scholarship deals with the issue,[98] which is covered only briefly here by reference to issues already raised.

In encouraging adaptive conceptualization, rule designers may consider rules that positively facilitate adaptation by including change processes and ways to frame rules to avoid creating barriers to important change. As with conceptualization generally, the less desirable alternative is to rely on courts to change how rules are interpreted to catch up (slowly) with changing times. At the same time, the cumulative context cautions against making a matter of concern too easy to reconceptualize, lest this invite frequent changes that would only serve to disguise shifting baselines.

All the dimensions of a conceptualization (Figure 4.1) might theoretically need to adapt over time. What matters and who matters might change in response to changed community values, changing populations or environments or simply better information about what already exists. The twentieth century saw water laws of many jurisdictions adapt to recognize water rights for environmental uses, as well as traditional consumptive uses like irrigation.[99] Climate change may make certain environments newly desirable as objects of legal protection as they become more ecologically valuable (e.g., aquatic refugia in environments predicted to become more arid) or more threatened (e.g., grasslands in regions predicted to become more valuable for farming and more subject to agricultural pressure). In relation to boundaries, rule designers should consider avoiding permanent static boundary delineations if a matter of concern might move, whether a species distribution or a natural feature like a river's course.[100] Rule designers should be alert to criticism that cumulative thresholds in biodiversity-related laws, such as species protection and protected area laws, focus excessively on historical preservation and restoration, reducing their power to "counter biodiversity

[98] E.g., Victor B. Flatt, "Adapting Laws for a Changing World: A Systemic Approach to Climate Change Adaptation" (2012) 64 *Florida Law Review* 269–293, 282–286; Craig Anthony Arnold, "Environmental Law, Episode IV: A New Hope: Can Environmental Law Adapt for Resilient Communities and Ecosystems" (2015) 21 *Journal of Environmental and Sustainability Law* 1–46; Robin Kundis Craig, "Stationarity Is Dead-Long Live Transformation: Five Principles for Climate Change Adaptation Law" (2010) 34 *Harvard Environmental Law Review* 9–73.

[99] Rebecca Nelson, "Allocations and Legal Trends in the 21st Century" in Josselin Rouillard and others (eds), *Water Resources Allocation and Agriculture: Transitioning from Open to Regulated Access* (IWA 2022) 25–36, 29–31.

[100] Matteo Nicolini, *Legal Geography: Comparative Law and the Production of Space* (Springer 2022) 69–72.

loss in a changing climate."[101] This may occur, for example, where climate change would make it impossible to return to historical conditions. An alternative approach would be to focus laws on sustaining biodiversity in the context of a changing climate, for example, delineating the boundaries of protected areas to allow species movement through "corridors" of connected areas.[102]

4.4 CONCLUSION

Rules for regulating cumulative harm depend on knowing: harm to what and whom? Rules can help to conceptualize what and who matter ("the matter of concern") for restoration or protection from cumulative harm as the basis for regulatory functions related to information, intervention, and coordination. These other functions, each the subject of a chapter that follows, interlink to the function of conceptualization to help contain cumulative change to the matter of concern to acceptable levels. In particular, since articulating what matters is fundamentally a question of values, it benefits from coordination – interactions among government and nongovernment bodies – that allows values to be contested in resolving a conceptualization.[103]

Matters of concern can vary widely, from a sacred place to the ambient concentration of a micropollutant. This chapter has suggested that rules for conceptualizing what matters should set out, or provide a process for setting out, the key dimensions of what and who matter, their spatial boundaries, and thresholds of acceptable conditions, each in a way that is clear and transparent as to underlying values. Clarity will usually require detail. That said, there is no universally "correct" way to specify elements, boundaries, and thresholds, or rules for doing so. This chapter has presented examples from around the world to illustrate some diverse possibilities. Rule designers should also be alert to the greater potential for ambiguity in matters of concern that are multidimensional and that link people and the environment (e.g., landscape, environmental justice, sustainability), which counsels even more attention to clarity. The case study on California groundwater (Chapter 8) analyzes these issues in more detail in a local context, with a focus on environmental justice as a challenging multidimensional matter of concern.

101 Alejandro E. Camacho, "De- and Re-Constructing Public Governance for Biodiversity Conservation" (2020) 73 *Vanderbilt Law Review* 1585–1642, 1611.

102 See generally Graeme L. Worboys, Wendy L. Francis and Michael Lockwood (eds), *Connectivity Conservation Management: A Global Guide* (Taylor & Francis 2010).

103 See Section 7.3.2.

5

Information

Laws for Producing, Sharing, Aggregating, and Analyzing Information

Links with Other Chapters

- Chapter 1 explains how examples used in this chapter were chosen.
- Chapter 2 synthesizes key challenges related to information and introduces the CIRCle Framework of regulatory functions for addressing cumulative environmental problems.
- Chapter 3 sketches the landscape of laws that may respond to cumulative environmental problems, including those that focus on information.
- Chapter 4 ("Conceptualization") discusses rules for articulating what and who we want to protect from cumulative impacts (the "matter of concern"), about which information is needed.
- Chapter 6 ("Regulatory intervention") discusses how rules can influence behavior to ensure that cumulative harm to the matter of concern stays within acceptable limits.
- Chapter 7 ("Coordination") covers coordinating between and among agencies and levels of government, nongovernment, and quasi-government entities, including to gather and share information.
- Each case study (Chapters 8–10) focuses on specific CIRCle Framework functions. Chapter 9 examines information in detail using the context of the health of the Great Barrier Reef, Australia. It focuses on strategic environmental assessment as a key tool for information, and explains its links to regulatory intervention.

5.1 INFORMATION AS A REGULATORY FUNCTION

Acting to restore or protect something that we care about (the "matter of concern") from unacceptable cumulative harm[1] depends on information. As described in Chapter 4, the matter of concern can take diverse forms, from a species, to an atmospheric concentration of greenhouse gases, or the ecological integrity of a river. I define information expansively as the outcome of analyzing data (quantitative or qualitative, including concepts and theories, produced in a Western scientific tradition or otherwise)[2] about the matter of concern, impacts to it, and rules and actors relevant to those impacts.[3] Information may be produced by governments, regulated entities, community members or other stakeholders, or it may be "co-produced" between multiple of these parties.[4]

Legal literature on the environment and information tends to focus on issues such as defining "best available" science or knowledge, or environmental impact assessment (EIA) laws, or, increasingly, the risks posed by technology related to environmental information.[5] I take a few steps back, and argue that laws for dealing with cumulative environmental problems should be information-making, not just information-taking. That is, rules can and should actively provide for producing, sharing, aggregating, and analyzing data to produce information that helps us understand the things we care about, and the cumulative threats that they face, so that rules for intervention can restore them or protect them from cumulative environmental harm.

As discussed earlier in this book,[6] effectively producing and using information to deal with cumulative environmental problems faces key challenges to which the design of information-related rules must respond. Impacts may accumulate in slow, complex, and sometimes nonlinear ways, which can

1 For the full definition of cumulative environmental problems used in this book, see Section 1.1.

2 Modified from National Research Council, *Using Science as Evidence in Public Policy* (National Academies Press 2012) 8.

3 Section 5.1.1 expands on this.

4 See further Section 5.2. For a general review of principles for knowledge coproduction and a review of the relevant literature, see Albert V. Norström and others, "Principles for Knowledge Co-Production in Sustainability Research" (2020) 3 *Nature Sustainability* 182–190.

5 E.g., see generally, Bruce Lindsay, Dru Marsh and Rebecca Nelson, "Conceptualising and Activating Knowledge in Environmental Protection Law" (2023) 46 *Melbourne University Law Review* 422–466; Jaap C. Hanekamp and Lucas Bergkamp, "The 'Best Available Science' and the Paris Agreement on Climate Change" (2016) 7 *European Journal of Risk Regulation* 42–48; Holly Doremus, "The Purposes, Effects, and Future of the Endangered Species Act's Best Available Science Mandate" (2004) 34 *Environmental Law* 397–450.

6 See Section 2.2.2.

make these problems hard to perceive. Generating information about the matter of concern and actions that cause relevant impacts can be costly and sharing it can encounter commercial, political, and community resistance. Contributors to the problem may be unwilling to share their data and information with government, and government may be unwilling to make information public or listen to community concerns about impacts and even ways of understanding what matters in the first place. This last point is especially important in the context of Indigenous and traditional knowledges, as this Chapter discusses further. Communities may raise concerns that collecting "big data" may harm privacy, or have potential discriminatory effects or a "chilling effect" on legitimate human activities.[7] These social issues related to information also deserve the attention of regulatory designers.[8] Finally, comparable data related to a matter of concern are often in short supply, making it difficult to build a picture of cumulative environmental change, and information can be subject to unavoidable uncertainty because of multiple, interacting, and complex cause-and-effect relationships.

Addressing these challenges is fundamentally about power, rather than just an instrumental technical issue about measuring things to understand them better. Rules for information about a cumulative environmental problem can address the power asymmetries that exist among the public, government, contributors to a problem, and those affected by it.[9] Gathering, aggregating, and making public the information about past, present, and future conditions of a matter of concern and impacts on it allow the public and decision-makers to see how the effects of multiple activities can aggregate to harm the environment. This is critical for environmental democracy, environmental justice, and the rule of law.[10] Information facilitates meaningful civic engagement and enables the public and affected communities to demand accountability and action from governments and

7 Nathan Young and others, "Ethical Ecosurveillance: Mitigating the Potential Impacts on Humans of Widespread Environmental Monitoring" (2022) 4 *People and Nature* 830–840, 833–835.

8 This chapter touches on some of these social matters, leaving others for attention in Chapter 7 (Coordination), and noting existing research on this topic, e.g. ibid.

9 Federica Fusi, Fengxiu Zhang and Jiaqi Liang, "Unveiling Environmental Justice through Open Government Data: Work in Progress for Most US States" (2023) 101 *Public Administration* 1088–1114, 1091.

10 See, e.g., Jesse Worker and Lalanath de Silva, *The Environmental Democracy Index: Technical Note* (World Resources Institute 2015); Swatanter Kumar and others, *Environmental Rule of Law: First Global Report* (United Nations Environment Programme 2019) 21, 63–70; Fusi, Zhang and Liang, "Unveiling Environmental Justice," 1092–1093.

contributors to the problem; information without an advocate may have little impact on intervention.[11]

Informed by these challenges, information is one of four central functions that this book argues that regulation must deliver to respond to cumulative environmental problems. These four functions, of conceptualization, information, regulatory intervention, and coordination, form the "CIRCle Framework" of regulatory functions advanced by this book.

This chapter begins by exploring the broad types of information needed to respond to cumulative environmental problems and regulatory methods of making links with conceptualization, regulatory intervention, and coordination. Section 5.2 then discusses a key factor likely to vary between cumulative environmental problems: the key actors involved in information. Section 5.3 considers types and examples of legal mechanisms to help address the key challenges associated with information outlined in Chapter 2: obtaining comprehensive, high-quality, and shareable data and analysis; allocating and reducing the associated costs; and sharing and accessing data and information. Chapter 7 (Coordination) then focuses on information as an important issue in coordination among governments and stakeholders.

5.1.1 *What Information Helps Address Cumulative Environmental Problems?*

We turn first to exploring the information required to deal with a cumulative environmental problem, summarized in Figure 5.1. Addressing cumulative environmental problems first requires understanding the matter of concern subject to cumulative change (see Chapter 4 "Conceptualization"). This means having information to establish cumulative threshold conditions – that is, the limits of acceptable conditions – against which a set of current or expected conditions or impacts can be compared to determine whether intervention is required. Monitoring ongoing environmental conditions is needed to reveal trends and unexpected changes in the condition of the matter of concern.

Dealing with cumulative environmental problems also requires attention to the other side of the picture: understanding impacts to the matter of concern caused by (1) actions that are regulated and lawfully undertaken, (2) actions

[11] For research that suggests this in the context of the Chapter 8 case study context of California groundwater, see Debra Perrone and others, "Stakeholder Integration Predicts Better Outcomes from Groundwater Sustainability Policy" (2023) 14:3793 *Nature Communications* 1–14, 9–10.

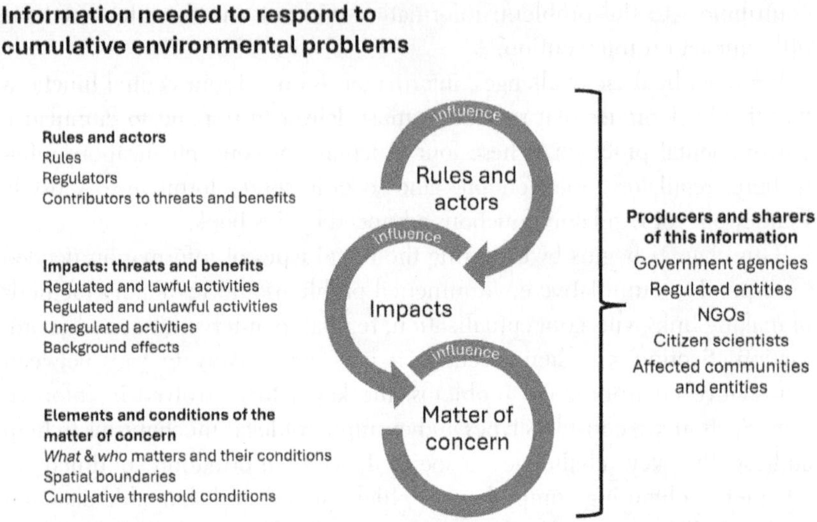

FIGURE 5.1 Information needed to analyze and respond to cumulative environmental problems using formal rules

that are regulated but carried out in a way that exceeds their authorization (e.g., emitting more pollution than an authorization permits) or that are carried out without required authorization (for brevity, "unlawful actions"), (3) actions that are not subject to regulation ("unregulated actions"), as well as (4) "background" effects that are difficult to attribute to an individual actor or action, but affect a matter of concern, for example, dust storms or wildfire affecting air quality, or invasive species affecting threatened species.[12] Sources of impact may be outside the spatial boundaries of the matter of concern – something that laws are not always good at recognizing.[13]

Addressing cumulative environmental problems may also involve predicting the likely cumulative impacts of proposed actions. This is especially important for cases in which, by the time significant change is detected, it can be difficult or impossible to reverse the environmental damage. Groundwater pollution, for example, may be practically impossible to remediate either due to cost or limitations of current technology.[14] EIA laws are an important, though not the only, area of law that provides for this type of predictive

[12] Commissioner for Environmental Sustainability Victoria, *Victorian State of the Environment 2023 Report: Summary Report* (2023) 46–47, 49–50.

[13] Rebecca Nelson, "Regulating Hidden Risks to Conservation Lands in Resource Rich Areas" (2021) 40 *University of Queensland Law Journal* 491–530, 500, 522–525.

[14] Nicholas P. Cheremisinoff, *Groundwater Remediation: A Practical Guide for Environmental Engineers and Scientists* (Scrivener 2017) 14.

analysis. Predictions of cumulative change at the regional scale, involving many actors, are also used in addressing cumulative environmental problems, for example, through strategic and regional environmental assessments and natural resources planning.[15] The resulting information can then be used to inform regulatory processes for individual future actions in these regions.

The outcome of understanding impacts – whether direct or indirect, anthropogenic or not, current or planned – is the ability to consider existing and potential interventions that seek to modify impacts or take other action to address unacceptable harm. This also requires information about the landscape of existing regulators and rules for regulatory interventions that "highlights their collective capacity to serve as a barrier to pressures" (i.e., their effectiveness).[16] Different types of intervention may produce different information needs, and there is theoretically a higher need for information about effectiveness for regulatory interventions that have relatively low outcome reliability.[17] For example, allowing an impact to go ahead with compensatory (offset) measures requires special attention to monitoring to ensure that those measures are effective and maintained over the long term.[18]

There will likely always be more data to gather, analyze, and share to better understand a problem. The important thing is not that the public or decision-makers know everything there is to know about the problem, but that the rules provide for having enough usable information to support the other interlinked functions of the CIRCle Framework. We turn now to distilling these connections.

5.1.2 *Information as an Integrated Regulatory Function in the CIRCle Framework*

Though legal scholars focus relatively rarely on data collection and analysis as the subject of rules,[19] many strands of regulatory theory assume that information has an important place in implementing regulatory

[15] See the case studies for examples: Chapter 8 in relation to groundwater planning and Chapter 9 in relation to strategic assessment. Chapter 3 describes the landscape of areas of law relevant to cumulative impacts.

[16] Effah Kwabena Antwi and others, "Risk Assessment Framework for Cumulative Effects (RAFCE)" (2022) 10 *Frontiers in Environmental Science* 1–23, 20.

[17] See Table 6.1.

[18] European Commission and Directorate-General for Environment, *Managing Natura 2000 Sites – The Provisions of Article 6 of the "Habitats" Directive 92/43/EEC* (Publications Office of the European Union 2019) 66.

[19] A notable exception is Eric Biber, "The Problem of Environmental Monitoring" (2011) 83 *University of Colorado Law Review* 1–82.

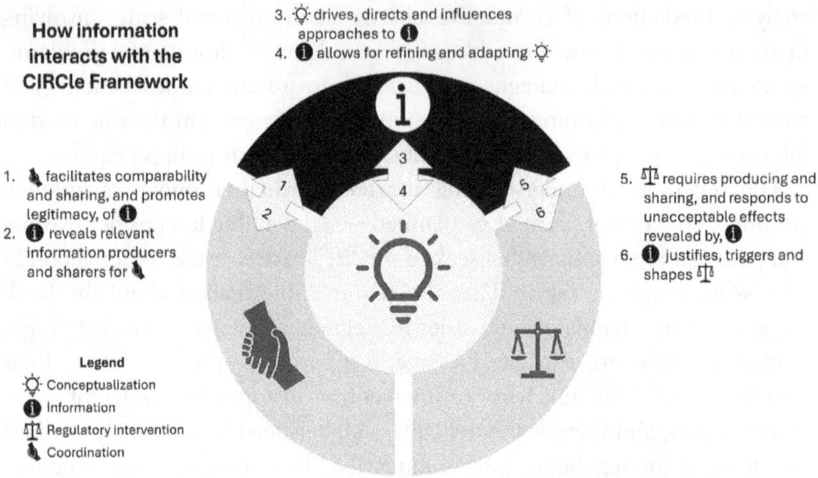

FIGURE 5.2 Integration of legal mechanisms for information with other CIRCle Framework functions, each necessary for regulating cumulative environmental problems

interventions.[20] Coglianese's "regulatory excellence" framework, for example, highlights the importance of regulators using trustworthy data supported by peer review processes and making the information that they use accessible to regulated entities and the public.[21] Risk-based regulation requires regulators to "continually gather and assimilate information to inform better strategy and tactics, and to inform the allocation of finite resources."[22] The use of technology to produce information is a prominent emerging theme more generally in regulatory theory.[23]

As shown in Figure 5.2 (building on Figure 2.1, which depicts basic links between regulatory functions), information may both influence and be influenced by regulatory functions related to conceptualization, intervention, and coordination – the other functions of the CIRCle Framework for rules to respond to cumulative environmental problems. First, the conceptualization of a cumulative environmental problem points to the information that must be gathered

[20] Information can also be used intentionally to change behavior as a regulatory "sermon," a form of intervention: see Section 6.3.

[21] Cary Coglianese, *Listening, Learning, Leading: A Framework for Regulatory Excellence* (University of Pennsylvania Law School 2015) xi, xii.

[22] Christopher Taylor and others, "Selecting Policy Instruments for Better Environmental Regulation: A Critique and Future Research Agenda" (2012) 22 *Environmental Policy and Governance* 268–292, 287.

[23] Neil Gunningham and Cameron Holley, "Next-Generation Environmental Regulation: Law, Regulation, and Governance" (2016) 12 *Annual Review of Law and Social Science* 273–293, 281–283.

about the characteristics of a matter of concern, its condition, and the actions and actors that impact it. Before generating information, it is important to have a clear initial idea of what the matter of concern is (Chapter 4 "Conceptualization"), recognizing that this conceptualization may change.[24] Information can also lead to refining and adapting how a matter of concern is conceptualized because processes for generating information may shift participants' values. Information collection and analyses undertaken in the context of cumulative environmental problems heighten this transformational potential because it engages values-rich questions about who is affected by environmental change in space and time, and what level of harm or change a society will accept.[25]

Secondly, information about cumulative environmental change may affect whether and how existing regulatory interventions address unacceptable change. Of course, decision-makers might ignore information about cumulative change in making decisions about interventions, but legal mechanisms can help counter this. Most national EIA laws around the world expressly require decision-makers to consider cumulative impacts.[26] This can theoretically affect the kind of assessment or the kind of mitigation measures required for a project, and whether the project will go ahead.[27] Outside the impact assessment context, interventions can draw on information in a range of context-specific ways, from extending the reach of endangered species laws if an endangered species is found in a new location to modifying a limit on groundwater withdrawals in response to new information about recharge rates. Information about environmental challenges can also influence how many people take up voluntary interventions ("regulatory carrots"), such as financial incentives for private land conservation, even where information is not designed for these persuasive purposes.[28]

Information about trends in environmental conditions might also trigger a change to interventions. Just as information about the number of babies born each year informs planning for school places to respond to anticipated demand[29], information about trends in cumulative environmental change

[24] As described in Chapter 7, forming this conceptualization involves resolving conflicting values associated with environmental disputes.

[25] Rebecca Nelson and L. M. Shirley, "The Latent Potential of Cumulative Effects Concepts in National and International Environmental Impact Assessment Regimes" (2023) 12 *Transnational Environmental Law* 150–174, 157–159.

[26] Ibid 160.

[27] See Section 3.2.2.

[28] Kaylan M. Kemink and others, "Exploring Motives for Participation in a Perpetual Easement Program: Going Beyond Financial Incentives" (2023) 284:110193 *Biological Conservation* 1–12, 8.

[29] B. Guy Peters, "Information and Governing: Cybernetic Models of Governance" in David Levi-Faur (ed), *The Oxford Handbook of Governance* (OUP 2012) 113–128, 120.

can be used to plan future regulatory change. This link might arise directly, because legal provisions expressly provide for it. Alternatively, the link might arise indirectly, when civil society, the media,[30] or independent scrutiny bodies (e.g., auditors-general, comptrollers, ombudsmen, and parliamentary or congressional committees) advocate for an intervention based on information about cumulative environmental change. Conversely, regulatory interventions themselves often require participants to collect and share information, for example, about compliance with a regulatory mandate or the performance of obligations required to obtain an incentive.

Finally, information about the matter of concern and about the actions that affect it points to the agencies, levels of government, and stakeholders that must coordinate to respond to a cumulative environmental problem because they regulate, carry out, or otherwise interact with those actions. Coordination processes themselves facilitate the sharing of data and information between stakeholders, agencies, and levels of government to facilitate standards for data comparability and data aggregation that will shed light on cumulative environmental problems. Coordination processes in relation to information can also increase the legitimacy of the resulting information and make it more likely that decision-makers will use it (both issues that are discussed in Chapter 7 "Coordination"). Coordinating about information can also create relationships between participants that are the basis for coordination more broadly.[31]

5.2 ACTORS AND INFORMATION FOR ADDRESSING CUMULATIVE ENVIRONMENTAL PROBLEMS

The question of who is involved in relation to information is just as important as what information is needed. As argued earlier, public access to information about cumulative environmental problems is necessary for democracy and the rule of law.[32] Accordingly, the public at large generally should be involved in being able to receive information. The question of who produces, shares, aggregates, and analyzes relevant data and information is more involved.

[30] E.g., media reporting on ineffective biodiversity offsets (a regulatory strategy discussed in Section 6.2.1), facilitated by public information about offsets, triggering formal inquiries and policy change: Caitlin Cassidy and Marni Cordell, "The Investigation that Blew the Lid off Sydney's Environmental Offsets" (*The Guardian* (Australia), May 29, 2023) www.theguardian.com/media/2023/may/29/the-investigation-that-blew-the-lid-off-sydneys-environmental-offsets.

[31] Dennis de Kool, "The Perceived Impacts of Monitoring Activities on Intergovernmental Relationships: Some Lessons from the Ecological Monitoring Network and Water in Focus" (2015) 187:689 *Environmental Monitoring and Assessment* 1–11; Andrea J. Reid and others, "'Two-Eyed Seeing': An Indigenous Framework to Transform Fisheries Research and Management" (2021) 22 *Fish and Fisheries* 243–261.

[32] See n 9.

While relevant actors will vary for different cumulative environmental problems, we can make some general observations.

Governments, regulated entities, nongovernment organizations, and individuals may all contribute to data collection and analysis in ways that are relevant to regulating cumulative environmental problems. Governments can, and do, collect data about background effects and the changing conditions of matters of concern that are the focus of regulation, including using participatory approaches that involve stakeholders to varying degrees.[33] Regulated entities are often required,[34] and are best placed, to collect data about the impacts of their operations, since they have access to relevant sites and management details. Since the impacts of unlawful actions will not usually be self-reported, governments must usually collect these data, sometimes supplemented by citizen scientists.

Nongovernment citizen science or "crowdsourcing" initiatives may collect relevant data, for example, using digital platforms that record individuals' observations, from recording birds or plants to air quality recordings.[35] Some citizen science initiatives deal with unlawful actions, such as illegal gold mining and logging, potentially contributing to enforcement actions,[36] and unregulated but potentially harmful actions, such as the construction of many small dams that reduce streamflow in a watershed.[37] Citizen science initiatives may also deal with background effects that cannot be attributed to an individual actor or activity and may be either unlawful or unregulated, like the spread of invasive alien species,[38] or light pollution at night.[39]

For some matters of concern, data and information collected voluntarily by nongovernment organizations and individuals is indispensable to addressing

[33] See generally, Aparna Bamzai-Dodson and others, "Engaging with Stakeholders to Produce Actionable Science: A Framework and Guidance" (2021) 13(4) *Weather, Climate, and Society* 1027–1041.

[34] E.g., Table 5.1, row 2.

[35] E.g., The Cornell Lab of Ornithology, eBird, https://ebird.org/home; iNaturalist, www.inaturalist.org; see generally, Sachit Mahajan and others, "Translating Citizen-Generated Air Quality Data into Evidence for Shaping Policy" (2022) 9:122 *Humanities and Social Sciences Communications* 1–18.

[36] E.g., World Resources Institute, Global Forest Watch, www.globalforestwatch.org; see generally, Anna Berti Suman, *Civic Monitoring for Environmental Law Enforcement* (Edward Elgar 2024).

[37] Rachel Clayton, "Suspected Unlicensed Dams Multiplying across Stressed River System Reveal Holes in Victoria's Water Compliance," *ABC News* (June 2, 2023) www.abc.net.au/news/2023-06-02/unlicensed-dams-devastating-the-moorabool/102411916.

[38] Petr Pyšek and others, "Scientists' Warning on Invasive Alien Species" (2020) 95 *Biological Reviews* 1511–1534, 1522–1524.

[39] E.g., NoirLab, *Globe at Night*, https://globeatnight.org.

cumulative environmental harm, for example, when a community experiences cumulative impacts of concern, or holds special knowledge that is central to understanding impacts, as with cultural heritage. Equally, data from citizen scientists can be important where government capacity, resources, or motivation fall short. From a social perspective, using nongovernment-sourced data – and including stakeholders and communities in processes relating to the analysis and use of government data – can help improve the legitimacy and credibility of the resulting information[40] and the regulatory interventions that it may trigger. This is the case for environmental problems in general. However, because cumulative environmental problems implicate so many actions – including those that are individually minor and not regulated, but may cause cumulatively significant harm – there is an especially pronounced need for community involvement and acceptance to counter the increased potential for political and public pushback to producing information.

These issues of the relevant actors, information sources, and types all arise in the crosscutting design features discussed next.

5.3 CROSSCUTTING DESIGN FEATURES

Ideally, data and information about matters of concern, changes in their condition, and cumulative pressures would be comprehensive, standardized, or otherwise made comparable where possible. They would widely be considered technically credible and socially legitimate. They would be either centralized or otherwise aggregated and easily available and understandable to the public and any agency that needed to use this information to inform its decision-making. These are the conditions that rules for information to help address cumulative environmental problems should be designed to create, while also addressing the social, political, and economic disincentives to achieving them.[41] This section deals with design features to address three key areas of regulatory challenge that cut across information contexts: obtaining comprehensive, high-quality data and analysis; allocating and reducing the associated costs; and sharing and accessing data and analysis.

Information-related provisions appear frequently in a wide range of legal situations dealing with cumulative environmental problems, from natural

[40] Ben Orlove and others, "Climate Decision-Making" (2020) 45 *Annual Review of Environment and Resources* 271–303, 17; see generally, Bamzai-Dodson and others, "Engaging with Stakeholders."

[41] See Section 2.2.2 for a discussion that leads to these design features.

resources allocation to pollution controls. Other relevant legal contexts – for example, human rights related to the environment – seem rarely to deal with information, though information is crucial to their operationalization.[42] The illustrative examples of regulatory solutions presented here are drawn from many areas of law, and a wide range of jurisdictions, recognizing that jurisdictions vary significantly in their appetite for regulatory detail in prescribed processes and public involvement.[43]

5.3.1 *Obtaining Comprehensive, High-Quality Data and Analysis*

Data about a cumulative environmental problem are comprehensive if they cover all the information needs relating to the matter of concern to understand and respond to cumulative threats.[44] In practice, though, regulations tend to overlook some important types of data. For example, rules more rarely provide for collecting data about actions that are not regulated than they do for regulated actions, even if both types of activities have the potential to cause significant cumulative harm. Table 5.1 provides examples of regulations that expressly address each of these key ongoing information needs. Additional research or information of a non-ongoing nature may also be needed to support conceptualization, for example, to establish "safe" levels of a pollutant, and intervention, for example, to understand the motivations and capacities to change behavior of contributors to cumulative impacts.[45]

Information that is high-quality for the purposes of cumulative environmental problems are produced using analytical methods that are transparently reported, appropriate to the subject matter, and robust (about which it is difficult to generalize, but which policy guidelines may flesh out, as discussed later). It may be unrealistic to avoid significant uncertainty about predicted future conditions of a matter of concern due to nonlinear and indirect effects, and analysis may involve potentially significant simplifications and assumptions.[46] Accordingly, regulations should provide mechanisms to ensure clarity and transparency about these matters, in particular.[47] Given its complexity,

[42] Emily Barritt, "The Aarhus Convention and the Latent Right to a Healthy Environment" (2024) 36 *Journal of Environmental Law* 67–84, 68, 81.

[43] Sheila Jasanoff, "Cultural Aspects of Risk Assessment in Britain and the United States" in Branden B. Johnson and Vincent T. Covello (eds), *The Social and Cultural Construction of Risk: Essays on Risk Selection and Perception*, vol. 3 (Springer 1987) 359–397, 361.

[44] See Section 5.1.1.

[45] See Section 6.3.

[46] See Section 2.2.2.3.

[47] The issue of how to ensure that uncertainty does not stand in the way of decision-making is dealt with in Chapter 6 on Intervention.

TABLE 5.1 *Mechanisms to fulfill information needs for addressing cumulative environmental problems*

Legal mechanism	Illustrative examples
Requirement to regularly collect data about the conditions of a matter of concern and report on aggregate effects over time	Chapter 9 of this book describes the integrated information system that informs interventions to protect the Great Barrier Reef, Australia. It includes a statutory obligation to produce a five-yearly, peer-reviewed "Outlook report" on the health of the Reef.[a]
Requirement to collect and report data about actions that are regulated and lawfully undertaken	Entities subject to hazardous waste reduction requirements in Indonesia must report periodically on how they implement this duty.[b]
Requirement to collect and analyze data about actions that are regulated by law but carried out in a way that exceeds their authorization (e.g., emitting more pollution than an authorization permits), or that are carried out without any authorization (for brevity, "unlawful actions")	Kenya's statutory National Environment Management Authority has duties to monitor compliance with a wide range of laws, including to monitor "activities that are likely to have a significant effect on the environment" (which is expressed notably broadly), compliance with pollution standards, resource use patterns, climate change duties, and carbon market compliance.[c] New York City's Citizens Air Complaint Program uses payment to incentivize third parties to report unlawfully idling vehicles.[d]
Requirement to collect data about activities that are not (or not yet) subject to regulation ("unregulated actions")	In Australia's Murray-Darling Basin, state governments write statutory plans that must provide for monitoring and assessing the potential of unregulated water uses (such as tree plantations and water withdrawals for domestic purposes) to have cumulatively significant impacts on the availability of water in rivers and aquifers.[e] A Seychelles multistage plan to recover populations of shark pursuant to its international obligations begins with identifying and recording (at that stage, unregulated) artisanal shark fishers, paving the way for phased interventions.[f]
Requirement to collect data about "background" effects that are difficult to attribute to an individual actor or activity	The recovery plan for the endangered California Condor, mandated under the US Endangered Species Act, plans information collection and associated measures in relation to damaging background effects such as habitat loss, poisoning by lead shot, collisions with structures, and natural predators.[g]

Legal mechanism	Illustrative examples
Requirement to collect data about indirect drivers of cumulative change, which may involve regulated, regulated but unauthorized, or unregulated actions	Italy's environmental accounting law, which requires annual natural capital accounts, is considered "advanced practice" in Europe.[h] Reports estimate subsidies that harm biodiversity[i] and must include proposals to phase out environmentally harmful subsidies.[j]

[a] Great Barrier Reef Marine Park Act 1975 (Australia) s 64.
[b] Peraturan Pemerintah Republik Indonesia nomor 22 tahun 2021 tentang Penyelenggaraan Perlindungan Dan Pengelolaan Lingkungan Hidup [Government Regulation no. 22 of 2021 on Environmental Protection, Organization and Management] (Indonesia) art. 284.
[c] Environmental Management and Co-ordination Act 1999, as amended (Cap. 387) (Kenya) ss 68 (1), 117(2); Climate Change Act 2016, as amended (Cap. 387A) (Kenya) ss 16–17; Climate Change (Carbon Markets) Regulations 2024 (Kenya); National Environment Management Authority (Kenya), "Development of the National Carbon Market Registry" (n.d.) www.nema.go.ke/index.php?option=com_content&view=article&id=412:development-of-the-national-carbon-market-registry&catid=10:news-and-events&Itemid=572#, last accessed March 18, 2025, archived at https://perma.cc/QP8C-3BWP.
[d] New York City Administrative Code § 24-163; NYC Environmental Protection, "Transportation Emissions: Citizens Air Complaint Program" (n.d.) www.nyc.gov/site/dep/environment/idling-citizens-air-complaint-program.page, last accessed March 18, 2025, archived at https://perma.cc/5KE4-YYRS.
[e] Basin Plan 2012 (Australia) ss 10.23–10.25; Rebecca Nelson, "Challenges to Improved Integrated Management of the Murray-Darling" in Barry Hart and others (eds), *Murray-Darling Basin, Australia: Its Future Management* (Elsevier 2021) 339–361, 349–350.
[f] Seychelles Fishing Authority, *National Plan of Action for the Conservation and Management of Sharks 2016–2020* (2016) 68, https://mofbe.gov.sc/wp-content/uploads/2021/09/National-Plan-of-Action-for-the-Conservation-and-Management-of-Sharks-2016-2020-3.pdf, archived at https://perma.cc/7XW9-VPLA; identified international obligations include those under the United Nations Convention on the Law of the Sea, December 10, 1982, Montego Bay, in force November 16, 1994, 1833 U.N.T.S. 396, among other laws: ibid 93.
[g] 16 U.S.C. §1533(f), Lloyd F. Kiff, Robert I. Mesta and Michael P. Wallace, *Recovery Plan for the California Condor* (3rd ed., 1996, US Fish and Wildlife Service) 30–33; see also US Fish and Wildlife Service, "California Condor Recovery Program" (n.d.) www.fws.gov/program/california-condor-recovery, last accessed March 18, 2025, archived at https://perma.cc/7HNM-HQ86.
[h] Directorate-General for Environment (European Commission), *Environmental Implementation Review 2022: Country Report – Italy (SWD/2022/275 Final)* (European Commission 2022) 3; Legge 28 dicembre 2015, n. 221 Disposizioni in materia ambientale per promuovere misure di green economy e per il contenimento dell'uso eccessivo di risorse naturali [Law on environmental provisions to promote green economy measures and to contain the excessive use of natural resources] (Italy) ("Italian Green Economy Law"), art. 67; Comitato per il Capitale Naturale, *Quinto Rapporto sullo Stato del Capitale Naturale in Italia* [Fifth Report on the State of Natural Capital in Italy] (Government of Italy 2022) www.mase.gov.it/sites/default/files/archivio/allegati/CapitaleNaturale/V_Rapporto_CN.pdf, archived at https://perma.cc/V59Q-ZC89.
[i] E.g., Comitato per il Capitale Naturale, *Quinto Rapporto*, 172–176; Italian Green Economy Law), arts. 67 (Natural Capital Committee), 68 (catalog of subsidies).
[j] Italian Green Economy Law, art. 68(2).

good cumulative impact analysis requires sufficient regulatory timelines to undertake modeling and coordination between multiple agencies to ensure access to expertise and robust work.[48] In addition to models and quantitative data, high-quality data may also include data produced outside Western scientific disciplines. This includes First Nations' knowledges, subject to appropriate protocols,[49] and qualitative information, a form that some cumulative impact analyses adopt.[50]

Regulatory approaches to ensuring high-quality data and analysis and addressing key risks tend to fall into two categories: those that use broadly worded *principles* to describe the kind of data and analysis that decision-makers must use (e.g., "best available science" and related terms) and those that prescribe *processes* to ensure certain aspects of quality or to head off risks. Principles for data analysis may expressly or implicitly require cumulative impact assessment (see Table 5.2).

Using principles ensures flexibility, the ability to evolve over time without amendment, and applicability to a diverse set of situations. A disadvantage of principles is that their precise meaning can be disputed.[51] The risk of such disputes may be heightened where the costs of comprehensive data collection or cumulative effects analysis would be significant. This suggests the value of combining principles and either more detailed guidance about what constitutes high-quality information or the protocols, processes, and institutions that produce it. Important types of processes and institutions that appear in rules include: using independent or nongovernment bodies and observers to avoid political pressure and executive capture; peer review, standards, and accreditation; requirements for transparency about uncertainty and assumptions; and regulatory timelines that are not so short that they prevent good analysis (see Table 5.2). Embedding these requirements in rules can help ensure stability in the face of cost or other pressures.

5.3.2 *Allocating and Reducing Costs Associated with Information*

Large-scale and with diverse contributors to change, cumulative environmental problems are data hungry, which heightens the costs of collecting data and

48 Emma E. Hodgson, Benjamin S. Halpern and Timothy E. Essington, "Moving Beyond Silos in Cumulative Effects Assessment" (2019) 7:211 *Frontiers in Ecology and Evolution* 1–8, 3 (discussing the need for agency-to-agency links).

49 Erin O'Donnell and Rebecca Nelson, "Shield Science for Robust Decisions" (2020) 3 *Nature Sustainability* 675–676, 676.

50 Emma E. Hodgson and Benjamin S. Halpern, "Investigating Cumulative Effects across Ecological Scales" (2018) 33 *Conservation Biology* 22–32, 27–28.

51 See, e.g., Doremus, "Purposes, Effects, and Future," 424–426 (discussing case law on the meaning of best available science).

TABLE 5.2 *Mechanisms to promote high-quality data and information for addressing cumulative environmental problems*

Legal mechanisms	Illustrative examples
Protocols for interface between Western and other knowledge systems in understanding a matter of concern	To avoid inappropriately integrating Indigenous knowledges into Western science as a "resource," some frameworks and protocols for knowledge generation, like Two-Eyed Seeing, Etuaptmumk (Miâ•Žkmaw; Eastern Canada), expressly seek to "remedy, rather than reinforce, existing power relations; respect differences, instead of suppress them; and uphold, as opposed to diminish, their unique strengths."[a]
Principle-based standards, like "best available science"	The US Endangered Species Act requires agencies to use "best available science" when determining whether a species is endangered[b] (i.e., determining the conditions of the matter of concern) and when formulating a "biological opinion,"[c] which must include cumulative effects.[d] This standard encompasses both scientific and commercial data.[e]
A "state of knowledge" standard for data collection and analysis	The "state of knowledge" that informs the standard of the environmental protection duty that applies to all persons in Victoria, Australia, includes information from business, government agencies, and independent and international organizations, including guidelines and standards.[f]
Regulatory independent scientific processes that ensure the integrity of data and analysis used by regulators[g]	Australian federal environmental law establishes an independent groundwater expert committee to review impact assessments, including cumulative impact assessments, of proposed coal mines and coal seam gas developments on water resources, and to advise on related bioregional assessments.[h] The committee was established specifically to enhance transparency and public confidence.[i]
Detailed policy guidance for undertaking rigorous cumulative impacts analysis	The US, Canada, and South Africa, among other jurisdictions, provide detailed general policy guidance for undertaking cumulative impacts analysis in general[j] and in specific contexts, e.g., transportation, chemical exposure.[k] Some industry sectors produce their own guidance on cumulative impact assessment.[l]

(*continued*)

TABLE 5.2 (*continued*)

Legal mechanisms	Illustrative examples
Independent observers of environmentally relevant activities	Papua New Guinea's fisheries legislation provides for independent at-sea observers to collect data for "scientific, management and compliance purposes" in relation to matters including fish taken, fishing methods, and the effects of fishing on the environment. Vessel operators and crew have an obligation to assist observers.[m]
Monitoring undertaken by communities potentially affected by cumulative impacts	Community conservancies, established under Namibia's nature conservation law, combine community development and wildlife protection.[n] A key feature of these arrangements is the community-led "Event Book System," under which conservancies design and undertake wildlife monitoring, trained by nongovernment organizations (NGOs), producing long-term data that are aggregated by government to guide interventions and compliance monitoring.[o] The Event Book System now also includes local-level climate change–related monitoring.[p]

[a] See generally Reid and others, "Two-Eyed Seeing," especially 246, 247.
[b] 16 U.S.C. § 1533(b)(1)(A).
[c] 50 C.F.R. § 402.14(d).
[d] 50 C.F.R. § 402.14(g)(3), (4).
[e] *San Luis & Delta-Mendota Water Authority v. Locke*, 776 F.3d 971, at 995 (9th Cir. 2014).
[f] Environment Protection Act 2017 (Victoria) ss 6(2), 25; Environment Protection Authority (Victoria, Australia), *Reasonably Practicable*, Publication 1856 (September 2020) 10, www.epa.vic.gov.au/-/media/epa/files/publications/1856-english.pdf, archived at https://perma.cc/Z6WK-PR7G. For examples of industry guidelines in relation to cumulative effects assessments, see note 70. See also generally Lindsay, Marsh and Nelson, "Conceptualising and Activating Knowledge in Environmental Protection Law."
[g] Coglianese, *Listening, Learning, Leading*, xi.
[h] Environment Protection and Biodiversity Conservation Act 1999 (Australia) ss 131AB, 505C, 505D.
[i] Australian Government, "About the Independent Expert Scientific Committee on Unconventional Gas Development and Large Coal Mining Development (IESC)" (n.d.) www.iesc.gov.au/about-us, last accessed March 18, 2025, archived at https://perma.cc/C7RU-C7SR.
[j] Council on Environmental Quality (US), *Considering Cumulative Effects under the National Environmental Policy Act* (1997) https://ceq.doe.gov/publications/cumulative_effects.html, archived at https://perma.cc/2HX5-C8SA; Impact Assessment Agency of Canada, *Policy Framework for Assessing Cumulative Effects under the Impact Assessment Act* (May 2023) www.canada.ca/en/impact-assessment-agency/services/policy-guidance/practitioners-guide-impact-assessment-act/policy-framework-assessing-cumulative-effects-under-impact-assessment-act.html, archived at https://perma.cc/EUU2-44PM; Department of Environmental Affairs and Tourism (South Africa), *Cumulative Effects Assessment, Integrated Environmental Management Information Series* 7 (2004) www.dffe.gov.za/sites/default/files/docs/series7_cumulative_effects_assessment.pdf, archived at https://perma.cc/32FV-262W.
[k] Transportation Projects: California Department of Transportation, *Guidance for Preparers of Cumulative Impact Analysis – Approach and Guidance* (2005) https://dot.ca.gov/-/media/dot-

media/programs/environmental-analysis/documents/ser/approach-and-guidance-a11y.pdf, archived at https://perma.cc/6YSU-F74C; US EPA, *Framework for Cumulative Risk Assessment* (2003) www.epa.gov/sites/default/files/2014-11/documents/frmwrk_cum_risk_assmnt.pdf, last accessed March 18, 2025, archived at https://perma.cc/V3F7-LTPK.
[l] RenewableUK, *Cumulative Impact Assessment Guidelines: Guiding Principles for Cumulative Impacts Assessment in Offshore Wind Farms* (2013) https://tethys.pnnl.gov/sites/default/files/publications/Cumulative-Impact-Assessment-Guidelines.pdf; American Association of Highway and Public Transportation Officials (AASHTO), *Practitioner's Handbook: Assessing Indirect Impacts and Cumulative Impacts under NEPA* (2016) https://wsdot.wa.gov/sites/default/files/2021-10/ENV-NSEPA_AASHTOCummHndbk.pdf, archived at https://perma.cc/QLF7-WLGH; Minerals Council of Australia, Cumulative Environmental Impact Assessment Industry Guide: Adaptive Strategies (July 2015) https://minerals.org.au/wp-content/uploads/2023/01/Cumulative_Environmental_Impact_Assessment_Industry_Guide_FINAL_0.pdf.
[m] Fisheries Management Act 1998 (Papua New Guinea) ss 50–55. A similar approach is used in Canada: Fishery (General) Regulations, SOR/93-53 (Canada) ss 39–40, 46–48.
[n] Nature Conservation Amendment Act 1996, No. 5 of 1996 (Namibia) s 3.
[o] Michael Wenborn and others, "Lessons on the Community Conservancy Model for Wildlife Protection in Namibia" (2022) 31 *The Journal of Environment & Development* 375–394, 384–389; Greg Stuart-Hill and others, "The Event Book System: A Community-Based Natural Resource Monitoring System from Namibia" (2005) 14 *Biodiversity and Conservation* 2611–2631, 2613.
[p] See generally, John Kazgeba Elijah Mfune and Kopang Bonadei Thekwane, "Empower to Adapt: Creating Climate Change Resilient Livelihoods through Community-Based Natural Resources Management (CBNRM) in Namibia: Final Independent Evaluation Report" (Green Climate Fund, 2023) www.greenclimate.fund/sites/default/files/document/fp024-final-independent-evaluation-report.pdf.

undertaking analysis,[52] and makes cost cutting and corner cutting significant risks. This puts issues of cost in focus: how to allocate costs, and how to contain costs in an absolute sense in a way that avoids the temptation to overlook impacts that may be individually minor but cumulatively significant. That, in turn, raises thorny issues associated with using technology.

A first element of the cost question is determining how to allocate the costs associated with data collection and analysis among contributors to a cumulative environmental problem and the state. As with standards for information quality, some jurisdictions use broad principles. Some focus on allocating costs to the contributors to a problem, like the "polluter pays" principle; others allocate costs to those who benefit from a resource or project, like the "beneficiary pays" principle; still others support a combined approach through principles like "shared responsibility" (Table 5.3). Governments with

[52] Hodgson and Halpern, "Investigating Cumulative Effects," 27 (in relation to mapping methods).

TABLE 5.3 *Mechanisms to share and reduce costs related to information*

Legal mechanism	Illustrative examples
Polluter pays principle – cost recovery for data collection based on cumulative risk	In Melbourne, Australia, municipal water service providers charge to accept trade waste into their sewerage systems; charges are based on a cumulative "risk rank" score, which considers the higher costs of more closely monitoring more complex types of discharges.[a]
Principle of shared responsibility to share costs among government and different categories of actions	In Canadian fisheries, "[t]he responsibility to pay for catch reporting and monitoring is shared between [the government agency Fisheries and Oceans Canada] and fish harvesters," with detailed policy for sharing specific costs between government, commercial fishers, recreational fishers, and Indigenous groups.[b]
Higher standard of information and burden of proof for proponent where existing cumulative impacts are close to cumulative threshold conditions	To protect streamflow that depends on groundwater, water law in the US state of Montana requires a permit applicant for a groundwater withdrawal right in a fully appropriated basin (in which no further surface water is available) to prove, using a hydrogeologic report, that any adverse effect on a connected stream would be offset.[c]
Stable source of government funding for data collection and sharing	Namibia's statutory Environmental Investment Fund was established to provide stable financial support to manage natural resources sustainably and gain associated benefits for local communities.[d] It receives money from parliamentary appropriations, statutory levies, and donations to fund activities that include "production, monitoring, use and dissemination of environmental information."[e]
Government data collection and analysis to support a regional intervention (e.g., regulatory limit on harm or resource use), used by a proponent to compare a project's impacts to the limit	The Office of Groundwater Impact Assessment (an independent statutory entity) in Queensland, Australia, undertakes regional and cumulative impact assessments for areas in which multiple tenures for unconventional gas developments overlap.[f] Development proponents use these models to identify their project's impacts for

Legal mechanism	Illustrative examples
	submission in environmental impact assessment (EIA) processes.[g]
Technology to reduce costs of collecting or analyzing data and planning compliance activities	Established under a presidential decree, Brazil's "Action Plan for the Prevention and Control of Deforestation in the Legal Amazon" uses satellite monitoring as a key component.[h] Empirical research suggests this monitoring has significantly improved targeted enforcement of illegal conversion of forests to pasture, both reducing deforestation and having positive economic effects.[i]
Prioritization of data collection to reduce costs	California's groundwater monitoring legislation sets out express criteria for prioritizing the implementation of the duty to monitor groundwater elevations. Relevant matters relate to dependence of the area on groundwater, growth projections, adverse impacts, and ecological matters.[j]

[a] Greater Western Water, *Greater Western Water (previously City West Water) Area – Pricing Handbook* 2021–22 (June 2021) 23–30, https://web.archive.org/web/20210809021133/https://www.citywestwater.com.au/sites/default/files/attachments/GWW%20(Previously%20CWW)%20Area%20-%20Pricing%20Handbook%20FY22.pdf.

[b] Government of Canada, "Fishery Monitoring Policy" (n.d.) www.dfo-mpo.gc.ca/reports-rapports/regs/sff-cpd/fishery-monitoring-surveillance-des-peches-eng.htm, last accessed March 18, 2025, archived at https://perma.cc/56RT-ABKX.

[c] Montana Code Ann. 85-2-360(1), (2), (3)(c). For further discussion of offsets, see Chapter 6.2.1.

[d] Environmental Investment Fund Act 2001 (Namibia) s 4.

[e] Ibid ss 3, 25(e).

[f] Water Act 2000 (Queensland) ch 3, 3A.

[g] Independent Expert Scientific Committee on Coal Seam Gas and Large Coal Mining Development (Australia), "Fact Sheet: Environmental Assessments" (n.d.) www.iesc.gov.au/publications/environmental-assessments, last accessed March 18, 2025, archived at https://perma.cc/KD6N-SLZL.

[h] Decreto nº 11.367, de 1º de janeiro de 2023 [Presidential Decree No. 11,637 of January 1, 2023] (Brazil) arts. 1, 4; Government of Brazil, *Action Plan for the Prevention and Control of Deforestation in the Legal Amazon (PPCDAm): Fifth Phase (2023–2027)* (2023) 110–112, www.gov.br/mma/pt-br/assuntos/combate-ao-desmatamento-queimadas-e-ordenamento-ambiental-territorial/controle-do-desmatamento-1/amazonia-ppcdam-1/ppcdam_5_en.pdf, last accessed March 18, 2025, archived at https://perma.cc/7FFC-DW4Q.

[i] See generally, Erik Merkus, "The Economic Consequences of Environmental Enforcement: Evidence from an Anti-Deforestation Policy in Brazil" (2024) 181(106646) *World Development* 1–12.

[j] Cal. Water Code §§ 10933(b), 10933.5.

scientific agencies may be better placed than individual project proponents to collect and analyze data on background effects, such as predicted climate change impacts or general environmental trends. Natural resources plans and strategic or regional environmental assessments can then include this information, to be used in assessing projects[53] (a kind of "tiering"). Regardless of where the responsibility falls, rules should provide clarity about who undertakes and pays for monitoring and analysis, and, ideally, consequences of not providing required information.[54]

A second key issue in relation to information and costs is how rules themselves can help reduce the costs of monitoring in an absolute sense. One way to do this is to support coordination between actors to reduce unnecessary duplication.[55] This can occur through tiering and by proponents sharing reusable data, which in some jurisdictions is rarely made publicly available in practice.[56] Another approach to containing costs is to prioritize data collection using a cumulative risk–based approach (Table 5.3) to help identify impacts that are "cross-cutting, multi-sector driven, and synergistic [and therefore] of greatest significance to a region and most urgently require effective management."[57] This can then drive intervention based on cumulative impact scores and ranks that include links to socioeconomic issues, guided by stakeholders, including communities.[58]

Rules can also support technology for monitoring, analysis, and targeting compliance activities to reduce the economic and environmental costs (Table 5.3) of collecting and processing data about large areas and many activities.[59] Bioacoustic monitoring of bird calls and machine learning to identify species,[60] and eDNA (environmental DNA), are examples. Technology can help monitor background levels of environmental stress, for example, vehicle sensors that can detect cumulatively significant local-level air pollution that may otherwise be missed, as used by the US Environmental

53 Antwi and others, "Risk Assessment Framework," 18.

54 Angus Morrison-Saunders and others, "Reflecting on, and Revising, International Best Practice Principles for EIA Follow-Up" (2021) 89:106596 *Environmental Impact Assessment Review* 1–10, 8.

55 Section 2.2.2.2.

56 Productivity Commission (Australia), *Resources Sector Regulation* (2020) 21–22.

57 Antwi and others, "Risk Assessment Framework," 7–9.

58 Ibid 8, 17–19.

59 For a review of large-scale monitoring and related processing technologies, see Alessio Fascista, "Toward Integrated Large-Scale Environmental Monitoring Using WSN/UAV/Crowdsensing: A Review of Applications, Signal Processing, and Future Perspectives" (2022) 22:1824 *Sensors* 1–65.

60 Zuzana Burivalova, Edward T. Game and Rhett A. Butler, "The Sound of a Tropical Forest" (2019) 363 *Science* 28–29.

Protection Agency.[61] Environmental monitoring can guide risk-based allocations of inspection resources to maximize the regulatory violations detected from inspections.[62] Satellite imagery, for example, has been used to detect potentially unlawful small dams[63] or water uses[64] that cumulatively reduce streamflows in Australia. The US Environmental Protection Agency considered the introduction of electronic reporting of permitted point source water pollution to be a "game changer."[65] That said, rules about environmental data collection should avoid rigidly requiring the use of any particular technology that might become superseded. Recalling the concerns discussed earlier,[66] the risks posed by technology deserve careful consideration and regulatory safeguards in terms of privacy or data protection laws, which go beyond the current scope of discussion.

Policy guidance about cumulative impact analysis and modeling can guide the use of analytical technology. Artificial intelligence provides a new way to understand complex interactions between impacts, including between climatic and more direct anthropogenic impacts; and to model the effects of a mix of types of interventions.[67] With appropriate safeguards, enforcement policies can contemplate the use of artificial intelligence and machine learning to reduce the time and cost of assessing large amounts of data to identify activities that may constitute noncompliance for further investigation by agencies. Making such predictions is a particularly prominent problem in the context of cumulative environmental effects because of the challenge of choosing where to direct compliance activities among numerous actors.

61 US Environmental Protection Agency, "Advanced Monitoring GMAP – Field Monitoring NEIC's Field Support Capabilities" (n.d.) www.epa.gov/sites/production/files/2018-05/documents/factsheet-neic-fb-advmonitoring.pdf, last accessed March 18, 2025, archived at https://perma.cc/2255-E2HR.

62 M. Hino, E. Benami and N. Brooks, "Machine Learning for Environmental Monitoring" (2018) 1 *Nature Sustainability* 583–588, 585.

63 See above n 37 and accompanying text.

64 Murray-Darling Basin Authority, Murray-Darling Basin Authority Communique (May 6, 2021) www.mdba.gov.au/news-and-events/newsroom/murray-darling-basin-authority-communique-may-2021, archived at https://perma.cc/6UBU-P58A.

65 Susan Bodine, Assistant Administrator for US EPA Office of Enforcement and Compliance Assurance, "The Enforcement Angle: EPA's Susan Bodine" (October 14, 2020) Podcast, eli.org/podcasts.

66 See Section 2.2.2.2.

67 Christian Simeoni and others, "Evaluating the Combined Effect of Climate and Anthropogenic Stressors on Marine Coastal Ecosystems: Insights from a Systematic Review of Cumulative Impact Assessment Approaches" (2023) 861:160687 *Science of The Total Environment* 1–18, 14.

5.3.3 *Sharing and Accessing Data and Information*

While access to government-held environmental information is a well-studied legal issue,[68] the cumulative effects incarnation of the issue is about sharing interoperable data from multiple sources, aggregating it, and accessing aggregated data and models or other systems that use it to predict effects, then accessing that information. Sharing data and information is not just technically desirable: Since cumulative impacts intersect with concerns about environmental justice and rights,[69] access to justice also requires access to information about cumulative environmental problems. Even where these problems most directly affect communities and justice, government data may omit important categories of impact, be unusable without special expertise, or not be aggregated.[70]

Law can play a central role in ensuring findable, accessible, interoperable, and reusable (FAIR) and contextualized data,[71] though this seems rarely recognized. Some laws lean in this direction: emerging natural capital and environmental accounting laws;[72] long-established impact assessment laws – EIA and strategic environmental assessment (SEA) – that require the public availability of impact assessment documents for a project or program; legal rights to environmental information, which sometimes link to human rights;[73] statutory "state of the environment" reporting; and legally mandated digital repositories that aggregate data from diverse sources, sometimes with the express rationale of better addressing cumulative impacts[74] (Table 5.4). To varying degrees, these mechanisms provide for synthesized information relevant to a particular matter of concern, as opposed to high-level overviews or reams of isolated documents; and sharing underlying data that are

68 For a recent notable example, see, e.g., Sean Whittaker, *The Right of Access to Environmental Information* (CUP 2021).

69 See generally, Office of General Counsel, US Environmental Protection Agency, *EPA Legal Tools to Advance Environmental Justice: Cumulative Impacts Addendum*, Pub. No. 360R22002 (2023) www.epa.gov/system/files/documents/2022-12/bh508-Cumulative%20Impacts%20Addendum%20Final%202022-11-28.pdf, last accessed March 18, 2025, archived at https://perma.cc/5HQ4-GVCQ; Barritt, "Aarhus Convention," 68, 81. See also Section 4.2.2.

70 Fusi, Zhang and Liang, "Unveiling Environmental Justice," 1096–1106.

71 See Section 2.2.2.2, especially n 55 and accompanying text.

72 E.g., see Table 5.1, last row.

73 E.g., Uzuazo Etemire, "Access to Environmental Information under EU Law" in Marjan Peeters and Mariolina Eliantonio (eds), *Research Handbook on EU Environmental Law* (Edward Elgar 2020) 117–132, 129–132; Barritt, "Aarhus Convention," 68, 81.

74 Department of Climate Change, Energy, the Environment and Water (Australia), Nature Positive Plan: Better for the Environment, Better for Business (Canberra, 2022), 1–50, 29–30, www.dcceew.gov.au/sites/default/files/documents/nature-positive-plan.pdf, archived at https://perma.cc/H5J8-9Q3V.

TABLE 5.4 *Mechanisms to promote sharing and access to FAIR data*

Legal mechanism	Illustrative example
Public right to access environmental information from public and private entities	Argentina's constitutional "right to a healthy, balanced environment" is supported by a statutory right to information[a] held by governments and public service companies (whether public or private) about "the state of the environment or one of its components, natural or cultural, including their mutual interactions, as well as to the activities and works which affect them or might affect them significantly" and to "policies, plans, programs and actions relating to the management of the environment."[b] South Africa's constitution allows third parties to request private environmental information if this is required to protect constitutional environmental rights.[c]
Regular publicly available government reports on the state of the environment	The independent statutory "Commissioner for Environmental Sustainability" in Victoria, Australia, must produce publicly available "state of the environment" reports.[d] These include recommendations for government action, to which the government must formally respond.[e] Such reports are also required in other jurisdictions,[f] and may prominently draw attention to cumulative impacts.[g]
Digital repository of information provided by agencies, regulated entities (including environmental impact assessment (EIA) documents) and citizen scientists to ensure accessibility	India's Biological Diversity Act of 2002 provides for a system of registering local knowledge related to biodiversity.[h] In Greece, reforms to EIA intended to increase transparency created a National Electronic Environmental Registry to manage and publish all EIA-related documents.[i]
Standardized data gathering and sharing for interoperability	Federal water regulations in Australia require public and some private entities to provide water data to a federal agency using standard units of measurement and providing detailed metadata.[j] The US Environmental Protection Agency's data standards policy[k] promotes transparency and the exchange and multiple use of data between that agency, states and tribes.

(*continued*)

TABLE 5.4 (*continued*)

Legal mechanism	Illustrative example
Requirements for accessible models and aggregated data	An express legislative purpose of California's groundwater monitoring legislation was to make groundwater level data "readily and widely available."[l] Online, freely available technical models support California's groundwater sustainability plans by predicting how much groundwater pumping depletes surface water.[m]
Environmental information sharing legislation prevails over barriers to information sharing based on commercial reasons	European Union law applies an irrebuttable presumption that it is in the public interest to disclose information about emissions to the environment, even if doing so may undermine commercial business interests or intellectual property rights.[n] Canadian case law implies an exception to copyright legislation in respect of disclosure requirements under recent oil and gas law.[o]
Time-limited confidentiality periods for environmental data with commercial value	UK legislation requires disclosure of oil and gas–related information either immediately, after two or five years or after expiration of a relevant licence.[p]

[a] Maria Onestini, "Human Right to Water: Argentine Cases, Human Rights – Are They Enforceable?" in Erkki J. Hollo (ed), *Water Resources Management and the Law* (Edward Elgar 2017) 118, 126–127 (citing art. 41 of the Argentine Constitution, and the 2016 Regimen De Libre Acceso La Información Pública Ambiental, Ley 25831).

[b] Ibid 127.

[c] Constitution of the Republic of South Africa 1996, ss 24, 32(1)(b).

[d] Commissioner for Environmental Sustainability Act 2003 (Victoria) ss 17–18A; Commissioner for Environmental Sustainability Victoria, *Victorian State of the Environment 2023 Report: Summary Report* (2023) www.ces.vic.gov.au/sites/default/files/2023-11/State%20of%20the%20Environment%202023%20Report_Summary%20Report_DIGITAL.pdf, archived at https://perma.cc/9QPB-YK3A.

[e] Commissioner for Environmental Sustainability Act 2003 (Victoria) s 17(5).

[f] European Environment Agency, *State of Nature in the EU: Results from Reporting under the Nature Directives 2013–2018* (2020) www.eea.europa.eu/en/analysis/publications/state-of-nature-in-the-eu-2020/state-of-nature-in-the-eu-2020/@@download/file, archived at https://perma.cc/8UGN-6TCB.

[g] E.g., European Environment Agency, *The European Environment – State and Outlook 2020: Knowledge for Transition to a Sustainable Europe* (2019) 74 ("key messages" for biodiversity), 134 ("key messages" for marine environment) www.eea.europa.eu/en/analysis/publications/state-of-nature-in-the-eu-2020, archived at https://perma.cc/D33K-7G3Q.

[h] Biological Diversity Act 2002 (India) s 36(5); Biological Biodiversity Rules 2024 (India) rr 11 (f)–(h); Laasya Shekar, "What Is a People's Biodiversity Register?" (July 7, 2024, Mongabay India) https://india.mongabay.com/2024/07/explainer-what-is-a-peoples-biodiversity-register.

[i] Νόμος αριθ 4014 (2011) "Περιβαλλοντική αδειοδότηση έργων και δραστηριοτήτων, ρύθμιση αυθαιρέτων σε συνάρτηση με δημιουργία περιβαλλοντικού ισοζυγίου και άλλες διατάξεις αρμοδιότητας Υπουργείου Περιβάλλοντος" [Law No. 4014 (2011) "Environmental Licensing of Works and Activities, Regulation of Illegal Constructions in Connection with Environmental Stability and Other

Provisions Falling Under the Competence of the Ministry of Environment"], art. 18, as amended; Kalliope Pediaditi and others, "Greece's Reformed EIA System: Evaluating Its Implementation and Potential" (2018) 73 *Environmental Impact Assessment Review* 90–103 (praising the design of the system, which was not implemented at that time); Ministry of Environment and Energy (Greece), "Access the Electronic Environmental Register" (n.d.) www.gov.gr/en/upourgeia/upourgeio-periballontos-kai-energeias/periballontos-kai-energeias/elektroniko-periballontiko-metroo-epm, last accessed March 18, 2025, archived at https://perma.cc/FM8U-TLSY.
[j] Water Regulations 2008 (Australia) regs 7.06, 7.10, 7.11.
[k] U.S. Environmental Protection Agency, "'Data Standards Policy," CIO 2133.0 (June 28, 2007) www.epa.gov/sites/default/files/2013-11/documents/21330.pdf, last accessed March 18, 2025, archived at https://perma.cc/3LPP-AJ76.
[l] California Water Code § 10920.
[m] California Department of Water Resources, "Data and Tools" (n.d.) https://water.ca.gov/Programs/Groundwater-Management/Data-and-Tools, last accessed March 18, 2025, archived at https://perma.cc/DT4T-XN26; see Chapter 8.
[n] Regulation 1367/2006 of the European Parliament and of the Council of September 6, 2006 on the application of the provisions of the Aarhus Convention on Access to Information, Public Participation in Decision-making and Access to Justice in Environmental Matters to Community institutions and bodies [2006] OJ L264/13, art. 6(1); Madrid, *Private Sector Environmental Information*, 194–195.
[o] Brown, "The Future of Intellectual Property," 122–123.
[p] Ibid 114–115 (citing Oil and Gas Authority (Offshore Petroleum) (Disclosure of Protected Material after Specified Period) Regulations 2018 (United Kingdom)).

enduringly accessible to enable aggregation to shed light on cumulative environmental problems.

As discussed in Chapter 2, political and commercial sensitivities may discourage governments and regulated entities from producing information that is FAIR, and sharing it. Regulated entities may resist attempts to standardize data collection if this imposes additional costs or is seen to pose risks. Agencies can consult regulated entities about standardization to find ways to reduce costs faced by these entities; this may be especially important for small recipients of regulatory "carrots," such as parties to land stewardship agreements that involve reporting requirements.[75]

Regulatory designers should also consider potentially perverse consequences of requiring data sharing: In the context of concerns about nutrient pollution of the Great Barrier Reef in Queensland, Australia, a proposed legal power to require farmers to provide data on fertilizer application, which would have indicated overapplication, led to the deletion of a decade's worth of voluntarily collected data.[76] But, in some cases, mandatory data sharing can

75 Byron Swift and others, "Private Lands Conservation in Latin America: The Need for Enhanced Legal Tools and Incentives" (2004) 19 *Journal of Environmental Law and Litigation* 85–140, 112.

76 Evan Hamman and others, "Regulating Land Use in the Catchment of the Great Barrier Reef" (2022) 115:106001 *Land Use Policy* 1–15, 7.

be welcomed by industry operators who benefit from accessing others' information.[77] One Australian information-sharing initiative to store and share data from project proponents is expected to reduce project application assessment times by six to twelve months.[78] Yielding to industry concerns, some jurisdictions exempt data that constitute business confidential information and trade secrets from environmental information sharing requirements, but this differs between jurisdictions and may give way to the values of public health and environmental protection.[79] Table 5.4 gives further examples of possible approaches.

5.4 CONCLUSION

Information is critical for understanding the things we care about and the cumulative threats that they face, so that rules for intervention can restore or protect them from cumulative environmental harm. This is about much more than just predicting cumulative impacts in the context of project-level EIA. It requires gathering and aggregating, in an ongoing way, comprehensive and high-quality data, analyzing it, allocating the costs of doing these things (probably with an eye to reducing those costs, given the data-hungry nature of cumulative environmental problems), and ensuring that information is shared and can be accessed by governments, affected communities, and other stakeholders. By drawing on formal rules from around the world, this chapter has illustrated diverse possibilities for designing rules to do these things and address the disincentives to gathering and sharing data and information that would otherwise threaten effective action to solve cumulative environmental problems.

More than just a technical issue about having good information to reveal problems and make decisions, information is about power and accountability. The knowledges that are accepted as legitimate and the practical accessibility of information about harm influence environmental democracy, environmental justice, and the rule of law. Regulatory systems, then, should not be mere information-*takers*, they should be information-*makers*. That is, rules should be actively designed not only to include – fairly – diverse sources of information already produced, which are needed to understand and respond to

[77] Abbe E. L. Brown, "The Future of Intellectual Property" in Daniel J. Gervais (ed), *Rights to Do, Rights to Prevent, and an Intersected Approach? Lessons from Intellectual Property, Information Control and Oil and Gas* (Edward Elgar 2021) 105–127, 120.

[78] Productivity Commission (Australia), *Resources Sector Regulation*, 378.

[79] Juliana Zuluaga Madrid, *Private Sector Environmental Information and the Law* (Routledge 2023) 158–202.

cumulative environmental problems, they should be designed to actively fill gaps in existing knowledge.

By themselves, rules for information cannot solve cumulative environmental problems. Cumulative environmental problems need advocates, both within and outside government, and those advocates need information both to act and to know that action is needed. Rules for information must also be integrated with the other functions of the CIRCle Framework, informing and responding to how the matter of concern is conceptualized, interventions are designed, and government and nongovernment actors come together to address the problem of cumulative environmental harm.

6

Regulatory Intervention

Laws for Influencing Cumulative Harm

Links with Other Chapters

- Chapter 1 explains how examples used in this chapter were chosen.
- Chapter 2 synthesizes key challenges related to regulatory intervention and introduces the CIRCle Framework of regulatory functions for addressing cumulative environmental problems.
- Chapter 3 sketches the landscape of laws that may respond to cumulative environmental problems.
- Chapter 4 ("Conceptualization") discusses rules for articulating what and who we want to protect from cumulative impacts (the "matter of concern"), which rules for intervention seek to protect or restore.
- Chapter 5 ("Information") discusses rules for collecting and analyzing data and information needed to inform regulatory intervention.
- Chapter 7 ("Coordination") covers coordinating interventions between levels of government, including involving nongovernment and quasi-government stakeholders.
- Each case study (Chapters 8–10) discusses links between intervention and one other CIRCle Framework function.

6.1 INTERVENTION AS A REGULATORY FUNCTION

Rules for regulatory intervention are probably what we come to first when we think about rules. The basic purpose of regulatory intervention is to change the impacts that accumulate to harm something that we care about – a "matter of concern."[1] The main argument of this chapter is that regulating cumulative environmental problems[2] requires a mix of formal rules[3] for intervention, combining different strategies and approaches from across the typologies developed here. The design of this mix should address key challenges (discussed in Chapter 2)[4] that make dealing with cumulative environmental problems difficult. To start with, these include challenges to perceiving the risks of many individually minor threats, a sense of futility and short-termism that can prevent intervention occurring. Then, even when intervention is on the cards, ethical ambiguity about how to allocate responsibility among many actors can hinder action. Finally, when interventions are in place, arguments about certainty and fairness, path dependence, risk aversion, and single action bias can impede adaptive management of interventions to suit changing circumstances and new information. To this catalog of difficulties, this chapter adds those posed by decision-making structures and interventions themselves, namely, legal silos that produce fragmented decision-making and administrative burdens. Although rules alone cannot solve a cumulative environmental problem, these challenges suggest rules will play an important role.[5]

This chapter explores[6] how rules for intervention can vary and the implications of this variation for addressing cumulative environmental problems. Section 6.2 develops a typology of regulatory "strategies" – harm-reducing, harm-offsetting, restoring, and coping – that focuses on how rules seek to change cumulative harm to the matter of concern. Section 6.3 expands a classic regulatory theory typology of "approaches" – regulatory sticks, carrots,

[1] As described in Chapter 4, matters of concern vary widely, from a species, to a pollutant, to a community's relationship with a place.

[2] For the full definition of cumulative environmental problems used in this book, see Section 1.1.

[3] Rules may be administrative, made by executive agencies, legislative, or even constitutional. The focus here is on substantive rules, rather than procedural rules that allow for challenges to administrative decision-making, which might also address multirisk impacts: Jonathan B. Wiener, "Learning to Manage the World" (2020) 40 *Risk Analysis* 2137–2143, 2139. This focus also excludes social controls outside formal rules and rules established by non-state actors. Note that Chapter 7 (Coordination) considers how quasi-governmental and nongovernmental actors can contribute to systems of rules for intervention in which the state is also an actor.

[4] See Section 2.2.3.

[5] See Sections 2.2.3 and 2.3.

[6] Note that this chapter has a slightly different structure to the foregoing chapters on the functions of conceptualization and information because of the prominent place of intervention as a purpose of rules.

and sermons – that focuses on how rules seek to change the activities of contributors to the cumulative harm or restoration (termed "contributors"). To these three approaches, I add "state rescue," where a state acts directly to address the harm rather than trying to influence others' behavior. Combining these typologies of strategies and approaches (Section 6.4) produces a matrix of formal rule-based interventions for dealing with cumulative environmental harms. Each individual "intervention" can be characterized by its "strategy" and regulatory "approach." This matrix helps identify diverse and some under-explored intervention opportunities. Section 6.5 then discusses crosscutting design features for interventions that respond to key challenges posed by cumulative environmental problems and presents examples of legal mechanisms that adopt them. These features involve ensuring that decision-making about individual activities is *connected* so that it reveals how harm accumulates, that intervention is *comprehensive* and appropriately enforced, that administrative *costs* are managed and that interventions can be adaptively *changed* where necessary, taking account of concerns about fairness. Throughout the chapter, the focus is on applying these ideas to cumulative environmental problems specifically, noting that extensive scholarship deals with design issues for different types of regulatory interventions in general and in relation to broader environmental issues.[7]

As emphasized in earlier chapters, each of the four functions of the CIRCle Framework advanced by this book (conceptualization, information, regulatory intervention and coordination) is needed to respond to cumulative environmental problems, and these functions are interlinked (Figure 2.1 depicts these basic links). Rules for *intervening* deal with potential or existing unacceptable cumulative harms to a *clearly conceptualized* matter of concern (Chapter 4), using *information* about something we care about (the "matter of concern") and the harms (Chapter 5), in a *coordinated* way (Chapter 8). Figure 6.1 summarizes these links in a more detailed way that is relevant to rules for intervention, and these links are explored further as the chapter proceeds.[8]

6.2 HOW CAN RULES AFFECT AGGREGATE HARM? A TYPOLOGY OF REGULATORY STRATEGIES

Our matrix of opportunities for regulatory intervention starts with regulatory strategies. This section develops a four-part typology of strategies by focusing on the matter of concern – what and who we want to protect from cumulative

[7] See notes 54 and 56 and accompanying text.
[8] See introductory paragraphs to Sections 6.2 and 6.3.

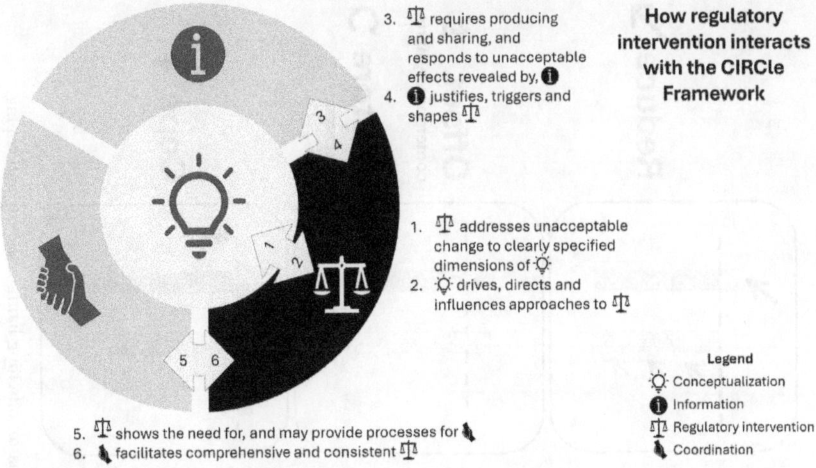

FIGURE 6.1 Integration of legal mechanisms for intervention with other CIRCle Framework functions, each necessary for regulating cumulative environmental problems

harm, or restore – and how rules try to influence cumulative change to its conditions. This closely links to thresholds of acceptable change that rules for conceptualization can formalize (cumulative threshold conditions lines, Figure 6.2),[9] supported by rules for information about the condition of the matter of concern relative to the threshold of unacceptable cumulative harm.[10] In addition to general regulatory literature, the typology of strategies developed here is loosely inspired by frameworks for responding to ecological transformation,[11] which implicitly address cumulative ecological harm; and prominent critiques of environmental offsets.[12]

Considering regulation by centering the matter of concern aligns with cumulative environmental impact analysis.[13] But focusing on the matter of concern differs from regulatory scholarship that tends to focus on how rules try to change the behavior of regulated parties, which has produced the typology of regulatory approaches discussed later.[14]

[9] See Section 4.3.3.

[10] See Section 5.1.1.

[11] E.g., Gregor W. Schuurman and others, "Navigating Ecological Transformation: Resist-Accept-Direct as a Path to a New Resource Management Paradigm" (2022) 72 *BioScience* 16–29.

[12] E.g., Laura J. Sonter and others, "Offsetting Impacts of Development on Biodiversity and Ecosystem Services" (2020) 49 *Ambio* 892–902.

[13] See Section 2.2.1.1.

[14] See Section 6.3.1.

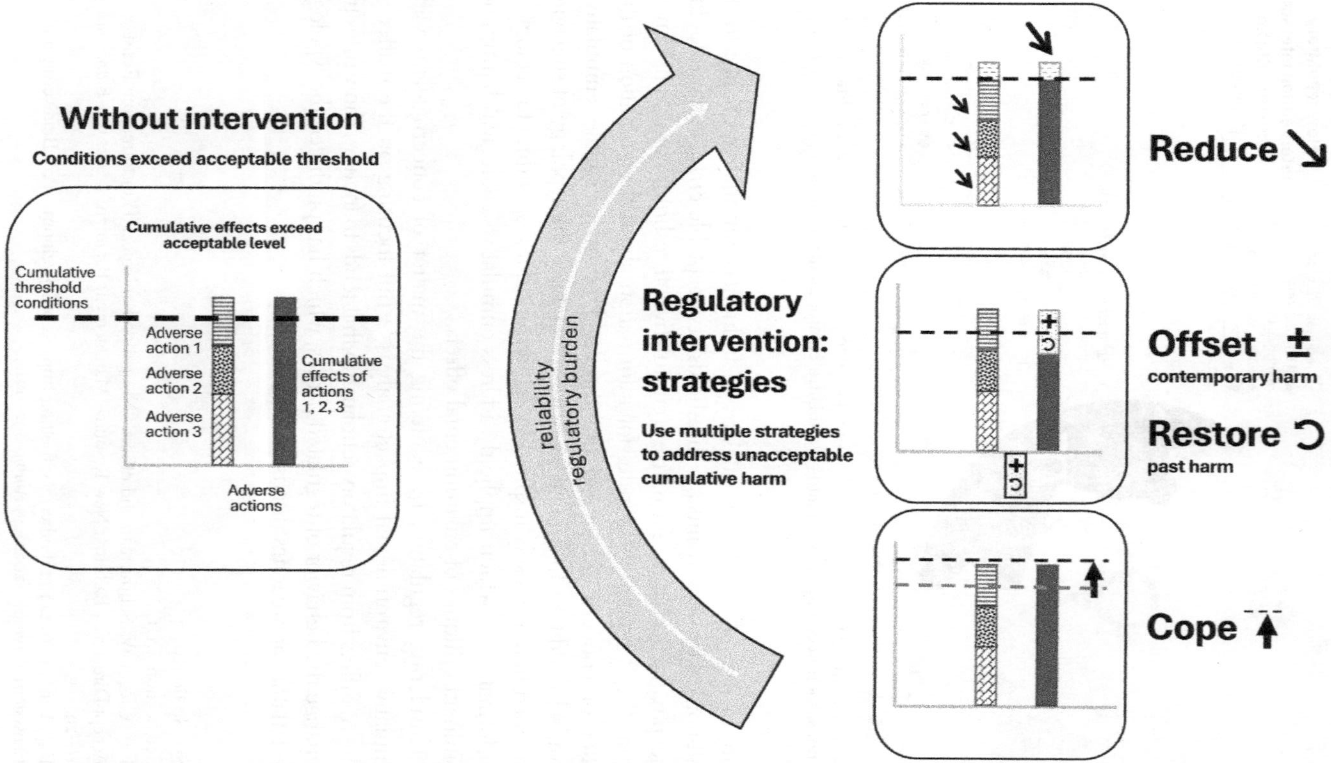

FIGURE 6.2 Four regulatory intervention strategies to ensure acceptable cumulative effects – reducing harm, offsetting harm, restoring, and coping

In sum, rules can adopt four main strategies to influence cumulative change to a matter of concern: reducing cumulative harm in absolute terms, by reducing or avoiding adverse effects; "neutralizing" or offsetting proposed negative effects by encouraging beneficial actions; restoring (reversing legacy harm that occurred in the past); and employing measures that help a matter of concern cope with change to reduce the harm caused by cumulative impacts without changing the activities that lead to impacts (Figure 6.2). Section 6.2.1 introduces each, and Section 6.2.2 assesses their advantages and disadvantages in addressing cumulative environmental problems.

6.2.1 *Harm-Reducing, Offsetting, Restoring, and Coping Strategies*

Rules that adopt a harm-reducing strategy seek to directly reduce the absolute level of cumulative harm by preventing or changing actions with adverse effects ("adverse actions") to reduce or avoid harm (Figure 6.2, top right). This is probably what comes to mind first when we think of rules relating to environmental harm. For example, rules mandate and incentivize farmers to reduce polluted runoff that affects the Great Barrier Reef ("Reef"), prohibit commercial fishing in certain zones, and facilitate controlling harmful invasive starfish.[15] In each case, the absolute level of harm to the Reef decreases if the rule is effective.

A harm-reducing strategy most clearly links to cumulative impacts if it takes the form of a "performance standard"[16] that limits cumulative change to a matter of concern. A rule may require polluters to change their behavior to meet ambient air quality standards (cumulative conditions) rather than require them to adopt a specific pollution-reducing technology. The former option adjusts the required behavior to account for increasing numbers of polluters, and pollution; the latter does not. Quantitative limits, a type of performance standard, can apply to traditionally regulated resources (e.g., total water withdrawals, ambient air pollution), as well as emerging issues (e.g., consumption of "domestic primary raw materials").[17] Developing quantitative limits is more challenging where it is harder to express in quantitative

[15] See Figure 9.1.

[16] Jody Freeman and Daniel A. Farber, "Modular Environmental Regulation" (2005) 54 *Duke Law Journal* 795–912, 819–820.

[17] E.g., see Section 6.5.1; Ministry of Economic Affairs and Employment and Ministry of the Environment (Finland), "Finland's Circular Economy Programme Sets Targets to Curb Overconsumption of Natural Resources" (Press release, April 8, 2021) https://valtioneuvosto.fi/en/-//1410903/circular-economy-programme-sets-targets-to-curb-overconsumption-of-natural-resources, archived at https://perma.cc/W2KU-M8JD.

terms what is important about the matter of concern – a challenge that can arise in the context of biodiversity, for example.[18]

A second strategy is offsetting, or encouraging actions with positive effects to "make room" for adverse actions.[19] Rather than reducing absolute harm, the aim is usually to achieve or maintain an acceptable net level of harm (Figure 6.2, middle right). This strategy is important where small but cumulatively significant harms cannot be reduced.[20] Offsetting applies in diverse contexts, such as land use, biodiversity, greenhouse gas emissions, water quality, and water withdrawals,[21] and can form an important part of cap-and-trade systems.[22] Offsetting implies that impacts are fungible, which is not always the case, and it will be more difficult and controversial to develop where it is hard to develop quantitative limits.[23]

When the harm occurred in the past, we can distinguish a related third strategy of restoring. This looks similar to offsetting in terms of the end effect (Figure 6.2, middle right), but restoring rules likely target someone other than the original contributor to the impact, who may be long gone or not identifiable. Dedicated nature restoration or "repair" laws are now emerging in diverse jurisdictions,[24] though they are a long-standing part of nature laws in some places.[25]

As an alternative to focusing on adverse impacts and benefits, a strategy may seek to intervene by helping the matter of concern to cope better[26] with the cumulative impacts of adverse actions (Figure 6.2, bottom right). This strategy

[18] See Section 4.2.

[19] Riki Therivel and Bill Ross, "Cumulative Effects Assessment: Does Scale Matter?" (2007) 27 *Environmental Impact Assessment Review* 365–385, 368.

[20] See Section 6.5.2.2 on small harms.

[21] See Kenneth R. Richards, "Environmental Offset Programmes," in Kenneth R. Richards and Josephine Van Zeben (eds), *Elgar Encyclopedia of Environmental Law Vol. VIII* (Edward Elgar 2020) 325–351.

[22] E.g., see discussion of carbon offsetting in Chapter 9 on the Great Barrier Reef.

[23] Sonter and others, "Offsetting Impacts," 894; Andy Lockhart, "Developing an Offsetting Programme: Tensions, Dilemmas and Difficulties in Biodiversity Market-Making in England" (2015) 42 *Environmental Conservation* 335–344, 339.

[24] E.g., Regulation (EU) 2024/1991 of the European Parliament and of the Council of June 24, 2024 on nature restoration and amending Regulation (EU) 2022/869, OJ L 2024/1991, July 29, 2024 ("EU Nature Restoration Law"); Nature Repair Act 2023 (Australia).

[25] See, e.g. Section 10.4.1.3 regarding laws for restoring grasslands in South Tyrol, Italy.

[26] The climate change literature is replete with discussion of concepts such as coping capacity, adaptive capacity, resilience, and vulnerability. These concepts are interconnected and not always used consistently between authors: see generally, A. R. Siders, "Adaptive Capacity to Climate Change: A Synthesis of Concepts, Methods, and Findings in a Fragmented Field" (2019) 10:e573 *WIREs Climate Change* 1–18. Importantly for present purposes, a coping strategy does not reduce gross or net cumulative impacts, rather, it reduces harm.

breaks the link between impacts and harm. Unlike the other strategies, this one allows activities to cause comparatively more impacts without unacceptably harming the matter of concern. In the California groundwater case study,[27] rules support funding a householder whose well has gone dry to deepen their well to enable them to cope with declining groundwater levels. The result is that agricultural groundwater users can continue pumping even when this causes groundwater levels to decline, because householders can cope with these impacts, maintaining their access to groundwater using deeper wells – though with risks discussed later.

For completeness, it is worth noting a final possible response to a problem: reconceptualizing the matter of concern to accept greater cumulative change. Rather than being an intervention tool, this relates to conceptualization. It may require changing legal rules about "what matters"[28] to accept more degraded conditions or to pursue novel conditions. Making reconceptualization too easy, though, especially where this can occur on a project-by-project basis, poses the critical risk of "shifting baselines"[29] and inadvertently increasing cumulative impacts. Adapting conceptualizations – and the importance of not conflating this with intervention – are addressed in Chapter 4 (Conceptualization). The remainder of this chapter discusses regulatory intervention using reducing, offsetting, restoring, and coping strategies.

6.2.2 *Assessing Regulatory Strategies*

The legal, economic, political, social, and physical feasibility of each strategy will vary with the jurisdiction and matter of concern. However, we can make some general observations about likely drawbacks of different strategies by considering two factors – how reliably a strategy changes cumulative environmental outcomes ("outcome reliability") and the degree to which a strategy burdens contributors to the harm ("regulatory burden") – and how they can be addressed. These factors are likely to influence political and social feasibility – a key challenge to regulating cumulative environmental problems.[30]

A harm-reducing strategy most reliably controls cumulative harms because it prevents adverse impacts in the first place (Figure 6.2, top right). It avoids the well-recognized risks that a beneficial action will not adequately counter

[27] See Chapter 8.
[28] See Section 4.3.1.
[29] See Section 2.2.2.1.
[30] Section 2.2.3.

adverse effects (i.e., nonequivalence),[31] uncertainty about whether measures to increase coping capacity will work,[32] and risks that offsetting, restoring, or coping measures might fail or might work initially but fail with time (as where wildfire affects a forest planted for carbon credits).[33] Even high-fungibility contexts such as carbon offsets can involve "durability risks" or "risks of reversal."[34] Some regulatory regimes recognize that incomplete offsetting is sometimes inevitable – a planted forest gains ecological function only over time – and require "overcompensation" for "interim losses."[35] Another common way to reduce risk is to allow offsetting only after impacts have been avoided and reduced as much as possible.[36] An important question for implementation is whether this avoids the risk that the mere fact that offsets are available might shut out the more reliable, but burdensome, strategy of reducing harm (i.e., "mitigation deterrence").[37] The severity of these risks related to offsetting, restoring, and coping strategies can vary with context and deserve careful consideration. Helping a small community cope with declining groundwater in California's Central Valley by drilling deeper wells using existing technology produces more reliable outcomes than helping the spatially extensive Great Barrier Reef cope better with climate heating using novel shading infrastructure.[38]

To avoid unintended harms related to offsetting, restoring, and coping strategies, it is especially important to appropriately conceptualize the matter of concern. Firstly, conceptualization may "lock in" ongoing cumulative effects if a goal that forms part of the conceptualization, for example, "no

[31] E.g., if mitigation is not required to be in effect at the time damage occurs, or if there is unintentional nonequivalence between the effect and compensatory actions (Martine Maron and others, "Taming a Wicked Problem: Resolving Controversies in Biodiversity Offsetting" (2016) 66 *BioScience* 489–498, 494–495), noting that some offset rules encourage nonequivalence in pursuit of environmental benefit: Rebecca Nelson, "Paying Back the River: A First Analysis of Western Groundwater Offset Rules and Lessons for Other Natural Resources" (2015) 34 *Stanford Environmental Law Journal* 129–194, 185–187.

[32] See generally, Siders, "Adaptive Capacity."

[33] E.g., Lockhart, "Developing an Offsetting Programme," 340 (re initial failure); Kaya Axelsson and others, "Oxford Principles for Net Zero Aligned Carbon Offsetting (Revised 2024)" (*Smith School of Enterprise and the Environment*, University of Oxford, 2024) 18, www.smithschool.ox.ac.uk/sites/default/files/2024-02/Oxford-Principles-for-Net-Zero-Aligned-Carbon-Offsetting-revised-2024.pdf (re inadvertent re-release of biologically stored carbon).

[34] Axelsson and others, "Oxford Principles," 18–20.

[35] European Commission and Directorate-General for Environment, *Managing Natura 2000 Sites – The Provisions of Article 6 of the "Habitats" Directive 92/43/EEC* (2019) 61.

[36] Ibid 58.

[37] See generally, Duncan McLaren, "Quantifying the Potential Scale of Mitigation Deterrence from Greenhouse Gas Removal Techniques" (2020) 162 *Climatic Change* 2411–2428.

[38] See Chapters 8 (California groundwater) and 9 (Great Barrier Reef).

net loss," is expressed relative to a "presumed trajectory of 'background' decline," rather than relative to a stable set of conditions.[39] Secondly, offsetting might simply not be feasible in some situations, for example, where demand for offsets exceeds supply,[40] which could create pressure to allow offsets that do not benefit the matter of concern as originally conceptualized (i.e., nonequivalence). A finite supply of offsets raises the need for rules about enabling equitable access to offsets among proponents of activities that would require them for their activities to proceed.[41]

Offsetting, restoring, or facilitating coping related to one matter of concern may also harm another thing that is not formally recognized to "matter" in a particular context. If a rule adopts ecosystem services, which benefit people, as a matter of concern, an offset strategy may allow harm to biodiversity that offers no readily identifiable benefits to people.[42] Related to this, environmental offsets without adequate safeguards may also harm people through, for example, direct and indirect impacts on Indigenous rights.[43] A funding scheme for well deepening will not increase the coping capacity of ecosystems affected by declining groundwater, or of well owners who experience barriers accessing the scheme.[44] To avoid harming other matters of concern, regimes for offsetting, restoring, or coping that are directed at one cumulative environmental problem (e.g., carbon offsets) might require safeguards in the form of, for example, no negative impact on the matter of concern at the heart of another cumulative environmental problem or social values (e.g., carbon offsets that do not harm biodiversity or traditional access to land).[45] Designing these safeguards requires coordination across regulators responsible for dealing with these different problems.[46] If well-designed, offsetting and

39 Maron and others, "Taming a Wicked Problem," 492. For a less risky approach to specifying cumulative threshold conditions, see Section 4.3.3.

40 Ken Henry and others, *Final Report: Independent Review of the Biodiversity Conservation Act 2016* (State of New South Wales, 2023) 50–52, www.parliament.nsw.gov.au/lc/tabledpapers/Pages/tabled-paper-details.aspx?pk=186428&houseCode=lc, archived at https://perma.cc/7NUU-TRJQ.

41 E.g., in the context of carbon offsets sourced from nature restoration, see generally, Kate Dooley, Zebedee Nicholls, and Malte Meinshausen, "Carbon Removals from Nature Restoration Are No Substitute for Steep Emission Reductions" (2022) 5(7) *One Earth* 812–824.

42 See generally, Sonter and others, "Offsetting Impacts."

43 E.g., see generally, Kathleen Birrell, Lee Godden and Maureen Tehan, "Climate Change and REDD+: Property as a Prism for Conceiving Indigenous Peoples' Engagement" (2012) 3 *Journal of Human Rights and the Environment* 196–216.

44 See Section 8.4.2.6

45 Axelsson and others, "Oxford Principles," 14.

46 See Chapter 7 (Coordination).

restoring may have co-benefits for other matters of concern, say, community development benefits, and coordination can help structure regulatory systems to create synergies between offset regimes for different matters of concern.[47]

Considering how strategies burden contributors reveals trade-offs between these burdens and outcome reliability. Requiring a contributor to change their operations to reduce their impacts (a harm-reducing strategy) likely burdens them more than if they operated as normal, on condition that they fund riskier measures to neutralize their impacts (harm-offsetting) or on condition that they act to increase the coping capacity of a matter of concern. But different ways of requiring harm reduction can change burdens on contributors and may make it easier for them to reduce harm. Performance standards, for example, allow greater flexibility and reduce cost compared to reducing harm using a specified technology that applies universally to contributors.[48] If a cumulative environmental problem has more numerous and diverse contributors, it will logically be easier to reduce aggregate harm if one contributor can pay another to offset, compared to a problem involving fewer, more homogeneous contributors: offsets will reduce costs more in the first situation (which has the characteristics of a cumulative environmental problem) than in the second. Depending on how the matter of concern is conceptualized, spatially diverse contributors to the same environmental problem may allow for selecting an offset location to increase environmental benefits.[49]

Administrative burdens to government, on the other hand, are less easy to generalize within and across different strategies. Different types of harm-reducing strategies may entail different costs for contributors to harm and regulators. For example, performance standards that refer to cumulative harm arguably best reflect cumulative impacts, and may reduce costs for contributors, but enforcing them may cost regulators more than enforcing technology standards (e.g., continuous pollution monitoring vs confirming the installation of specified technology).[50] Scientific uncertainty will also influence administrative cost. If there is uncertainty about what activities cause harm, or whether

[47] Peter J. Whitehead, *Indigenous Livelihoods: Background Paper* (NAILSMA Knowledge Series, North Australian Indigenous Land and Sea Management Alliance 2012) 54–56, https://nailsma.org.au/uploads/resources/KS-011-Indigenous-Livelihoods-background-paper-Whitehead.pdf, archived at https://perma.cc/9YSR-5Y9R; Section 9.5.4.

[48] Cary Coglianese and Shana M. Starobin, "Social Science and the Analysis of Environmental Policy" (2020) 37 *Review of Policy Research* 578–604, 589–590.

[49] Deqiang Ma, Jonathan R. Rhodes and Martine Maron, "The Consequences of Coastal Offsets for Fisheries" (2022) 59 *Journal of Applied Ecology* 1157–1167, 1164.

[50] Cary Coglianese, "The Limits of Performance-Based Regulation" (2017) 50 *University of Michigan Journal of Law Reform* 525–564, 547–552.

an offsetting or coping strategy will work, justifying a strategy may require research and more intensive monitoring to verify the outcome,[51] increasing administrative burdens. Since legal regimes are not traditionally established to facilitate environment-related coping, relative to other strategies, more regulatory barriers may obstruct rules for coping.[52]

6.3 HOW CAN RULES INFLUENCE BEHAVIOR THAT HAS CUMULATIVE EFFECTS? A TYPOLOGY OF REGULATORY APPROACHES

While regulatory strategies focus on how rules affect cumulative harm relative to a level of acceptable conditions, regulatory approaches focus on contributors to the harm, and how rules try to change their behavior. Regulatory theorists have developed many ways of classifying regulatory approaches, none of which is universally accepted.[53] Section 6.3.1 uses the simple framework of mandatory "sticks," incentive-based "carrots," and information-based "sermons,"[54] adding an option that sidesteps influencing the behavior of contributors in favor of the state directly taking action ("state rescue") (Figure 6.3). A further important adjustment reflects this book's focus on formal rules: Each approach is based on enforceable rules.[55] Since regulatory theory[56] says little directly about cumulative effects, Section 6.3.2 applies a

[51] Robin Kundis Craig and J. B. Ruhl, "Designing Administrative Law for Adaptive Management" (2014) 67 *Vanderbilt Law Review* 1–87, 13 (citations omitted).

[52] E.g., in relation to the Great Barrier Reef, see generally, Pedro Fidelman and others, "Regulatory Implications of Coral Reef Restoration and Adaptation under a Changing Climate" (2019) 100 *Environmental Science and Policy* 221–229.

[53] Arie Freiberg, "Authority Tools: Pervasive, Persistent and Powerful" in Michael Howlett and Ishani Mukherjee (eds), *Routledge Handbook of Policy Design* (Taylor & Francis 2018) 243–260, 243.

[54] This simple typology, originally advanced by Bemelmans-Videc, Rist and Vedung (Marie-Louise Bemelmans-Videc, Ray C. Rist and Evert Vedung (eds), *Carrots, Sticks & Sermons: Policy Instruments and Their Evaluation* (Transaction Publishers 1998)) and much cited thereafter, suits present purposes for its parsimony, given the present purpose of constructing a matrix of both approaches and strategies. Other more complex regulatory typologies also exist, e.g., see Coglianese and Starobin, "Social Science and the Analysis of Environmental Policy," 588–592; James Salzman, "Teaching Policy Instrument Choice in Environmental Law: The Five P's" (2013) 23(2) *Duke Environmental Law and Policy Forum* 363; Karoline S. Rogge and Kristin Reichardt, "Policy Mixes for Sustainability Transitions: An Extended Concept and Framework for Analysis" (2016) 45 *Research Policy* 1620–1635. This chapter discusses some of the variation revealed by these more complex typologies within the categories of the simpler overall typology used here.

[55] Accordingly, this discussion does not include entirely self-regulatory approaches that include no role for the state. See also the description of this book's scope in Section 1.3.

[56] For useful references on regulatory theory, see, e.g., Michael Howlett and Ishani Mukherjee (eds), *Routledge Handbook of Policy Design* (Taylor & Francis 2018); Michael Howlett,

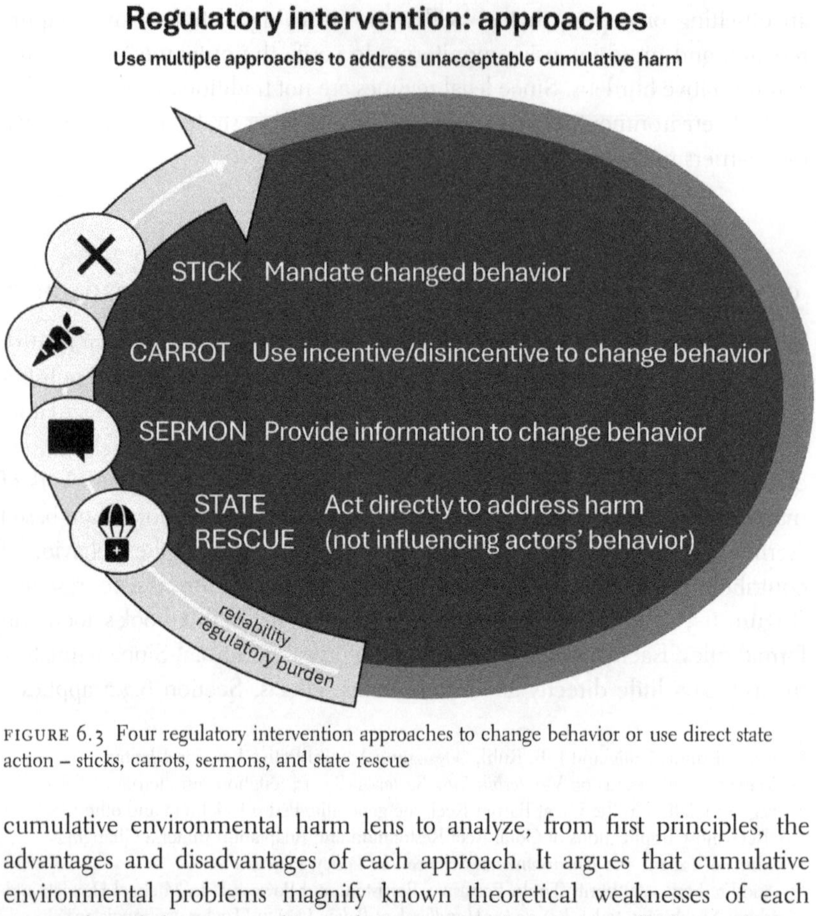

FIGURE 6.3 Four regulatory intervention approaches to change behavior or use direct state action – sticks, carrots, sermons, and state rescue

cumulative environmental harm lens to analyze, from first principles, the advantages and disadvantages of each approach. It argues that cumulative environmental problems magnify known theoretical weaknesses of each approach and that no single regulatory approach is universally best suited to dealing with cumulative environmental problems.

Designing an approach to intervention based on the categories discussed in this section depends on and links with rules for information about which actions affect the matter of concern, and are likely to do so in the future. Choosing between regulatory approaches requires information about the many heterogeneous contributors to the problem: their diverse activities; motivations; capacities to change their behavior; and the palatability to them of different regulatory approaches under different

Designing Public Policies: Principles and Instruments (2nd edn, Routledge 2019); Robert Baldwin, Martin Cave and Martin Lodge, *Understanding Regulation: Theory, Strategy, Practice* (OUP, 2nd edn, 2012); Cary Coglianese (ed), *Achieving Regulatory Excellence* (Brookings Institution Press 2017); Peter Drahos (ed), *Regulatory Theory: Foundations and Applications* (ANU 2017).

conditions.[57] In addition, coordinating actors that design and implement rules for intervention, as well as those subject to them, and affected communities, has numerous potential benefits. It can reveal the types of information just discussed, promote regulatory consistency, avoid inefficient duplication in rules, and may reveal potentially antagonistic or counterproductive rules.[58]

6.3.1 *Regulatory Sticks, Carrots, Sermons, and State Rescue*

The historically dominant (and enduringly popular[59]) approach to environmental governance is the regulatory stick used to "command and control." Traditionally, this approach involves imposing precisely specified and uniformly applied, court-enforceable obligations to control environmentally harmful behavior, supported by penalties for noncompliance.[60] Regimes might license polluting emissions, and perhaps allow licenses to be traded; prohibit or restrict specified activities or land uses in certain areas or in general; or allocate rights to access a natural resource such as water, fish, or timber.

Regulatory "carrots" use rules to incentivize behavior changes to alter environmental impacts, offering either material or symbolic incentives.[61] Rule-based subsidies, grants, and even government procurement rules reward those who undertake activities aligned with policy goals. Payments to farmers may encourage extensive pastoralism to preserve grasslands.[62] Legal rules can support conservation easements accompanied by tax benefits,[63] or confer formalized awards or other forms of praise.[64] Conversely, taxes, charges, or

57 Eric L. Windholz, *Governing through Regulation: Public Policy, Regulation and the Law* (Routledge 2018) 112–113, 192–193.

58 Ibid; see generally, P. M. Grabosky, "Counterproductive Regulation" (1995) 23 *International Journal of the Sociology of Law* 347–369. For a discussion of the regulatory function of coordination in the CIRCle Framework, see Chapter 7.

59 Neil Gunningham and Cameron Holley, "Next-Generation Environmental Regulation: Law, Regulation, and Governance" (2016) 12 *Annual Review of Law and Social Science* 273–293, 275.

60 Howlett, *Designing Public Policies*, 32, 192.

61 Frans L. Leeuw, "The Carrot: Subsidies as a Tool of Government – Theory and Practice" in Marie-Louise Bemelmans-Videc, Ray C. Rist and Evert Vedung (eds), *Carrots, Sticks and Sermons* (Transaction Publishing 1998) 77–102, 77–79. See generally P. N. Grabosky, "Regulation by Reward: On the Use of Incentives as Regulatory Instruments" (1995) 17 *Law and Policy* 257–282.

62 Section 10.4.1.2.

63 E.g., "Claiming Conservation Covenant Concessions," Australian Taxation Office (April 4, 2023) www.ato.gov.au/businesses-and-organisations/not-for-profit-organisations/gifts-and-fundraising/in-detail/fundraising/claiming-conservation-covenant-concessions, archived at https://perma.cc/FJ2J-B9TP.

64 Grabosky, "Regulation by Reward," 261–262. This might also be considered a carrot-sermon hybrid.

levies (for simplicity, "levies") direct behavior by making less harmful options cheaper, in a relative sense, consistently with the polluter pays principle[65] (I exclude charges that raise revenue without being designed to influence behavior). As discussed here, mandatory levies are not "sticks" because they do not directly mandate a change in the behavior that causes relevant harm – the contributor could pay the levy and continue their normal behavior.

Understood broadly, regulatory carrots can also encourage desired behavior in other ways. Management-based regulation obliges contributors to write plans rather than achieve substantive goals, which tends to encourage leading firms, though not laggards, to exceed minimum performance.[66] Other rules can support infrastructure that encourages behavioral change, for example, rules to promote electric vehicle charging infrastructure to encourage take-up of electric rather than gasoline vehicles.[67] Some rules pair a carrot with a stick, for example, reducing license fees for regulated activities that exceed a minimum regulatory standard.[68]

Regulatory sermons involve rules that require the state or contributors to provide information that aims to change the behavior of the information provider or receivers.[69] Such rules include requiring a state entity to run training or educational programs to persuade participants to change environmentally adverse behavior; or rules related to consumer-directed environmental information about products, including environmental certification schemes[70] or public-facing pollution

[65] Priscilla Schwartz, "The Polluter-Pays Principle" in Ludwig Krämer and Emanuela Orlando (eds), *Elgar Encyclopedia of Environmental Law, Vol VI* (Edward Elgar 2018) 260–271, 261–262 (contributors to environmental harm bear the cost of preventing or remedying the harm). The principle could also inform offset mechanisms and fees for licenses: ibid 265–267.

[66] Coglianese, "Limits of Performance-Based Regulation," 536; Gunningham and Holley, "Next-Generation Environmental Regulation," 279.

[67] E.g., see generally, Regulation (EU) 2023/1984 of the European Parliament and of the Council of September 13, 2023, on the deployment of alternative fuels infrastructure [2023] OJ L234/1.

[68] Environment Protection Authority (New South Wales), *Regulatory Policy* (2024) 31, www.epa.nsw.gov.au/Publications/About/2024p4550-Regulatory-Policy, archived at https://perma.cc/8TPD-DMUB.

[69] Chapter 5 discusses information issues not directly associated with changing behavior (e.g., a state's environmental condition reports). Note that some aspects of regulatory sermons may be enforceable, e.g., traceability recordkeeping required in relation to product labeling: e.g., Decreto Ministeriale 26 luglio 2017, n. 57167 Disposizioni nazionali per l'attuazione del regolamento (UE) n. 1151/2012 e del regolamento delegato (UE) n. 665/2014 sulle condizioni di utilizzo dell'indicazione facoltativa di qualita' «prodotto di montagna» [Ministerial Decree 57167 on national provisions for the implementation of Regulation (EU) No. 1151/2012 and Delegated Regulation (EU) No. 665/2014 on the conditions of use of the optional quality indication "mountain product"] (Italy), as amended art. 4.

[70] See generally, Thomas Vogelpohl, "Transnational Sustainability Certification for the Bioeconomy? Patterns and Discourse Coalitions of Resistance and Alternatives in Biomass Exporting Regions" (2021) 11:3 *Energy, Sustainability and Society* 1–13.

information.[71] There is growing global enthusiasm for mandatory and voluntary "environmental, social, governance" reporting and "environmental accounting" by firms and governmental units.[72] These systems recognize and publicize the economic importance of environmental assets, indirectly encouraging their protection.

Other regulatory sermons echo environmental impact assessment (EIA): The Taskforce on Nature-Related Financial Disclosures recommends that firms disclose their impacts on specific ecosystems and species, including cumulative impacts.[73] Under some circumstances, this approach may have binding force through company directors' duties.[74] Some "carrots" support "sermons," for example, incentives to provide public information about toxic releases.[75]

Finally, in some situations, rules may provide for the state to parachute in a solution to cumulative environmental harm without trying to influence the behavior of the contributors – here termed "state rescue." That is, the activities that cause impacts still happen, but the state adopts a strategy that affects the overall level of harm that results. In practice, this can be important to address harm from legacy activities that continue to cause impacts long after they have ceased being "active," or to address the impacts of activities that must continue, where the contributor lacks the capacity to change their behavior. Rules might, for example, provide for the state to remediate pollution from an abandoned mine site.[76] More controversially, rules might provide for the state

[71] E.g., Stuart Johnston Edwards and Tony R. Walker, "An Overview of Canada's National Pollutant Release Inventory Program as a Pollution Control Policy Tool" (2020) 63 *Journal of Environmental Planning and Management* 1097–1113, 1098.

[72] See generally, Rutger Hoekstra, How Natural Capital Accounting Can Help Accelerate Finance for Nature (Metrics for the Future 2022) https://seea.un.org/sites/seea.un.org/files/how-nca-can-help-accelerate-finance-for-nature.pdf; Taskforce on Nature-related Financial Disclosures, *Recommendations of the Taskforce on Nature-Related Financial Disclosures* (2023) 29–31, 122, https://tnfd.global/wp-content/uploads/2023/08/Recommendations_of_the_Taskforce_on_Nature-related_Financial_Disclosures_September_2023.pdf.

[73] Taskforce on Nature-related Financial Disclosures, *Recommendations of the TNFD*, 29–31, 122.

[74] Sebastian Hartford-Davis and Zoe Bush, Joint Memorandum of Opinion: Nature-Related Risks and Directors' Duties (October 24, 2023) 1–3, https://commonwealthclimatelaw.org/wp-content/uploads/2023/11/Joint-Memorandum-of-Opinion-Nature-related-risks-and-directors-duties.pdf.

[75] See generally, Robert Innes and Abdoul G. Sam, "Voluntary Pollution Reductions and the Enforcement of Environmental Law: An Empirical Study of the 33/50 Program" (2008) 51 *Journal of Law and Economics* 271–296 (where the primary, implicit, incentive was reduced inspections and enforcement proceedings, together with technical assistance).

[76] E.g., under the Comprehensive Environmental Response, Compensation and Liability Act, 42 U.S.C. §§ 9601–9675: U.S. Environmental Protection Agency, "Abandoned Mine Land and Federal Facilities" (2024) www.epa.gov/enforcement/abandoned-mine-land-and-federal-facilities, archived at https://perma.cc/M243-YVVU.

to undertake geoengineering to remove carbon dioxide[77] if regulatory approaches to influencing the behavior of greenhouse polluters fail.

6.3.2 *Assessing Regulatory Approaches*

Regulatory literature finds clear differences in how reliably sticks, carrots, and sermons achieve policy goals, and their regulatory cost, which is influenced by how flexibly they apply to heterogeneous regulated entities.[78] This section applies a cumulative environmental harm lens to these issues, assessing the advantages and disadvantages of each approach from this perspective.

Regulatory sticks are traditionally perceived as rigid and inefficient, imposing uniform obligations (e.g., technology standards)[79] on entities with varying costs of compliance.[80] However, they offer certainty for regulated entities[81] and relatively high outcome reliability if well enforced. In practice, though, regulatory sticks can be more flexible than they appear due to "pervasive" negotiation between regulators and regulated entities.[82] This not only reduces burdens for diverse contributors with the resources to negotiate but may also make enforcement more variable and affect the reliability of environmental outcomes.

Contemporary "sticks" use design features that do a better job of accommodating the diverse contributors typical of cumulative environmental problems.[83] Performance-based or outcomes-based regulation increases flexibility and reduces costs for contributors[84] by letting them choose how they achieve preset goals, sometimes through collaborating with other contributors.[85] However, the fact that obligations vary may make monitoring and enforcing performance more burdensome.[86] Reliability also decreases if standards are loosely specified (which increases decision-makers' discretion), or if

77 E.g., see generally, Jan McDonald and others, "Greenhouse Gas Removal in Australian Climate Law: A Positive Role for Negative Emissions" (2023) 46 *UNSW Law Journal* 79–110.
78 E.g., Coglianese, "Limits of Performance-Based Regulation," 532, 545.
79 Gunningham and Holley, "Next-Generation Environmental Regulation," 276.
80 Robert N. Stavins, "The Problem of the Commons: Still Unsettled after 100 Years" (2011) 101 *The American Economic Review* 81–108, 94; Dave Owen, "The Negotiable Implementation of Environmental Law" (2023) 75 *Stanford Law Review* 137–203, 145–149.
81 Gunningham and Holley, "Next-Generation Environmental Regulation," 277.
82 Owen, "The Negotiable Implementation of Environmental Law," 153–184.
83 Gunningham and Holley, "Next-Generation Environmental Regulation," 278–279.
84 Coglianese, "Limits of Performance-Based Regulation," 532, 545.
85 Therivel and Ross, "Cumulative Effects Assessment," 368.
86 Coglianese, "Limits of Performance-Based Regulation," 549–550, 558–549. See Chapter 5 in relation to information about enforcement.

performance is specified as averages across multiple sites[87] (which may inadvertently cause significant localized cumulative harm).[88]

Regulatory carrots and sermons tend to be more palatable to governments and regulated entities than regulatory sticks because accepting an incentive and changing behavior in response to a levy or information is voluntary.[89] Nonetheless, participants must still expend effort to understand the rules. The state may also bear significant burdens in designing, monitoring, and enforcing the regime to ensure that participants deliver incentivized benefits, pay levies, and provide accurate information.[90] However, information-based instruments may cost less to administer than sticks or carrots.[91] The state generally pays for incentives, the costs of which are inefficient if recipients would have acted in the desired way anyway,[92] but gains revenue from levies.

However, carrots and sermons are also theoretically less reliable than well-enforced regulatory sticks because their voluntariness means they may cause fewer contributors to change their behavior than needed to ensure cumulative harm is acceptable.[93] Among diverse contributors, some will lack interest, willingness, or capacity to respond to monetary or, probably to a greater extent, information-based motivations.[94] Sometimes, individual nonparticipant "holdouts" in incentive schemes may significantly reduce outcome reliability if they compromise goals that depend on high participation in specific spatial areas for ecological reasons, such as habitat corridors.[95]

State rescue emerges with quite a different report card. Since it does not try to change contributors' behavior, it does not represent a burden for them, but it does for the state – and perhaps a significant one. Reliability-wise, the same considerations do not arise as for the other approaches because state rescue does not depend on the actions of non-state contributors. Rather, outcome

87 E.g., Charles Halvorson, "Deflated Dreams: The EPA's Bubble Policy and the Politics of Uncertainty in Regulatory Reform" (2019) 93 *Business History Review* 25–49.

88 Coglianese, "Limits of Performance-Based Regulation," 537–541 (describing many variables in specifying performance standards).

89 E.g., Brian Murray and Jonas Monast, "Carrots, Sticks, and the Evolution of U.S. Climate Policy" (2024) 11 *Texas A&M Law Review* 431–450, 447.

90 Gunningham and Holley, "Next-Generation Environmental Regulation," 280.

91 Yayun Shen and Michael Faure, "Behavioural Instruments in Environmental Law and Policy: Potential and Challenges" (2024) 33 *Review of European, Comparative and International Environmental Law* 3–18, 7–8.

92 Leeuw, "The Carrot," 79–80.

93 Gunningham and Holley, "Next-Generation Environmental Regulation," 279.

94 Ibid 280; Shen and Faure, "Behavioural Instruments," 10–11.

95 E.g., Edwin Alblas and Josephine van Zeben, "'Farming out' Biodiversity: Implementing EU Nature Law through Agri-Environmental Schemes" (2023) 17:100180 *Earth System Governance* 1–10, 6.

reliability suffers if there are gaps or weaknesses in the capability of the state to deliver the "rescue" solution. This might happen because of overstretched budgets, changes in political appetite to act, and the like. Depending entirely on state rescue also means relying entirely on the state to deal with potential increases in cumulative harms from contributors, which are not subject to intervention in a direct way.

Overall, well-enforced regulatory sticks provide greater scope reliably to change the behavior of heterogeneous contributors to cumulative environmental harm, in exchange for imposing higher burdens on some of them and confronting potentially higher associated political and social barriers. The voluntariness of carrots and sermons involves lower burdens for contributors, who retain the option of not changing their behavior, but for the same reason, these approaches produce less reliable outcomes. State rescue removes burdens from contributors to the problem and places it on the state, exposing reliable outcomes to risks from politics and government budgets rather than contributors' failure to act. This high-level assessment of reliability is naturally premised on important assumptions about enforcement and acceptability. These factors need to be considered in a local context, perhaps including, as discussed earlier, harnessing coordination with stakeholders representing regulated entities and affected communities.[96]

6.4 MIXING REGULATORY INTERVENTIONS FOR CUMULATIVE ENVIRONMENTAL PROBLEMS

Real-world regulatory interventions are more complex than an individual strategy or approach, firstly, because a single mechanism for intervention combines both elements, and secondly, because addressing a cumulative environmental problem likely requires more than one type of intervention. This section discusses each of these issues in turn.

6.4.1 *A Matrix of Strategies and Approaches*

Combining regulatory strategies (Section 6.2) and approaches (Section 6.3) produces a matrix of theoretical modes of regulatory interventions. Table 6.1 gives corresponding examples, showing that sticks, carrots, and sermons are each flexible enough to accommodate the full range of harm-reducing, offsetting, restoring, and coping strategies. State rescue may apply to the last three approaches (since, as conceived here, state rescue involves the state

96 See paragraph preceding Section 6.3.1. See also Section 6.5.2.3 regarding enforcement.

TABLE 6.1 *Options for increasing diversity of regulatory interventions: four strategies and four approaches to address cumulative environmental problems, with characteristics and examples.*

Approaches/ strategies	Mandating (Stick)	Incentivizing (Carrot)	Informing and persuading (Sermon)	State rescue
Harm-reducing	Reduce plastic pollution by limiting production of single-use plastic items (Vanuatu)[a]	Reduce total water withdrawals by buying and retiring farmers' water rights (Australia) [b]	Reduce air pollution via mandated emissions disclosure (Canada) [c]	N/A
Harm-offsetting (for contemporary impacts)	Reduce net biodiversity loss by requiring developers to offset loss[d] in one place by gain in another (Uganda)[e]	Reduce net wetland loss by facilitating aggregated wetland restoration through for-profit "banking" (US)[f]	Reduce net greenhouse gas emissions using a voluntary public "net zero" reporting framework (Australia)[g]	Reduce net groundwater depletion from ongoing groundwater pumping by the state undertaking aquifer recharge (Spain)[h]
Restoring (for past impacts)	Remediate legacy soil contamination by imposing obligation to remediate on landowner, even if they did not cause contamination (Japan).[i]	Restore biodiversity by providing incentives to landowners to rewet peatland (European Union).[j]	(Indirectly) counter urban heat islands by reporting on cool green spaces using ecosystem accounting to inform investment in further spaces (Australia)[k]	Reduce pollution by the state remediating abandoned mine sites (US).[l]
Coping	Require gas developers to "make good" effects on landowners affected by groundwater level declines drying up their wells (Australia)[m]	Assist species to disperse to cope with climate change by paying farmers to connect habitat (UK)[n]	Assist communities to adapt to climate change by requiring agency to publish climate vulnerability atlases (Mexico)[o]	Assist communities to cope with sea level rise using rules that facilitate the state building a sea wall (Maldives).[p]

TABLE 6.1 (*continued*)

Key: Arrows indicate the direction in which the intervention approach or strategy tends to involve (all else being equal) more reliable outcomes, less voluntariness, and a higher burden for contributors to harm

[a] Waste Management Regulations Order No. 15 of 2018 (Vanuatu) s 2.

[b] Rebecca Nelson, "Breaking Backs and Boiling Frogs: Warnings from a Dialogue between Federal Water Law and Environmental Law" (2019) 42 *University of New South Wales Law Journal* 1179–1214, 1209–1210.

[c] Canadian Environmental Protection Act 1999 (Canada) ss 46–50; Government of Canada, "National Pollutant Release Inventory" (n.d.) www.canada.ca/en/services/environment/pollution-waste-management/national-pollutant-release-inventory.html, archived at https://perma.cc/WC2A-8S9M. See also Johnston Edwards and Walker, "An Overview of Canada's National Pollutant Release Inventory Program."

[d] See generally, Sonter and others, "Offsetting Impacts."

[e] National Environment Act 2019 (Uganda) ss 115, 122 (2)(d), 179 (2)(c).

[f] J. B. Ruhl and James Salzman, "No Net Loss? The Past, Present, and Future of Wetlands Mitigation Banking" (2022) 73 *Case Western Reserve Law Review* 411–439, 420–422, 428–429.

[g] Clean Energy Regulatory (Australia), "Corporate Emissions Reduction Transparency Report 2023" (2024) https://cer.gov.au/markets/reports-and-data/corporate-emissions-reduction-transparency-report/corporate-emissions-0, archived at https://perma.cc/CU53-TU9Y.

[h] Jose David Henao Casas and others, "Managed Aquifer Recharge as a Low-Regret Measure for Climate Change Adaptation: Insights from Los Arenales, Spain" (2022) 14:3703 *Water* 1–22. This is formally facilitated under a royal decree: ibid 4. Another example is state provision of coral-friendly public vessel moorings on the Great Barrier Reef to reduce damage from anchoring: Minister for the Environment and the Great Barrier Reef, Minister for Science and Minister for Multicultural Affairs, "New Moorings Enhance Protection for the Great Barrier Reef" (Media statement, November 16, 2023) https://statements.qld.gov.au/statements/99162, archived at https://perma.cc/3NNE-G9PV.

[i] 土壌汚染対策法 [Soil Contamination Countermeasures Act] 2002 (Japan), as amended, art. 7(1); Miho Ishimaki, "Soil Protection Law in Japan" in Harald Ginzky and others (eds), *International Yearbook of Soil Law and Policy 2022* (Springer 2024) 227–242, 237–238. Obligations to remediate others' pollution may also be imposed under negotiated conditions of water pollution discharge permits in the US: e.g., Rhett Larson, "Orphaned Pollution" (2013) 45 *Arizona State Law Journal* 991–1032, 1001–1004.

[j] EU Nature Restoration Law 2024, art. 11.

[k] Phil Cryle and others, *Practical Guidance Notes for Urban Ecosystem Accounting: A Draft Report by Working Group on Urban Ecosystem Accounting in Australia*, Prepared for the Interjurisdictional Environmental-Economic Accounting Steering Committee (2021) 70, www.dcceew.gov.au/sites/default/files/documents/practical-guidance-notes-urban-ecosystem-accounting.pdf, archived at https://perma.cc/52D2-PR2Y.

[l] See n 76.

TABLE 6.1 (*continued*)

[m] Water Act 2000 (Queensland) s 409; see Rebecca Nelson, "Regulating Cumulative Impacts in Groundwater Systems: Global Lessons from the Australian Experience" in Cameron Holley and Darren Sinclair (eds), *Reforming Water Law and Governance: From Stagnation to Innovation in Australia* (Springer 2018) 237–256, 246–248.

[n] Department for Environment, Food and Rural Affairs (UK), "Environmental Land Management (ELM) Update: How Government Will Pay for Land-Based Environment and Climate Goods and Services" (2023) www.gov.uk/government/publications/environmental-land-management-update-how-government-will-pay-for-land-based-environment-and-climate-goods-and-services/environmental-land-management-elm-update-how-government-will-pay-for-land-based-environment-and-climate-goods-and-services, archived at https://perma.cc/QFD8-2C3R.

[o] Marco Heredia and Beatriz Corral, "Climate Governance and Federalism in Mexico" in Alan Fenna, Sébastien Jodoin and Joana Setzer (eds), *Climate Governance and Federalism: A Forum of Federations Comparative Policy Analysis* (CUP 2023) 218–240, 228.

[p] Geronimo Gussmann and Jochen Hinkel, "A Framework for Assessing the Potential Effectiveness of Adaptation Policies: Coastal Risks and Sea-Level Rise in the Maldives" (2021) 115 *Environmental Science and Policy* 35–42, 39–40; Environment Protection and Preservation Act of Maldives 1993 (Maldives) s 3 (providing for guidelines); *Guidelines for Climate Risk Resilient Coastal Protection in the Maldives* (2015) www.environment.gov.mv/v2/en/download/13722, archived at https://perma.cc/GR3W-KW5G.

acting in respect of others' harms; if the state directly causes harm, it is a contributor, and rules that adopt any of the four approaches could apply). However, the relative difficulty of finding examples that pursue some forms of coping strategy and sermon approach (Table 6.1) suggests anecdotally that these categories are less developed.

Overall, this matrix suggests that more modes of intervening are available to address cumulative environmental problems than are commonly recognized, and that some common concepts and categories contain more diverse ways of intervening than is first apparent. Take "market-based mechanisms." The term can refer to diverse things: a water rights market that allows governments to "buy back" rights to reduce aggregate consumptive withdrawals to sustainable levels (reducing harm);[97] permits that allow "trading" of protected habitat for habitat that will be harmed by a development (offsetting harm);[98] and a project condition that requires a project proponent to pay into a fund to develop heat-tolerant coral (coping).[99] Each provides economic incentives to contributors, and is likely to be more politically palatable than a regulatory stick alone. However, the merits of a market in regulating a cumulative environmental problem cannot be assessed without understanding *how* the market is used to change cumulative harm – the *strategy*. For the reasons discussed earlier, the harm-reducing strategy of the water rights market will more reliably achieve the desired aggregate outcome than the harm-offsetting strategy of habitat trading or the coping strategy of developing heat-tolerant coral. The matrix, then, allows for a more nuanced view of the risks of a particular intervention in addressing cumulative environmental problems.

The matrix also demonstrates how the choice of regulatory approach and strategy can exacerbate risks where both the approach and the strategy attract the same type of risk. This helps highlight when regulatory designers should pay special attention to making sure that a rule includes features to help combat the challenges that arise. Take burdens to contributors. The combination of regulatory approach and regulatory strategy can exacerbate these burdens (highest at upper left side, Table 6.1). In this case, regulatory designers have comparatively higher need to consider ways to reduce costs to ensure a rule is politically and socially palatable.

97 Daniel H. Cole, "Explaining the Persistence of 'Command-and-Control' in US Environmental Law" in Kenneth R. Richards and Josephine van Zeben (eds), *Elgar Encyclopedia of Environmental Law* Vol. VIII (Edward Elgar 2020) 157–169, 157.

98 J. B. Ruhl, "Regulation by Adaptive Management – Is It Possible?" (2005–2006) 7 *Minnesota Journal of Law Science and Technology* 21–57, 43–46.

99 See Section 9.5.3.

Conversely, consider risks associated with reliably addressing cumulative impacts, that is, risks to outcome reliability (highest at lower right side, Table 6.1). Rules that take a carrot approach, for example, entail a relatively high risk to outcome reliability in influencing the behavior of contributors. A rule that sought to incentivize an unproven coping strategy would compound this risk with the further risk that even successful behavior change would not result in the desired ultimate effect – that the matter of concern could cope with higher cumulative impacts without experiencing unacceptable harm. Here, regulatory designers have comparatively higher need to use rules for intervening adaptively[100] to deal with these risks. Another way to address these realizations of heightened risk is to use a mix of regulatory interventions, so that mechanisms that are highly risky on one parameter are balanced by less-risky regulatory options – the topic to which we now move.

6.4.2 *The Need for a Mix of Regulatory Interventions*

Over two decades of scholarship argues that "policy mixes" offer flexibility and backup where one approach proves less effective, and help to accommodate conditions of uncertainty, complexity, and different types of target actors.[101] As suggested earlier, this rationale also supports using a mix of interventions that adopt different regulatory approaches and strategies to address cumulative environmental problems, for which these conditions are prominent.

Cumulative environmental problems have characteristics that inherently suggest a mix of regulatory interventions, either used concurrently or adaptively in sequence,[102] is likely to be more effective than a single strategy and approach. Firstly, contributors are heterogeneous, with different motivations, capacities to change behavior, and types of impact. This changes their receptivity to different regulatory designs. Individual petrol vehicle drivers, cattle farmers, and coal-burning electricity generators all produce greenhouse gas emissions, but their diversity requires different regulatory designs. A single rule or even type of rule could not conceivably address the many types of impact that affect the Great Barrier Reef: water pollution,

[100] See Section 6.5.4.

[101] Raul Pacheco-Vega, "Environmental Regulation, Governance, and Policy Instruments, 20 Years after the Stick, Carrot, and Sermon Typology" (2020) 22 *Journal of Environmental Policy and Planning* 620–635, 622–625; John Braithwaite, "Regulatory Mix, Collective Efficacy, and Crimes of the Powerful" (2020) 1 *Journal of White Collar and Corporate Crime* 62–71, 69.

[102] See Section 6.5.4 regarding adaptive interventions.

climate change, growth in invasive species, direct damage to habitat and fauna from vessels, and so on.[103]

Secondly, from a pragmatic view, cumulative environmental problems will inevitably involve a mix of interventions. These problems tend to engage multiple levels of government,[104] and even single levels of government often use multiple regulatory approaches, creating a regulatory mix across levels.[105] Reform costs and path dependence mean it will rarely be possible to engage in a regulatory "revolution" to wipe clean an existing regulatory slate and start again.[106] Regulatory mixes are also often inevitable as a result of "policy layering" over time,[107] so improving how they perform is critical. This highlights the value of being aware of potential weaknesses of each approach in a cumulative context and designing regulation in a way that combats these weaknesses. Combining interventions from the same corner of the matrix risks compounding disadvantages, whereas selecting interventions from across the matrix provides for counteracting risks.

Thirdly, theories of "smart regulation" and "new environmental governance" suggest that complex, dynamic environmental problems with low availability of centralized knowledge[108] benefit from engaging nongovernment regulatory actors and adaptively escalating to more interventionist approaches as needed.[109] This requires multiple regulatory approaches, both to allow for escalation and because different types of interventions will suit different nongovernment regulatory actors. Coordination with nongovernment actors is discussed in more detail in a later chapter.[110]

Finally, a mix of interventions can help address some key reasons why it is hard to deal with cumulative environmental problems.[111] Voluntary measures can surmount political and social to regulatory sticks, the ethical ambiguity of dealing with individually small actions, and causal uncertainty. Combining voluntary approaches with backup "sticks" helps reduce reliability risks of voluntary approaches. Combining strategies can help avoid similar problems.

[103] See Figure 9.1.
[104] See Section 2.2.4.1.
[105] Christopher Taylor and others, "Selecting Policy Instruments for Better Environmental Regulation: A Critique and Future Research Agenda" (2012) 22 *Environmental Policy and Governance* 268–292, 282.
[106] See generally, Cole, "Explaining the Persistence of 'Command-and-Control'."
[107] Michael Howlett, Ishani Mukherjee and Jeremy Rayner, "Understanding Policy Designs over Time: Layering, Stretching, Patching and Packaging" in Michael Howlett and Ishani Mukherjee (eds), *Routledge Handbook of Policy Design* (Taylor & Francis 2018) 136–144, 137 (citations omitted).
[108] Gunningham and Holley, "Next-Generation Environmental Regulation," 284.
[109] Ibid 280–281.
[110] See Chapter 7 ("Coordination").
[111] See Section 6.1 for a summary, and Section 2.2.3 for a fuller discussion.

In the Murray-Darling Basin, Australia, legal rules support a harm-reducing strategy, whereby governments "buy back" water rights from farmers to reduce aggregate water withdrawals to an "environmentally sustainable level of take."[112] Farmers lobbied to add a less burdensome but more costly coping strategy, now implemented through rules for artificially watering wetlands and using infrastructure to help ecosystems cope with less water.[113]

At the same time, as for other types of problems, mixes of interventions to deal with cumulative environmental problems must be designed with potential antagonistic effects in mind.[114] This issue is addressed further in Chapter 7 (Coordination).

Though compelling arguments support using a mix of regulatory interventions to regulate cumulative environmental problems, existing literature provides little guidance on designing them to deal with these problems, and calls for empirical testing.[115] Chapters 9 and 10 examine the way that combinations of regulatory interventions address case studies of cumulative environmental problems in Australia (the Great Barrier Reef) and Italy (Alpine grasslands).

6.5 CROSSCUTTING DESIGN FEATURES

Even a mix of carefully chosen interventions may strike significant challenges in addressing cumulative environmental problems. The effectiveness of tools for dealing with cumulative impacts can be compromised by various challenges – disconnected decision-making and legal silos, loopholes in coverage, excessive cost to administer, and difficulty adapting to changed circumstances.[116] This section takes up the issue of design features that cut across regulatory strategies and approaches to address these challenges.

Each section starts with a reflection on connections between the relevant challenge and the matrix of interventions advanced earlier, and then illustrates the diversity of potential regulatory design solutions with real-world examples.

6.5.1 *Connected Decision-Making*

To the already significant list of challenges related to intervention discussed in Chapter 2, law itself adds another: fragmented decision-making and laws that

[112] See Nelson, "Breaking Backs" and note b to Table 6.1.

[113] Water Act 2007 (Australia) ss 23A, 23B, 28–31; Basin Plan 2012 (Australia) ss 7.09–7.27; Nelson, "Breaking Backs," 1209–1210.

[114] See n 58.

[115] Gunningham and Holley, "Next-Generation Environmental Regulation," 281, 284.

[116] See Section 2.2.3.

consider sectors, impacts, and actions in isolation, unconnected to the effects of other actions that aggregate to affect the same matter of concern. Scholars and governments alike frequently observe that environment-related law comprises "hard, impermeable, organizational and institutional silos that prevent coordination or integration of laws and policies across systems and scales," or complaints to that effect, across diverse jurisdictions.[117] This is a key problem for addressing cumulative impacts: Taking a blinkered view of individual impacts in isolation does not reveal their cumulative context, and misrepresents their significance to decision-makers and the public.[118]

Legal mechanisms can "connect" decision-making about an individual action to other relevant actions in three key ways: requiring consideration of cumulative environmental principles ("principles"), applying aggregate limits and targets for impact ("limits") that will take effect immediately or in the future,[119] or using comprehensive management plans and strategic assessments ("plans") that assess how multiple existing and new impacts accumulate in a region.[120] Limits should relate to the cumulative threshold conditions for the matter of concern,[121] ensuring that this threshold is not crossed. Rules should also connect across impact types relevant to a matter of concern. Where the matter of concern is the ecological health of a water resource, carefully managing river flows but ignoring problematic invasive species will not produce the desired result.[122] Making these connections across impact

[117] Craig Anthony Arnold, "Environmental Law, Episode IV: A New Hope: Can Environmental Law Adapt for Resilient Communities and Ecosystems" (2015) 21 *Journal of Environmental and Sustainability Law* 1–46, 15. See also, e.g., European Environment Agency, *The European Environment – State and Outlook 2020: Knowledge for Transition to a Sustainable Europe* (2019) 374–375, www.eea.europa.eu/en/analysis/publications/soer-2020/soer-2020/@@download/file, archived at https://perma.cc/D33K-7G3Q; Nelson, "Breaking Backs," 1188; generally Margaret A. Young, "Fragmentation" in Lavanya Rajamani and Jacqueline Peel (eds), *The Oxford Handbook of International Environmental Law* (OUP 2021) 86–101.

[118] Rebecca Nelson and L. M. Shirley, "The Latent Potential of Cumulative Effects Concepts in National and International Environmental Impact Assessment Regimes" (2023) 12 *Transnational Environmental Law* 150–174, 152.

[119] E.g., Great Britain's zero emission vehicle mandate, which will phase out sales of non-zero emission cars and vans: Holly Edwards, Iona Stewart, Becky Mawhood and Paul Bolton, Electric Vehicles and Infrastructure, Commons Library Research Briefing CBP-7480 (UK House of Commons, July 12, 2024) 27–28, https://researchbriefings.files.parliament.uk/documents/CBP-7480/CBP-7480.pdf.

[120] For a discussion of different kinds of strategic environmental assessment (SEA), see Bram Noble and Kelechi Nwanekezie, "Conceptualizing Strategic Environmental Assessment: Principles, Approaches and Research Directions" (2017) 62 *Environmental Impact Assessment Review* 165–173, 167–170.

[121] For a discussion on cumulative threshold conditions, see Section 4.3.3.

[122] Rebecca Nelson, "Challenges to Improved Integrated Management of the Murray-Darling Basin" in Barry Hart and others (eds), *Murray-Darling Basin, Australia: Its Future*

types is feasible using principles and plans, but more difficult for limits unless the limit uses an index that aggregates different kinds of impacts, such as cultural health indices, cumulative exposure maps for ecosystems, or environmental justice index maps.[123] Table 6.2 gives illustrative examples of these "connecting" tools across different regulatory approaches.

Specificity and clarity are key to these approaches. Principles need policy guidance to encourage effective implementation and to constrain administrative discretion to avoid inconsistent approaches between individual decisions,[124] supported by adequate public sector capacity. Clearer and more specific limits provide greater certainty, for example, quantitatively rather than qualitatively expressed limits (though the former have the disadvantage of requiring intentional amendment to adapt to new circumstances). Notably, unlike targets for impacts, targets for positive actions (which adopt an offsetting or restoring strategy), without more, do not directly address cumulative harm because negative impacts may continue growing. Targets for renewable energy sources,[125] in contrast to regulatory carbon budgets,[126] demonstrate this difference.

To ensure that limits and plans influence and link individual actions, rather than "stay on the shelf,"[127] rules should apply limits and plans to project approvals,[128] or risk them being used inconsistently or overlooked entirely in the context of new projects.[129] Conversely, approval processes for individual

Management (Elsevier 2021) 339–361, 351. See Chapter 9 (Great Barrier Reef) for analysis that contrasts treatment of different activities and impact types (coal mining and cattle grazing; water pollution and climate change).

123 See Section 4.3.3 (cultural health indicators); Table 6.2, row 1; Section 9.4.2 (cumulative exposure of the Great Barrier Reef).

124 Melissa M. Foley and others, "The Challenges and Opportunities in Cumulative Effects Assessment" (2017) 62 *Environmental Impact Assessment Review* 122–134, 128.

125 E.g., Directive 2018/2001 of the European Parliament and of the Council of December 11, 2018 on the promotion of the use of energy from renewable sources [2018] OJ L328/82, as amended, art. 3 (targets for share of energy to be derived from renewable sources).

126 E.g., Ron Levy, "Fixed Constitutional Commitments: Evaluating Environmental Constitutionalism's 'New Frontier'" (2022) 46 *Melbourne University Law Review* 82–122, n 11 and accompanying text (five-yearly UK carbon budgets).

127 Nataly Escobedo Garcia and Nicola Ulibarri, "Plan Writing as a Policy Tool: Instrumental, Conceptual, and Tactical Uses of Water Management Plans in California" (2022) 12 *Journal of Environmental Studies and Sciences* 475–489, 484.

128 See generally, Riki Therivel and Ainhoa González, "'Ripe for Decision': Tiering in Environmental Assessment" (2021) 87:106520 *Environmental Impact Assessment Review* 1–10. See Chapter 9 (Great Barrier Reef, Section 9.5.1) for an example of a relative lack of clarity under the Cumulative Impacts Management Policy.

129 Julia Dehm, "Coal Mines, Carbon Budgets and Human Rights in Australian Climate Litigation: Reflections on *Gloucester Resources Limited v Minister for Planning and Environment*" (2020) 26 *Australian Journal of Human Rights* 244–273, 253–254.

TABLE 6.2 *Mechanisms for connected decision-making about cumulative environmental impacts*

Legal mechanism	Illustrative examples
Cumulative environmental principle	Grants under California's statutory Transformative Climate Communities program (a "carrot" that incentivizes projects to reduce greenhouse gas emissions and achieve other community benefits) are prioritized for communities that face significant cumulative environmental burdens based on the CalEnviroScreen cumulative environmental justice tool.[a] This tool "connects" across several types of impacts, including multiple dimensions of air and water pollution, traffic, and solid waste, but omits water sustainability issues that could compromise access to water.[b]
Limit that requires reduced impacts	Danish building regulations employ a progressively decreasing limit on the embodied carbon of new buildings.[c]
Target for restoration	Kenyan environmental law seeks to "achieve and maintain a tree cover of at least ten per cent of the land area of Kenya," which is pursued by measures including a system of payments for ecosystem services.[d]
Qualitative limits on aggregate effects	A legal right to a healthy environment implicitly caps adverse impacts to a level that remains "healthy" but leaves for case-by-case determination key elements like the boundaries of the "environment," for whom it must be healthy, and whether proportionality justifies limiting a right, e.g., if beneficial effects of a limitation to the right outweighs its negative effects.[e]
Plan that manages aggregate effects on natural resources	Withdrawals of water in Australia's Murray-Darling Basin must reflect an "environmentally sustainable level of take" that is quantified in a federal regulatory "Basin Plan," which constrains state-administered water allocation regimes. The limit may be reached by reducing withdrawals and may be changed by measures that increase coping capacity.[f] The Basin Plan connects across water quality and water quantity impact types, but is constrained in considering impacts associated with land use.[g]
Link between strategic and project-level assessment	Strategic assessment of land use plans (as is required by European law, for example) inherently involves tiering between the assessment, the land use plan, and the authorizations given for development under

Legal mechanism	Illustrative examples
	the plan, which may themselves require project-level environmental impact assessment (EIA); this context has produced a cumulative effects-focused strategic assessment of zoning options for the peri-urban areas of Milan, Italy.[h]

[a] California Statutes 2012 ch 830 (SB 535) §§ 2–4; California Strategic Growth Council, Transformative Climate Communities Program Round 5 Final Program Guidelines FY 2022–2023 (2023), 9, 13, 31, https://sgc.ca.gov/grant-programs/tcc/docs/20240906-TCC_Round_5_Guidelines .pdf, archived at https://perma.cc/77MT-A5WQ. See also Chapter 10 note 92 and accompanying text.
[b] See generally, Lauren Zeise and Jared Blumenfeld, *CalEnviroScreen 4.0* (California Environmental Protection Agency 2021) https://oehha.ca.gov/media/downloads/calenviroscreen/report/calenviroscreen40reportf2021.pdf, archived at https://perma.cc/8YG9-FXCQ. See also Section 8.3.2.2.
[c] Freja Nygaard Rasmussen and others, "Embodied Carbon in Building Regulation – Development and Implementation in Finland, Sweden and Denmark" in Rahman Azari and Alice Moncaster (eds), *The Routledge Handbook of Embodied Carbon in the Built Environment* (Routledge 2023) 85–102, 87; Minister of Social Affairs and Housing (Denmark), "New Agreement Sets Ambitious Climate Requirements for New Construction" (Press release, May 30, 2024) www.sm.dk/nyheder/nyhedsarkiv/2024/maj/ny-aftale-stiller-ambitioese-klimakrav-til-nyt-byggeri, archived at https://perma.cc/84BZ-8GE8.
[d] Environmental Management and Co-ordination Act 1999 Cap. 387, as amended (Kenya), ss 9(2)(q), (r); Gordana Petrovska Dojchinovska and Alex Lyons, "Natural Resources Management in Kenya (Water and Forest): Centralised Policies, Between Exclusion and Participation of the Local Population" in Marie-Aude Fouéré, Marie-Emmanuelle Pommerolle and Christian Thibon (eds), *Kenya in Motion 2000–2020* (AfricaE, 2021) 223–248, 231–234.
[e] For issues relevant to proportionality assessment, see Grant Huscroft, Bradley W. Miller and Grégoire Webber (eds), *Proportionality and the Rule of Law: Rights, Justification, Reasoning* (CUP 2014).
[f] See note *b* to Table 6.1 and accompanying text in table.
[g] See generally, Nelson, "Challenges to Improved Integrated Management."
[h] Ainhoa González, "Strategic Environmental Assessment of Spatial Land-Use Plans" in Thomas B. Fischer and Ainhoa González (eds), *Handbook on Strategic Environmental Assessment* (Edward Elgar 2021) 142–163, 158–159; see generally, Chiara Bragagnolo and Davide Geneletti, "Dealing with Land Use Decisions in Uncertain Contexts: A Method to Support Strategic Environmental Assessment of Spatial Plans" (2014) 57 *Journal of Environmental Planning and Management* 50–77.

projects should trigger the formulation of a limit or plan where the process reveals potentially unacceptable accumulating harm (two-way influence termed "tiering").[130]

[130] Therivel and González, "'Ripe for Decision': Tiering." For a more comprehensive summary of the relationships between tiers, see Thomas B. Fischer, "Strategic Environmental Assessment and Transport Planning: Towards a Generic Framework for Evaluating Practice and Developing Guidance" (2006) 24 *Impact Assessment and Project Appraisal* 183–197, 189.

6.5.2 *Comprehensiveness: Regulatory Coverage and Enforcement*

To avoid the risk of unregulated, cumulative harm, a set of regulatory interventions must comprehensively – that is, without "gaps" in regulatory coverage – consider all activities capable of causing cumulatively significant impacts to a matter of concern. Gaps can stem from how the coverage of a regulatory intervention is specified, and how it is enforced. Imagine that activities in categories A, B, C, and D accumulate to harm a matter of concern. A rule may be specified, or interpreted, to apply only to categories A and B, allowing category C and D activities to cause unregulated cumulative impacts (a "gap by omission"). Or, the rule may be specified to apply to all activities other than category D activities, which are intentionally exempt (a "gap by exemption"). Finally, inadequate enforcement and inadequate response to voluntary tools may mean that some activities in one or more categories may cause cumulatively significant impacts in practice, even if many rules are in place. The discussion that follows considers regulatory design solutions to each of these types of gaps. Coordination mechanisms are necessary to deal with gaps that would emerge because a regulator lacks jurisdiction to cover all relevant impacts; I address this separately later in the book.[131]

6.5.2.1 Gaps by Omission

Gaps by omission arise in many ways. Rules may cover only specific sectors or types of actions, only some types of relevant impacts, or only direct human activities and not other impacts or "background effects" that are difficult to attribute to individual actors, such as invasive species and wildfire.[132] Limits that are expressed per person do not prevent overshoot of a cumulative target caused by population growth. Interventions may apply to actions above specified size thresholds, missing the cumulative impacts of smaller actions, for example, laws that require EIA for "intensive rearing of poultry ... with more than ... 60 000 places for hens"[133] Most significantly, individual rules or an entire area of law (like land use planning) may apply only to new activities, overlooking the ongoing impacts of existing activities. Table 6.3 sets out examples of diverse ways to avoid and reduce gaps by omission. In each case, the mechanism is specified

[131] See Chapter 7 on Coordination.

[132] Nelson, "Challenges to Improved Integrated Management," 351–352.

[133] Directive 2011/92/EU of the European Parliament and of the Council of December 13, 2011, on the assessment of the effects of certain public and private projects on the environment [2012] OJ L26/1, as amended, art. 4(1), annex I point 17(a).

TABLE 6.3 *Mechanisms for comprehensive regulatory intervention: avoiding gaps by omission*

Legal mechanism	Illustrative examples
Environmental impact assessment (EIA) requirements determined by considering cumulative impacts	Under the EU EIA Directive's "screening process," EIA requirements apply to listed project types, and additional projects, taking into consideration certain criteria, including "the cumulation of the impact with the impact of other existing and/or approved projects."[a] This approach covers projects that would not otherwise require assessment due to their cumulative impacts.[b]
Duty that specifies impacts or risks, not individual types of actions	A general environmental duty in Victoria, Australia, requires any person "engaging in an activity that may give rise to risks of harm to human health or the environment from pollution or waste [to] minimise those risks, so far as reasonably practicable."[c] Gaps are minimized, based on practicability.[d] This duty was formulated to capture the cumulative effects of smaller pollution sources.[e]
Area-based management boundaries that encompass broader adverse impacts	Wildlife Management Areas established under Tanzania's wildlife law provide for communities to undertake conservation outside "core" protected areas, guided by model bylaws, management plans developed in a participatory manner, and benefit sharing arrangements.[f] A key objective is to "mainstream" and facilitate conservation planning across wider connected landscapes than traditional protected conservation areas allow, including communal and private lands, which brings challenges related to governance, capacity, equity, and enforcement.[g]

[a] Directive 2014/52/EU of the European Parliament and Council of April 16, 2014, amending Directive 2011/92/EU on the assessment of the effects of certain public and private projects on the environment [2014] OJ L124/1, art. 4(3), annex III point 3(g). For a similar approach, see Decree on Environmental Impact Assessment No. 112/PM 2010 (Lao People's Democratic Republic) art. 6(2), noting that this approach is no longer adopted in the decree currently in force, Decree on Environmental Impact Assessment No. 329 of 2022 (Lao People's Democratic Republic), which nonetheless requires cumulative impact assessment: arts. 3(9), 22(4), 23(7).

[b] Nelson and Shirley, "Latent Potential," 16.

[c] Environment Protection Act 2017 (Victoria) s 25(1).

[d] See generally, Bruce Lindsay, Dru Marsh and Rebecca Nelson, "Conceptualising and Activating Knowledge in Environmental Protection Law" (2023) 46 *Melbourne University Law Review* 422–466.

[e] Ibid 426.

[f] Wildlife Conservation Act 2009, as revised 2022, Cap. 283 R.E. 2022 (Tanzania) ss 31–34.

[g] Ministry of Natural Resources and Tourism (Tanzania), *National Wildlife Management Areas Strategy* 2023–2033 (n.d.) 10–11, 22–24, https://maliasili.go.tz/assets/pdfs/DOC-20230601-WA0038_230705_135553_compressed.pdf, last accessed March 19, 2025, archived at https://perma.cc/725H-KFQ4.

in a way that is intended to apply more broadly than is common for laws of that type, but this can, in turn, raise challenges with implementation and enforcement.[134]

6.5.2.2 Gaps by Exemption and Derogation

Regulatory mechanisms also create gaps through express exemptions, which are also termed waivers or carve-outs, or derogations from rules that would otherwise apply. These may be thought necessary because an impact is small or low risk;[135] or socially desirable or necessary (e.g., small-scale agriculture,[136] military activities in the national interest,[137] activities intended to produce environmental benefits or adapt to climate change,[138] or activities undertaken during emergencies[139]). Rule makers may want to avoid burdening long-established activities, producing "grandfathering" exemptions that may apply to diverse impacts (e.g., exempting existing power plants from new air pollution standards[140] or existing building construction from environment-related requirements[141]). Relevant to all regulatory approaches, another motivation for exempting activities is to reduce administrative and enforcement costs for regulators.[142]

[134] See Section 6.5.3.

[135] Martin Z. P. Olszynski, "Ancient Maxim, Modern Problems: De Minimis, Cumulative Environmental Effects and Risk-Based Regulation" (2015) 40 *Queen's Law Journal* 705–740, 718–721, *contra* Albert C. Lin, "Unifying Role of Harm in Environmental Law" (2006) *Wisconsin Law Review* 897–986, 902.

[136] Chris Wood, *Environmental Impact Assessment: A Comparative Review* (Routledge 2003) 109 (exemption from EIA requirements).

[137] Mark P. Nevitt, "Environmental Law in Military Operations," in Geoffrey S. Corn, Rachel E. VanLandingham, and Shane R. Reeves (eds), *U.S. Military Operations: Law, Policy, and Practice* (2015) 401–436, 405–413.

[138] E.g., "overriding beneficial consequences for the environment" under art. 6(4) of the EU Habitats Directive: Commission and Directorate-General for Environment, *Managing Natura 2000 Sites*, 67.

[139] See generally, Victor B. Flatt, "Holding Polluters Accountable in Times of Climate and Covid Risk: The Problems with 'Emergency' Enforcement Waivers" (2020–2021) 12 *San Diego Journal of Climate and Energy Law* 1–18.

[140] See generally, Richard L. Revesz and others, "Grandfathering Coal: Power Plant Regulation under the Clean Air Act Dialogue" (2016) 46 *Environmental Law Reporter News and Analysis* 10541–10551.

[141] E.g., exemptions from some UK minimum energy efficiency requirements apply to some historical buildings, but selling or renting a property usually triggers a regulatory "sermon" in the form of an energy performance certificate: Chamara Panakaduwa, Paul Coates and Mustapha Munir, "Identifying Sustainable Retrofit Challenges of Historical Buildings: A Systematic Review" (2024) 313:114226 *Energy and Buildings* 1–10, 7.

[142] E.g., Barbara Schreiner and Barbara van Koppen, "Hybrid Water Rights Systems for Pro-Poor Water Governance in Africa" (2020) 12 *Water* 155, 4–5 (concern re billing small-scale irrigators in Kenya for water use). Other factors may also be locally important, e.g., associating

Rules can reduce the risk of excluded activities having cumulatively significant impacts in diverse ways. The first is simply removing the exemption so that the "regular" intervention applies to at least some formerly excluded activities, perhaps adding an element (extra time to comply, one-off compensation) to reduce the burden. A variation is to simplify a regulatory process to "reduce red tape". However, global experience simplifying EIA alerts us to the dangers of "ultra-simplification" removing public participation requirements in a way that affects the basic requirements of EIA,[143] and relying on inadequate impact assessments that fail to prevent cumulative environmental impacts.[144] An alternative is to maintain the exemption and deal with the resulting cumulative impacts in other ways, either through state rescue or incentivizing action from others, using a coping strategy, or focusing on data collection as an interim measure, to inform future intervention (Table 6.4).

6.5.2.3 Implementation and Enforcement Gaps

Even if a regulatory mechanism is comprehensive in its coverage on paper, gaps in implementation – lower than desirable take-up of voluntary tools and noncompliance – can create a comprehensiveness challenge. This creates risks of uncontrolled cumulative harm. Under incentive- and information-based interventions (regulatory carrots and sermons), gaps arise where small contributors face barriers to accessing a scheme, including lack of awareness and insufficient resources to engage with complex regimes.[145] In this case, the impacts of their activities are not covered in practice even though they are eligible to participate. This may also be the case for state rescue mechanisms aimed at communities that must apply for them, but face barriers to doing so.[146] Regulatory interventions may include express mechanisms to address this by reducing administrative barriers to entry. The current EU Common Agricultural Policy, which provides subsidies to small farmers that are linked

a regulatory tool with colonialism: ibid, 5. For responses to challenges of enforcement capacity see Section 6.5.2.3.

[143] Álvaro Enríquez-de-Salamanca, "Simplified Environmental Impact Assessment Processes: Review and Implementation Proposals" (2021) 90:106640 *Environmental Impact Assessment Review* 1–8, 6.

[144] Sara Elizabeth Da Silveira and Marlene De Paula Pereira, "Os Princípios Ambientais Na Licença Ambiental Simplificada" (2023) 16:e1200 *Revista Foco* 1–19, 12–13, 15.

[145] Neil Gunningham "Regulating Small and Medium Sized Enterprises" (2002) 14 *Journal of Environmental Law* 3–32, 3–4, 21–22.

[146] See Section 8.4.2.6.

TABLE 6.4 *Burden-reducing alternatives to exemptions to increase regulatory comprehensiveness, in order of most to least similar to the "regular" intervention applied to nonexempt activities*

Legal mechanism	Illustrative examples
Use a version of the regulatory intervention, modified to…	
… make the regulatory approach less stringent	South African law provides for a limited monthly supply of a volume of water free of charge, without significant impact on overall consumption; where volumetric charges usually apply to water use, a tiered tariff system makes available a quantity of water at a lower rate for basic household needs, with a higher rate for higher use.[a]
… use a more collaborative/voluntary regulatory approach	Despite famously strong attachment to property rights, some western US water laws (e.g., Utah) explicitly accept that cumulatively significant groundwater depletion can justify restricting both existing and proposed withdrawals if users agree.[b]
… use a different regulatory strategy: offsetting	Rather than being exempt from regulation, individually minor activities (like vessel moorings, which damage seagrass) in the Great Barrier Reef Marine Park, Australia, require permission; a permit may be granted on condition of paying a monetary offset, which enables pooling of funds to repair or mitigate damage to the Marine Park.[c]
Maintain exemption, but …	
… ensure the derogation benefits the cumulatively impacted matter of concern	New Jersey's Environmental Justice Law prohibits approving a facility that would add to disproportionate cumulative environmental stressors for an overburdened community, unless necessary to "serve an essential environmental, health, or safety need of the host overburdened community" (noting that economic benefit cannot be considered).[d]
… apply a cumulative limit that includes activities with special status	Fish harvest agreements negotiated between the federal government and tribes in British Columbia, Canada reserve a percentage of the total allowable catch (a cumulative limit) for the relevant tribe.[e]
… use a coping strategy	The city of Adelaide in Australia deals with high cumulative vehicle noise by subsidizing improved window glazing for occupants of affected houses,[f] as distinct from regulating vehicles or traffic.

Legal mechanism	Illustrative examples
… collect data on cumulative impact for possible or planned future intervention	A Seychelles multistage plan to recover populations of shark pursuant to its international obligations begins with identifying and recording artisanal shark fishers, paving the way for phased interventions.[g]

[a] Constitution of the Republic of South Africa 1996, s 27(1)(b); Water Services Act 108 of 1997 (South Africa) ss 2(a), 3, 5; Andrea Szabó, "The Value of Free Water: Analyzing South Africa's Free Basic Water Policy" (2015) 83 *Econometrica* 1913–1961, 1913, 1914.

[b] E.g., Utah Code § 73-5-15(4)(a)(iii), (c) (regarding state regulation of withdrawals pursuant to voluntary arrangements between water users).

[c] Great Barrier Reef Marine Park Regulations 2019 (Australia) s 117(2)(j); Great Barrier Reef Marine Park Zoning Plan 2003 (Australia) s 2.2.4(l)(iii); regarding offsets for seagrass damage, see generally, Ma, Rhodes and Maron, "The Consequences of Coastal Offsets."

[d] New Jersey Admin. Code § 7:1C-9.2; New Jersey Department of Environmental Protection, "Environmental Justice Rules Frequently Asked Questions" (2023) 18–19, https://dep.nj.gov/wp-content/uploads/ej/docs/ej-rule-frequently-asked-questions.pdf, archived at https://perma.cc/ZYW7-D97M.

[e] E.g., Nisga'a Nation Harvest Agreement between Canada, British Columbia and the Nisga'a Nation, May 11, 2000, art. 2, available at Government of Canada, "Nisga'a Harvest Agreement" (May 11, 2000) www.rcaanc-cirnac.gc.ca/eng/1100100031747/1543410863980, archived at https://perma.cc/97AU-NT8C.

[f] E.g., City of Adelaide, "Noise Management Incentives" (n.d.) www.cityofadelaide.com.au/about-council/grants-sponsorship-incentives/noise-management-incentives, last accessed March 19, 2025, archived at https://perma.cc/CLF6-RMFH. This is sometimes framed as integrating consideration of the victims of the problem: Ruth Wiedemann and Karin Ingold, "Solving Cross-Sectoral Policy Problems: Adding a Cross-Sectoral Dimension to Assess Policy Performance" (2022) 24 *Journal of Environmental Policy and Planning* 526–539, 530.

[g] Seychelles Fishing Authority, *National Plan of Action for the Conservation and Management of Sharks 2016–2020* (2016) 68, https://mofbe.gov.sc/wp-content/uploads/2021/09/National-Plan-of-Action-for-the-Conservation-and-Management-of-Sharks-2016-2020-3.pdf, archived at https://perma.cc/7XW9-VPLA; identified international obligations include those under the United Nations Convention on the Law of the Sea, December 10, 1982, Montego Bay, in force November 16, 1994, 1833 U.N.T.S. 396), among other laws: ibid 93.

to environmental conditions, expressly requires member states to plan to reduce burdens for farmers.[147]

Risks of noncompliance affect not just regulatory sticks (e.g., enforcing conditions of a pollution authorization) but also regulatory carrots (e.g., enforcing conditions of a stewardship payment) and regulatory sermons

[147] Regulation 2021/2115 of the European Parliament and of the Council of December 2, 2021, on Common Agricultural Policy Strategic Plans [2021] OJ L435/1 (CAP Regulation), art. 139 (3)(f); see generally, Mirta Alessandrini and others, "Smallholder Farms in the Sustainable Food Transition: A Critical Examination of the New Common Agricultural Policy" (2024) 33 *Review of European, Comparative and International Environmental Law* 124–135. See Chapter 10 for a case study in which the CAP is a key intervention.

(e.g., ensuring the accuracy of information about impacts provided to regulators or the public). While the focus of this book is regulatory design, this section touches on enforcement briefly and narrowly, drawing out selected issues that are pronounced for cumulative environmental problems and that pose regulatory design issues.

Since cumulative environmental problems involve numerous, diverse contributors, they can stretch enforcement resources.[148] Some common strategies for responding to this will not necessarily suit cumulative environmental problems. For example, relying on third-party enforcement will be difficult if causation is hard to prove, there are numerous activities, and the third party is resource-poor. Guiding discretion to best use scarce resources using "risk-based" enforcement principles[149] can be problematic if principles focus solely on an individual contributor's risk of noncompliance and overlook the cumulative risk of noncompliance to a matter of concern. Enforcement discretion can also be a challenge because cumulative environmental problems are relatively hard to perceive, more diffuse, and require engagement with scientific complexity,[150] and so are more likely to "fly under the radar" of regulators. Providing regulators with information and training geared to these challenges is one possible solution. Rules can address these enforcement problems by using cumulative impact principles directly or indirectly to guide regulatory discretion, facilitating enforcement by relatively resource-rich third parties, or providing for automatic enforcement for categories of contributors that are numerous and homogeneous (Table 6.5).

6.5.3 *Administrative Cost and Using Cumulative Impact Concepts to Reduce It*

In addition to burdens on regulated parties,[151] administrative costs to government can be a significant challenge to regulating problems that involve many different actors. Considering alternatives among regulatory sticks, carrots, sermons, and state rescue may reveal ways to reduce administrative costs, though the choice may trade off more reliable outcomes.[152] One solution is

[148] See also Section 6.5.3 on administrative cost.

[149] E.g., *Independent Inquiry into the Environment Protection Authority* (State of Victoria, 2016) [4.3.2], https://apo.org.au/sites/default/files/resource-files/2016-03/apo-nid72340.pdf, archived at https://perma.cc/R934-UX6W. See Peter Mascini, "Why Was the Enforcement Pyramid So Influential? And What Price Was Paid?" (2013) 7 *Regulation and Governance* 48–60, 54.

[150] See discussion in Section 2.2.2.3.

[151] See Section 6.2.2 (re strategies) and 6.3.2 (re approaches).

[152] See Table 6.1.

TABLE 6.5 *Mechanisms for considering cumulative environmental impacts in enforcement*

Legal mechanisms	Illustrative examples
Enforcement policy that prioritizes responding to risks of cumulative impacts	Under formal policy, California's environmental agencies must prioritize enforcement in communities that suffer disproportionate burdens of cumulative environmental harm.[a]
Power of affected communities to guide or displace regulators' enforcement discretion (cf. direct third-party enforcement)	Contemporary Texas groundwater law allows an "affected person" to petition a state body to review a local groundwater conservation district's failure to enforce its rules.[b]
	Past Nebraska groundwater law allowed well owners to petition to shift enforcement powers to the state if local districts failed to enforce rules in a "control area" to protect against cumulative depletion.[c]
Power to enforce of non-state actors or other states with significant resources	Under the Equator Principles, signatory financiers require project developers to comply with national environmental impact assessment (EIA) requirements (which often include cumulative impact assessment).[d] Financiers can then enforce these requirements as a contractual obligation, independent of state enforcement.
	For cumulative environmental problems with a transnational element, extraterritorial action may avoid domestic barriers to enforcement, e.g., Japan's timber legislation and Papua New Guinea's fisheries legislation disallow importing specimens from other nations that prohibit their export.[e]
Technology that supports enforcement capacity for numerous contributors	To address pollution from poorly maintained vehicles and enforce air pollution requirements, Hong Kong's vehicle emissions control measures involve remote sensors to detect noncompliant vehicle emissions more cost-effectively than testing each vehicle during a roadworthiness examination.[f]
Displacement of obligation to change behavior to a smaller set of different parties to reduce enforcement burden	Vanuatu bans the production of disposable plastic items rather than relying solely on banning littering of plastic items.[g]

[a] Section 8.3.2.2, notes 95–98 and accompanying text.

[b] Texas Water Code § 36.3011 and 30 Texas Administrative Code § 293.23.

[c] Nebraska Laws 1975 (LB 577), s 12.

[d] Nelson and Shirley, "Latent Potential," 163.

(*continued*)

TABLE 6.5 (*continued*)

[e] Lydia Slobodian, "Shifting the Burden of Wildlife Protection: The Role of Extraterritorial Jurisdiction in Implementing CITES" in Marie-Claire Cordonier Segger, David Andrew Wardell and Alexandra Harrington (eds), *CITES as a Tool for Sustainable Development* (CUP 2023) 49–78, 66.
[f] Air Pollution Control (Vehicle Design Standards) (Emission) Regulations 1992, Cap. 311 sub. leg. J, as amended (Hong Kong SAR); Legislative Council Panel on Environmental Affairs (Hong Kong SAR), *Improvement of Roadside Air Quality*, LC Paper No. CB(1)(949/16-17(03) (2017) [9]–[12] www.legco.gov.hk/yr16-17/english/panels/ea/papers/ea20170522cb1-949-3-e.pdf, archived at https://perma.cc/4E6H-ZUQ2; Environmental Protection Department (Hong Kong SAR), "Strengthened Emissions Control for Petrol and LPG Vehicles" (n.d.) www.epd.gov.hk/epd/english/environmentinhk/air/guide_ref/remote_sensing_Petrol_n_LPG.html#Vehicle%20Emissions%20Standard, last accessed March 19, 2025, archived at https://perma.cc/P5ER-PSY5. See also the discussion of information and technology in Section 5.3.2.
[g] See Waste Management Regulations Order No. 15 of 2018 (Vanuatu) s 2.

to design rules so that a single regulatory decision influences multiple activities – a sort of regulatory "economy of scale" (Table 6.6). These mechanisms carry benefits for regulating cumulative impacts beyond reducing administrative cost. They promote connected decision-making[153] by considering many contributors at once. They may also make it easier to manage adaptively,[154] since a single decision can modify requirements that apply to multiple contributors, for example, reducing the "cap" in a cap-and-trade system.[155]

Conversely, issues of scale and participation present risks. Cumulative performance standards that apply to large areas may inadvertently allow "hot-spots" of cumulative impact that are locally significant.[156] The alternative, considering the impacts of sources of harm individually, though, would increase uncertainty for participants and costs for regulators.[157] A lower cost but lower precision option to prevent hotspots is to use trading zones (Table 6.6). The types of "bulk" regulatory mechanisms included in Table 6.6 also tend to restrict public participation requirements[158] to the single "aggregated" decision rather than inviting comment about individual impacts (e.g., decision to issue multisource permit, decision to set trading

153 See Section 6.5.1.

154 See Section 2.2.3.3.

155 For a broader guidance on the establishment of cap and trade systems, see, e.g., Richard Schmalensee and Robert N. Stavins, "Lessons Learned from Three Decades of Experience with Cap and Trade" (2017) 11 *Review of Environmental Economics and Policy* 59–79.

156 33 C.F.R. § 330.5(c) (regarding regional conditions); US Army Corps of Engineers, "Reissuance and Modification of Nationwide Permits [FR Doc #2021-00102]" (January 13, 2021) 86 *Federal Register (USA)* 2744–2878, 2758. Note that the conditions may only be made stricter through regional conditions: 33 C.F.R. § 330.1(d).

157 Schmalensee and Stavins, "Lessons Learned," 63, 72.

158 Terence J. Centner, "Challenging NPDES Permits Granted without Public Participation" (2011) 38 *Boston College Environmental Affairs Law Review* 1–40, 20–23.

TABLE 6.6 *Mechanisms for reducing administrative costs by applying a single decision to multiple sources of impact*

Legal mechanisms	Illustrative examples
Single permit for multiple impact sources under the same control	A "bubble" policy under the US Clean Air Act applied an average performance standard and an aggregate emissions limit to multiple air pollution points controlled by the same person in the same industrial grouping, considering them a single "source."[a]
Single opt-in permit for a sector or pollution type	"General" permits under the US Clean Water Act place conditions on a sector or discharge type in a geographic area (e.g., cranberry production, industrial stormwater sources).[b] This reduces processing times for authorizing cumulatively minor activities[c] (though concerns have arisen about the supporting cumulative impact analyses[d]). An individual discharger opts in to be covered,[e] and in some circumstances requires an individual permit.[f]
Cumulative performance standard applied to similar activities across sectors	German "dynamic environmentally sensitive traffic management systems" (*dynamisches umweltsensitives Verkehrsmanagement*) alter legally binding road speed limits in response to local (cumulative) air quality conditions.[g]
Cap-and-trade system that limits aggregate impacts (a cumulative performance standard), with local trading rules to prevent cumulative impact hotspots	Cap-and-trade systems limit aggregate adverse effects or resource use in diverse environmental contexts (e.g., air pollution, water use, land use development rights[h]), while enabling contributors to trade individual rights to cause impacts or use resources. Zone-based trading rules that prevent trades from downstream/downwind to upstream/upwind seek to prevent local hotspots, e.g., under Australian water trading rules designed to protect local water-dependent environments and California's Regional Clean Air Incentives Market to prevent hotspots of NO_x and SO_2 caused by trade.[i]

[a] Coglianese, "Limits of Performance-Based Regulation," 540. Note that other elements of the bubble policy, and some of its fine details, made it controversial and uncertain for firms, and ultimately take-up was not high: see generally, Halvorson, "Deflated Dreams."

[b] 33 C.F.R. Ch. II Pt. 330, 40 C.F.R. § 122.28(a).

[c] U.S. Army Corps of Engineers, "Reissuance and Modification of Nationwide Permits," 2762.

[d] Ibid 2751.

[e] 40 C.F.R. § 122.28(b)(2).

[f] 40 C.F.R. § 122.28(b)(3)(i)(A), (G).

[g] See generally, Volker Diegmann and others, Dynamisches umweltsensitives Verkehrsmanagement (Bundesanstalt für Straßenwesen, 2020) https://bast.opus.hbz-nrw.de/frontdoor/index/index/docId/2335 (report in German, summary in English), archived at https://perma.cc/WX96-ZHD9.

[h] See generally, Schmalensee and Stavins, "Lessons Learned."

[i] Ibid 64.

rules within a cap). This suggests the need for more frequent review to guard against unintended consequences.[159]

6.5.4 *Adaptive Intervention to Respond to Accumulating Impacts*

Regulating cumulative environmental problems inherently requires adapting rules[160] for intervening and adapting how they apply to individual contributors when actual or predicted cumulative impacts approach maximum acceptable levels ("intervening adaptively," for short).[161] Contributors to the problem or their activities may change, introducing new impacts or types of impacts; and scientific complexity and unpredictability mean new information about the matter of concern or the harm will likely emerge with time. This need to adapt environment-related rules is well-established, pointing to regulatory design for flexibility and iterative evaluation, including "provisional decision making, monitoring, and adjustment."[162] Here, then, the focus is exploring implications and options in the cumulative impact context.

Intervening adaptively in anticipation of serious cumulative impacts finds support in diverse formulations[163] of the precautionary principle. Notably, this principle appears in legislation,[164] policy guidance,[165] and judicial decisions

[159] See intervening adaptively in Section 6.5.4.

[160] B. Guy Peters, "Information and Governing: Cybernetic Models of Governance" in David Levi-Faur (ed), *The Oxford Handbook of Governance* (OUP 2012) 113–128, 116; Howlett, *Designing Public Policies*, 64–66 ("evidence-based policy"). See also Section 2.2.3.3.

[161] Understanding when this level is reached requires information as a trigger: Martin A. Nie and Courtney A. Schultz, "Decision-Making Triggers in Adaptive Management" (2012) 26 *Conservation Biology* 1137–1144, 1138, 1141–1142. See Chapter 5 (Information). Note that other elements of the CIRCle Framework also require an adaptive approach, e.g., adapting how the matter of concern is conceptualized: see Section 6.5.4.

[162] Alejandro E. Camacho, "De- and Re-Constructing Public Governance for Biodiversity Conservation" (2020) 73 *Vanderbilt Law Review* 1585–1642, 1613; Jonathan H. Adler, "Dynamic Environmentalism and Adaptive Management: Legal Obstacles and Opportunities" (2015) 11 *Journal of Law Economics and Policy* 133–162, 147.

[163] Eloise Scotford, "Environmental Principles across Jurisdictions: Legal Connectors and Catalysts" in Emma Lees and Jorge E. Viñuales (eds), *The Oxford Handbook of Comparative Environmental Law* (OUP 2019) 651–677, 660; Jonathan B. Wiener, "*Precautionary Principle*" in Ludwig Krämer and Emanuela Orlando (eds), *Elgar Encyclopedia of Environmental Law* Vol. VI (Edward Elgar 2023) 174–185, 175–179.

[164] See, e.g., Impact Assessment Act 2019 (Canada) s 6(2); Directive 2008/56/EC of the European Parliament and of the Council of June 17, 2008, establishing a framework for community action in the field of marine environmental policy [2008] OJ L164/19, preamble (27), (44), art. 8(1)(b)(ii).

[165] E.g., G. Hegmann and others, *Cumulative Effects Assessment Practitioners Guide Prepared for Canadian Environmental Assessment Agency* (1999) 48, https://publications.gc.ca/site/eng/9.647223/publication.html, archived at https://perma.cc/XN7W-R544; "Navigating the

dealing with cumulative impacts.[166] In its original form, the principle facilitates preventive regulatory intervention without conclusive proof about the cause-and-effect relationship between pollution and harm.[167] More broadly, the principle holds that scientific uncertainty should not justify postponing preventive action in the case of potential serious environmental harm. Uncertainty about precise effects does not preclude regulatory measures, and early actions are "provisional and should be updated over time in light of learning."[168]

Intervening adaptively can mean either changing how an administrative decision applies to an entity (Section 6.5.4.1); or changing an element of an existing rule, or introducing a new rule to the mix (Section 6.5.4.2). Adapting may be triggered by actual or predicted cumulative impacts approaching maximum acceptable levels (i.e., cumulative threshold conditions[169]).

6.5.4.1 Adapting an Administrative Decision

Some areas of law and some regulatory approaches[170] provide more scope for adapting administrative decisions in response to cumulative effects than others. EIA laws focus resources and scrutiny at the proposal stage,[171] including predicting cumulative effects, rather than follow up once an activity commences,[172] which would allow for adaptation. By contrast, "decentralized behavior-coordinating mechanisms" such as markets involve iterative decision-making by individual actors,[173] and inherent scope for contributors to change their impacts. Regulatory sermons are also inherently adaptive in that regularly provided information about impacts changes with time. The focus of this section is therefore adapting mandatory regulatory approaches ("regulatory sticks"), which tend to strike prominent barriers to adaptation.[174]

Implementation Impasse: Enabling Interagency Collaboration on Cumulative Effects" (July 2019) Aotearoa Cumulative Effects (ACE) Framework, 5, www.sustainableseaschallenge.co.nz/tools-and-resources/ace-framework/, archived at https://perma.cc/9323-P2EM.

166 Tom Kaveney, Ailsa Kerswell and Andrew Buick, *Cumulative Environmental Impact Assessment Industry Guide* (Minerals Council of Australia 2015) 48–49 (describing several Australian state-level judicial decisions).

167 Noga Morag-Levine, "Is Precautionary Regulation a Civil Law Instrument? Lessons from the History of the Alkali Act" (2011) 23 *Journal of Environmental Law* 1–43, 3.

168 Wiener, "Precautionary Principle," 179.

169 See Section 4.3.3.

170 See Section 6.3.

171 Ruhl, "Regulation by Adaptive Management," 35.

172 See generally, ibid.

173 Ibid 27.

174 See Section 2.2.3.3.

Rules can help address concerns that changes unfairly frustrate regulated parties' "legitimate expectations"[175] by forewarning them of the potential need to adapt,[176] and using transparent, predetermined triggers for adaptation. Table 6.7 sets out examples of rules that facilitate adapting individual decisions in response to concerns about cumulative impacts, with key variables being how frequently change is anticipated to occur, and the parties that may trigger the review that leads to adaptation.

As well as positively facilitating adaptation (Table 6.7), regulatory mechanisms should avoid elements that impede adaptation, keeping in mind the characteristics of the relevant cumulative environmental problem. For example, where there is uncertainty about precisely how impacts aggregate to cause harm,[177] rules for adapting a decision should avoid requiring conclusive proof of a causal link between a specific activity and a harm. Instead, they could simply require adaptation in response to an indicator of cumulative environmental effect (e.g., ambient air quality);[178] frame a regulatory requirement around avoiding risk, rather than an actual effect (e.g., a general environmental duty);[179] or apply a presumption about a causal link.[180]

6.5.4.2 Adapting a Regulatory Intervention or Regulatory Mix

Larger-scale adaptation occurs by changing the rules, or the set of rules, themselves. Increasing impacts may require adjusting a performance standard to keep cumulative impacts acceptable. New rules might be needed to improve regulatory "comprehensiveness" to cover previously unregulated activities,[181] or respond to a realization that a riskier regulatory intervention has not effectively addressed cumulative impacts.[182] Adopting rules for this kind of adaptation usefully forewarns the public of possible future change, potentially reducing concerns about legitimate expectations and fairness.

[175] Fergus Green, "Legal Transitions without Legitimate Expectations" (2020) 28 *Journal of Political Philosophy* 397–420.

[176] Ruhl, "Regulation by Adaptive Management," 49.

[177] See Section 2.2.2.3.

[178] E.g., Table 6.6, row 3.

[179] E.g., Table 6.3, row 2. See also Environment Protection Act 2017 (Victoria) s 25(1); Lindsay, Marsh and Nelson, "Conceptualising and Activating Knowledge."

[180] E.g., a presumption of hydraulic connectivity between groundwater proposed to be withdrawn and a river, which applies to proposed withdrawals within a specified distance from a river and leads to measures to protect surface water rights from interference: Oregon Administrative Rules Ch. 690, Div. 9.

[181] See Section 6.5.2.

[182] See Section 6.4.1.

TABLE 6.7 *Mechanisms that facilitate adapting a decision in response to cumulative impacts*

Legal mechanisms	Illustrative examples
Frequent (e.g., annual) reviews to adapt rights to take resources	Making an annual "seasonal determination" of water availability in Victoria, Australia, affects the water available to be taken under different categories of water entitlements (which are expressed as a proportion of the total) and responds to the cumulative conditions of water resources.[a]
	Malawi's water law requires a water license holder to update an impact assessment before the expiration of a license (which must last for at least five years), to be reviewed by the National Water Resources Authority.[b]
Time-limited approvals to implement lower-frequency (e.g., five-yearly) review and adaptation	Nationwide general permits under the US Clean Water Act expire after five years unless they are modified or reissued.[c] They may be modified at any time if the cumulative effect of the activities would be more than minimal;[d] reissuance expressly may consider climate change.[e]
Ad hoc review using a stakeholder-initiated process in response to changed conditions	In Chile, if environmental conditions change significantly compared to predictions, a project proponent or a directly affected person may request revisions to an environmental permit ("resolución de calificación ambiental") for projects that required full impact assessment documentation.[f]
Review by the state using an approval condition to respond to specified unacceptable cumulative effects	Water law in Oregon, US, requires conditions on water rights to allow the state to reduce allowable water use if future data shows that flows in scenic waterways have cumulatively reduced more than a specified threshold.[g]

[a] Water Act 1989 (Victoria) ss 33AC, 64GB. For an explanation of the place of seasonal determinations in Victoria's water allocation system, see Department of Energy, Environment and Climate Action (Victoria), "How Is Water Managed?" (n.d.) https://accounts.water.vic.gov.au/water-explained/how-is-water-managed/, last accessed March 20, 2025, archived at https://perma.cc/27YC-42RR.

[b] *Water Resources Act 2013*, ch 72:03 (Malawi) ss 61, 62. It is unclear whether this provision is implemented. Water law in Western Australia also provides for renewable, time-limited water licenses, guided by water allocation plans: Rights in Water and Irrigation Act 1914 (Western Australia) s 5C, Sch. 1, cll. 7(2), 22; Quantum Management Consulting and Assurance, *Report for the Economic Regulation Authority Inquiry into Water Resource Management and Planning Charges*, Department of Water's Processes (2010) 32, www.erawa.com.au/inquiries/completed-inquiries/2009-inquiry-into-water-resource-management-and-planning-charges, archived at https://perma.cc/8RPS-LYVC.

(*continued*)

TABLE 6.7 (*continued*)

[c] 33 C.F.R. § 330.6(b).
[d] 33 C.F.R. §§ 330.1(d), 330.5. See also US Army Corps of Engineers, "Reissuance and Modification of Nationwide Permits," 2751.
[e] Ibid 2755.
[f] Ley sobre Bases Generales del Medio Ambiente, Ley No. 19300 [Law on the General Bases of the Environment, Law No. 19300], 1994, as amended, art. 25 quinquies; Kay Bergamini and Cristian Pérez, "Environmental Impact Assessment Follow-up Institutional and Regulatory Frameworks: Lights and Shadows of the Chilean Experience" (2022) 40 *Impact Assessment and Project Appraisal* 423–436, 429.
[g] Oregon Revised Statutes §§ 390.835(9)(g), 390.835(12).

Openly flagging different trajectories of intervention might also, perhaps, reduce the effects of path dependence.

Scholars have advanced general ways in which law can facilitate adaptation, while ensuring appropriate stability, such as formally allowing for ad hoc or recurring amendment, relying on inherently evolutionary forms of law like the common law, and using more easily changed standards and delegated powers.[183] Table 6.8 directs this question to the situation of cumulative environmental problems, giving examples of mechanisms for adapting rules in response to cumulative impacts.

6.6 CONCLUSION

Diverse rules can influence cumulative impacts. In analyzing rules for intervention, it helps to consider the *strategy* employed by a rule (harm-reducing, harm-offsetting, restoring, and coping), which focuses on how the rule seeks to change harm to the matter of concern; and the rule's *approach* (stick, carrot, sermon, or state rescue), which focuses on how the rule seeks to change the behavior of contributors to the harm – or avoid the need to do this by relying on the state. Combining these two dimensions produces a matrix of rule types, some of which seem less used than others, presenting options for further developments. Some combinations give rules characteristics that compound weaknesses such as burdens on contributors to harm or riskiness of the outcome. This points to issues that need attention in regulatory design. No single type of rule will be universally effective to address all aspects of a cumulative environmental problem.

A major way of dealing with the weaknesses of certain types of rules for intervention is to use a mix of rules so that some can compensate for the

[183] E.g., Robin Kundis Craig and others, "Balancing Stability and Flexibility in Adaptive Governance: An Analysis of Tools Available in U.S. Environmental Law" (2017) 22(2):3 *Ecology and Society* 1–15, 8–9.

TABLE 6.8 *Mechanisms that facilitate adapting a set of rules in response to cumulative impacts*

Legal mechanism	Illustrative examples
Sequenced, predetermined regulatory designations and rule changes in response to escalating cumulative impacts	To increase regulatory controls, groundwater law in Arizona, US, provides for converting the designation of an area within which controls apply to groundwater withdrawals from an "irrigation non-expansion area" (less restrictive, relatively) to an "active management area" (more restrictive).[a]
Regular assessment of regional cumulative impacts, linked to considering new rules, without specifying the nature of the rules	In Australia's multistate Murray-Darling Basin, states are required to identify broad risks to the condition or continued availability of water resources in ten-yearly plans, before identifying strategies to address them (which expressly may include regulation).[b]
Regular review of whether a rule is effectively controlling cumulative impacts to trigger adaptation	To assess the impact of the Common Agricultural Policy,[c] an agricultural subsidy program that is intended to reduce impacts on the environment and climate,[d] the European Commission uses a rule-based "performance framework" based on set indicators.[e] These include "context" indicators of aggregate (cumulative) environmental conditions and trends.[f]
Self-updating standard (e.g., responsive to monitoring, or adaptive interpretation)	German "dynamic environmentally sensitive traffic management systems" adjust traffic speed limits to respond to cumulative impacts in real time; the content of a "general environmental duty," as used in Victoria and Queensland, Australia, adjusts relevant standards through interpretation.[g]

[a] Arizona Revised Statutes § 45-439. See generally, "Active Management Area'" Arizona Department of Water Resources (US), "AMAs 101" (n.d.) www.azwater.gov/sites/default/files/2025-02/AMA101_2025.pdf, last accessed March 19, 2025, archived at https://perma.cc/BJS9-BA5G.

[b] Water Act 2007 (Australia) s 22(1) items 3, 5; Basin Plan 2012 (Australia) chapter 4.

[c] CAP Regulation arts. 141–143.

[d] Ibid preamble (30).

[e] Ibid annexes I, XIV; EU CAP Network, "EU level CAP Evaluation Framework" (n.d.) https://eu-cap-network.ec.europa.eu/support/evaluation/evaluation-framework_en#paragraph-8970, last accessed March 19, 2025, archived at https://perma.cc/ML8Z-CM9Z.

[f] E.g., "water quality," "greenhouse gas emissions from agriculture," "percentage of species and habitats of Community interest related to agriculture with stable or increasing trends": ibid annex I, indicators C.37, C.39, C.44.

[g] See Environment Protection Act 2017 (Victoria) s 25(1); Lindsay, Marsh and Nelson, "Conceptualising and Activating Knowledge," 443; and Diegmann and others, Dynamisches umweltsensitives Verkehrsmanagement. Note that the Queensland duty is supported by codes of practice that require active change: Environmental Protection Act 1994 (Queensland) ss 319, 551; see also Queensland Government, "Environmental Codes of Practice for Industry" (n.d.) www.business.qld.gov.au/running-business/environment/industry-codes, last accessed March 19, 2025, archived at https://perma.cc/A9NS-SYJW.

weaknesses of others. A mix is also necessary to accommodate heterogeneous contributors to the cumulative environmental harm and the multiple levels of government, with different powers and capacities, that are inevitably involved.

In designing rules for intervention, key issues are ensuring connected decision-making so that individual actions are not considered in isolation; comprehensiveness, so that few or no actions that could cause cumulatively significant impact are unaddressed; manageable costs associated with intervention; and adaptive interventions, so that the rules and their implementation can change as impacts accumulate or new circumstances arise. Numerous examples from around the world illustrate how rules can be designed with these challenges in mind. Inevitably, tensions arise in balancing different objectives for intervention rules and in bridging what is desirable and what is possible in designing a rule. Chapters 9 and 10 examine some key issues discussed here in case studies of interventions to address cumulative environmental problems in Australia and Italy.

7

Coordination

Laws for Making Links

Links with Other Chapters

- Chapter 1 explains how examples used in this chapter were chosen.
- Chapter 2 synthesizes key challenges related to coordination and introduces the CIRCle Framework of regulatory functions for addressing cumulative environmental problems.
- Chapter 3 sketches the landscape of laws that may respond to cumulative environmental problems.
- Chapter 4 ("Conceptualization") discusses rules for articulating what and who we want to protect from cumulative impacts (the "matter of concern") – a key issue for coordination.
- Chapter 5 ("Information") discusses rules for collecting and analyzing data and information about cumulative harm, which requires coordination.
- Chapter 6 ("Intervention") discusses how rules can influence behavior to ensure that cumulative harm stays within acceptable limits.
- Chapter 10 analyzes a detailed case study on the Alpine grasslands in South Tyrol, Italy, focused on vertical intergovernmental coordination.

7.1 COORDINATION AS A REGULATORY FUNCTION

Dealing with cumulative environmental harm to a matter of concern – from a national park to an aquifer used for drinking water – often means dealing with multilayered laws. These laws engage a constellation of actors with relevant roles distributed across multiple vertical levels of government and across agencies of the same level of government, as well as with nongovernment entities. This makes coordination vital. Except in the simplest of situations, it is likely neither practical nor desirable to deal with cumulative environmental problems by relying on a single institution or level of government.[1] The Alpine case study (Chapter 10) points to this complexity: In the deceptively simple context of protecting grasslands, agencies at the level of municipalities, multi-municipality districts, the province, the Italian State, the European Union, and multiple international treaty bodies are potentially involved in relevant rules that span agriculture, nature, impact assessment, and landscapes.

Coordination is part of a broader framework of interlinking core functions that form the "CIRCle Framework" advanced by this book for regulatory systems to respond to cumulative environmental problems.[2] As well as coordination, regulating cumulative environmental problems requires conceptualizing the matter of concern, which is the focus of protection or restoration; gathering and sharing information about the matter of concern and threats to it, and undertaking regulatory intervention to address these threats to ensure that cumulative environmental harm stays within acceptable limits. This chapter lays out how mechanisms for coordination bring together relevant actors to advance these other three functions of conceptualization, information, and regulatory intervention, and resolve disputes and "drift" that arise along the way.

By focusing on legal mechanisms for coordination and how they can serve different functions that are important to addressing cumulative environmental problems, this chapter draws and builds on diverse literatures: multilevel governance typologies that tend to focus on coordination writ large (rather than in relation to specific functions);[3] regulatory literature that addresses conflict, undermining, and synergies between the different elements of an instrument mix for intervention,[4] and that analyzes the regulatory authority of

[1] Stefano Ponte, Christine Noe and Asubisye Mwamfupe, "Private and Public Authority Interactions and the Functional Quality of Sustainability Governance: Lessons from Conservation and Development Initiatives in Tanzania" (2021) 15 *Regulation and Governance* 1270–1285, 1272. See also Chapter 10.

[2] See Section 2.4 for an elaboration of the CIRCle Framework.

[3] E.g., Liesbet Hooghe and Gary Marks, "Types of Multi-Level Governance" in Henrik Enderlein Sonja Wälti and Michael Zürn (eds), *Handbook on Multi-Level Governance* (Edward Elgar 2010) 17–31.

[4] E.g., Michael Howlett, *Designing Public Policies: Principles and Instruments* (2nd edn, Routledge 2019) 260–263.

public institutions by reference to functions;[5] and legal literature on intergovernmental relations[6] and distributions of legislative competencies between levels of government and collaboration at "peak level moments" of decision-making such as rulemaking and adjudication.[7]

Section 7.1 explains, for present purposes, what coordination means in general (Section 7.1.1), and in the contexts of each of the other three CIRCle Framework functions: conceptualization, information, and regulatory intervention (Section 7.1.2). Section 7.2 then explores the key government actors involved in coordination and how legal systems implicate different relevant actors depending on how they distribute powers; and the role of nongovernment actors. Section 7.3 distils key legal approaches to supporting coordination for each CIRCle Framework function, and dealing with disagreements related to cumulative environmental problems, with a focus on resolving "vertical" disputes between levels of government. This vertical dispute resolution context is then illustrated in the European Alps case study.[8]

7.1.1 *What Is Coordination?*

As used in this book, coordination refers to links across laws and structures for repeated interactions among government agencies, levels of government, quasi-governmental, and nongovernmental actors (together, "actors") to address a cumulative environmental problem, facilitated by legal mechanisms. I use the term "coordination" to encompass interactions along a wide spectrum, from maintaining enthusiastic partnerships to resolving disputes among antagonists. Legal mechanisms may support coordination by providing a structure and an incentive for repeated interactions between actors in a general sense, or specifically in coordinating the carrying out of the CIRCle Framework functions of conceptualization, information, or regulatory intervention.

5 See, e.g., Alejandro E. Camacho and Robert L. Glicksman, "Designing Regulation across Organizations: Assessing the Functions and Dimensions of Governance" (2021) 15(S1) *Regulation and Governance* S102–S122.

6 E.g., Johanne Poirier and Cheryl Saunders, "Comparative Experiences of Intergovernmental Relations in Federal Systems" in Johanne Poirier, Cheryl Saunders and John Kincaid (eds), *Intergovernmental Relations in Federal Systems: Comparative Structures and Dynamics* (OUP 2015) 440, 479.

7 E.g., Jody Freeman and Daniel A. Farber, "Modular Environmental Regulation" (2005) 54 *Duke Law Journal* 795–912, 824–825.

8 See Chapter 10, especially Section 10.4.2.3 (re Natura 2000 sites).

Nonlegal factors will influence whether coordination is successful – among them, leadership, resources, and motivation.[9] Informal coordination is also important.[10] But legal mechanisms can help create conditions for success by addressing inherent disincentives to coordination.[11] Important disincentives include a problem being caused by many diverse contributors to harm, potentially with competing interests; engaging multiple and perhaps many government agencies with different goals that may pertain to narrow domains (e.g., biodiversity, water management, geoscientific information); and involving complex and prolonged accumulation of impacts, all of which make it difficult to establish and maintain fruitful interactions.

Coordination as used here relates to not just domestic government agencies but also includes quasi-governmental organizations, international and supranational institutions, and domestic and transnational nongovernment actors whose activities intentionally link with domestic government action (Figure 7.1). Other broader types of coordination can be important to deal with cumulative environmental problems, but lie beyond the focus of this book. This includes coordination that relates solely to private parties, such as groups of nongovernment stakeholders (outside scope since the present focus is public law regulation) and general public participation in government decision-making more broadly[12] (outside scope since large-scale cumulative problems can make direct participation by heterogeneous individuals, rather than groups and representatives, difficult and rare in practice[13]).

7.1.2 *Coordination as an Integrated Regulatory Function in the CIRCle Framework*

Across the functions of conceptualization, information, and regulatory intervention, coordination among actors provides opportunities to promote three characteristics that are critical to dealing with central challenges associated

[9] This is a central issue addressed by collaborative governance literature, e.g., Scott Douglas and others, "Pathways to Collaborative Performance: Examining the Different Combinations of Conditions under Which Collaborations Are Successful" (2020) 39 *Policy and Society* 638–658.

[10] See, e.g., Nicole Bolleyer and Tanja A. Börzel, "Non-Hierarchical Policy Coordination in Multilevel Systems" (2010) 2 *European Political Science Review* 157–185.

[11] For a fuller discussion of these disincentives, see Section 2.2.4.2.

[12] For a discussion of approaches to public participation in environmental contexts in domestic laws around the world, see Swatanter Kumar and others, *Environmental Rule of Law: First Global Report* (United Nations Environment Programme 2019) 116–131.

[13] Richard D. Margerum, "A Typology of Collaboration Efforts in Environmental Management" (2008) 41 *Environmental Management* 487–500, 493–494.

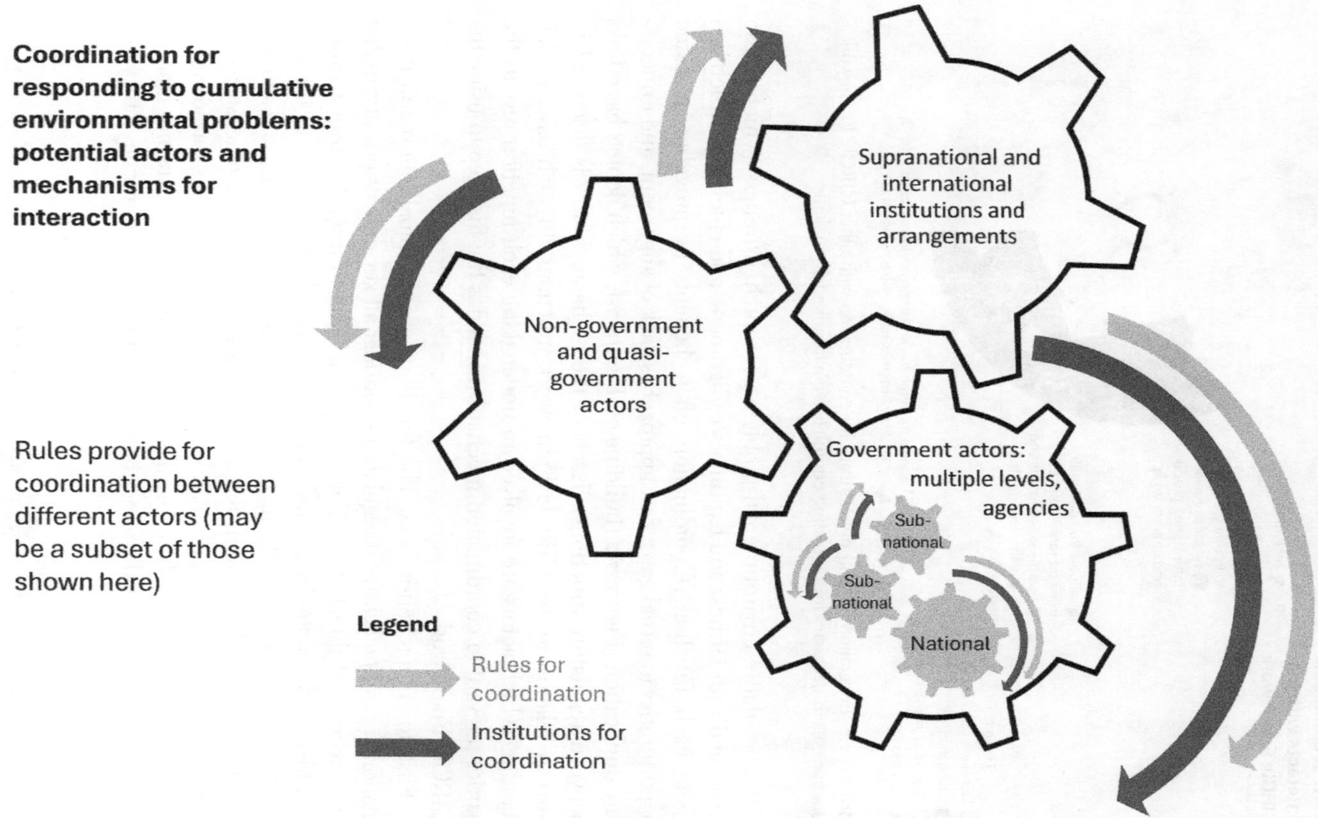

FIGURE 7.1 Coordination for responding to cumulative environmental problems: potential actors and interactions

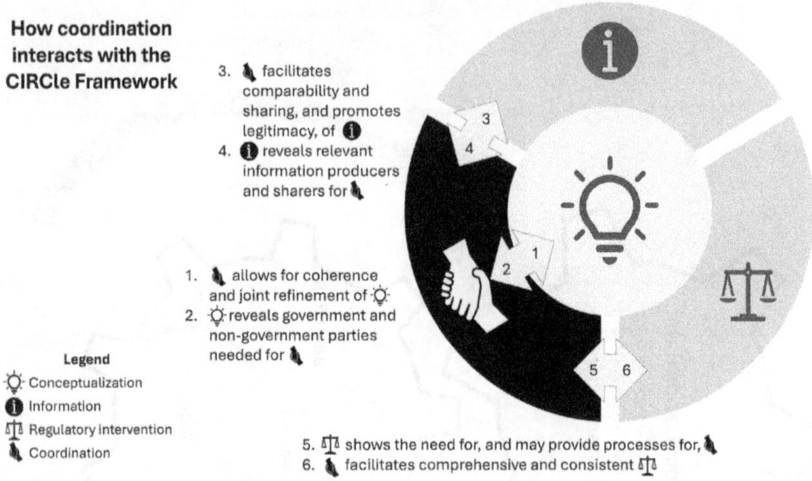

FIGURE 7.2 Integration of legal mechanisms for coordination with other CIRCle Framework functions, each necessary for regulating cumulative environmental problems

with cumulative environmental problems: comprehensiveness (which is also associated with fairness and legitimacy), alignment, and efficiency, which can affect each function. Coordination offers benefits by providing repeated opportunities to reveal gaps, new approaches, lack of alignment, and unnecessary duplication (Figure 7.2 (building on Figure 2.1, which depicts basic links between regulatory functions). Each of these characteristics is discussed in turn in relation to the CIRCle Framework functions. In each case, understanding which actors are involved in undertaking each function reveals the parties relevant to coordination mechanisms, and is the first step to using the CIRCle Framework.[14]

First, to comprehensiveness. The functions of conceptualization and information are *comprehensive* if regulations consider all key dimensions of a matter of concern and threats to it. For example, seeking to protect a river requires considering the watershed[15] and connected groundwater as well as the river itself, and providing for collecting information about these aspects and activities and threats that affect them. Regulatory intervention is comprehensive if all actions that may have cumulatively significant impacts are considered in designing interventions. In particular, comprehensiveness means not ignoring actions that are individually minor or traditionally exempt from rules if they may

[14] See Chapter 11 (Guidelines).

[15] Rebecca Nelson, "Sick City Streams: New Approaches to Legal Treatments" (2020) 43 *Melbourne University Law Review* 748–821, 770.

have cumulative impacts that would cause unacceptable harm.[16] Coordinating actors helps make these functions of conceptualization, information, and regulatory intervention more comprehensive by letting actors share information about the condition of matters of concern and threats to these matters, and share expertise and knowledge about innovative approaches to intervention.[17]

Coordination between levels of government and with nongovernment actors may also indirectly increase the comprehensiveness of functions by creating an awareness of other viewpoints – including by revealing motivations of contributors to cumulative problems, and the likely degree of resistance to a proposed regulatory intervention – and providing an opportunity to build legitimacy to support rules. This information-revealing role is also important as regards the public. If the distance between a regulatory actor and a local public is too great, a regulatory actor may misconceptualize the matter of concern in a way that omits important public views, overlooks key local information, or risks significant noncompliance with a regulatory intervention that is locally considered illegitimate.[18] If too close, a regulatory actor may omit the "bigger picture" of cumulative change in conceptualizing the problem, collecting and analyzing information about it, and intervening.

Secondly – alignment. I use this as a "catch-all" term for the following kinds of conditions: The conceptualization function is carried out coherently[19] such that the relevant actors conceptualize the matter of concern in a mutually reinforcing way, or at least not in a mutually undermining way; data and information are collected and analyzed in a way that is interoperable to facilitate aggregation to understand cumulative change;[20] multiple regulatory interventions are consistent in that they enhance, or at least do not reduce, each other's effectiveness. Coordination that allows actors to negotiate improves implementation of interventions by building support for aligned outcomes,[21] such as a shared understanding of what matters, interoperable information systems, and acceptable interventions. Policy alignment[22] becomes more challenging with more regulatory actors and as delegation

[16] See Section 6.5.2 re comprehensiveness of intervention.

[17] Sarah Fox, "Localizing Environmental Federalism" (2020) 54 *UC Davis Law Review* 133–194, 155, 180, 190, 193.

[18] Margerum, "A Typology of Collaboration Efforts," 496.

[19] This use of the term "coherence" in the context of conceptualization mirrors its use in the policy design literature to describe alignment of policy goals (see Section 1.2.1), though here, conceptualization has a more specific meaning than "goals"; see Chapter 4.

[20] See Section 5.3.3.

[21] Margerum, "A Typology of Collaboration Efforts," 495 (citing many other works), 498.

[22] Ibid 496–497.

grants discretion to an implementing government.[23] Chapter 8 reveals regulatory incoherence between different conceptualizations of "who matters" in the management of groundwater in California. Chapter 10 shows regulatory consistency between interventions designed to preserve and restore Alpine grasslands in South Tyrol, Italy.

Thirdly – efficiency. Coordination can reveal unnecessary duplication between the efforts of different actors. Duplication can be inefficient if a regulatory actor goes to significant effort to undertake information or intervention functions in the same way as another.[24] Importantly, what amounts to duplication is case specific. While overlapping responsibilities may cause conflict and tension between actors who hold them,[25] redundancy may also valuably enhance democracy and insure against agency capture and policy instability.[26] Valuably, agencies or levels of government with overlapping responsibilities may also address different parts of the problem in space (corresponding to their territorial jurisdiction) or use diverse but synergistic regulatory interventions directed toward different categories of contributors to the cumulative environmental problem.

The issue of transaction costs associated with coordination is also important. However, research on complex governance arrangements suggests that different parties to coordination arrangements will face different transaction costs (especially if the problem involves heterogeneous interests), and that these will also vary with local contexts.[27] Accordingly, other than noting the issue, the question of designing legal mechanisms to deal with the cost of coordination for each of the CIRCle Framework functions remains for future empirical research.

[23] Robert D. Cooter and Michael D. Gilbert, *Public Law and Economics* (OUP, 2022) 265 (delegation increases "diversion of purpose").

[24] Kristen A. Goodrich and others, "Toward Improved Sediment Management and Coastal Resilience through Efficient Permitting in California" (2023) 72 *Environmental Management* 558–567, 565 (in relation to permitting processes for intervention). This definition of duplication should be distinguished from the way that term is used by some scholars to indicate that multiple regulatory actors have regulatory authority relevant to the same matter. That situation would not necessarily be classified as duplication here because different actors may address different parts of the problem in space using synergistic regulatory interventions, as discussed next in the text.

[25] E.g., Ponte, Noe and Mwamfupe, "Private and Public Authority Interactions," 1279–1280.

[26] Camacho and Glicksman, "Designing Regulation across Organizations," 26; section 8.3.2.2 in relation to changing priorities in relation to the cumulative concept of environmental justice at the US federal level compared to California. See also Chapter 10, n 126 and accompanying text.

[27] See generally, Mark Lubell and others, "Transaction Costs and the Perceived Effectiveness of Complex Institutional Systems" (2017) 77 *Public Administration Review* 668–680.

In relation to coordinating regulatory intervention, there is also an argument for coordination based on fairness. Cumulative environmental problems involve diverse actors undertaking diverse activities that likely involve different regulators and other affected communities. This introduces the real risk that without some degree of coordination, different sorts of activities will attract interventions that vary in the burdens they place on contributors to the problem and affected communities in ways that are not clearly justified and may be unfair. This points to coordination for regulatory intervention considering the distributional impacts of interventions.[28]

While laws do not guarantee consensus or otherwise successful coordination, which is influenced by many factors, such as leadership and trust,[29] formal rules can provide precision and clarity about responsibilities and a formal requirement or incentive initially to come to the table and to keep coming back. Efforts at formalizing coordination arrangements should, however, consider existing informal rules that deal with certain elements of the problem, both to learn from them and to avoid undercutting existing, effective measures.[30] In some cases, legal mechanisms may formalize existing informal arrangements,[31] whereas in other cases, laws may establish these mechanisms for the first time.[32]

7.2 COORDINATION WITHIN, BETWEEN, AND BEYOND GOVERNMENTS: KEY ACTORS

To establish the context for discussing legal mechanisms for coordination, we first ask: Which government actors have competencies related to the environment? Answering these questions involves examining constitutional distributions of power, other horizontal and vertical distributions of lawmaking power,

[28] Philippa England, "Leaders, Laggards and Blame Games: Responsive Regulation and Environmental Change in the Catchments of the GBR" (2021) unpublished manuscript 25.

[29] Nicola Ulibarri and others, "Drivers and Dynamics of Collaborative Governance in Environmental Management" (2023) 71 *Environmental Management* 495–504, 499.

[30] Note that sometimes informal arrangements are established after formal arrangements: see Section 10.4.2.3.

[31] E.g., the multilevel Interagency Review Team used to review mitigation banks under the US Clean Water Act: Palmer Hough and Rachel Harrington, "Ten Years of the Compensatory Mitigation Rule: Reflections on Progress and Opportunities" (2019) 49 *Environmental Law Reporter News and Analysis* 10018, 10021.

[32] E.g., the planned establishment of a new Australian federal agency, Environment Information Australia, in part to facilitate access to environmental data across governments: Department of Climate Change, Energy, the Environment and Water (Australia), "Budget 2023–2024: Protecting, Repairing and Better Managing the Environment" (2023) 2–3, www.dcceew.gov.au/sites/default/files/documents/protecting-repairing-and-better-managing-the-environment-fs.pdf, archived at https://perma.cc/HK7Q-C7ZQ.

and intersections between government actors and quasi-governmental and nongovernmental actors. Each relevant agency identified must have legal authority to collaborate to support more specific coordination mechanisms.

7.2.1 *Constitutional Responsibilities Related to the Environment*

Constitutions vary in how they allocate power related to the environment among levels of government.[33] Environmental protection is an objective for both the federal and Länder governments in Germany.[34] Italy's national government has exclusive power to protect the environment and ecosystems, though it legislates to grant autonomy to some Regions for this purpose and there are some areas of concurrent power, such as fishing and agriculture.[35] Canada's constitution reveals a "patchwork" of federal powers relating to the environment, based on navigation and shipping, criminal law, and trade and commerce, overlaid on a "carpet" of broader provincial powers relating to property and civil rights and ownership of most natural resources.[36]

Allocations of legislative power over the environment, and the degree to which it is exercised by different levels of government, can change. Accordingly, intergovernmental coordination to address cumulative environmental problems may need to adapt over time. Shifts in power over the environment may occur with evolving statutory implementation of express constitutional environmental provisions, which are now widespread,[37] or with negotiated federalism that stems from constitutional allocations of power affected by uncertainty or "gray areas," as in the United States.[38] Regulatory authority may expand in scope in response to actions that give content to another legislative power. This occurs in Australia, where the federal legislature relies significantly on the government's ratification of international environ-

[33] See generally, e.g., Mariachiara Alberton and Francesco Palermo (eds), *Environmental Protection in Multi-Layered Systems: Comparative Lessons from the Water Sector* (Koninklujke Brill NV 2012); Francesco Palermo and Karl Kössler, *Comparative Federalism* (Hart 2017); Kalyani Robbins (ed), *The Law and Policy of Environmental Federalism* (Edward Elgar 2015).

[34] Palermo and Kössler, *Comparative Federalism*, 391–393.

[35] Ibid 393–396.

[36] Sari Graben and Eric Biber, "Presidents, Parliaments, and Legal Change: Quantifying the Effect of Political Systems in Comparative Environmental Law" (2017) 35 *Virginia Environmental Law Journal* 357–419, 374, citing Meinhard Doelle and Chris Tollefson, *Environmental Law: Cases and Materials* (Carswell 2nd edn, 2013).

[37] Roderic O'Gorman, "Environmental Constitutionalism: A Comparative Study" (2017) 6 *Transnational Environmental Law* 435–462, 437.

[38] Erin Ryan, "Negotiating Environmental Federalism: Dynamic Federalism as a Strategy for Good Governance" (2017) *Wisconsin Law Review* 17–39, 37.

mental treaties, which attracts power to legislate to implement them.[39] Political changes at national or state levels may lead governments to preempt lower-level interventions or withdraw from policy areas, enabling other levels to intervene. This was illustrated when the US federal government's withdrawal from the Paris Agreement triggered state-level attention to emission reductions.[40]

7.2.2 *Vertical and Horizontal Regulatory Complexity beyond Allocations of Competencies*

Consistent with observations in multilevel governance scholarship,[41] cumulative environmental problems often engage a much more complex constellation of regulatory actors vertically and horizontally than constitutional arrangements reveal. Environment-related laws may divide responsibilities for different dimensions of a problem among multiple different actors, vertically and horizontally. Like constitutional arrangements, these divisions may change with time and political developments.[42] An agency may have responsibility influenced by, for example:

1. the *location* of a matter of concern relative to jurisdictional and property boundaries, for example, on federal, state, or local public land, or on private land in a territorial jurisdiction;
2. the *designation* of the matter of concern, for example, species that are listed as endangered or have other similar status, or land or water that has a special conservation status such as a national park or protected water body;
3. types of *impacts* or *actions*, including omissions and background effects that impact the matter of concern, for example, withdrawing and using water, polluting the air, failing to control feral animals, or increased peak heat due to climate change; and
4. types of *entities* that undertake activities that threaten a matter of concern, for example, roads authorities, private corporations, special-purpose local districts, or owners/lessees of land, which may involve different corresponding government actors with responsibilities in relation to these entities.

39 Lee Godden and Jacqueline Peel, *Environmental Law: Scientific, Policy and Regulatory Dimensions* (OUP 2010) 127.

40 Fox, "Localizing Environmental Federalism," 145–146.

41 E.g., Paul Stephenson, "Twenty Years of Multi-Level Governance: 'Where Does It Come From? What Is It? Where Is It Going?'" (2013) 20 *Journal of European Public Policy* 817–837, 817.

42 Moritz Reese, "Distribution of Powers" in Emma Lees and Jorge E. Viñuales (eds), *The Oxford Handbook of Comparative Environmental Law* (OUP 2019) 678–702, 690.

Vertically, different levels of government may be engaged by even a spatially limited matter of concern, as the case study on Alpine grasslands demonstrates: four levels of domestic regulation and supranational and international laws influence relevant matters across nature, landscape, agriculture, and impact assessment laws.

Regulatory authority related to a cumulative environmental problem may also span agencies at the same level, triggering a need for horizontal coordination.[43] This may be a side effect of jurisdictional boundary-drawing that does not match an environmental resource, for example, as demonstrated in the well-studied problem of interjurisdictional water resources.[44] Horizontal regulatory fragmentation may also be intentional. In Queensland, Australia, separating mining and environment agencies is intended to help agencies transparently pursue conflicting economic and environmental policies in influencing mine authorizations.[45]

7.2.3 *Nongovernmental and Quasi-governmental Actors*

Much environmental legal scholarship dealing with nongovernment actors focuses on their role in challenging administrative decisions, but nongovernment actors may also play important ongoing roles in regulatory systems for responding to cumulative environmental problems.[46] They may seek to intervene to address the problem or represent those undertaking activities that contribute to the problem or are affected by it in coordination initiatives to

[43] E.g., Gwen Arnold, "When Cooperative Federalism Isn't – How US Federal Interagency Contradictions Impede Effective Wetland Management" (2015) 45 *Publius – The Journal of Federalism* 244–269, 245–246; Dave Owen, "Cooperative Subfederalism" (2018) 9 *University of California Irvine Law Review* 177–227.

[44] Mark Elder and Christian Loewe, "Introduction and Context – Global Environment Outlook (Geo-6): Healthy Planet, Healthy People" in Paul Ekins, Joyeeta Gupta and Pierre Boileau (eds), *Global Environment Outlook (GEO-6): Healthy Planet, Healthy People* (United Nations Environment Programme 2019) 3–19, 11; Palermo and Kössler, *Comparative Federalism*, 383; Arvind Lakshmisha and Andreas Thiel, "Legitimacy, Shared Understanding and Exchange of Resources: Co-Managing Lakes Along an Urban–Rural Gradient in Greater Bengaluru Metropolitan Region, India" (2023) 71 *Environmental Management* 523–537, 530.

[45] Jacqueline Peel, "An Environmental Revolution in the Queensland Mining Industry or Just a Changing of the Guard – An Analysis of the New Regime for the Environmental Regulation of Mining under the Environmental Protection Act (Qld)" (2001) 20 *Australian Mining and Petroleum Law Journal* 137–147, 140. See also Rebecca Nelson, "Regulating Hidden Risks to Conservation Lands in Resource Rich Areas" (2021) 40 *University of Queensland Law Journal* 491–530, 504–514.

[46] See, e.g., Will Reisinger, Trent A. Dougherty and Nolan Moser, "Environmental Enforcement and the Limits of Cooperative Federalism: Will Courts Allow Citizen Suits to Pick up the Slack?" (2010) 20 *Duke Environmental Law and Policy Forum* 1–62.

solve it. Nongovernment actors can bring together heterogeneous local stakeholders and contribute local knowledge and resources.[47] Organizations that represent contributors to a cumulative problem can offer governments important information about likely resistance to or acceptability of regulatory interventions. Some organizations may act as intermediary organizations that "buffer" community distrust of government[48] or build legitimacy, although the relationship between stakeholder participation and legitimacy is not straightforward.[49] Nongovernment actors are not confined to the divisions and silos that affect government actors, and they may draw on norms beyond legal rules, for example, in the case of faith-based environmental organizations.[50]

Interactions between private and public actors may be complementary (pursuing shared or aligned goals), competitive (involving struggles to monopolize political authority or displace another's interventions), or coexistent (involving divergent goals and strategies, and sometimes overlapping interventions),[51] and their nature may change with time.[52] The focus here is on the use of legal mechanisms that support involving nongovernment actors in legal systems for addressing cumulative environmental problems in an ongoing complementary way. This applies a legal lens to what Cashore and others term "collaboration" in the sense of "active, voluntary and conscious partnership between public and private governance … established through direct communication."[53]

Between nongovernment actors and public actors lie quasi-government actors, such as state-owned enterprises, quasi-autonomous nongovernment

[47] E.g., see generally Lakshmisha and Thiel, "Legitimacy, Shared Understanding and Exchange of Resources."

[48] Casey L. Taylor, "Partnerships, Lawsuits, and Competing Accountabilities in CCAA Agreements" (2023) 71 *Environmental Management* 655–669, 663–664.

[49] E.g., Alba Mohedano Roldán, Andreas Duit and Lisen Schultz, "Does Stakeholder Participation Increase the Legitimacy of Nature Reserves in Local Communities? Evidence from 92 Biosphere Reserves in 36 Countries" (2019) 21 *Journal of Environmental Policy and Planning* 188–203, 198–199.

[50] E.g., Jens Koehrsen, "Muslims and Climate Change: How Islam, Muslim Organizations, and Religious Leaders Influence Climate Change Perceptions and Mitigation Activities" (2021) 12:e702 *WIREs Climate Change* 1–19, 7–12.

[51] Benjamin Cashore and others, "Private Authority and Public Policy Interactions in Global Context: Governance Spheres for Problem Solving" (2021) 15 *Regulation and Governance* 1166–1182, 1172.

[52] Margerum, "A Typology of Collaboration Efforts," 494; Cashore and others, "Private Authority and Public Policy Interactions," 1167–1168, 1176.

[53] Cashore and others, "Private Authority and Public Policy Interactions," 1173. See also Mary Gleason and others, "A Transactional and Collaborative Approach to Reducing Effects of Bottom Trawling" (2013) 27 *Conservation Biology* 470–479, 478. See also note e in Table 7.3 and accompanying text.

organizations (NGOs established and given authority by a government),[54] and importantly for present purposes, associations of local districts and inter-jurisdictional bodies. In the context of cumulative environmental problems, they provide for coordination either by linking up public and private entities or by helping small jurisdictional units to voice common concerns.[55]

7.3 COORDINATING KEY FUNCTIONS TO ADDRESS CUMULATIVE ENVIRONMENTAL PROBLEMS

Environment-related laws and administrative arrangements around the world present a rich trove of real-world coordination mechanisms to address cumulative environmental problems. This section opens with overarching reflections on broad approaches to coordination – institutions and rules. It then illustrates diverse approaches to coordinating actors in relation to each of the key CIRCle Framework functions of conceptualization, information, and regulatory intervention, in turn. As for other chapters, the examples provided here are illustrative. They draw out diversity in geography and approach, rather than attempting to be comprehensive or to uncover the most successful or best performing options, the demonstration of which would require further empirical work. The chapter concludes by discussing legal mechanisms for resolving disagreements and disputes, with a focus on coordinating government actors.

It is important to acknowledge the implications of aspiring to coordination for dealing with cumulative environmental problems. Coordination takes time, sometimes a long time.[56] Some would argue that where cumulative harms are urgent, there is no time to coordinate or build consensus among many diverse actors. Rather than urgency justifying ignoring coordination and taking a regulatory steamroller to any of the functions discussed here, an alternative is to use precaution – responding to an urgent need with an urgent but temporary response that allows more time for proper coordination efforts, as discussed further later.

54 Howlett, *Designing Public Policies*, 170–176.

55 The issue of rules for the design of these organizations goes beyond the present scope, but is an area of active research. See, e.g., Saba N. Siddiki and others, "How Policy Rules Shape the Structure and Performance of Collaborative Governance Arrangements" (2015) 75 *Public Administration Review* 536–547; Michael Kiparsky and others, "The Importance of Institutional Design for Distributed Local-Level Governance of Groundwater: The Case of California's Sustainable Groundwater Management Act" (2017) 9(1):755 *Water* 1–17.

56 E.g., Patricia N. Manley, Jonathan W. Long and Robert M. Scheller, "Keeping up with the Landscapes: Promoting Resilience in Dynamic Social-Ecological Systems" (2024) 29(1):3 *Ecology and Society* 1–13, 7.

7.3.1 *Overarching Reflections: Institutions versus Rules and Power Structures in Coordination Mechanisms*

Across all the mechanisms discussed here, two major formal approaches to coordination emerge. One centers on general or special-purpose institutions tasked with coordination, the other on rules and power structures for coordination. Institutions may support interactions between actors, usually, though not always, across multiple functions. Institutions include intergovernmental councils,[57] executive forums, joint institutions and specialized agencies, and some kinds of intergovernmental agreements.[58] They allow for regular "vertical" meetings of federal and subnational representatives, "horizontal" meetings of representatives at the same level of government, or both.[59] In some cases, a specific agency or bureaucrat may be tasked with coordinating the consideration of environmental effects across government agencies.[60] By contrast, rules-based coordination is associated with one or more legal mechanisms that support specific functions in the CIRCle Framework without creating a separate coordinating institution. Coordinating rules may appear in the form of detailed joint planning processes, or less detailed duties to cooperate with, consult or notify other actors, such as a requirement of agencies generally to "proactively engage" underserved communities and nongovernmental actors to inform regulatory plans.[61]

Considering the challenges that characterize cumulative environmental problems[62] permits some theoretical observations about possible advantages and disadvantages of coordinating institutions versus rules. Institutions that deal with multiple CIRCle Framework functions provide theoretically greater scope for integrating functions – a vital element of the CIRCle Framework[63] – compared to rules that appear in narrower contexts. Integrating functions is especially important where change requires adaptation, for example, where information about new impacts

57 Johanna Schnabel, *Managing Interdependencies in Federal Systems: Intergovernmental Councils and the Making of Public Policy* (Palgrave Macmillan 2020) 3.

58 See generally, ibid.

59 Ibid, 3. See also Anika Klafki, "Legal Harmonization through Interfederal Cooperation: A Comparison of the Interfederal Harmonization of Law through Uniform Law Conferences and Executive Intergovernmental Conferences" (2018) 19 *German Law Journal* 1437–1460, 1451–1454.

60 E.g., State Development and Public Works Organisation Act 1971 (Queensland) s 25.

61 Joseph R. Biden, "Modernizing Regulatory Review (Executive Order 14094)" (April 6, 2023) 88 Federal Register (US) 21879 s 2(c), now revoked by Donald J. Trump, "Initial Rescissions of Harmful Executive Orders and Actions (Executive Order 14148)" (January 20, 2025) 90 Federal Register (US) 8237 s 2. 88 Federal Register 21879 (USA) s 2(c), now revoked by Executive Order 14148 of January 20, 2025, 90 Federal Register 8237 (USA).

62 See generally, Chapter 2.

63 Section 2.4.

requires new interventions. However, cumulative environmental problems that accumulate slowly may not attract the sustained attention of coordination institutions that deal with a wide range of issues, including some that seem more pressing or prominent. Duty-based mechanisms require fewer resources than institutional mechanisms because they do not involve resourcing a dedicated institution, and they are inherently adaptable because they lack a defined structure. However, a duty by itself cannot create a meeting mechanism in the same way as more detailed arrangements, nor can it provide funding or staff to facilitate ongoing interactions.

A further overarching observation relates to the different distributions of power among relevant coordinating actors. As the examples show, some coordination mechanisms reflect equality and require consensus, while others compel lower-level governments to act consistently with higher-level governments, or vice versa, in relation to a regulatory function. Some even repose powers in independent bodies rather than any one level of government.

It is not possible to pick a universal "winner" among these approaches. Designing the right mechanism will depend on contextual factors, including the environmental problem itself, resource availability, the diversity and number of relevant actors, how environmental legal competencies are allocated, the political system, and the function at issue. Coordinating interventions to respond to the cumulative effects of waste disposal in the federal nation of Palau (with 22,000 people across 16 states and a vast, largely maritime territory)[64] will necessarily involve different considerations than those most relevant to regulating the gathering, sharing, and analysis of data and information about cumulative environmental effects on faunal biodiversity in the quasi-federal state of Italy (with fifty-nine million people and numerous layers of government across a relatively small territory).[65] Additionally, collaborative governance literature highlights the dynamic nature of collaborations,[66] which raises the possibility that different legal mechanisms may best serve coordination at different stages or levels of maturity of coordinating actions to deal with a cumulative environmental problem.

7.3.2 *Coordinating in Conceptualizing a Cumulative Environmental Problem*

Conceptualizing a matter of concern involves developing a clear idea of what matters, its spatial boundaries, and cumulative threshold conditions that

64 Palau Government, "States" (n.d.) www.palaugov.pw/states/, last accessed March 20, 2025, archived at https://perma.cc/69P6-YEMT; United Nations, "UNdata: Palau" (n.d.) https://data.un.org/en/iso/pw.html, last accessed March 20, 2025.

65 United Nations, "UNdata: Italy" (n.d.) https://data.worldbank.org/country/italy, last accessed March 20, 2025; Section 10.3.2.

66 Ulibarri and others, "Drivers and Dynamics," 501.

distinguish acceptable from unacceptable conditions.[67] Where multiple actors are involved, this requires articulating and adjudicating the conflicting values that underlie environmental disputes,[68] and reaching shared understandings of goals among those seeking to solve a joint problem.[69]

Table 7.1 sets out legislative examples of coordination processes associated with formally articulating the key dimensions of conceptualization, noting that stakeholder engagement per se is important but not unique to cumulative environmental problems, so lies outside the present scope. The examples involve different configurations of vertical and horizontal coordination by governmental agencies, quasi-governmental agencies, and nongovernmental actors at different scales, from a small water body to jurisdiction-spanning aquifers, to a species over its entire distribution.

7.3.3 *Coordinating in Relation to Information*

The intergovernmental relations literature tends to view information sharing as the lowest form of commitment to intergovernmental coordination,[70] at least when pursued in isolation and in a generic rather than a problem-specific context. Without coordination about information, though, the design of interventions to address cumulative environmental problems may overlook key contributors to the problem or declining trends in the condition of the matter of concern, or actors may collect information with inefficient duplication or in a way that precludes aggregation to reveal cumulative impacts. Information sharing may also be a politically palatable starting point for broader coordination.[71]

Mechanisms that facilitate general information sharing, such as the public data clearinghouses discussed in Chapter 5 on Information, and further

67 See Chapter 4.

68 See generally, Daniel Sarewitz, "How Science Makes Environmental Controversies Worse" (2004) 7 *Environmental Science and Policy* 385–403.

69 E.g., Albert V. Norström and others, "Principles for Knowledge Co-Production in Sustainability Research" (2020) 3 *Nature Sustainability* 182–190, 186; Taylor, "Partnerships, Lawsuits," 662–663; Chris Ansell and Alison Gash, "Collaborative Governance in Theory and Practice" (2008) 18 *Journal of Public Administration Research and Theory* 543–571, 560. See also Chapter 2.

70 Schnabel, *Managing Interdependencies*, 60.

71 Miranda A. Schreurs, "Multi-Level Governance the ASEAN Way" in Henrik Enderlein, Sonja Walti and Michael Zurn (eds), *Handbook on Multi-Level Governance* (Edward Elgar 2010) 308–320, 311; Rebecca Nelson and Meg Casey, "Beyond the Traditional Governance of Trans-Jurisdictional Groundwater: Unconventional Approaches to Cross-Boundary Aquifer Management in the United States" in Janice Gray, Cameron Holley and Rosemary Rayfuse (eds), *Trans-Jurisdictional Water Law and Governance* (Routledge (Earthscan) 2016) 138–156, 142–145.

TABLE 7.1 *Mechanisms for coordination to conceptualize cumulative environmental problems*

Legal mechanism	Illustrative examples
Coordination in designating a matter of concern, including spatial elements	In India, the Andhra Pradesh Water, Land and Trees Authority, which is comprised of representatives from multiple state government agencies, independent experts, Indigenous groups, Scheduled Castes and women, may declare "over exploited areas" of groundwater, which triggers a time-limited moratorium on new wells.[a] It may delegate this function to a variety of local authorities.[b]
	The designation of a biocultural Biodiversity Heritage Site in India engages its complex multitiered system of statutory biodiversity entities: a subnational State Biodiversity Board recommends a site to the state government, which designates the site after having consulted a Biodiversity Management Committee that may be constituted at a variety of local levels; rules for the site are determined by the state government in consultation with the Central Government.[c] Though its implementation is perceived as slow, this system is praised for its biocultural and participatory approach.[d]
Coordination in developing shared goals/thresholds for a common matter of concern	In the US state of Texas, multiple local-scale groundwater conservation districts that overlie groundwater management areas undertake joint planning processes to determine "desired future conditions" for groundwater.[e] A state agency uses locally determined desired future conditions to provide each local district with scientific information on available water corresponding to these conditions as the basis of local planning.[f]
Coordination in setting restoration goals	A quasi-government organization, Melbourne Water, develops a statutory strategic plan to restore the Yarra/Birrarung River in Melbourne, Australia. The strategic plan must give effect to a "long-term community vision document" prepared using community codesign. Among other things, that vision document identifies community values and priorities for land adjoining the river. An independent Birrarung Council with membership drawn from

Legal mechanism	Illustrative examples
	Aboriginal, environmental, agricultural, and community groups advises the government on the development of the strategic plan, which translates the community vision into performance objectives.[g]

[a] Andhra Pradesh Water, Land and Trees Act 2002 (Andhra Pradesh, India) ss 3, 11.
[b] Ibid s 7.
[c] Biological Diversity Act 2002 (India) ss 37, 41, as amended by the Biological Diversity (Amendment) Act 2023 (India) s 27.
[d] Aparna Watve and Vishwas Chavan, "Conceptualising Framework for Local Biodiversity Heritage Sites (LBHS): A Bio-cultural Model for Biodiversity Conservation in Maharashtra" (2020) 22 *Asian Biotechnology and Development Review* 61–82, 65–66.
[e] Texas Water Code § 36.108.
[f] Texas Water Code § 36.1084.
[g] Yarra River Protection (Wilip-gin Birrarung murron) Act 2017 (Victoria, Australia) ss 17, 20(1)(a), 48. See also Nelson, "Sick City Streams," 768–770.

described here, also give regulatory actors and stakeholders access to information. However, they do not necessarily allow for coordination involving interaction, which makes it more likely that the information produced will be used in decision-making processes.[72] More interactive information-related mechanisms include intergovernmental agreements, joint agencies established to address a specific problem, and coordination arrangements that apply to specific decision-making processes about cumulative impacts, such as project-level and strategic impact assessments. Nongovernmental actors may play an important role in triggering or facilitating information coordination between governments, or partnering with governments using these mechanisms.[73]

Table 7.2 sets out examples, including those that provide for general advisory functions as a form of coordination of information, noting that there is some overlap with advice about intervention, discussed next. Chapter 9 describes the coordination that produced the strategic assessment of cumulative impacts on the Great Barrier Reef, triggered by an environmental NGO sharing with the World Heritage Committee information about growing unaddressed cumulative impacts on the Reef; a subsequent research and development program for climate adaptation and restoration is cofunded by governments and NGOs.[74]

72 Norström and others, "Principles for Knowledge Co-Production," 186.
73 E.g., Table 7.4 row 2.
74 Sections 9.3.1 and 9.5.3.

TABLE 7.2 *Mechanisms for coordinated information initiatives to address cumulative environmental problems*

Legal mechanism	Illustrative example
Intergovernmental advisory council/ agreements to share information	Germany's *Umweltministerkonferenz* is a formally constituted, multilevel environmental ministerial conference with many working groups undertaking activities that are transparently communicated.[a] Its activities include coordination relating to information, e.g., developing uniform indicators on the impact of climate change on the water sector.[b]
Problem-specific intergovernmental advisory body	For Pacific Island nations, multi-stakeholder, multilevel advisory councils are central to informing climate change adaptation measures.[c] Tuvalu's statutory National Advisory Council on Climate Change advises on matters related to climate change, disasters, and sustainable development. Its members include representatives from a wide range of government agencies, umbrella groups for nongovernment organizations, and a church representative.[d]
Multilevel agency with information-related functions	An agreement between a dozen federal and state agencies and stakeholder groups for water allocation and management in California's Bay Delta involved creating a position of Lead Scientist and an Independent Science Board to develop credible information, in part to deal with "combat science" and distrust of data produced by different agencies.[e] A multiagency, multilevel Data Assessment Team met weekly to analyze technical data about water quality, fish, and flows, and make recommendations about interventions.[f] Ultimately, a statutory "Bay-Delta Authority" was created as "an honest broker, a source of information, and a procurer of science," with membership from state and federal agencies, the public, and others.[g]
Joint intergovernmental committee dedicated to information issues	A formal Compact between the US National Park Service and the state of Montana establishes a federal–state Technical Oversight Committee to assess the cumulative impacts of development affecting the hydrothermal system that supports geysers in Yellowstone National Park (an information function) and makes associated intervention-related recommendations about groundwater appropriations proposed under state law.[h]
Duty of cooperation in assessing cumulative impacts of a project	In considering cumulative and other impacts under Canada's federal Impact Assessment Act, government has a duty of consultation and cooperation[i] that applies

Legal mechanism	Illustrative example
	to jurisdictions with relevant powers, duties or functions; the term "jurisdiction" is defined broadly to include agencies, bodies, authorities, Indigenous governing bodies, a government of a foreign state, or an international organization.[j]
Coordinated strategic planning requirements and a multilevel, interagency coordination committee	South Africa's National Environmental Management Act ("NEMA") requires intergovernmental coordination and harmonization of policies, legislation, and actions relating to the environment. Certain national departments and every province prepare plans for this purpose and to promote consistency in the exercise of environmental functions. Every organ of the state must exercise its functions in accordance with the plans. Under an earlier version of the legislation, a statutory Committee for Environmental Co-ordination also sought to "promote the integration and co-ordination of environmental functions" by state organs and advance the objectives of the coordination plans.[k]

[a] "Konferenz der Umweltminister des Bundes und der Länder (UMK)" (n.d.) www .umweltministerkonferenz.de/, last accessed March 19, 2025, archived at https://perma.cc/U5JU-CHPW.

[b] Umweltministerkonferenz, Circular Resolution 26/2023, "LAWA-Konzept Klimafolgenmoni toring für den Wassersektor – Schlussbericht der LAWA-KG Klimaindikatoren" (2023) www .umweltministerkonferenz.de/umlbeschluesse/umlauf2023_26.pdf, archived at https://perma.cc/7SHQ-4GDK.

[c] See generally, Kate Morioka and others, "Applying Information for National Adaptation Planning and Decision Making: Present and Future Practice in the Pacific Islands" (2020) 20:135 *Regional Environmental Change* 1–12.

[d] Climate Change Resilience Act 2019 (Tuvalu) ss 19–20; "NACCC – National Advisory Council on Climate Change," Tuvalu Climate Change Portal (n.d.) www.tuvaluclimatechange.gov.tv/naccc-national-advisory-council-climate-change, last accessed March 19, 2025, archived at https://perma.cc/959B-5R69.

[e] Freeman and Farber, "Modular Environmental Regulation," 845–846.

[f] Ibid 850.

[g] Ibid 855–856.

[h] Montana Code Annotated 85-20-401 art. IV(J)(1) (US National Park Service - Montana Compact) See *Progress Report: Yellowstone Controlled Groundwater Area Technical Oversight Committee 2014–2018* (2019) https://dnrc.mt.gov/_docs/water/controlled-ground-water-areas/191212_5-year_Report_2018-web-sm.pdf, archived at https://perma.cc/4UKA-J67Q.

[i] Impact Assessment Act 2019 (Canada) s 21.

[j] Ibid ss 2 ("jurisdiction"), 21, 22(1)(a)(ii) (considering cumulative effects).

[k] NEMA 1998, as amended (South Africa) ss 7 (now repealed), 11(1), (2), 12(a), 16(1), (a) (the plans are known as environmental implementation plans and environmental management plans). See also E. Couzens and M. Dent, "Finding NEMA: The National Environmental Management Act, the De Hoop Dam, Conflict Resolution and Alternative Dispute Resolution in Environmental Disputes" (2006) 9(3) *Potchefstroom Electronic Law Journal* 1–51, 15, citing NEMA s 2(4)(l).

7.3.4 *Coordinating Regulatory Intervention among Governments, Legal Areas, and Cumulative Environmental Problems*

Coordination can promote synergies and comprehensiveness in regulatory intervention, help discover and address inconsistencies, and avoid unnecessary duplication and gaps in responding to cumulative environmental problems.[75] Table 7.3 includes examples of both institutions and rules for these purposes.

Coordination mechanisms can also encourage structured intergovernmental and government–NGO interactions that deal with intervention (Table 7.3). Nongovernment and quasi-government actors can support regulatory intervention by government in various ways. As a preliminary matter, they can help define the regulatory modes (strategies and approaches)[76] that constitute acceptable interventions. The Intergovernmental Panel on Climate Change is tasked with identifying climate change response strategies, which involves advising on plausible mitigation pathways through their assessment reports, including as to technologies such as geoengineering and carbon capture and storage as well as reducing emissions.[77] Nongovernment actors may also reinforce the use of regulatory sticks or facilitate local take-up of regulatory carrots and advice to fill gaps in the implementation of regulatory interventions (in both cases, promoting comprehensiveness[78]). Governments may broadly encourage this role, for example, through incentives for NGOs to fund private protected areas to complement public lands dedicated to conservation purposes.[79] Local nongovernmental collectives or transnational NGOs can help deliver incentive payments that governments or they themselves fund; and governments may link with private sustainability standards – a form of regulatory sermon – through environmental agreements, arbitration, trade, or energy policies.[80]

[75] For a discussion of these points, see Section 7.1.2.

[76] See Sections 6.2 to 6.4.

[77] United Nations General Assembly, Resolution on Protection of Global Climate for Present and Future Generations of Mankind, December 6, 1988 (UN Doc A/RES/43/53); Intergovernmental Panel on Climate Change, "Reports" (n.d.) www.ipcc.ch/reports/, last accessed March 20, 2025.

[78] For a discussion of comprehensive intervention, see Section 6.5.2.

[79] Nelson, "Regulating Hidden Risks," 494–496.

[80] For a synthesis of key themes in the literature on private standards organizations, see Luc Fransen, "Beyond Regulatory Governance? On the Evolutionary Trajectory of Transnational Private Sustainability Governance" (2018) 146 *Ecological Economics* 772–777, especially at 773 for links with governments. See also Duncan J. Snidal and Kenneth W. Abbott, "The Governance Triangle: Regulatory Standards Institutions and the Shadow of the State" in Kenneth W. Abbott and Duncan J. Snidal (eds), *The Spectrum of International Institutions: An Interdisciplinary Collaboration on Global Governance* (Routledge 2021) 52–91, 55 (coordination in the context of standards).

TABLE 7.3 *Mechanisms to recognize regulatory inconsistency and promote synergies in coordinating interventions to address cumulative environmental problems*

Legal mechanism	Illustrative examples
Interagency institutional mechanism to consider interactions between interventions	In the United States, the national-level Office of Information and Regulatory Affairs was established to consider how regulatory interventions interact through a communication and review process for existing regulation; a process for agencies to notify the Office of their regulatory plans so that other agencies could alert the Office to potential conflicts; and a centralized review process for "significant" regulations, about which the Office could advise in relation to consistency with policies and actions of other agencies.[a]
Rules to consider interactions between interventions	In the US state of Washington, legislation directs the Department of Ecology to consider the potential for existing statutes to conflict with the policies of "water resource programs" and to submit proposed statutory modifications to resolve any issues.[b]
Plan to assess consistency of interventions	The European Common Agricultural Policy requires each member state to adopt a national "CAP Strategic Plan". A Plan must set out the interventions that the member state uses to meet environment-related objectives, expressly demonstrating how interventions are "mutually coherent and compatible" for individual objectives, and how interventions are consistent and complementary *across* objectives.[c]
Coordinated intervention by governmental and nongovernmental actors	With an agreement in place for ongoing funding from international nongovernmental organizations (NGOs) to offset a loss in commercial fishing revenue, the Republic of Kiribati declared a 410,500-km² marine protected area in the uninhabited Phoenix Islands, including a no-take zone.[d] An NGO-funded trawl permit buyout has also occurred in the United States.[e]

[a] William J. Clinton, "Regulatory Planning and Review (Executive Order 12866)" (September 30, 1993) 58 *Federal Register* (US) 51375 ss 2(f), 4(c)(2)–(4), 5, 6(b); Office of Information and Regulatory Affairs (US), "OIRA" (n.d.) www.reginfo.gov/public/jsp/Utilities/faq.myjsp#oira, last accessed March 19, 2025, archived at https://perma.cc/BBM3-CDX3.

(*continued*)

TABLE 7.3 (*continued*)

[b] Revised Code of Washington § 90.54.040(3). For a similar example in South Australian land use legislation, see Planning, Development and Infrastructure Act 2016 (South Australia) s 57(1).
[c] Regulation 2021/2115 of the European Parliament and of the Council of December 2, 2021 on Common Agricultural Policy Strategic Plans, [2021] OJ L435/1 (CAP Regulation), preamble (101), (102), arts. 104, 109(1)(c), 118(2), 139(3)(b).
[d] Phoenix Islands Protected Area Conservation Trust Act 2009, as amended (Kiribati) ss 6, 26; Rebecca L. Gruby and others, "Policy Interactions in Large-Scale Marine Protected Areas" (2021) 14:e12753 *Conservation Letters* 1–9, 4–6.
[e] Gleason and others, "A Transactional and Collaborative Approach," 476–478.

While considering these potential benefits, regulatory designers should be attuned to the potential for NGO involvement to create conflict and inconsistency between regulatory interventions. For example, regulatory carrots that funnel revenue to powerful NGOs rather than resource-poor communities may exacerbate power imbalances, causing conflict,[81] and private standards may undermine state regulatory instruments.[82]

Coordination mechanisms can also address interventions at the interface of different cumulative environmental problems (Table 7.3). This raises the challenge of anticipating and dealing with connections between problems in the first place. These connections can arise in different ways. Sometimes the same activity contributes to two different cumulative environmental problems, which invites considering "stacked" interventions that deal with both problems. We see this in the Great Barrier Reef case study: Both grazing and coal mines lead to greenhouse pollution and water quality threats to the Reef,[83] with the potential to better link interventions dealing with these impacts. In other cases, an intervention to deal with one cumulative environmental problem makes it more difficult to deal with another (as in the Alps case study: Rewilding initiatives that reintroduce large predators to their historical ranges are perceived to discourage traditional grazing that is required to maintain biodiverse grasslands[84]). Responses at the interface between cumulative environmental problems might involve prioritizing interventions that fulfill multiple objectives and avoiding or compensating for interventions that adversely affect the nontarget problem.[85]

81 See generally, Ponte, Noe and Mwamfupe, "Private and Public Authority Interactions."
82 E.g. Pablo Pacheco and others, "Governing Sustainable Palm Oil Supply: Disconnects, Complementarities, and Antagonisms between State Regulations and Private Standards" (2020) 14 *Regulation and Governance* 568–598, 576–578.
83 See Section 9.2.2.
84 See Section 10.5.
85 Guy Pe'Er and others, "How Can the European Common Agricultural Policy Help Halt Biodiversity Loss? Recommendations by over 300 Experts" (2022) 15:e12901 *Conservation Letters* 1–12, 6.

7.3.5 *Resolving Disputes, Gaps, and Drift in and through Coordination*

Finally, legal mechanisms for coordination can also address the potential for resolving disputes about inconsistent approaches, implementation gaps, or "drift" where multiple levels of government play different roles in addressing a cumulative environmental problem (e.g., lower-level government implementing higher-level mandate). Perhaps most prominently, rules for preemption give one level of government the power to override another.[86] In some jurisdictions (e.g., the United States, Australia, Germany, Brazil, and Canada), federal law generally overrules inconsistent state law.[87] Similarly, local laws may be overridden by provincial or central laws – as sometimes occurs in relation to local rights for nature laws[88] and some classic problems of cumulative impact, such as plastic bag bans and pesticide restrictions.[89] By contrast, non-preemption or "gold-plating" allows concurrent intervention where more protective local approaches prevail (Table 7.4). Such rules do not remove the need for coordination, though, since alignment and integration are also required in situations and for functions that are less likely to attract rules of preemption, such as rules for information.

Implementation gaps and drift are different problems that can arise where administrators may have significant discretion as to implementation.[90] Some European member states can be reluctant to implement and enforce European environmental directives.[91] Local-level Chinese governments face stronger individual incentives to promote economic development than implement national environmental laws,[92] as may US states, which share some

[86] Fox, "Localizing Environmental Federalism," 152.

[87] Sandra Zellmer, "Federal Pre-Emption and Displacement of Environmental Statutes and Common Law Claims," in Nicholas S. Bryner, Robert L. Glicksman and LeRoy C. Paddock (eds), *Elgar Encyclopedia of Environmental Law* Vol. II (Edward Elgar 2016) 96–107, 99.

[88] E.g., Elizabeth Kronk Warner and Jensen Lillquist, "Laboratories of the Future: Tribes and Rights of Nature" (2023) 111 *California Law Review* 325–393, 386–388; Peter Doran and Rachel Killean, "Rights of Nature: Origins, Development and Possibilities for the Island of Ireland" (Environmental Justice Network Ireland Civil Society Briefing Paper, January 2022) 2, https://ejni.net/wp-content/uploads/2022/01/EJNI-Briefing-Paper-Rights-of-Nature-Jan-2157.pdf.

[89] Fox, "Localizing Environmental Federalism," 154.

[90] See, e.g., Andrew Macintosh and Lauren Waugh, "Compensatory Mitigation and Screening Rules in Environmental Impact Assessment" (2014) 49 *Environmental Impact Assessment Review* 1–12, 1, 8–11.

[91] Sara Dillon, "The Mirage of EC Environmental Federalism in a Reluctant Member State Jurisdiction" (1999) 8 *NYU Environmental Law Journal* 1–73, 8–9, 12.

[92] Huiyu Zhao and Robert Percival, "Comparative Environmental Federalism: Subsidiarity and Central Regulation in the United States and China" (2017) 6 *Transnational Environmental Law* 531–549, 544–547.

TABLE 7.4 *Mechanisms to address drift, implementation gaps and disputes in coordinated interventions for cumulative environmental problems*

Mechanism	Illustrative legal example
Avoiding drift by retaining central role in cumulative impact decision-making	In Australia, statutory "bilateral agreements" allow a state to conduct environmental impact assessments and approve developments for the purposes of national law.[a] However, the national legislation expressly precludes agreements that would allow a state to approve the narrow categories of developments that require national cumulative impact assessment,[b] in the context of concerns that these developments require a higher level of accountability.[c]
Higher-level step-in power to remedy lack of lower-level implementation	In Canada, the national government may take emergency action to protect an endangered species if a provincial government fails to do so, and the relevant minister must make a recommendation to do so if "the species faces imminent threats to its survival or recovery."[d] In practice, emergency orders are rarely made, and only in response to nongovernmental organization (NGO) agitation, but national intervention may also result in voluntary conservation agreements between the provincial and national government to address the problem without issuing a formal order.[e]
"Fallback" higher-level intervention in the absence of coordinated multilevel, multi-stakeholder intervention	In the US state of Washington, state law imposes a default volumetric limit on permit-exempt groundwater wells used for domestic purposes due to cumulative impacts on salmon streams in certain watersheds. Local plans can lift these limits if they provide for offsetting the impacts on streamflow of permit-exempt water use. A plan must be agreed upon by federally recognized Indian tribes, the state departments of ecology and of fish and wildlife, each relevant county and city, the largest irrigation district, water service provider, and representatives of residential construction and agricultural and environmental interests. The state department of ecology may "step in" if no plan is approved by a deadline,[f] which has occurred on several occasions.[g]

Mechanism	Illustrative legal example
Right to non-preemption or stricter lower-level intervention than required	The exercise of environmental powers by the European Union (EU) does not prevent member states applying "more stringent protective measures."[h] This occurs in practice, e.g., various member states have adopted pollution limits on nitrogen dioxide, particulates, sulfur dioxide, and benzene that are stricter than EU air quality law requires.[i]
General multilevel oversight and dispute resolution in environmental coordination	Under South Africa's National Environmental Management Act (also discussed earlier), the Director-General of the National Environmental Management Authority monitors how public organs comply with coordination plans prepared by national and provincial governments.[j] Noncompliance is addressed through a conflict management process involving conciliation and arbitration.[k]

[a] Environment Protection and Biodiversity Conservation Act 1999 (Australia) s 3(2)(b), (c), pt 5; Department of Climate Change, Energy, the Environment and Water (Australia), "Shared Environmental Assessments with States and Territories" (n.d.) www.dcceew.gov.au/environment/epbc/approvals/state-assessments, last accessed March 19, 2025, archived at https://perma.cc/YQV5-6FP8.

[b] Environment Protection and Biodiversity Conservation Act 1999 (Australia) s 46(1). National cumulative impact assessment requirements only apply to unconventional gas and large coal mining developments: Rebecca Nelson, "Breaking Backs and Boiling Frogs: Warnings from a Dialogue between Federal Water Law and Environmental Law" (2019) 42 *University of New South Wales Law Journal* 1179–1214, 1195–1196.

[c] Stephen Hunter, *Independent Review of the Water Trigger Legislation* (Commonwealth of Australia, 2017) 24, https://oia.pmc.gov.au/sites/default/files/posts/2017/09/independent_review_of_the_water_trigger_legislation.pdf, archived at https://perma.cc/KCU7-TMUJ.

[d] Species at Risk Act 2002 (Canada) s 80.

[e] Julee Boan and Rachel Plotkin, "In a Rut: Barriers to Caribou Recovery" in Andrea Olive, Chance Finegan, and Karen F. Beazley (eds), *Transformative Politics of Nature: Overcoming Barriers to Conservation in Canada* (University of Toronto Press, 2023), 85–106.

[f] Revised Code of Washington § 90.94.030(3)(h).

[g] E.g., Nooksack, Snohomish, Cedar-Sammamish, Deschutes, Kennedy-Goldsborough and Kitsap: Department of Ecology (State of Washington), "Watershed Planning" (n.d.) https://ecology.wa.gov/water-shorelines/water-supply/improving-streamflows/watershed-planning, last accessed March 19, 2025, archived at https://perma.cc/2NFT-EQDQ.

[h] Consolidated version of the Treaty on the Functioning of the European Union [2016] OJ C202/1, art. 193. For similar examples in the context of Australian water law and US air pollution law, see Water Act 2007 (Australia) s 40, and Palermo and Kössler, *Comparative Federalism*, 385.

[i] Lorenzo Squintani, *Beyond Minimum Harmonisation: Gold-Plating and Green-Plating of European Environmental Law* (CUP 2019) 79.

[j] NEMA ss 16(1)(a), (2).

[k] NEMA chapter 4. For a similar interjurisdictional dispute resolution example in the context of Australian water law, see Water Act 2007 (Australia) Sch 1 (Murray-Darling Basin Agreement), cl 140.

environmental enforcement responsibilities with the federal government under a cooperative federalism approach.[93]

Solutions to implementation gaps and drift include introducing meaningful oversight between coordinating parties.[94] This might mean, for example, allowing one level of government to "step in" to undertake a function if a lower level fails to do so, as the state is empowered to do in response to local failures in the California groundwater case study.[95] Oversight may be supported by "fallback" legislative arrangements that apply even if coordination fails, including by facilitating action by "outsiders", such as a nongovernmental actor or even another nation that is free from relevant political pressures (Table 7.4). More pointed disputes in coordinating regulatory intervention are addressed by dispute resolution mechanisms established by legislation or intergovernmental agreements (Table 7.4).

7.4 CONCLUSION

This chapter has set out the key roles and benefits of coordination for dealing with cumulative environmental problems and important categories of coordinating actors: government agencies and quasi-governmental actors at all levels, and nongovernment actors representing those contributing to, affected by, or seeking to deal with the problem. It has presented a diverse range of rules and institutions to support coordination in relation to each CIRCle Framework function: conceptualization, information, and intervention, as well as dispute resolution generally. These examples represent diversity in many ways: geography, the actors they bring to the table, their reliance on institutions versus rules, and the power dynamics they reflect.

That the examples are numerous supports the basic proposition that it is valuable to give regulatory form to structures for coordination. However, their existence does not necessarily mean that they are used in ways that effectively address cumulative environmental problems. Challenges may still remain even with formal coordination mechanisms, and important empirical questions arise about how the forms of coordination discussed here deal with issues such as transaction costs and sustaining fruitful interactions over the long term. But formal coordination mechanisms should help address key disincentives to coordination that are pronounced in cumulative environmental problems, helping not only to bring key actors to the table but also to keep them coming back.

93 Reisinger, Dougherty and Moser, "Environmental Enforcement," 6–7, 16–27.

94 Edwin Alblas and Josephine van Zeben, "'Farming out' Biodiversity: Implementing EU Nature Law through Agri-Environmental Schemes" (2023) 17 *Earth System Governance* 100180, 7.

95 Section 8.4.2.7.

8

Not a Drop to Drink

Conceptualizing Environmental Justice in California Groundwater

8.1 INTRODUCTION

For anyone coming to California groundwater issues for the first time, it is not long before they see the grainy "telephone pole" picture.[1] Hydrologist Joseph Poland of the US Geological Survey stands beside a dirt road in the San Joaquin Valley of California, next to an impressively tall pole. The pole is marked with dates: at the top, nine meters up, and at about five times Mr. Poland's height, 1925; in the middle, 1955; and at his feet, 1977. The signs show how much the ground had sunk progressively due to overpumping of groundwater. They point to the problem at the heart of this chapter: groundwater depletion. But the focus here is how depletion affects what you can hardly see in the photo – off in the distance, blurs of small white houses, presumably part of a rural community that depends on aquifers for their drinking water.

This chapter analyzes how California law conceptualizes two dimensions of groundwater sustainability: first, groundwater depletion as a physical problem; and second, the effects of groundwater depletion in causing underprivileged households and communities to lose access to drinking water. Both dimensions are inherently cumulative: On one hand, the aggregate impacts of many groundwater withdrawals and drought cause physical depletion; and, on the other hand, communities experience an

[1] Richard Ireland, "Land Subsidence in the San Joaquin Valley (Photograph)" (U.S. Geological Survey, 1977) www.usgs.gov/media/images/land-subsidence-san-joaquin-valley, archived at https://perma.cc/R2P5-GYWQ.

accumulation of harm from socioeconomic vulnerabilities and environmental stresses, one of which is groundwater depletion that jeopardizes drinking water supplies. Conceptualizing what and who matter is a central function of regulating cumulative environmental problems.[2] *Conceptualization*, in turn, links to other functions for which law can provide: structuring what and where *information* is generated and shared, what types of *regulatory intervention* are used to deal with harm, and who is heard and involved in *coordination* to do these things (together, the CIRCle Framework of regulatory functions). This case study serves as an introduction to using the CIRCle Framework advanced by this book to assess legal mechanisms in a real-world context, by focusing on rules for conceptualization and their links with these other functions.

The key legal mechanism in focus here is statutory planning under California's 2014 Sustainable Groundwater Management Act (SGMA), the state's first attempt at a comprehensive statewide groundwater regulatory system. Locally developed and implemented groundwater sustainability plans under SGMA are broadly analogous to resource management plans used around the world.[3] Though recent, the plans have attracted great scholarly interest for how they relate to what are usually termed "disadvantaged communities" in California – a term that I also use here because of its statutory source, while acknowledging its sensitivity for some.[4] Existing work that has studied plan development reveals, for example, that few representatives from disadvantaged communities are represented on the local decision-making bodies that make the plans;[5] few small farmers, who are usually excluded from large agricultural groupings, participate;[6] and plans rarely discuss the quality of drinking water, which can be contaminated by nitrates and pose a

[2] See Chapter 4 on Conceptualization.

[3] See Section 3.2.3.

[4] A widely accepted alternative term has not yet emerged: Oceana Haaland and Pablo Ortiz, *Disadvantaged Communities Nomenclature within the State of California: Findings and Conclusions* (California Department of Water Resources 2022) 6, https://water.ca.gov/-/media/DWR-Website/Web-Pages/About/Tribal/Files/IRWM/URC-Nomenclature-Whitepaper.pdf, archived at https://perma.cc/8LEZ-8MP8.

[5] See generally, Kristin B. Dobbin and Mark Lubell, "Collaborative Governance and Environmental Justice: Disadvantaged Community Representation in California Sustainable Groundwater Management" (2021) 49 *Policy Studies Journal* 562–590.

[6] See generally, Linda Estelí Méndez-Barrientos and others, "Farmer Participation and Institutional Capture in Common-Pool Resource Governance Reforms. The Case of Groundwater Management in California" (2020) 33 *Society and Natural Resources* 1486–1507.

major concern for disadvantaged communities.[7] Scholars have also shown that planning efforts that better engage disadvantaged communities tend to produce quantified sustainability goals that seek to better protect those communities.[8] This chapter builds on this focus on disadvantaged communities from a legal perspective, emphasizing the Central Valley of California (see Figure 1.2), where these concerns are heightened.

Section 8.2 describes the importance of groundwater as drinking water, the challenges faced by disadvantaged communities that rely on groundwater, and how this context presents pronounced challenges for conceptualizing what and who matter in regulating cumulative harms. Section 8.3 demonstrates how, before the introduction of SGMA, the patchwork of groundwater-related laws that applied in California had a significant gap in its view of "what matters." It focused largely on groundwater pollution as a matter of concern, with groundwater depletion a notably threadbare patch. Across different laws, multiple different conceptualizations of "who matters" emerged. Some focused simply on low-income communities, and others focused on communities that faced significant cumulative environmental and socioeconomic burdens. Section 8.4 analyzes, in detail, the degree to which SGMA changes what and who matter in groundwater sustainability, and how its provisions for conceptualization link to other CIRCle Framework functions. It argues that while SGMA focuses strongly on groundwater depletion, its attention to disadvantaged communities is variable, showing differences between provisions that deal with different regulatory functions. In addition, by preferring a simple rather than cumulative view of who matters, SGMA misses an opportunity to maximize the likely effectiveness of interventions.

8.2 CONTEXT AND CHALLENGES

8.2.1 *The Threat to Community Drinking Water of Declining Groundwater Levels*

California's Central Valley is one of the world's thirty-seven "mega aquifers": very large subsurface reservoirs of underground water that generally span

[7] See generally, Emel G. Wadhwani, "Fertilizers and Nitrates in Drinking Water: State Water Board Tackles the Public Health Threat of Contaminated Groundwater" (2018) 24 *Hastings Environmental Law Journal* 237–251.

[8] See generally, Debra Perrone and others, "Stakeholder Integration Predicts Better Outcomes from Groundwater Sustainability Policy" (2023) 14:3793 *Nature Communications* 1–14.

political boundaries and, together, account for most of the world's groundwater resources.[9] Central Valley groundwater is notoriously overused,[10] and the most intensely depleted in the United States.[11] It supports one of the world's most productive agricultural regions and a growing population,[12] including many disadvantaged communities. Satellite data show that cumulative losses of Central Valley groundwater are accelerating, largely driven by agricultural withdrawals.[13] Yet California has historically taken a "hands-off" regulatory approach to groundwater use, including in the economically muscular agriculture sector. Rather than requiring a permit to pump groundwater (as do most western US states and nearly three-quarters of the world's nations),[14] California relies on ad hoc court-based processes to quantify rights to pump groundwater, which have not been used in the Central Valley.[15]

Groundwater depletion manifests as declining water table levels, which may put groundwater levels beyond the reach of wells such that they run dry, and water can no longer be pumped to the surface. The combined effect of groundwater withdrawals and drought caused around one-fifth of wells in the Central Valley to run dry between 2013 and 2018.[16] Because

9 Jean Margat and Jac van der Gun, *Groundwater around the World: A Geographic Synopsis* (CRC 2013) 37, 44, 47, app 3.

10 Ibid 135.

11 Leonard F. Konikow, "Long-Term Groundwater Depletion in the United States" (2015) 53 *Groundwater* 2–9, 6–7.

12 Thomas E. Reilly and others, *Ground-Water Availability in the United States*, US Geological Survey Circular 1323 (2008) 44.

13 Pang-Wei Liu and others, "Groundwater Depletion in California's Central Valley Accelerates during Megadrought" (2022) 13:7825 *Nature Communications* 1–11, 6–7.

14 John Kemoli Sagala and Zachary A. Smith, "Comparative Groundwater Management: Findings from an Exploratory Global Survey" (2008) 33 *Water International* 258–267, 262; see generally, Gabriel Eckstein and others, *Groundwater Laws and Regulations: Survey of Sixteen U.S. States*, vols. I and II (Texas A&M University School of Law 2022).

15 California Department of Water Resources, *Sustainable Groundwater Management Act 2019 Basin Prioritization: Process and Results* (May 2020) app 5 (*SGMA Basin Prioritization*) https://data.cnra.ca.gov/dataset/13ebd2d3-4e62-4fee-9342-d7c3ef3e0079/resource/ffafd27b-5e7e-4db3-b846-e7b3cb5c614c/download/sgma_bp_process_document.pdf, archived at https://perma.cc/28VU-98ME. Note that under California's groundwater basin and subbasin numbering system, basins in the Central Valley all commence with the number 5: Department of Water Resources (California), *California's Groundwater: Working toward Sustainability: Bulletin 118 – Interim Update 2016* (2016) fig B-2, https://cawaterlibrary.net/wp-content/uploads/2017/05/Bulletin_118_Interim_Update_2016.pdf, archived at https://perma.cc/42W2-5X4X.

16 Scott Jasechko and Debra Perrone, "California's Central Valley Groundwater Wells Run Dry during Recent Drought" (2020) 8:e2019EF001339 *Earth's Future* 1–12, 9 (based on wells constructed since 1975). See also Clara MacLeod and Linda Estelí Méndez-Barrientos,

small municipal and household wells tend to be relatively shallow, they are especially vulnerable to drying out as water levels decline. Deeper, high-capacity wells – typically agricultural wells – are less vulnerable: They can continue to withdraw significant volumes of groundwater, further increasing water level declines and worsening water quality problems.[17]

Depletion-related threats to drinking water may prove cumulatively more significant for households and communities that lack the resources to find alternatives and that face cumulative environmental burdens. Data from California's dry well reporting system illustrate the issues: One householder reports "well is dry (no longer producing water)," and that they lacked money to fix the well while battling stage 4 cancer;[18] many others who reported wells that were dry or "pumping sand" noted they were trucking in water, "getting water from our neighbors with a hose," purchasing bottled water, and frequently, that they "cannot afford to finance solutions."[19]

8.2.2 *Conceptualization and Its Links to Information, Intervention, and Coordination*

This chapter explores whether and how law conceptualizes groundwater availability ("what matters") for disadvantaged communities who depend on it ("who matters") (together, "the matter of concern") as the object of protection from cumulative harm. The "what matters" part of this conceptualization puts groundwater levels in focus, because the most straightforward way to ensure that groundwater is available is to make sure that levels do not fall below the base of wells[20] used to access it. If they do, wells will run dry.

"Groundwater Management in California's Central Valley: A Focus on Disadvantaged Communities" (2019) 3 *Case Studies in the Environment* 1, 1–2, 10.

17 See generally, Zeno F. Levy and others, "Critical Aquifer Overdraft Accelerates Degradation of Groundwater Quality in California's Central Valley during Drought" (2021) 48 *Geophysical Research Letters* e2021GL094398.

18 California Natural Resources Agency, "Dry Well Reporting System Data" (*California Natural Resources Agency*, 2024) (report ID #20240) https://data.cnra.ca.gov/dataset/dry-well-reporting-system-data, archived at https://perma.cc/F4UD-YF3N.

19 See generally, ibid.

20 To be precise, wells will run dry if groundwater levels fall below the level of the pump, which will be at least a little above the base of the well.

Recall Chapter 4 (Conceptualization)

Key design features of regulatory mechanisms for conceptualization are using rules to clearly and transparently specify, or provide a process for specifying: **what matters** and **who matters** (together, the "matter of

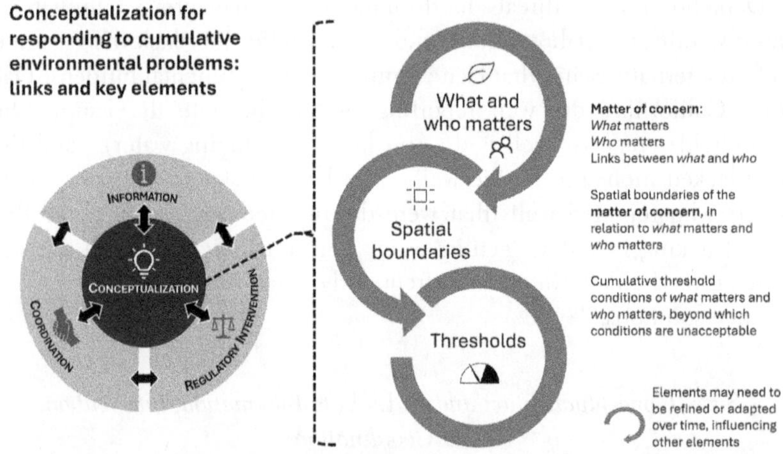

FIGURE 8.1 Conceptualization for responding to cumulative environmental problems: links and key dimensions, discussed further in Chapter 4

concern") for restoration or protection from cumulative harm, and **how they are linked** (together, the "matter of concern"); their **spatial extent**; and **threshold acceptable conditions**, which may involve a temporal element (see Figure 8.1).

The "who matters" part of this conceptualization requires determining what constitutes a disadvantaged household or community that depends on groundwater, where they are, and which groundwater body they rely on. Where levels are currently declining, this signals potential intervention to stabilize or increase levels – either by artificially recharging the aquifer with floodwater or another source or foregoing some pumping.[21] Combining what and who matters lets us then conceptualize cumulative threshold conditions: groundwater levels, beyond which cumulative harm would be unacceptable. History makes setting threshold conditions challenging. The fact that groundwater levels across many parts of

[21] Nicola Ulibarri and others, "Assessing the Feasibility of Managed Aquifer Recharge in California" (2021) 57:e2020WR029292 *Water Resources Research* 1–18, 8, 14.

California's Central Valley have been declining for decades[22] means there is no obvious objective answer to the question of what a good groundwater level is. The answer depends on who groundwater is intended to benefit. Those with deep wells can maintain access to a declining groundwater resource for longer than those with shallow wells. Specifying these things clearly and transparently is the fundamental challenge of conceptualization.[23]

The way that law conceptualizes what and who matter centrally affects each of the other three regulatory functions of the CIRCle Framework for dealing with a cumulative environmental problem (Figure 8.1) – the information that is generated and shared about the matter of concern and threats to it, intervention to address threats, and coordination mechanisms that determine who is heard and who makes decisions about doing these things. Section 8.4.2 analyzes these links in more detail in the context of SGMA.

8.3 CONCEPTUALIZATION ACROSS THE REGULATORY LANDSCAPE

Until the passage of SGMA, a patchwork of statutes dealt with narrow elements of the issue of groundwater and drinking water supplies, each conceptualizing the matter of concern differently with respect to the physical characteristics of groundwater (what matters) and its end users (who matters). Together, these conceptualizations left a weakness: the risk of groundwater levels lowering, and its effects on disadvantaged communities and households reliant on groundwater. This part analyzes this patchwork of laws, and the various ways in which they conceptualize what and who matter. This has two purposes: First, to demonstrate surveying the regulatory landscape[24] (the preliminary stage of the analytical process to use the CIRCle Framework); and, second, to lay the foundation for the following analysis of the ways in which SGMA filled – and did not fill – this gap. Since many laws are involved, these analyses are necessarily brief.

8.3.1 *Conceptualizing What Matters: The Groundwater Level Gap*

Putting SGMA to one side, California's other groundwater-related laws primarily focus on the availability and quality of water supplied by larger water utilities ("piped water"), rather than water availability for those who lack a utility service. General water planning laws cover groundwater in specific contexts, such as agriculture, urban, and integrated water management. Land use and environmental impact assessment ("EIA") laws also deal with groundwater in relatively

[22] Liu and others, "Groundwater Depletion," 4–5.

[23] See Chapter 4 (Conceptualization)

[24] See Chapter 11 (Guidelines). Chapters 9 and 10 take a more detailed approach to this surveying process, using the "compass" approach presented in Figure 3.1 to analyze regulatory interventions: see Tables 9.1 and 10.1.

narrow ways. But before SGMA, other than an early voluntary form of planning, California lacked a generally applicable law that regulated groundwater sustainability, conceptualized as relating to groundwater levels. Traditionally, then, those with typically shallower wells – household well owners and smaller water suppliers – were exposed to the risks of falling groundwater levels and wells going dry.

8.3.1.1 Drinking Water Laws: Quality of Utility-Supplied (Piped) Water

The US Safe Drinking Water Act has long regulated the quality of drinking water from public water supply systems by establishing national primary drinking water regulations that limit contaminant levels.[25] California implements these federal rules[26] under its own Safe Drinking Water legislation. More recent California law creates a fund to support grants for expanding piped water service[27] and providing replacement water and system repairs where needed.[28] A legally required "aquifer risk" map, which influences how the fund is spent, includes groundwater quality and a drought-driven focus on aquifer levels but does not focus on depletion in general.[29] In this legal view, it is the quality of piped water that matters.

California's human right to "safe, clean, affordable, and accessible" water for consumption, cooking, and sanitary purposes further supports these laws.[30] State agencies are required to consider this "policy" when "revising, adopting, or establishing policies, regulations, and grant criteria" pertinent to water use. This right to "safe, clean" water clearly covers water quality, but "accessible" water only ambiguously links to water quantity; it is unclear whether the reference is to piped water service being available or to water in aquifers that is accessible because groundwater levels have not declined too far. A related "human right to water data tool" clearly emphasizes the quality of water supplied by small utilities.[31] It currently considers "accessibility" only as

[25] The federal Safe Drinking Water Act (Safe Drinking Water Act of 1974 (P.L. 93-523), as amended, codified as 42 U.S.C. §§300f to 300j-10) also protects aquifers used for drinking water from injection of contaminated fluids (42 U.S.C. §§ 300h to 300h-9), but this is a minor role that is not discussed further here.

[26] 42 U.S.C. § 300g-2 (state primary enforcement responsibility).

[27] Cal. Health and Safety Code §§ 116766, 116768 (purposes of fund expenditure plan), 116769 (contents of fund expenditure plan).

[28] Cal. Health and Safety Code §§ 116770, 116767 (definition of "replacement water").

[29] See State Water Resources Control Board, *2024 Aquifer Risk Map Methodology* (2024), www.waterboards.ca.gov/water_issues/programs/gama/docs/armmethods24.pdf, archived at https://perma.cc/2Z3H-CKXR.

[30] Cal. A.B. 685 of 2012 (Cal. Stats.2012, c. 524, §1), codified as Cal. Water Code §106.3.

[31] California Office of Environmental Health Hazard Assessment, "The Human Right to Water in California" (January 28, 2021) https://oehha.ca.gov/water/report/human-right-water-california, archived at https://perma.cc/L8ES-T3LB.

vulnerability to utility water outages,[32] though future amendments may include depletion.[33] Such amendments would align with evolving understandings of the human right to water internationally, which are shifting from considering the right as a water services issue, to considering the human right to "raw water at the source."[34] This move would expand the conceptualization of the matter of concern to include groundwater levels, beyond access to piped water.

8.3.1.2 Water Pollution Laws: Quality of Groundwater in Aquifers

Water pollution laws regulate discharges of pollution into waters. Both the federal Clean Water Act[35] and California's Porter-Cologne Act[36] regulate pollution discharges. These statutes require California's state and regional Water Boards to protect all beneficial uses of water, including municipal or domestic water sources,[37] using "total maximum daily loads" of pollutants[38] and a mix of planning and permitting tools, and funds for water pollution projects[39] and water treatment systems.[40] The federal Clean Water Act's permitting requirements are restricted to point source discharges to "waters of the United States," a category that excludes groundwater.[41] For present purposes, the law's main effect is to restrict federal funding for actions that may pollute designated sole source aquifers.[42] Only California's Porter-

[32] Carolina Balazs and others, *Achieving the Human Right to Water in California: An Assessment of the State's Community Water Systems* (Office of Environmental Health Hazard Assessment, California EPA, 2021) 49, https://oehha.ca.gov/sites/default/files/media/downloads/water/report/hrtwachievinghrtw2021f.pdf, archived at https://perma.cc/TW4S-CT68.

[33] Note that there are plans to incorporate additional indicators relating to sufficiency, continuity of supply, and vulnerability to drought in the future, including information about overdraft: ibid 58.

[34] Stefano Burchi, "The Future of Domestic Water Law: Trends and Developments Revisited, and Where Reform Is Headed" (2019) 44 *Water International* 258–277, 274.

[35] Federal Water Pollution Control Act Amendments of 1972, as amended (33 U.S.C. § 1251 et seq.).

[36] Porter-Cologne Water Quality Control Act (Cal. Water Code Div. 7, § 13000 et seq.)

[37] Cal. Water Code §§ 13241, 13263(a), 13050(f) and (h).

[38] 33 U.S.C. § 1313(d).

[39] Cal. Water Code Div. 7, esp. § ;13477 State Water Resources Control Board, "Financial Assistance Funding – Grants and Loans" (n.d.) www.waterboards.ca.gov/water_issues/programs/grants_loans/, last accessed March 20, 2025, archived at https://perma.cc/V33L-XN9J.

[40] Cal. Stats. 2017, c. 438 (A.B.277), now codified as Cal. Water Code §§ 13486–13489 (Water and Wastewater Loan and Grant Program).

[41] An exception applies in the narrow circumstance that pollutants discharged from a point source arrive at navigable waters through groundwater: *County of Maui, Hawaii v. Hawaii Wildlife Fund*, 140 S. Ct. 1462, 206 L. Ed. 2d 640 (2020).

[42] 42 U.S.C. § 300h-3(e) ("an aquifer which is the sole or principal drinking water source for the area").

Cologne Water Quality Control Act directly controls pollution discharges to groundwater, dealing with both point- and nonpoint sources such as agricultural nitrate pollution.[43] Nonpoint pollution is the main source of water quality impairment in California.[44] The Porter-Cologne Act is silent on groundwater levels. In this case, it is groundwater quality that matters.

8.3.1.3 Pre-SGMA Water Planning Laws: Quality and Availability of Piped Water

Water supply reliability emerges as a key concern through state legislation for integrated water resources planning, and planning for municipal and agricultural uses.[45] Integrated regional water management plans[46] identify water management demand and supply strategies, including "[g]roundwater storage and conjunctive water management" to provide "long-term, reliable, and high-quality water supply and protect the environment."[47] In relation to drinking water, though, the integrated planning legislation only focuses on water quality.[48] Other legislation provides for agricultural water management plans and urban water management plans, which are required of large water suppliers that provide service for these purposes, and focus on water quality, water use efficiency and supply reliability.[49] Drinking water for disadvantaged communities unserved by a utility is outside their scope.

[43] Cal. Water Code § 13263.

[44] Ellen Hanak and others, *Managing California's Water: From Conflict to Reconciliation* (Public Policy Institute of California 2011) 285. For this reason, some other laws relevant to water pollution are not considered here, e.g., the US federal Comprehensive Environmental Response, Compensation, and Liability Act of 1980, which deals with hazardous waste sites, and the US Toxic Substances Control Act of 1976, which regulates toxic chemicals.

[45] Note that I categorize well construction laws together with land use laws, since they do not deal with management of the resource in that they do not regulate the volume of water that can be withdrawn, as distinct from technical standards that apply to the construction of well casings, and so on.

[46] Cal. Water Code §§ 10530–10550 (Integrated Regional Water Management Planning Act), added by Stats.2007–2008, 2nd Ex.Sess., c. 1 (S.B.1).

[47] Cal. Water Code §§ 10534, 10537.

[48] Cal. Water Code § 10540(c)(2).

[49] Agricultural Water Management Planning Act of 1986 (Cal. Stats.1986, C. 954, §1), codified as Cal. Water Code §§ 10800–10853 (1986), especially §§ 10825, 10826 (quality and quantity of source water), 10853 (agricultural: supplying water to 25,000 irrigated acres or more); Urban Water Management Planning Act of 1983, Cal. Stats.1983, C. 1009, §1, codified as Cal. Water Code §§10610–10657 (1983), especially §§ 10617 (urban: supplying water for municipal purposes to more than 3,000 customers or more than 3,000 acre-feet of water annually), 10631 (groundwater, demand management), 10631(b) (quantify sources), 10634 (quality), 10635 (reliability).

8.3.1.4 Land Use and EIA Laws: Quality and Availability of Groundwater

Local land use-related laws influence groundwater by zoning and permitting land uses that may pollute groundwater or build over recharge zones, affecting groundwater availability. State land use planning laws require cities and counties to adopt general plans for land use that include conservation and open space elements.[50] These consider how development affects the quality and availability of groundwater in aquifers, though not expressly in a drinking water context.[51] Cities and counties may also regulate small-scale domestic septic systems and improperly constructed wells to prevent pollution.[52]

Federal and state EIA laws provide for assessing the impacts of individual projects that may use groundwater or have the potential to pollute it. The federal National Environmental Policy Act ("NEPA") obliges federal agencies to prepare statements on "environmental impacts" of proposed major federal actions.[53] This is purely procedural, not imposing a stand-alone approval requirement. The California Environmental Quality Act requires lead agencies to assess the impacts of any project "they propose to carry out or approve that may have a significant effect on the environment."[54] In this case, assessments are linked to a prohibition on agencies "approving projects with significant environmental effects if there are feasible alternatives or mitigation measures that would substantially lessen or avoid those effects."[55] Both groundwater quality and quantity are relevant to EIA laws that define "effects" and the "environment" broadly.[56]

8.3.2 *Conceptualizing Who Matters: Communities of Concern*

Groundwater-related legal provisions also adopt different broad approaches to describing who matters. Some are simple in the sense that they make a one-dimensional determination of who matters. This may take the form of "everyone matters," "low-income communities matter" (usually using the term

[50] Cal. Government Code § 65302(a), (d).

[51] Governor's Office of Planning and Research, *General Plan Guidelines Including Updated Element on Environmental Justice* (2020) 55, 112–114, 303, https://lci.ca.gov/docs/20200706-GPG_Chapter_4_EJ.pdf, archived at https://perma.cc/4P6U-K97K.

[52] E.g., Fresno County Code of Ordinances §§14.04.050, 14.09.030, 14.12.030.

[53] 42 U.S.C. § 4332.

[54] Cal. Public Resources Code §21100(a) (state agencies), 21151(a) (local agencies).

[55] Kamala D. Harris, *Environmental Justice at the Local and Regional Level* (State of California Department of Justice 2012) 4, https://oag.ca.gov/sites/all/files/agweb/pdfs/environment/ej_fact_sheet_final_050712.pdf, archived at https://perma.cc/GD2S-6MBB.

[56] 40 C.F.R. § 1508.1(i)(4); Cal. Public Resources Code § 21060.5.

"disadvantaged communities," defined as an area in which the median household income is less than 80 percent of the median household income level[57]), or "no-one in particular matters" (where a law is silent on the question). Only the second approach recognizes the special vulnerability of population subgroups, albeit based on the single criterion of income. A less common alternative to these simple approaches to determining who matters is the idea of "environmental justice communities," which describes populations that suffer a disproportionate cumulative burden of multiple kinds of impacts, including environmental burdens of which water-related stress is just one component, alongside pronounced socioeconomic vulnerability.[58] Importantly, as discussed later, there are varying legal and policy definitions of "environmental justice" and "disadvantaged communities," not only between state- and federal-level laws but also among different state-level laws and even within a single law. In practice, this incoherence in an important element of conceptualization creates significant confusion for communities.[59]

How a law describes who matters is important. It determines who the law "sees and hears" for the purposes of collecting information, designing interventions, and inviting them to participate and coordinate. The outcome might mean, for example, being eligible for a grant to restore your water supply (or not); explaining and having your community's circumstances considered in a water plan or a project assessment (or not); or being protected in regulating activities that affect groundwater (or not).

8.3.2.1 Simple Views of Who Matters

At one end of the spectrum of simple views of who matters, California's human right to "clean, safe, affordable, and accessible" water applies to all humans, implicitly with the same minimum standards for water quality, affordability, and accessibility for all. As written, the right does not highlight any particular population, though associated policy tools focus on low-income disadvantaged communities.[60]

[57] Cal. Health and Safety Code § 116275(aa). In a "severely disadvantaged community," the median household income is less than 60 percent of the statewide median household income: Cal. Water Code § 13476(j).

[58] Haaland and Ortiz, *Disadvantaged Communities Nomenclature*, 19–23.

[59] Ibid 4, 6, 8, 19–20.

[60] E.g., California's main drinking water fund, which prioritizes grants for disadvantaged communities, is expressed to be directed at realizing the human right to water: California State Water Resources Control Board, 2024 *Drinking Water Needs Assessment* (2024) 18, 19, www.waterboards.ca.gov/drinking_water/certlic/drinkingwater/needs.html, archived at https://perma.cc/8VXY-9N9T.

Many other groundwater-related laws focus expressly on disadvantaged communities defined solely with reference to income. This is common in the areas of drinking water, water information and resource management, and land use. Though drinking water quality standards do not distinguish between communities, grant-making provisions that aim to remedy noncompliance with these standards focus on disadvantaged communities. This is the case for federal programs[61] under which communities become eligible and are prioritized for funding.[62] Similarly, grants under California's main drinking water fund prioritize funding for failing water supply systems and domestic wells[63] based on disadvantage defined by income and groundwater pollution risks.[64] Smaller state grant programs[65] and information tools[66] adopt a similar focus.

In the planning context, integrated regional water management plans must identify and consider the water-related needs of low-income "disadvantaged communities,"[67] and include them in public participation processes.[68] Projects that would benefit disadvantaged communities are prioritized,[69] with special attention to contaminated areas.[70] Finally, land use laws focus on disadvantaged communities[71] by requiring general plans to identify such communities outside city boundaries and

[61] 42 U.S.C. §§ 300j-12(a)(2)(G)(ii)(I), (d)(3), (d)(1)(A), (f)(1)(C) (Drinking Water State Revolving Fund), 300j-19a (Assistance for Small and Disadvantaged Communities Program); see also Misbah Husain and Melissa Scanlan, "Disadvantaged Communities, Water Justice and the Promise of the Infrastructure Investment and Jobs Act" (2022) 52 *Seton Hall Law Review* 1513–1530, 1519.

[62] E.g., 42 U.S.C. § 300j-19a(a)(2), (c)(2)(A), (d).

[63] Cal. Health and Safety Code § 116769.

[64] "Low income" is defined as "a single household with an income that is less than 200 percent of the federal poverty level": Cal. Health and Safety Code §§ 116767(k), 116769(b) ("needs assessment"), 116772 (aquifer risk map); State Water Resources Control Board, *2024 Aquifer Risk Map Methodology*; State Water Resources Control Board, Aquifer Risk Map, https://gispublic.waterboards.ca.gov/portal/apps/experiencebuilder/experience/?id=18c7d253f0a44fd2a5c7bcfb42cc158d, last accessed March 20, 2025, archived at https://perma.cc/US7Z-4MJW.

[65] E.g., Water and Wastewater Loan and Grant Program: Cal. Water Code §§ 13488, 13489 (requiring income at or below 120 percent of the statewide median household income).

[66] E.g., a nonstatutory "human right to water data tool" highlights disadvantaged communities defined by income: Balazs and others, *Achieving the Human Right to Water*, 105–108.

[67] Cal. Water Code §§ 10534, 10540(c)(7).

[68] Cal. Water Code § 10541(g)(12).

[69] Cal. Water Code § 10551. Note that this provision ceased to have effect on January 1, 2025.

[70] Cal. Water Code § 10545.

[71] "'Disadvantaged unincorporated community' means a fringe, island, or legacy community in which the median household income is 80 percent or less than the statewide median household income.": Cal. Government Code § 65302.10(a)(2).

their "water . . . needs or deficiencies,"[72] and review financing options for extending services to them.[73]

A final, "simple" approach to defining who matters is to omit to say that anyone in particular matters, in favor of focusing on solely technical, physical issues. This is the approach of key elements of drinking water laws, water pollution laws, and water information and resource management laws. Federal sole source aquifer provisions make no reference to community vulnerabilities that might affect the importance of an aquifer to the population that depends on it. California's water pollution permitting provisions[74] mention no particular human population.[75] Agricultural water management planning processes require public participation without mentioning who should be involved.[76]

Some other laws inch toward recognizing people, but not in a way that really defines who matters. Although drinking water quality standards apply the same way everywhere, the standard setting process "may" consider physiologically vulnerable communities such as children and pregnant women.[77] Urban water suppliers preparing their plans must encourage the participation of "diverse social, cultural and economic elements of the population,"[78] but they need neither involve nor consider the circumstances of any specific population.

8.3.2.2 A Cumulative View of Who Matters: Environmental Justice Communities

Less commonly, rather than taking a "simple" view of who matters, groundwater-related laws focus on environmental justice communities defined by cumulative environmental burdens. That is, instead of using a single income criterion to decide who matters, they determine who matters by aggregating indicators of different kinds of environmental and socioeconomic stresses. Land use laws, a statutory drinking water fund, and EIA laws take this

[72] Cal. Government Code § 65302.10(b).

[73] Governor's Office of Planning and Research, *General Plan Guidelines*, 67. See also Nelia Sperka, *Technical Advisory: Senate Bill 244: Land Use, General Plans, and Disadvantaged Communities* (Office of Planning and Research (California) 2013), https://lci.ca.gov/docs/SB244_Technical_Advisory.pdf, archived at https://perma.cc/H5DY-65HV.

[74] Cal. Water Code Div. 7 chapter 4 ("regional water quality control").

[75] E.g., considerations relevant to the establishment of water quality objectives and waste discharge requirements: Cal. Water Code §§ 13241, 13263.

[76] Cal. Water Code §10841.

[77] Cal. Health and Safety Code § 116365.2. See also § 116365.

[78] Cal. Water Code § 10642.

approach, as discussed later. Overall, though, the idea of environmental justice communities advanced by these laws does not consider declining groundwater levels to be an environmental justice issue, focusing instead on pollution. Equally strikingly, there is no coherent idea of environmental justice communities across these legal areas, with differences in the indicators used at state and federal levels.

Of all the laws discussed here, California's land use laws use environmental justice most prominently. Local "general plans" for land use must include an environmental justice component that identifies "disadvantaged communities,"[79] this time defined cumulatively by demographic vulnerabilities, income, and environmental stressors.[80] The objectives and policies of a plan must aim to "reduce the unique or compounded health risks in disadvantaged communities," including by measures directed at pollution exposure, food access, and safe homes.[81]

In other laws, a cumulative conceptualization of environmental justice emerges more tangentially in a way that is specific to a regulatory function – information, regulatory intervention, or coordination. We turn first to EIA laws, which chiefly serve a regulatory information function. Before recently being revoked, NEPA regulations expressly defined and required consideration of environmental justice, drawing attention to income, race, color, national origin, tribal affiliation and disability, and "the cumulative impacts of environmental and other burdens, and the legacy of racism or other structural or systemic barriers" and "access to a healthy, sustainable, and resilient environment."[82] In its detail, and in linking environmental justice to a sustainable environment, this went significantly beyond older executive orders requiring consideration of environmental justice.[83] A US Environmental Protection Agency ("EPA") mapping tool, EJScreen,

79 Cal. Government Code § 65302(h)(1).

80 Cal. Government Code § 65302(h)(4)(A), (C), referring to definition in Cal. Health and Safety Code § 39711.

81 Cal. Government Code § 65302(h)(1)(A).

82 40 C.F.R. § 1508.1(m). In February 2025, these regulations were revoked: Council on Environmental Quality (US), "Removal of National Environmental Policy Act Implementing Regulations" (February 25, 2025) 90 Federal Register (USA) 10610.

83 William Clinton, "Federal Actions to Address Environmental Justice in Minority Populations and Low-Income Populations" (February 11, 1994) 59 *Federal Register (USA)* 7629, s1–101; William Clinton, "White House Memorandum for the Heads of All Departments and Agencies: Executive Order on Federal Actions to Address Environmental Justice in Minority Populations and Low-Income Populations" (February 11, 1994). See also US Environmental Protection Agency, "Environmental Justice and the National Environmental Policy Act" (n.d.) www.epa.gov/environmentaljustice/environmental-justice-and-national-environmental-policy-act, last accessed March 21, 2025, archived at https://perma.cc/RQB2-D6ZP.

supported considering environmental justice by showing spatial disparities in environmental, demographic, health, climate risk, and service gap indicators.[84] However, no clear resource sustainability indicators were included. At the time of writing, it appears that a federal administrative priority is to terminate all of these federal environmental justice tools and measures.[85]

Demonstrating the value for policy stability of policy redundancy across government levels,[86] California's EIA laws continue to embed environmental justice; they will likely provide a conceptual safety net for environmental justice concepts even with federal policy change. A California Attorney-General's memorandum sees environmental justice embedded in an EIA law provision under which a project may be deemed environmentally significant if it will cause "substantial effects on human beings,"[87] considering any human receptors more sensitive to the effect. That is, an effect will be more significant for populations already subject to other environmental stresses or vulnerabilities.[88] A California EPA mapping tool, CalEnviroScreen,[89] aggregates environmental, health, and socioeconomic indicators into scores that show how cumulative environmental burdens and vulnerabilities vary across space.[90] Confusingly, though, CalEnviroScreen uses different criteria from those in the US EPA's EJScreen.

Second, in the context of regulatory intervention as a function, environmental justice emerges in the design of "state rescue" mechanisms (which involve the state stepping in to deal with a cumulative problem, rather than seeking to

84 See generally, US Environmental Protection Agency, *EJScreen Technical Documentation for Version 2.3* (2024) www.epa.gov/system/files/documents/2024-07/ejscreen-tech-doc-version-2-3.pdf, archived at https://perma.cc/EZ6R-P2R7.

85 Office of the Attorney General (US), Memorandum for All Department Employees: Rescinding "Environmental Justice" Memoranda (February 5, 2025) www.justice.gov/ag/media/1388551 archived at https://perma.cc/CZ2C-DWHU; Angela C. Jones, "Trump Administration Environmental-Justice-Related Executive Orders: Potential Implications for EPA Programs" (Congressional Research Service, February 24, 2025) www.congress.gov/crs-product/IF12922.

86 See Section 7.1.2, especially n 26 and accompanying text.

87 Cal. Public Resources Code, § 21083(b)(3); see also CEQA Guidelines, 2 Cal. Code Regs. § 15126.2.

88 Harris, *Environmental Justice at the Local and Regional Level*, 3–4, citing *Kings County Farm Bureau v. City of Hanford* (1990) 221 Cal.App.3d at 661, *Los Angeles Unified School Dist. v. City of Los Angeles* (1997) 58 Cal.App.4th 1019, 1025; see also CEQA Guidelines, 14 Cal. Code Regs. § 15300.2.

89 California Office of Environmental Health Hazard Assessment, "Uses of CalEnviroScreen" (n.d.) https://oehha.ca.gov/calenviroscreen/how-use, last accessed March 20, 2025, archived at https://perma.cc/8KVY-G2F4.

90 E.g., cleanup sites, traffic impacts, pesticide use, drinking water contaminants: see generally, Lauren Zeise and Jared Blumenfeld, *CalEnviroScreen 4.0* (California Environmental Protection Agency 2021), https://oehha.ca.gov/media/downloads/calenviroscreen/report/calenviroscreen40reportf2021.pdf, archived at https://perma.cc/8YG9-FXCQ.

change behavior that causes cumulative harm[91]) that support communities. Statutory funds for drinking water projects invest in communities affected by cumulative burdens based on "geographic, socioeconomic, public health, and environmental hazard criteria."[92] The use of a power to consolidate underperforming utilities[93] expressly may be prioritized by considering historical overburden by "pollution and industrial development or … other environmental justice hurdles."[94] We also see environmental justice communities in regulatory enforcement policies, even if not directly in the corresponding laws. Thus, California's water quality enforcement policy requires enforcement to "integrate environmental justice consideration."[95] Among other things, this involves improving data about violations and enforcement for "minority communities and low-income populations"; considering informal approaches to compliance and enforcement to avoid economic hardships for these communities;[96] and prioritizing enforcing violations that contaminate drinking water sources.[97] More broadly, the California Department of Justice's Bureau of Environmental Justice, established in 2018, litigates to assist low-income and minority communities affected by disproportionate pollution.[98]

At the level of formal policy, the California EPA's environmental justice strategy[99] defines environmental justice as "the fair treatment of people of all races, cultures, and income levels, including minority populations and low-income populations in the state."[100] In line with its pollution-focused mission,[101]

[91] For discussion of state rescue mechanisms as a form of regulatory intervention, see Section 6.3.

[92] Cal. Health and Safety Code §§ 39711(a)), 39719(b)(3).

[93] Cal. Health and Safety Code § 116682.

[94] Cal. Health and Safety Code § 116682(l).

[95] State Water Resources Control Board, *Water Quality Enforcement Policy* (2017) 4, www.waterboards.ca.gov/board_decisions/adopted_orders/resolutions/2017/040417_9_final%20adopted%20policy.pdf, archived at https://perma.cc/V2JS-JXXN.

[96] Ibid 4.

[97] Ibid.

[98] Xavier Becerra, *Attorney General Becerra Establishes Bureau of Environmental Justice* (February 22, 2018), https://oag.ca.gov/news/press-releases/attorney-general-becerra-establishes-bureau-environmental-justice, archived at https://perma.cc/5QFF-GVS6.

[99] Cal. Public Resources Code § 71113; California Environmental Protection Agency, *Intra-Agency Environmental Justice Strategy* (2004) 1, https://calepa.ca.gov/wp-content/uploads/2017/01/EnvJustice-Documents-2004yr-EnglishStrategy.pdf, archived at https://perma.cc/VZS9-UUBC. This applies to the State Water Resources Control Board, which is a department of CalEPA, and which implements the Porter-Cologne Water Quality Control Act.

[100] Cal. Public Resources Code § 71110(a); see also Cal. Government Code § 65040.12 (definition of environmental justice as related to "environmental laws, regulations and policies").

[101] E.g. "About Us" (n.d.) https://calepa.ca.gov/about/, last accessed March 23, 2025, archived at https://perma.cc/N4CU-PNQP.

the strategy's distributive justice elements focus on pollution (e.g., a "clean environment" and "health hazards").[102] Its only reference to resources depletion is to recite a statutory obligation to identify "differential patterns of consumption of natural resources" among different socioeconomic groups.[103]

Finally, several different coordination mechanisms expressly advance environmental justice by bringing together different levels of government or agencies across government in institutions. In California, this occurs pursuant to statute (through a function of the Office of Planning and Research)[104] as well as policy (under CalEPA's environmental justice strategy).[105] Until early 2025, multiple nonstatutory environmental justice groups existed at the federal level, including the Interagency Working Group on Environmental Justice,[106] US EPA's National Environmental Justice Advisory Council, and the White House Environmental Justice Advisory Council.[107] None, however, had an express mission related to groundwater.

Strikingly, across these numerous formal arrangements that recognize the cumulative burden of environmental stresses and socioeconomic disadvantage in defining who matters, the corresponding view of what matters is pollution. Pollution is the central and almost exclusive environmental focus. When it comes to protecting access to natural resources – preventing groundwater depletion to protect access – the concept of environmental justice is largely missing in action.

8.4 RECONCEPTUALIZING GROUNDWATER SUSTAINABILITY UNDER SGMA

When it was passed in 2014, SGMA filled a critical gap in conceptualizing what mattered in state groundwater-related law by focusing on "chronic lowering" of groundwater levels[108] as one of several elements of a

[102] California Environmental Protection Agency, *Intra-Agency Environmental Justice Strategy*, 8–9 ("environmental justice integration").

[103] Ibid 2.

[104] Cal. Government Code § 65040.12.

[105] E.g., California Environmental Protection Agency, *Intra-Agency Environmental Justice Strategy*, 10.

[106] Clinton, "Federal Actions to Address Environmental Justice," s1–s102.

[107] US EPA, "White House Environmental Justice Advisory Council" (n.d.) https://bidenwhitehouse.archives.gov/environmentaljustice/white-house-environmental-justice-advisory-council/, last accessed March 23, 2025 (referring to both the White House Environmental Justice Advisory Council and the National Environmental Justice Advisory Council); see also note 85 and accompanying text.

[108] Sustainable Groundwater Management Act of 2014, Cal. Stats. 2014, C. 346, §3, codified as Cal. Water Code, Div. 6, pt. 2.74 § 10721(x)(1).

multidimensional view of "sustainability."[109] As written, SGMA also facilitates identifying disadvantaged communities that rely on groundwater as part of "who matters" in groundwater management. However, rather than taking a cumulative view of vulnerability, in implementing SGMA, agencies have focused simply on low income. Considering links between conceptualization and the other regulatory functions under SGMA suggests that this difference may reduce its effectiveness.

Section 8.4.1 introduces the key elements of SGMA after reviewing a closely related predecessor groundwater law, which lay the foundations for how SGMA conceptualizes matters of concern relevant to groundwater levels. Section 8.4.2 then analyzes how SGMA provides for conceptualizing what and who matter in its different elements, and how these elements link conceptualization to the other regulatory functions of the CIRCle Framework: information, regulatory intervention, and coordination.

8.4.1 *Emergence of SGMA*

California's first, brief, voluntary groundwater management planning law appeared in 1992.[110] It established a template for maximum local control of groundwater, and an expectation that locals be responsible for determining what matters in their local jurisdiction through the development of management plans. SGMA followed this template, in modified form, over two decades later. The framework for these voluntary plans was comparatively less stringent than those under preexisting water planning laws.[111] The 1992 law allowed and incentivized, but did not require, local agencies to adopt groundwater management plans. Among other things, plans could provide for mitigating overdraft,[112] which causes declining groundwater levels. Though the law led to over 100 plans, local agencies tended to adopt plans to head off the risk of future state intervention in groundwater management, and to fulfill state funding requirements, rather than necessarily because they were committed to implementing the plans.[113] There seems to be no evidence that the legislation fundamentally changed groundwater sustainability outcomes.

109 For more on multidimensional versus reductionist views of matters of concern, see Section 4.2.1.

110 Groundwater Management Act, Cal. A.B. 3030 of 1992, Cal. Stats. 1992, C. 947, § 2, codified as Cal. Water Code Pt. 2.75 of Div. 6 (1992).

111 Rebecca L. Nelson, "Assessing Local Planning to Control Groundwater Depletion: California as a Microcosm of Global Issues" (2012) 48:W01502 *Water Resources Research* 1–14, 4.

112 Cal. Water Code § 10753.8.

113 Nelson, "Assessing Local Planning to Control Groundwater Depletion," 4–5.

Then, during the southwest US "megadrought" of the early twenty-first century,[114] California passed its first laws for state-centralized monitoring of groundwater quality and levels.[115] This established the framework for conceptualizing and prioritizing groundwater basins that SGMA was to continue, and successfully focused the state's legislative mind on groundwater levels for the first time.

In 2014, the successful passage of SGMA created a new local groundwater planning mechanism with higher and more detailed minimum standards set by the state, relative to the earlier planning law. Continuing to emphasize local control,[116] SGMA provides for establishing local "groundwater sustainability agencies" (for brevity, "local agencies") for spatially defined groundwater basins, with one or more existing local agencies typically assuming the role.[117] Local agencies write groundwater sustainability plans that are either mandatory or discretionary, depending on the basin's "priority" status. The plans must be designed to achieve "sustainable groundwater management" over twenty years (and use a planning horizon of 50 years) which means avoiding "undesirable results"[118] in several categories, supported by monitoring and the possibility of state intervention. As explained next, multiple elements of SGMA contribute to conceptualizing what and who matter in pursuing groundwater sustainability, and, in doing so, these elements include regulatory mechanisms for information, regulatory intervention, and coordination.

8.4.2 *Conceptualizing What and Who Matter under SGMA*

SGMA provides for conceptualizing what and who matter through seven key elements (Figure 8.2), from delimiting and prioritizing groundwater basins, to the state potentially intervening to enforce minimum state requirements for local plans. In addition to determining what and who matter (summarized in Table 8.1), other linked elements of conceptualization – spatial boundaries

[114] See generally, A. Park Williams, Benjamin I. Cook and Jason E. Smerdon, "Rapid Intensification of the Emerging Southwestern North American Megadrought in 2020–2021" (2022) 12 *Nature Climate Change* 232–234.

[115] Groundwater Quality Monitoring Act of 2001, A.B. 599, Cal. Stats. 2001, C. 522, §2, as amended, codified as Cal. Water Code §§ 10780–10783 (2001); Groundwater Monitoring Program Act, Cal. S.B. 6 of 2009, Cal. Stats.2009–2010, 7th Ex.Sess., C. 1, §1, codified as Cal. Water Code §§10920–10936 (2009).

[116] Sustainable Groundwater Management Act of 2014, Cal. Stats.2014, C. 346, §3, codified as Cal. Water Code, Div. 6, pt. 2.74 § 10720.1.

[117] Cal. Water Code § 10723, 10723.6.

[118] Cal. Water Code § 10721(v); 23 Cal. Code of Regs. § 354.24.

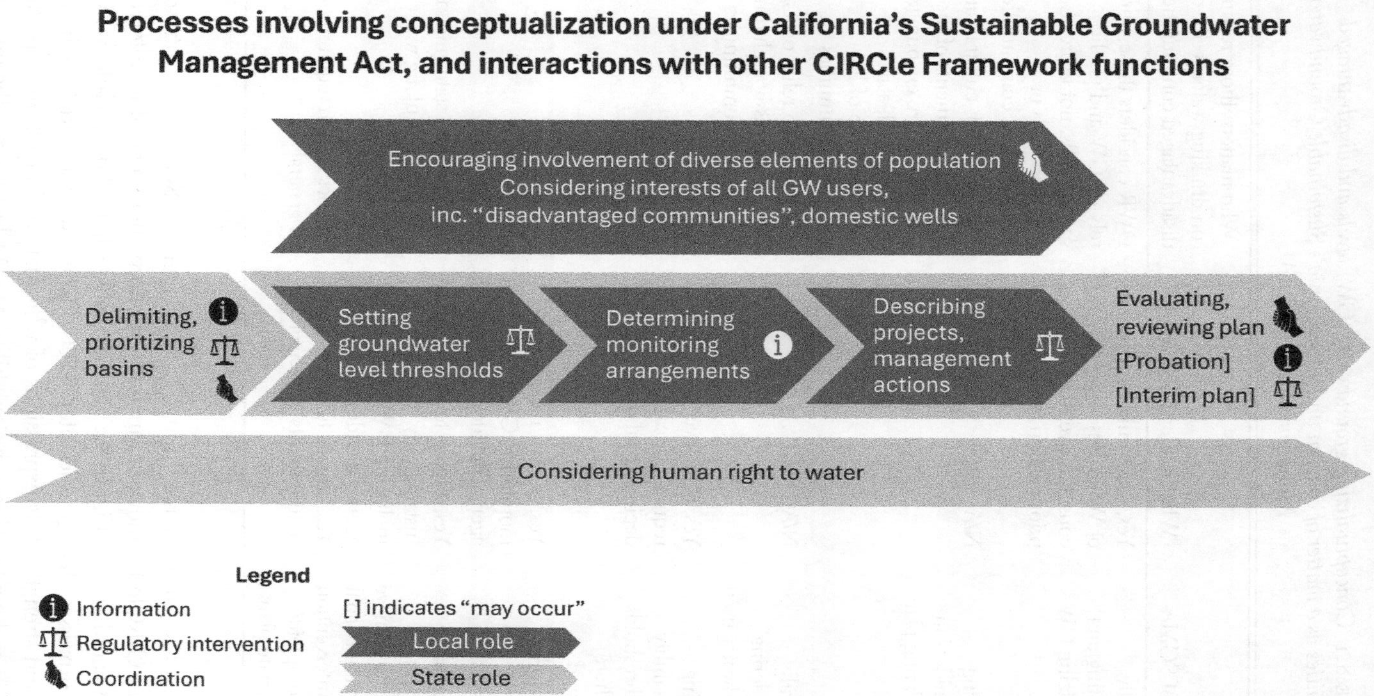

FIGURE 8.2 Elements of SGMA involved in conceptualizing what matters and who matters in groundwater sustainability, and links to other CIRCle Framework functions of information, regulatory intervention, and coordination

TABLE 8.1 *Conceptualizing groundwater (GW) levels and disadvantaged communities as a matter of concern under California's Sustainable Groundwater Management Act (SGMA)*

Element of SGMA	What matters: GW levels?	Who matters: those relying on drinking water wells, or disadvantaged communities?
(1) Spatially delimiting and prioritizing GW basins	Yes, California Department of Water Resources (DWR) considers overdraft in prioritization	DWR considers those who rely on GW and public supply wells, not expressly domestic wells or disadvantaged communities
(2) Involving stakeholders in formulating plan	N/A	"diverse social, cultural, and economic elements of the population" are encouraged to be involved; state promotes map of low-income communities
(3) Generally "considering" groundwater users	N/A	Everyone who relies on GW matters, expressly including low-income communities
(4) Defining sustainability goals/thresholds and where measured	Yes, GW level goals required; local agency decides local thresholds	All GW users
(5) Monitoring network	Yes, SGMA requires monitoring GW levels; local agency decides sites	All GW users
(6) Projects and management actions to achieve sustainability goal	Yes, applies to all sustainability indicators, including GW levels; local agency decides local actions	All GW users; state guidance focuses on drinking water wells
(7) State intervention re incomplete/ inadequate plan	Yes, applies to plan requirements in general	Applies to plan requirements in general

and thresholds – also emerge through these elements of SGMA, and intersect with other CIRCle Framework functions of information, regulatory intervention, and coordination (Figure 8.2). As the analysis here shows, while SGMA strongly expresses that groundwater levels matter, we see variation in the content and strength of its expressions of who matters. Indeed, in important respects, in seeking to achieve sustainability, SGMA leaves open the question of "*for whom?*"[119] Moreover, it appears that these legal weaknesses are driving real-world risks for disadvantaged communities, briefly discussed here by drawing on earlier coauthored work analyzing 108 published plans, over half of which are in the Central Valley (for brevity, "Perrone and others work"[120]) and additional analysis.

8.4.2.1 Prioritizing Basins

A foundational aspect of SGMA is the spatial delimitation and prioritization of groundwater basins. Basin boundaries affect how local agencies form and coordinate, since multiple agencies overlying a basin must either coordinate their plans or come together in a partnership to develop a single plan.[121] Thus, though setting basin boundaries appears to be a dry, technical aspect of conceptualization (where are the limits of the aquifer?), rules[122] provide for adapting boundaries in response to both scientific criteria and to "promote[] sustainable groundwater management," including processes for public input (though without specifying any particular populations).[123] In practice, local political factors, such as local maneuvering to "get more heft or independence" and protect local agency "little fiefdoms" influenced basin boundaries.[124] Complex local decision-making included considering whether to coordinate or "go it alone" for the 190 single and 74 multiple-entity local agencies that ultimately formed.[125] In these processes, then, we see a link between delimiting basin boundaries, the spatial element of *conceptualizing* the matter of concern, and *coordination* among local agencies.

California's Department of Water Resources ("Department"), a technical agency, prioritized groundwater basins as high, medium, low, or very low

[119] This is a central point made in relation to domestic wells by Darcy Bostic and others, *Sustainable for Whom? The Impact of Groundwater Sustainability Plans on Domestic Wells* (Center for Regional Change at the University of California, Davis 2020).

[120] Perrone and others, "Stakeholder Integration."

[121] Cal. Water Code §§ 10723, 10727.6.

[122] Cal. Water Code § 10722.2, 23 Cal. Code Regs. §§ 340–346.6.

[123] 23 Cal. Code Regs. §§ 342.4, 343.12, 344.16.

[124] Felicity Barringer, "To Manage Groundwater, California Must First Get Basin Boundaries Right," *& The West* (November 29, 2016, Bill Lane Center for the American West, Stanford University) https://andthewest.stanford.edu/2016/to-manage-groundwater-california-must-first-get-basin-boundaries-right. For a database of boundary revisions, see California Department of Water Resources, "SGMA Portal – Basin Boundary Modification Request System" (n.d.) https://sgma.water.ca.gov/basinmod/modrequest/submitted, last accessed March 20, 2025.

[125] See generally, Anita Milman and others, "Establishment of Agencies for Local Groundwater Governance under California's Sustainable Groundwater Management Act" (2018) 11 *Water Alternatives* 458–480.

priority.[126] This determined whether a groundwater sustainability plan was mandatory (only for high- and medium-priority basins) and its due date, or voluntary[127] – a fundamental influence on regulatory intervention. The main statutory prioritization criteria were set by earlier groundwater monitoring legislation.[128] The criteria include overdraft (where withdrawals exceed recharge, leading to groundwater level declines[129]) and reliance on groundwater (including public supply wells, but not domestic wells[130]), but no particular human population.

The statute did permit the Department to consider other relevant factors when prioritizing basins,[131] but in practice, it did not consider disadvantaged communities,[132] even in the Central Valley, where disadvantage is so prominent. Thus, in prioritizing basins, we see the convergence of three regulatory functions: prioritization influences *regulatory intervention*, involves *conceptualizing* what matters in a way that includes groundwater levels, using monitoring *information* produced pursuant to a formal rule. However, the process provides little clarity about who matters as an element of conceptualization.

8.4.2.2 Engaging the Public

In developing and implementing a plan, SGMA requires an agency to "encourage the active involvement of diverse social, cultural, and economic elements of the population,"[133] and document how this was done.[134] The Department supports local agencies through professional facilitators,

[126] Cal. Water Code § 10722.4.
[127] Cal. Water Code § 10720.7.
[128] See Section 8.4.1.
[129] Cal. Water Code § 10933(b)(7); California Department of Water Resources, *SGMA Basin Prioritization*, 2; California Department of Water Resources, "Basin Prioritization" (n.d.) https://water.ca.gov/programs/groundwater-management/basin-prioritization, last accessed March 20, 2025, archived at https://perma.cc/865F-CRLL.
[130] Cal. Water Code § 10933(b)(3), (6).
[131] Cal. Water Code § 10933(b)(8).
[132] Department of Water Resources (California), *California Groundwater Elevation Monitoring: Basin Prioritization Process* (2014) app A (last table, column headed "other information comments," which related to issues such as impacts on fisheries, the importance of agriculture, and industrial growth), archived at https://web.archive.org/web/20190324094650/https://water.ca.gov/-/media/DWR-Website/Web-Pages/Programs/Groundwater-Management/Basin-Prioritization/Files/CA_GW-Basin-Prioritization_07-10-14.pdf.
[133] Cal. Water Code § 10727.8.
[134] 23 Cal. Code Regs. § 354.10(d)(3).

translators, and interpreters, and guidance on stakeholder engagement.[135] The guidance makes a brief reference to "disadvantaged communities" and "environmental justice groups" as examples of stakeholder groups, with little elaboration on what these terms mean and how they differ.[136] This is problematic, given the confusion that attends the many different versions of these terms.[137] The guidance simply directs agencies to a tool that maps "disadvantaged communities" defined by low income.[138] A local agency may also appoint an advisory committee, but it need not include any specific stakeholder group.[139]

In this element, then, we see implementation tools designed to support linguistically diverse groups to participate and to help agencies identify the spatial locations of low-income communities (the "simple" view of disadvantaged communities). But we see no clear legislative view of who matters as a community of concern, and no reference to the cumulative view that would include other environmental burdens on communities, which is prominent in relation to pollution concerns.

8.4.2.3 Considering Groundwater Users

An overarching "consideration" requirement indirectly influences the substance of local groundwater sustainability plans. A local agency must describe in its plan,[140] and "consider the interests of all beneficial uses and users of groundwater," including agricultural users, domestic well owners, municipal well operators, public water systems, and "disadvantaged communities" reliant

[135] California Department of Water Resources, "Assistance and Engagement" (n.d.) https://water.ca.gov/Programs/Groundwater-Management/Assistance-and-Engagement, last accessed March 20, 2025, archived at https://perma.cc/HFF2-8NXD.

[136] California Department of Water Resources, *Stakeholder Communication and Engagement* (2018) 7, https://water.ca.gov/-/media/DWR-Website/Web-Pages/Programs/Groundwater-Management/Assistance-and-Engagement/Files/Guidance-Doc-for-GSP—Stakeholder-Communication-and-Engagement.pdf, archived at https://perma.cc/XWX5-AD7W. See also California Department of Water Resources, "Guidance on Engaging and Communicating with Underrepresented Groundwater Users" (2021) https://water.ca.gov/-/media/DWR-Website/Web-Pages/Programs/Groundwater-Management/Assistance-and-Engagement/Files/DWR—Underrepresented_Users_v3.pdf, archived at https://perma.cc/A78V-RUL5.

[137] See n 57 and accompanying text.

[138] California Department of Water Resources, "Mapping Tools: Disadvantaged Communities" (n.d.) https://water.ca.gov/Work-With-Us/Grants-And-Loans/Mapping-Tools, last accessed March 20, 2025, archived at https://perma.cc/27B8-FRB6; California Department of Water Resources, "Underrepresented Groundwater Users," 2.

[139] Cal. Water Code § 10727.8.

[140] 23 Cal. Code Regs. § 354.10(a).

on groundwater.[141] This element represents an "everyone matters" view of who matters. In practice, domestic use is widely recognized to be important: Perrone and others show that around 80 percent of plans describe domestic well users to varying degrees.[142] However, there is no direct, express link between this general obligation to "consider" and the other provisions described here.

8.4.2.4 Setting Groundwater Level Thresholds

A plan confronts the issues of groundwater levels and communities through its core enforceable sustainability goal, which links the cumulative threshold element of *conceptualization* to *interventions* to achieve the goal. A plan must describe current and historical groundwater levels[143] to inform the statutory sustainability goal of a plan, which is defined by the absence of "undesirable results" that are "significant and unreasonable."[144] SGMA sets out key general "sustainability indicators," which include degraded water quality and chronic lowering of groundwater levels.[145] Local agencies are left to quantify relevant thresholds, where they are measured, and what effects groundwater users can expect at these thresholds.[146] The legislation lacks minimum protections[147] or a hierarchy for considering user groups, even though state law in California has considered domestic water use the "highest" use of water for over eighty years.[148]

In practice, this approach to the sustainability goal has delivered weak protections for domestic wells, and even weaker protections for domestic wells in low-income communities. In the Central Valley's most critically overdrafted areas, plans may allow continued groundwater declines to 350 feet or more below ground level.[149] Perrone and others find that only 29 percent of

[141] Cal. Water Code § 10723.2; 23 Cal. Code Regs. § 354.26(b)(3) (potential effects of "undesirable results" on groundwater users).

[142] Perrone and others, "Stakeholder Integration," 4 (fig. 2).

[143] 23 Cal. Code Regs. § 354.16(a).

[144] Cal. Water Code § 10721(x); 23 Cal. Code Regs. § 354.24.

[145] Cal. Water Code § 10721(x); 23 Cal. Code Regs. § 354.26.

[146] 23 Cal. Code Regs. §§ 351(t), 354.28 (minimum thresholds). See also Cal. Water Code § 10727.2(b)(1), (2); 23 Cal. Code Regs. § 354.30 ("measurable objectives").

[147] The accompanying regulations state merely that the Department must consider the state policy on the human right to water when implementing the regulations: 23 Cal. Code Regs. § 350.4(g).

[148] Cal. Water Code § 106.

[149] EKI Environment & Water, "Estimated Numbers of Californians Reliant on Domestic Wells Impacted as a Result of the Sustainability Criteria Defined in Selected San Joaquin Valley Groundwater Sustainability Plans and Associated Costs to Mitigate Those Impacts (White Paper Prepared for the Water Foundation)" (*Water Foundation*, April 9, 2020) fig. 4, https://waterfdn.org/wp-content/uploads/2020/05/Domestic-Well-Impacts_White-Paper_2020-04-09.pdf archived at https://perma.cc/V2AD-NXPF.

plans adopt minimum thresholds that protect more than half of domestic wells in their territory, and many plan areas that fail to provide even this degree of protection are located in the Central Valley.[150] Significantly fewer domestic wells in (low-income) disadvantaged communities are protected than domestic wells in communities that are not so designated.[151] This is perhaps unsurprising, given that less than a quarter of all plans consider stakeholders in setting minimum thresholds, as opposed to factors such as lowest historical well levels.[152]

8.4.2.5 Monitoring Groundwater Levels

A plan must provide for a monitoring network to monitor groundwater conditions relative to enforceable goals, including those related to groundwater levels, and to monitor impacts on groundwater users.[153] These requirements are closely linked to minimum thresholds, and link *information* to *intervention*. The locations of sites chosen for monitoring contribute to the spatial element of *conceptualization*. These locations matter because groundwater levels vary across a basin. Levels that are monitored far from a community and deemed acceptable do not necessarily reliably describe conditions for that community. This means that monitoring sites "cover" the surrounding communities, but not others, in the sense of revealing declining groundwater levels relevant to compliance with enforceable goals.[154]

SGMA's monitoring provisions do not expressly require that monitoring locations be chosen to shed light on the groundwater conditions being experienced in disadvantaged communities, though the density and frequency of the sites and measurements must be based on impacts to groundwater users in a general sense.[155] Empirically, though, there is little difference between the percentage of wells in low-income communities close to key monitoring sites compared to wells outside these communities[156] – although, as described earlier, domestic wells within disadvantaged communities are less protected by minimum thresholds.

[150] Perrone and others, "Stakeholder Integration" 5, fig. 3.

[151] Ibid 8, fig. 6, supplementary table 4.2.

[152] Ibid 5.

[153] Cal. Water Code § 10727.2(e), (f); 23 Cal. Code Regs. § 354.34(b)(2), (3), (c)(1). See also 23 Cal. Code Regs. § 354.38(e)(3) (monitoring management action effectiveness where there are adverse impacts to groundwater users).

[154] Perrone and others, "Stakeholder Integration," 2.

[155] 23 Cal. Code Regs. § 354.34(f)(3).

[156] Perrone and others, "Stakeholder Integration," 8.

8.4.2.6 Designing Interventions

Having set sustainability goals, a plan must describe projects and management actions (*intervention*) to achieve them, including those that would be triggered when locally determined minimum thresholds are exceeded or "undesirable results have occurred or are imminent."[157] In other words, what interventions will prevent threshold conditions being exceeded (linking *conceptualization* to *intervention*)? These provisions do not expressly distinguish between disadvantaged and other groundwater users, but the Department has issued formal, though nonbinding, guidance on identifying and addressing impacts on drinking water wells.[158] Even so, it mentions disadvantaged communities only once, suggesting that a local agency should, at minimum, "disclose anticipated conditions" such as risks of wells going dry, and "work with" other entities to respond, or "implement projects and management actions to assist the identified users or avoid the adverse conditions."[159] The guidance document recommends adopting measures to "promote long-term sustainability," rather than short-term projects such as providing bottled water to households that lose access to drinking water.[160] The guidance further cautions that agencies pursuing programs to mitigate impacts for those who lose access to drinking water from wells not "arbitrarily or inequitably" exclude users based on the characteristics of their well, "socioeconomic status, demographics, and other relevant factors."[161]

To the extent that this guidance counsels a strategy to intervene to reduce cumulative impacts (reducing groundwater level decline) rather than just help communities cope with greater declines, such a strategy would better protect those that face cumulative stresses. Intervention to reduce cumulative impacts would deal with the root problem (declining groundwater levels) rather than depending on coping mechanisms that are potentially unreliable or practically inaccessible given other forms of disadvantage, such as language and health barriers.

157 23 Cal. Code Regs. § 354.44(a), (b).

158 California Department of Water Resources, "Considerations for Identifying and Addressing Drinking Water Well Impacts" (2023) https://water.ca.gov/-/media/DWR-Website/Web-Pages/Programs/Groundwater-Management/DrinkingWater/Files/ConsiderationsForIdentifyingandAddressingDrinkingWaterWellImpacts.pdf, archived at https://perma.cc/83QL-W2C3.

159 Ibid 6–7.

160 Ibid 14.

161 California Department of Water Resources, "Considerations for Identifying and Addressing Drinking Water Well Impacts," 11.

In practice, though, plans in the Central Valley sometimes include coping mechanisms that rely on uncertain future funding and that may be unfeasible for cumulatively burdened communities. Such measures may involve lowering a pump or deepening or replacing a well. This may require a tenant to persuade the landowner to be a claimant; and a claimant to be confident enough to approach a government entity (which may not be the case for undocumented residents), to have sufficient data to verify a claim, to fill out a claim form and to understand and sign legal agreements.[162] Using these approaches reduces the comprehensiveness of intervention if those who need them cannot take them up.[163] In addition, pumping from deeper down can involve more maintenance, higher pumping costs, and the need to treat lower-quality water.[164] In other words, the coping mechanism may place an ongoing burden on claimants if it is even accessible in the first place, fundamentally changing its effectiveness.

8.4.2.7 Coordinating across Levels and State Oversight

While most of the activity under SGMA is at the local level, the state has guidance, enforcement, and ongoing review roles. This also brings in the overlay of considering the human right to water, discussed earlier.[165] The Department evaluates plans and may find that a plan is incomplete and requires resubmission, or that it is inadequate if deficiencies are not remedied.[166] In evaluating plans, the Department must consider whether the local agency has considered groundwater users' interests (expressed generally).[167] If a local agency fails to resolve deficiencies, the State Water Resources Control Board (a department of the EPA) may place a basin in "probationary" status to resolve deficiencies, ultimately with the potential to use an interim

[162] See, e.g., "Delano-Earlimart Irrigation District GSA Mitigation Plan, Version 4.0" (*Delano-Earlimart Irrigation District*, July 2024) www.deid.org/wp-content/uploads/2023/03/deid-gsa-pilot-mitigation-plan-and-tm-122222.pdf, archived at https://perma.cc/WQ2Z-FPSW; Lower Tule River Irrigation District Groundwater Sustainability Agency and Pixley Irrigation District Groundwater Sustainability Agency, "Groundwater Sustainability Plan Impact Mitigation Plan" (n.d.) www.ltrid.org/wp-content/uploads/2023/06/ltrid-mitgation-plan-updated-6.29.23.pdf, archived at https://perma.cc/FT2H-XCZY.

[163] See Section 6.5.2.3.

[164] EKI Environment & Water, "Estimated Numbers of Californians Reliant on Domestic Wells," 3, 9.

[165] See Section 8.3.1.1.

[166] 23 Cal. Code Regs. § 355.2.

[167] 23 Cal. Code Regs. §§ 355.4(b)(4), 355.6(c)(4).

plan written by the state to collect further information and intervene to comply with the sustainability goal.[168]

In practice, it is this state–local *coordination* through oversight that has shone the most powerful spotlight on disadvantaged communities who risk losing access to their drinking water supplies due to declining groundwater levels. The Department found that multiple plans in six basins – all in the Central Valley – were deficient in their goals for groundwater levels and their consideration of disadvantaged communities.[169] In some cases, this led to corrections to plans that the Department later accepted as adequate.[170] In other cases (as of January 2025), the State Board emphasized considerations of equity and disadvantage and, at the time of writing, appears poised to declare "probationary" basins.[171] It considers that "[t]he primary intent of SGMA is to protect people who live in the basins from the devastating consequences of losing access to groundwater."[172] This has the potential to ensure that, at least in those basins, SGMA produces a conceptualization of what matters that includes not only groundwater levels but also disadvantaged communities that rely on the resource – though apparently taking a simple rather than a cumulative view of the burden they face.

Overall, as summarized in Table 8.1, legal provisions for each of these SGMA elements clearly focus on groundwater levels as a matter of concern. This fills a crucial gap in how California's legal system conceptualizes groundwater sustainability. Local agencies are empowered to define the

[168] Cal. Water Code § 10735.2.

[169] California State Water Resources Control Board, "Groundwater, the Sustainable Groundwater Management Act, and State Intervention" (October 12, 2023) 8–9, www.waterboards.ca.gov/water_issues/programs/sgma/docs/groundwater-sgma-state-intervention-faqs.pdf, last accessed March 20, 2025, archived at https://perma.cc/W37V-KLMD.

[170] E.g., Letter from Paul Gosselin to Ronnie Samuelian, "Re: Approved Determination of the Revised Groundwater Sustainability Plans Submitted for the San Joaquin Valley – Kings Subbasin" (*California Department of Water Resources*, August 4, 2023) https://sgma.water.ca.gov/portal/gsp/assessments/22, archived at https://perma.cc/64T9-56RR.

[171] E.g., State Water Resources Control Board, "Kern County Subbasin Probationary Hearing Final Staff Report" (January 2025) 42–43, 124, www.waterboards.ca.gov/water_issues/programs/sgma/docs/kern/202501-kern-final-staff-report.pdf, archived at https://perma.cc/AU6F-ELNM (noting the potential for disproportionate impacts on economically disadvantaged communities and communities of color caused by overdraft affecting shallow wells); State Water Resources Control Board, "Continuation of Hearing Regarding Designation of the Kern County Groundwater Subbasin as Probationary Under the Sustainable Groundwater Management Act," Resolution No. 2025–0007 (February 20, 2025), www.waterboards.ca.gov/board_decisions/adopted_orders/resolutions/2025/rs2025-0007.pdf.

[172] California State Water Resources Control Board, "Groundwater, the SGMA and State Intervention," 9.

amount of decline that matters in a local context, but there is no state "safety net" of maximum decline.

Provisions that define who matters, though, are expressed weakly in relation to disadvantaged communities. Disadvantaged communities were ignored in prioritizing basins, with the risk that groundwater declines that are significant enough to affect shallow wells, but not other users, will escape the groundwater planning mandate that only applies to high- and medium-priority basins. Where groundwater planning is required, local agencies must "consider" low-income disadvantaged communities and "encourage" diverse participation, but no outcome is mandated. Provisions dealing with intervention – controlling cumulative harm from declining groundwater levels – do not expressly protect vulnerable communities, though policy guidance points weakly in this direction. Considering low-income disadvantaged communities might lead to protections for domestic wells to prevent them going dry. Statutory "best management practices" guidance suggests somewhat tentatively that a local agency "may decide, for example, that … basinwide loss of domestic well pumping capacity due to lowering of groundwater levels are both significant and unreasonable conditions."[173] Perhaps it is more surprising that the opposite conclusion is also apparently possible.

Though SGMA includes low-income disadvantaged communities in its view of "who matters," it does not reliably protect them from falling groundwater levels, and it fails to take a cumulative view of burdens in determining who matters. The cumulative approach would recognize that losing access to drinking water may compound other environmental burdens that communities experience and contribute to environmental injustice more generally. This contrasts with the cumulative view of who matters taken by other groundwater-related laws and policies, as in the contexts of EIA, land use laws, statutory drinking water project grants, and EPA enforcement policy.[174] Notably, California's EIA legislation does not apply to the preparation and adoption of groundwater sustainability plans,[175] so environmental justice considerations under that legislation[176] are not engaged. Taking a simple (income-based) rather than cumulative view of who matters risks

[173] This guidance is still in draft as at January 2025: California Department of Water Resources, "Best Management Practices for the Sustainable Management of Groundwater: Sustainable Management Criteria (Draft)" (2017) https://water.ca.gov/-/media/DWR-Website/Web-Pages/Programs/Groundwater-Management/Sustainable-Groundwater-Management/Best-Management-Practices-and-Guidance-Documents/Files/BMP-6-Sustainable-Management-Criteria-DRAFT_ay_19, archived at https://perma.cc/N7SL-VCLG, 6.

[174] See Section 8.3.2.2.

[175] Cal. Water Code § 10728.6.

[176] See Section 8.3.2.2.

exacerbating vulnerabilities for communities of concern, because it ignores factors that reduce the feasibility of interventions in cumulatively burdened communities, such as education, language, and health.

8.5 CONCLUSION

In California's traditional regulatory landscape for groundwater as drinking water, what matters is groundwater pollution and how it might impact people who receive water service from a utility. The question of who matters in this landscape, when it comes to disadvantaged communities, is answered in different ways. A key distinction is between a "simple view" of disadvantaged communities based mostly or solely on low income and a "cumulative view" that sees the aggregate burden posed by multiple forms of socioeconomic disadvantage and environmental stresses.

This pre-SGMA view of what and who matter was largely silent on groundwater levels. SGMA tried to fill that silence, answering that groundwater levels matter too. But, in the end, despite its detailed provisions and processes for conceptualization, and their links to information, intervention, and coordination, the SGMA view of who matters is, at best, expressed vaguely and at varying volume through its various key elements. It also seems entirely to overlook the cumulative view of disadvantaged communities. This is important, because a solution that might effectively support a low-income householder who has lost access to their drinking water supply may not work for someone who also faces the other kinds of burdens that pollution-oriented laws consider under the banner of "environmental justice," such as poor health, language barriers, low educational attainment, and other environmental stressors. SGMA does not expressly prevent a local agency setting its groundwater level goals at the lowest recorded historical level, or lower, and promising to mitigate impacts on affected disadvantaged communities by "coping" measures that might simply prove infeasible for cumulatively burdened communities. Using the lens of environmental justice to understand the cumulative burdens that communities experience can help evaluate the real-world feasibility of these measures.

The implementation of SGMA's state–local coordination provisions, which allow the state to step in to remedy inadequate local plans, seems to be giving a louder voice to concerns about vulnerable communities losing access to their drinking water than does SGMA on paper. At the same time, federal termination of environmental justice initiatives shows that it may be preferable to rely on strong, clear, and coherent formal laws for conceptualizing "who matters" rather than relying heavily on agency willpower to provide structure and certainty. This raises the possibility of expanding SGMA's conceptualization of who matters in the context of groundwater depletion, and making this conceptualization coherent across its provisions. Expanding "who matters" to reflect a cumulative, environmental justice view, as occurs in the context of groundwater quality concerns, would guide the state to more calibrated solutions to groundwater depletion problems for those most vulnerable to its effects.

In the scheme of this book, the analysis of California's traditional regulatory landscape for groundwater illustrates the first phases of an evaluation of how a legal system responds to a cumulative environmental problem.[177] The analysis of SGMA illustrates how conceptualization centers and links to regulatory functions for information, regulatory intervention, and coordination, which are explored in the case studies that follow. It shows the potential for incoherent approaches (such as ignoring disadvantaged communities in prioritizing basins, but not in public participation processes), to which regulatory designers should be alert.

Beyond this, the California case study also suggests the value of conceptualizing what matters for the purposes of addressing a cumulative environmental problem in a way that is, itself, cumulative. Environmental justice indices that aggregate socioeconomic and environmental stressors, and inform regulatory schemes, are a prominent example of this approach. California's environmental justice index is currently limited to socioeconomic burdens and pollution-oriented environmental stressors, but indicators of access to natural resources, such as groundwater, would be a valuable extension. Outside the groundwater context, and in other places, a similar cumulative approach could embrace other access issues, from access to urban green space to access to resources for adapting to climate change. An ecological take on this approach is to map cumulative exposure to different forms of stress, an approach discussed in the Great Barrier Reef case study.[178] Ultimately, though, it is not just how a matter of concern is conceptualized, but how it links to the other regulatory functions required to address cumulative environmental problems that influences how laws can protect it from a thousand cuts.

[177] See Chapter 11 (Guidelines).
[178] See Section 9.4.2.

9

Coral, Coal, and Cattle

Cumulative Impacts and the Great Barrier Reef

9.1 INTRODUCTION

Like other World Heritage–listed sites, superlatives feature prominently in official descriptions of Australia's Great Barrier Reef ("Reef"). The "outstanding universal values" of this, the world's "most extensive coral reef ecosystem," include both natural beauty, as "the most spectacular maritime scenery in the world" and "amazing" biodiversity as "one of the richest and most complex natural ecosystems on earth."[1] The Reef is also a vital part of Aboriginal and Torres Strait Islander Peoples' culture and heritage, with some seventy Traditional Owner groups having cultural authority in the Reef area.[2]

Since its World Heritage listing in 1981,[3] however, the Reef has experienced "a historical sequence of compounding pressures that are steadily escalating," involving polluted agricultural runoff, coastal development, the effects of climate change, and fishing.[4] Indeed, the Reef has become a flash point for the effects of climate change nationally and internationally. These cumulative impacts have triggered significant evolution in the Reef's "globally

[1] "Great Barrier Reef: Description" (*UNESCO*, n.d.) https://whc.unesco.org/en/list/154/, last accessed March 24, 2025.

[2] Great Barrier Reef Marine Park Authority, "Reef Traditional Owners" (2022) www2.gbrmpa.gov.au/learn/traditional-owners/reef-traditional-owners, archived at https://perma.cc/6VFS-TU79.

[3] World Heritage Committee, Decision 5 COM VIII.15, Report of the Fifth Session of the UNESCO World Heritage Committee, October 26–30, 1981, CC-81/CONF/003/6 (January 5, 1982) 5.

[4] Terry P. Hughes, Jon C. Day and Jon Brodie, "Securing the Future of the Great Barrier Reef" (2015) 5 *Nature Climate Change* 508–511, 509, 510.

iconic governance regime,"[5] administered jointly by Australia's national government (the "Commonwealth") and the adjoining state of Queensland (see Figure 1.2).

The Reef offers a critical case study of the problems and potential of key legal mechanisms for dealing with cumulative impacts. The problems are profound. The Reef is highly vulnerable to climate change.[6] Long-established legal silos divide the regulation of adverse effects along jurisdictional lines, and between impact types, such as water quality and climate change, and make it hard to see the big picture. But there is also potential: As World Heritage, the Reef has high political salience and the highest level of legal protection for ecosystems in Australia. Reef governance has produced a central strategic environmental assessment (SEA) – often argued to be the most appropriate way to assess and manage cumulative impacts.[7] It seems like one of the likeliest places to find successful regulation of cumulative impacts, at least for problems at this scale.

A decade on from the SEA, this chapter evaluates its legacy of influence on the regulatory landscape of mechanisms for undertaking two key functions that are critical to regulating cumulative environmental problems: producing information about cumulative impacts on the Reef and advancing regulatory intervention to address those impacts. These are two of the four key interlinking functions of the CIRCle Framework of functions that this book argues benefit from being based on formal rules to help address cumulative environmental problems.[8] This chapter shows how the SEA, an information tool, paved the way for regulatory interventions that are unlikely to have happened without it. Because there are so many diverse types of activities and impacts on the Reef, this chapter focuses on an important subset. It contrasts mechanisms that apply in relation to sediment pollution and climate change as contributed by two major sectors, cattle grazing and coal mining. This reveals the influence of the SEA on individual regulatory tool bundles that apply to these impacts. In addition, it shows the potential of the Reef SEA to integrate regulatory mechanisms between different types of impacts, and between the

[5] Tiffany H. Morrison, "Evolving Polycentric Governance of the Great Barrier Reef" (2017) 114 *Proceedings of the National Academy, USA* E3013–E3021, E3014.

[6] See generally, Terry P. Hughes and others, "Coral Reefs in the Anthropocene" (2017) 546 *Nature* 82–90.

[7] Morten Bidstrup, Lone Kørnøv and Maria Rosário Partidário, "Cumulative Effects in Strategic Environmental Assessment: The Influence of Plan Boundaries" (2016) 57 *Environmental Impact Assessment Review* 151–158, 151 (citing numerous studies that make this argument).

[8] See Section 2.4 for an introduction to the CIRCle Framework.

siloed cumulative environmental problems of climate change and the broader range of impacts to the Reef.

These forms of influence – integrating information and regulatory intervention, changing regulatory tool bundles, and forming links across regulatory silos – go beyond the common perception that SEA has a technical-informative role in assessing the impacts of a program at a point in time, often disconnected from decision-making.[9] Rather, this kind of influence aligns with a view of SEA as providing a strategic framework that influences decision-making broadly, even beyond the land use, development, and spatial planning contexts typically discussed in the international literature.[10]

Section 9.2 provides context, describing how coal mines and cattle grazing contribute to water and greenhouse pollution that impacts the Reef, and the challenges that arise in managing these cumulative impacts. Section 9.3 gives an overview of the regulatory landscape around the Reef SEA, and the scope of the SEA. Sections 9.4 and 9.5 analyze its influence on legal mechanisms dealing with the cumulative impacts of coal mining and cattle grazing from the perspective of information and intervention, respectively.

9.2 CONTEXT AND CHALLENGES

9.2.1 *Key Threats to the Reef: Climate Change and Water Pollution*

As I write, the Reef is undergoing its fifth mass coral bleaching event in a decade – an effect of stress caused by a marine heat wave.[11] The damage accumulates with harms from diverse other causes, from invasive species to water pollution to cyclones.[12] The health of the Reef has been a prominent issue in Australia, due at least in part to its implications for the Reef's significant tourism industry.[13]

9 Victor Lobos and Maria Partidario, "Theory versus Practice in Strategic Environmental Assessment (SEA)" (2014) 48 *Environmental Impact Assessment Review* 34–46, 40, 45.

10 See generally, Bram Noble and Kelechi Nwanekezie, "Conceptualizing Strategic Environmental Assessment: Principles, Approaches and Research Directions" (2017) 62 *Environmental Impact Assessment Review* 165–173.

11 Great Barrier Reef Marine Park Authority (GBRMPA), *Aerial Surveys Confirm Widespread Bleaching across the Great Barrier Reef* (March 8, 2024) www2.gbrmpa.gov.au/news/aerial-surveys-confirm-widespread-bleaching-across-great-barrier-reef, archived at https://perma.cc/NFG3-5G25.

12 GBRMPA, "Reef Snapshot: Summer 2022–2023" (2023) 4, https://hdl.handle.net/11017/4002.

13 See GBRMPA, *Great Barrier Reef Region Strategic Assessment: Strategic Assessment Report* (GBRMPA 2014) 5-26 to 5-30, https://hdl.handle.net/11017/2861.

Climate change and fine sediment in catchment runoff ("sediment pollution") feature among the highest risk threats among the cumulative pressures on the Reef.[14] Climate change impacts are diverse: altered ocean currents affect the transport of coral eggs, more frequent and intense cyclones physically damage coral, ocean acidification compromises coral skeleton building, and higher sea temperatures cause heat stress and reduce available oxygen.[15] These effects are felt worldwide: Even if ambitious global targets of 1.5°C of global mean warming are met, over 90 percent of coral reefs are likely to be lost, increasing to 99.7 percent at 2.0°C.[16]

Sediment pollution reduces available light and affects how corals grow and reproduce, making it more difficult for them to recover from disturbances, and even smothering Reef organisms entirely.[17] Waterborne sediment increases turbidity, which also increases ocean temperatures and reduces oxygen levels for Reef organisms.[18]

These pressures have similarities and differences in the challenges they pose to regulating them as cumulative threats. They are similar in that legacies of greenhouse gases and sediment both continue to cause adverse effects for years after their emission.[19] This means that the benefits of contemporary interventions may take many years to be seen and addressing cumulative impacts means repairing historical damage. A key difference between these pressures is that while greenhouse gases emitted globally cause climate change that affects the Reef, sediment pollution is entirely sourced within Queensland's territory – from the thirty-five major river basins, together larger than the size of Japan,[20] which discharge to the Reef.

[14] Ibid 6–47 (with respect to impacts on coral habitats; noting that crown-of-thorns starfish and nutrients from catchment runoff also receive the same rating of "very high" effects). Note that risks from sediment were originally categorized as "catastrophic," later revised to "major": GBRMPA, *Great Barrier Reef Region Strategic Assessment: Supplementary Report* (2014) 70, https://hdl.handle.net/11017/2864.

[15] GBRMPA, *Reef Authority Strategic Assessment*, 6-10 to 6-15.

[16] Adele M. Dixon and others, "Future Loss of Local-Scale Thermal Refugia in Coral Reef Ecosystems" (2022) 1:e0000004 *PLOS Climate* 1–20, 5.

[17] GBRMPA, "Position Statement: Water Quality" (2020) https://hdl.handle.net/11017/3683; GBRMPA, *Reef Authority Strategic Assessment*, 6–22.

[18] Department of State Development Infrastructure and Planning (Queensland) (DSDIPQ), *Great Barrier Reef Coastal Zone Strategic Assessment Supplementary Report* (July 2014) 35, https://hdl.handle.net/11017/3166.

[19] GBRMPA, "Position Statement: Water Quality," 3 (citations omitted).

[20] Department of Environment and Science (Queensland) (DESQ), *Great Barrier Reef River Basins End-of-Basin Load Water Quality Objectives* (2019) 3, https://environment.des.qld.gov.au/__data/assets/pdf_file/0023/99320/gbr-river-basins-eob-load-wqos.pdf, archived at https://perma.cc/HVV5-J5UC.

Making the cumulative problem even more difficult, the pressures of climate change and sediment pollution interact. Climate change increases the likelihood of more intense rainfall events that cause soil erosion and sedimentation, making water quality management more challenging.[21] They also act together to exacerbate other effects: crown of thorns starfish, an invasive coral-eating species that also damages the Reef, benefits from turbid water and higher sea temperatures.[22]

9.2.2 *Coal and Cattle*

Cattle grazing and coal mining each emit greenhouse gas emissions that contribute to climate change and increase sediment in catchment runoff, which both affect the Reef. Both industries have characteristics that produce political, social, and economic challenges to intervention and concerns about regulatory burdens. Other agricultural enterprises, especially sugarcane growing, also contribute to water pollution via pesticides and nutrients[23] though those are not discussed further here.

As one of the world's largest exporters of coal,[24] Australian coal mines, most of which are in Queensland, contribute significantly to global greenhouse gas emissions.[25] They emit greenhouse pollution directly when the coal is mined, and indirectly, when it is burnt in Australia or overseas.[26] Mines contribute sediment-laden runoff to the Reef through earthworks and construction activities and rock blasting that result in dust deposition,[27] as well as a small amount of point-source pollution.[28] Multinational companies own most

[21] DESQ, *Reef 2050 Water Quality Improvement Plan 2017–2022* (2018) 14, www.reefplan.qld.gov.au/__data/assets/pdf_file/0017/46115/reef-2050-water-quality-improvement-plan-2017-22.pdf, archived at https://perma.cc/4VHM-TB4X ("*WQIP*").

[22] GBRMPA, *Great Barrier Reef Region Strategic Assessment: Supplementary Report*, 67.

[23] GBRMPA, "Position Statement: Water Quality," 2. See also n 40.

[24] Geoscience Australia, "Coal: Production," *Australia's Energy Commodity Resources 2023* (2023) www.ga.gov.au/digital-publication/aecr2023/coal, archived at https://perma.cc/42H2-TA7F.

[25] Jacqueline Peel, "The *Living Wonders* Case: A Backwards Step in Australian Climate Litigation on Coal Mines" (2024) 36 *Journal of Environmental Law* 125–132, 130.

[26] In relation to fugitive emissions, see Department of Climate Change, Energy, the Environment and Water (Australia) (DCCEEW), *Quarterly Update of Australia's National Greenhouse Gas Inventory: September 2024* (2025) 19–20, www.dcceew.gov.au/sites/default/files/documents/nggi-quarterly-update-september-2024.pdf, archived at https://perma.cc/493M-6VSJ.

[27] DSDIPQ, *Great Barrier Reef Coastal Zone Strategic Assessment Supplementary Report*, 35–37.

[28] DSDIPQ, *Great Barrier Reef Coastal Zone Strategic Assessment 2013: Strategic Assessment Report (Draft for Consultation)* (2013) 4-135, 5-165 to 5-166, https://hdl.handle.net/11017/3138.

Queensland coal mines,[29] and have recently earned "extraordinary revenue" due to high coal prices.[30] Coal mining also contributes significantly to state revenue and rural employment, which produces polarized political views about it in Australia.[31]

Australia is also among the world's largest beef exporters,[32] and cattle and calves are Queensland's largest agricultural export.[33] Queensland has Australia's largest cattle herd, with family-run operations dominating the industry.[34] Cattle grazing in northern Australia is large scale, with an average property size of 24,000 ha, and some properties over 1 million ha, but around half of grazing operations are not financially sustainable.[35] Sediment pollution of the Reef, which has more than quintupled since the 1850s, is driven largely by soil erosion associated with clearing native vegetation to establish pasture for grazing, and overgrazing.[36] Queensland has the highest rate of land clearing in Australia, and as of 2023, its rate of deforestation is significant worldwide.[37] Gully, streambank, and other forms of erosion caused by past land management practices continue

29 Industry Queensland, "Coal Mines Qld" (n.d.) https://industryqld.com.au/coal-mines-qld/, archived at https://perma.cc/2TAP-F576.

30 Queensland Treasury, *Queensland's Coal Industry and Long-Term Global Coal Demand* (2022) 9, https://s3.treasury.qld.gov.au/files/Queensland%E2%80%99s-Coal-Industry-and-Long-Term-Global-Coal-Demand_November-2022.pdf, archived at https://perma.cc/N4AQ-R5AF.

31 See generally, Bruce Tranter and Kerry Foxwell-Norton, "Only in Queensland? Coal Mines and Voting in the 2019 Australian Federal Election" (2021) 7 *Environmental Sociology* 90–101.

32 OECD and FAO, *Agricultural Outlook 2024–2033 Database* (2024), https://data-explorer.oecd.org (available under agricultural trade and markets, select all countries as "reference area," "beef and veal" as "commodity" and "exports" as "measure"), archived at https://perma.cc/87ZN-VWA9.

33 Department of Agriculture and Fisheries (Queensland), "Primary Industries Data" (2025) www.daf.qld.gov.au/news-media/campaigns/data-farm/primary-industries, archived at https://perma.cc/7PNN-YYCT.

34 Ernst & Young, *The Queensland Beef Supply Chain* (Queensland Department of Agriculture 2018) 13, www.publications.qld.gov.au/dataset/investment-outlook-for-the-queensland-beef-supply-chain, archived at https://perma.cc/63B2-ZVK5.

35 Steven Bray and others, "Climate Clever Beef: Options to Improve Business Performance and Reduce Greenhouse Gas Emissions in Northern Australia" (2016) 38 *The Rangeland Journal* 207–218, 208.

36 GBRMPA, *Reef Authority Strategic Assessment* 5-18 to 5-19 and 6-22; Fanny Douvere and Tim Badman, *Mission Report: Reactive Monitoring Mission to Great Barrier Reef (Australia), 6th to 14th March 2012* (UNESCO World Heritage Centre and IUCN June 2012) 26, https://whc.unesco.org/en/documents/117104.

37 Environmental Defenders Office, *Analysis of Vegetation Management Regulatory Frameworks in Australia: WWF Trees Scorecard 2023: Evidence Collection* (July 2023) 117, www.edo.org.au/wp-content/uploads/2023/08/EDO-Report-Analysis-Vegetation-Management-Regulatory-Frameworks.pdf.

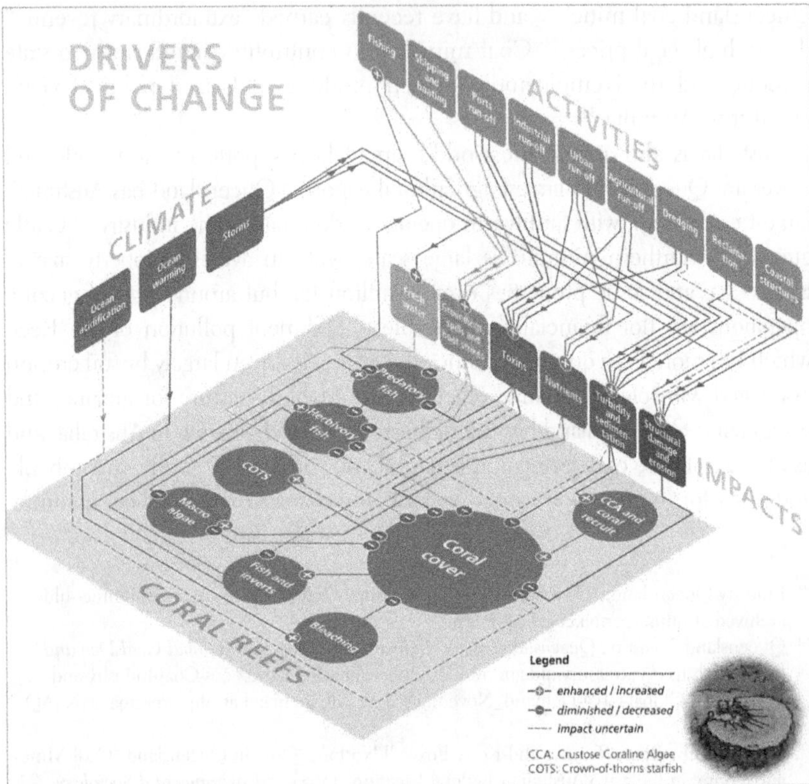

FIGURE 9.1 Qualitative model of cumulative impacts on coral, as assessed by the Reef SEA, omitting greenhouse gas emissions contributing to climate change
Source: © Commonwealth of Australia (GBRMPA, *Reef Authority Strategic Assessment*, 6–57), 2014

to contribute sediment to the Reef.[38] Cattle also contribute directly to greenhouse gas emissions through enteric fermentation and manure, and indirectly through other land management practices associated with cattle grazing, including savanna burning.[39]

Climate change and sediment pollution are an important subset of the pressures and impacts that accumulate to affect the Reef (Figure 9.1). Both cattle grazing and coal mining impact the Reef in other ways, and other activities and factors contribute to sediment pollution and climate change.[40]

[38] DSDIPQ, *GBR Coastal Zone Strategic Assessment Report*, 4-135.

[39] Bray and others, "Climate Clever Beef," 208. Note that when undertaken in specific ways, savanna burning is considered to reduce greenhouse gas emissions: see n 166 and accompanying text.

[40] E.g., waterborne nutrient pollution from sugarcane: see generally, Evan Hamman and Felicity Deane, "The Control of Nutrient Run-Off from Agricultural Areas: Insights into Governance from Australia's Sugarcane Industry and the Great Barrier Reef" (2018) 7 *Transnational Environmental Law* 451–468.

9.2.3 *Challenges: Information, Intervention, and Intersecting Problems*

Coal mines and cattle grazing, and their impacts, highlight the importance and challenges associated with two functions of regulation under the CIRCle Framework advanced by this book:[41] collecting, aggregating, and analyzing data and information about conditions of the Reef and threats to it; and intervening to change behavior to reduce cumulative harm. As shown by Chapters 5 and 6, respectively, diverse regulatory mechanisms can support these functions.

The large size of the Reef and its catchments, the dispersed nature of farming activities, and the difficulty of accessing parts of the Reef and its catchments and identifying species pose challenges in collecting data about its condition and relevant impacts.[42] It is also difficult to monitor sediment and greenhouse gas emissions and their effects, because they are diffuse (widely dispersed in space, rather than "point" sources) and because of legacy effects of past decades' and centuries' activities. So it is to gather information about regulatory interventions, compliance, and even government policies and programs in a complex regulatory landscape. Bringing all this information together when different laws address these issues is the overarching challenge. Section 9.4 takes up these information-related challenges.

Regulatory intervention is challenging when contributors to a cumulative environmental problem are politically or economically weighty, such as cattle grazing and coal mining, and known for a "culture of independence" and resentment of government restrictions.[43] In contrast to coal mining companies, graziers have more diverse financial positions and willingness to change practices.[44] This spotlights potential debates about approaches and strategies for intervention that reduce regulatory burden and increase social and political palatability, but that tend to reduce the reliability with which interventions pursue their objectives,[45] such as regulatory incentives ("carrots") and offset strategies. As discussed in Section 9.5, both carrots and

[41] See Section 2.4 for a brief description of the CIRCle Framework.

[42] E.g., A. J. Cheal and M. J. Emslie, *Supplementary Report to the Final Report of the Coral Reef Expert Group: S3. Synopsis of Current Coral Reef Monitoring on the Great Barrier Reef* (GBRMPA 2020) 18–19, https://hdl.handle.net/11017/3565 (hereafter "*Coral Monitoring Supplementary Report*").

[43] Neil Gunningham, Peter Grabosky and Darren Sinclair, *Smart Regulation: Designing Environmental Policy* (Clarendon Press, 1998) 289–290.

[44] Philippa England, "Leaders, Laggards and Blame Games: Responsive Regulation and Environmental Change in the Catchments of the GBR" (2021) unpublished manuscript, on file with author.

[45] Sections 6.2 to 6.4 of Chapter 6 ("Intervention") characterize different regulatory approaches and strategies in view of these aspects.

offsets appear in the regulatory landscape for the Reef. The diversity among graziers also raises questions about the fairness of the burdens imposed on different contributors across types of cumulative impact.[46]

A larger intervention-related challenge emerges in the intersection of two cumulative environmental problems. On one hand lies the aggregation of multiple types of impacts, including sediment pollution and climate change, on the Reef; and on the other hand is the cumulative impact of multiple types of activities that produce greenhouse gas emissions on the climate. This raises the challenge of dealing with greenhouse-polluting activities at the intersection of these problems: How might regulatory actors intervene in relation to activities undertaken in Queensland that produce greenhouse gases in the context of cumulative impacts on the Reef, given that others outside the jurisdiction and outside its control also contribute to this problem? Section 9.4 takes up these intervention-related challenges.

By contrast, the other two functions of regulation under the CIRCle Framework – conceptualization and coordination – are relatively less problematic in the Reef context, though not entirely straightforward. Conceptualizing the Reef as a matter of concern for regulatory purposes is largely settled due to its World Heritage listing, though some aspects are still variably implemented and contested.[47] Significant initiatives have developed a long-term vision for the Reef, expressing desired future conditions – a key component of conceptualization.[48] Similarly, while regulating pressures on the Reef is a multilevel governmental exercise, as discussed in Section 9.3, responsibilities and formal coordination structures are well studied[49] and well established, the product of a tumultuous history of federal-state conflict over the Reef.[50] Indeed, current approaches to regulating cumulative impacts on the Reef evolved significantly as a result of international action that coalesced in a multilevel (state/national) SEA, discussed next.

46 England, "Leaders, Laggards and Blame Games."

47 E.g., Douvere and Badman, *Mission Report: Reactive Monitoring Mission*, 35–36 (variable attention to outstanding universal values, as opposed to values generally). For a discussion on conceptualizing the matter of concern, see Chapter 4.

48 See generally, Australian Government and Queensland Government, *Reef 2050 Long-Term Sustainability Plan 2021–2025* (2021) www.dcceew.gov.au/parks-heritage/great-barrier-reef/publications/reef-2050-long-term-sustainability-plan-2021-25, archived at https://perma.cc/8DWU-Y6YY. See Chapter 4 (Conceptualization).

49 See, e.g., Pedro Fidelman and others, "Regulatory Implications of Coral Reef Restoration and Adaptation under a Changing Climate" (2019) 100 *Environmental Science and Policy* 221–229, 223; Morrison, "Evolving Polycentric Governance."

50 For an overview of the early history, see Lorne K. Kriwoken, "Great Barrier Reef Marine Park: Intergovernmental Relations" (1991) 15 *Marine Policy* 349–362.

9.3 OVERVIEW OF THE REGULATORY LANDSCAPE AND THE REEF SEA

This section sets the scene for analyzing regulatory functions related to information and intervention and how the SEA influenced them. It explains how Australia distributes regulatory responsibility for environmental matters between states and the Commonwealth (Section 9.3.1), how international attention drove the Reef SEA that was developed cooperatively[51] between both levels (Section 9.3.2), and how the Reef SEA was scoped (Section 9.3.3).

9.3.1 *Setting the Scene: Regulatory Responsibilities and International Influence*

As a constitutional and practical matter, cumulative impacts on the Reef have long been managed by different levels of government, with overarching coordination. Australian states are primarily responsible for environmental matters, including pollution and land use planning; the federal Parliament may legislate to implement international treaties signed by the government.[52] These include the Climate Change Convention[53] and the World Heritage Convention,[54] which provides for listing and protecting areas that are "the priceless and irreplaceable assets, not only of each nation, but of humanity as a whole."[55] This international link grants the Commonwealth Parliament powers to regulate activities on the Reef itself (e.g., fishing, tourism), projects

[51] While regulatory mechanisms for coordination lie outside the scope of this chapter, note that the Reef SEA triggered extensive coordination mechanisms: Australian Government and Queensland Government, *Reef 2050 Long-Term Sustainability Plan* (Australian Government 2015) 49–50, https://hdl.handle.net/11017/2934; Australian National Audit Office, *Reef Trust – Design and Implementation* (2016) 32, www.anao.gov.au/sites/default/files/ANAO_Report_2016-2017_27.pdf, archived at https://perma.cc/H2MB-4JDY.

[52] For a discussion of the development of Australian federal and state legislative responsibilities in relation to the environment in the context of cumulative impact concerns, see Rebecca Nelson, "Breaking Backs and Boiling Frogs: Warnings from a Dialogue between Federal Water Law and Environmental Law" (2019) 42 *University of New South Wales Law Journal* 1179–1214, 1186–1191.

[53] United Nations Framework Convention on Climate Change (adopted May 9, 1992, entered into force March 21, 1994) 1771 U.N.T.S. 107. Note that while other treaties ratified by Australia are also relevant to the Great Barrier Reef, they are not discussed here for reasons of brevity and because they are less directly influential.

[54] Convention Concerning the Protection of the World Cultural and Natural Heritage (adopted November 16, 1972, Paris, entered into force December 17, 1975) 1037 U.N.T.S. 151.

[55] UNESCO, *Operational Guidelines for the Implementation of the World Heritage Convention* (WHC.21/01 edn, UNESCO 2021) 11. For a practical description of the operation of the World Heritage Convention, see ibid.

that may affect it, and climate change, while Queensland regulates land use and pollution produced in the Reef's catchments. The Commonwealth and Queensland governments coordinate under an intergovernmental agreement that expressly recognizes that climate change and catchment-sourced water pollution harm the Reef.[56]

In 2009, an international information mechanism jolted this system of shared responsibility, ultimately producing a key overarching legal mechanism for managing cumulative effects: the Reef SEA. The World Heritage Committee learned that – contrary to international guidelines[57] – Australia had failed to notify it that a large liquefied natural gas plant was being constructed on Curtis Island, inside the Reef World Heritage area.[58] This triggered formal discussions and a "reactive monitoring mission," both of which emphasized threats from diffuse water quality impacts, climate change, and cumulative impacts. The Committee urged Australia to undertake a strategic assessment of the Reef to formulate a long-term sustainability plan[59] and a framework for assessing development proposals in a way that considered cumulative impacts.[60]

The Committee backed these exhortations with indications it might list the Reef as "World Heritage in danger," a threat that continues even now.[61] Since such a listing would undermine tourism and damage Australia's international reputation, the threat worked to focus bureaucratic minds on the problem. Scholars consider that the SEA would likely never have happened without the Committee's request.[62] The Committee's involvement made mandating

56 DSDIPQ, *Great Barrier Reef Coastal Zone Strategic Assessment: Program Report* (2014) 16, https://hdl.handle.net/11017/3165.

57 UNESCO, *Operational Guidelines* [172].

58 This omission was apparently caused by jurisdictional confusion about the boundaries of the WHA: Evan Vaughan Hamman, "The Role of Non-State Actors in Promoting Compliance with the World Heritage Convention: An Empirical Study of Australia's Great Barrier Reef" (Thesis, Doctor of Philosophy, Queensland University of Technology 2017) 35–36.

59 World Heritage Committee, Decision 35 COM 7b.10 Great Barrier Reef (Australia) (N 154), Decisions Adopted by the World Heritage Committee at Its 35th Session, June 29–29, 2011, WHC-11/35COM/20 (July 7, 2011) 55; Douvere and Badman, *Mission Report: Reactive Monitoring Mission*, 7–8, 17–20, 23, 26, 31, 32, 45, 47, 49, 50 (esp. recommendations 2, 4, 7, 8). For a fuller description of the Reef SEA, see generally, Evan Hamman, Karen Vella and Umberto Baresi, "Cumulative Impacts and Strategic Environmental Assessment: Policy Development for Australia's Great Barrier Reef" in Jill A. E. Blakley and Daniel M. Franks (eds), *Handbook of Cumulative Impact Assessment* (Edward Elgar 2021) 123–139.

60 Douvere and Badman, *Mission Report: Reactive Monitoring Mission*, 6–7 (recommendation 5).

61 World Heritage Committee, "Great Barrier Reef (Australia) (N 154)" in UNESCO (ed), *State of Conservation of Properties Inscribed on the World Heritage List*, *WHC/24/46com/7badd* (2024) 59–64.

62 Hamman, Vella and Baresi, "Cumulative Impacts and Strategic Environmental Assessment," 135.

agricultural pollution interventions "politically palatable,"[63] illustrating how involving more regulatory actors can change feasible interventions to address cumulative impacts.[64] The resulting assessment (2014) and its associated plans and policies (2015–2018) (together, the "Reef SEA") became the overarching mechanism for dealing with cumulative impacts on the Reef.

9.3.2 *Framework for the Reef SEA*

The Reef SEA was undertaken under discretionary provisions of Australia's national environmental legislation[65] that are used relatively rarely. These provisions are often criticized as too narrow, or merely a vehicle for bulk approval of projects.[66] Usefully, though, they can offer a two-part structure that directly links assessment (information) and regulatory intervention. The first component, a "strategic assessment report," is an information-focused assessment of environmental matters and the effectiveness of management arrangements. The second component is a "program report" that proposes improved management arrangements, possibly including mechanisms for information and intervention. The Commonwealth Environment Minister considers the program report for endorsement, which indicates that it adequately addresses impacts on relevant nationally protected matters (here, World Heritage values).[67] This raises the expectation that the formal commitments in the program, for example, information and intervention initiatives, are needed to address impacts on federally protected matters. While the program may not directly legally bind governments, arrangements that deviate significantly from it would raise the possibility of contravening federal legal protections.

While the Reef SEA is also not directly legally binding on coal or cattle proponents, it raised the potential to influence their activities in two ways: first, by connecting information about their impacts to existing laws that apply to their activities, changing how these laws are implemented; and, second, by

[63] Rowena Maguire, Evan Hamman and Justine Bell-James, *Environmental Planning and Climate Law in Queensland* (LexisNexis Butterworths 2020) 155, 230.

[64] See Section 2.2.4.1.

[65] Environment Protection and Biodiversity Conservation Act 1999 (Australia) pt 10 ("EPBC Act").

[66] This requires approving actions undertaken in accordance with an endorsed program, which is not what occurred here: ibid s 146B. See, e.g., Simon Marsden, "A Critique of Australian Law Reform for Strategic Environmental Assessment" (2013) 32 *University of Tasmania Law Review* 276, 280–281. For a recent summary of critiques of national SEA in Australia, see Tanya Burdett and Carolyn Cameron, "Strategic Environmental Assessment in Australia" in Thomas B. Fischer and Ainhoa González (eds), *Handbook on Strategic Environmental Assessment* (Edward Elgar 2021) 284–304, 292–294.

[67] EPBC Act s 146(2)(f).

triggering the formulation and adaptation of new and existing regulatory interventions, respectively, diversifying the regulatory mix. The degree to which the Reef SEA regime fulfilled this theoretical potential was influenced significantly by how it was scoped, discussed next.

9.3.3 *Scope of the Reef SEA*

The scope of a SEA in terms of sectors, space, and time, critically affects its analysis of cumulative impacts.[68] In this case, narrow and ambiguous language hampered the Reef SEA's potential comprehensively to gather information and influence regulatory interventions in relation to climate change and water pollution. This ultimately constrained its ability to connect the intersecting cumulative environmental problems of impacts on the Reef and climate change generally.

Without legislative criteria for adequacy, or detailed guidance from the World Heritage Committee,[69] formal terms of reference set the scope of the Reef SEA. Reflecting jurisdictional responsibilities, the Reef SEA was split in two. A Commonwealth agency, the Great Barrier Reef Marine Park Authority ("Reef Authority"), was to assess marine areas, with discretion to include other places if the Reef was "affected by actions in those places."[70] The Reef Authority was to assess (among other things) Reef conditions, cumulative impacts and "the likely impacts of climate change," and the effectiveness of management arrangements, including to "adapt to reasonable climate change scenarios."[71] But it was only to cover "management arrangements within the Authority's jurisdiction" and work jointly with Queensland in relation to water quality.[72] Queensland, on the other hand, was to assess "threats from both within and outside the strategic assessment area"[73] and the effectiveness of its management, planning and development framework in a 5-km wide, 2,300-km-long coastal strip, and catchment areas "to the extent that water quality management arrangements apply."[74]

68 See generally, Bidstrup, Kørnøv and Partidário, "Cumulative Effects in Strategic Environmental Assessment."

69 Hamman, Vella and Baresi, "Cumulative Impacts and Strategic Environmental Assessment," 132.

70 GBRMPA, *Great Barrier Reef Region Strategic Assessment: Terms of Reference* (GBRMPA 2012) 1, 2, https://hdl.handle.net/11017/2859.

71 Ibid 6, 7.

72 Ibid 1, 2.

73 Queensland Government, *Great Barrier Reef Coastal Zone Strategic Assessment: Background and Final Terms of Reference* (2012) 7, www.statedevelopment.qld.gov.au/__data/assets/pdf_file/0012/11316/great-barrier-tor.pdf, archived at https://perma.cc/2PZT-9FMD.

74 Ibid 1–2.

The SEA terms of reference included catchment-sourced water pollution and adapting to climate change, but excluded climate mitigation. The Queensland government, which grants coal mining leases and associated environmental approvals,[75] assessed the impacts of mining that "directly affect the GBR coastal zone," including water quality impacts, but considered that "climate change cannot be addressed by the Program due to its global nature."[76] Commonwealth-level climate change regulators were not involved in the Reef SEA and the Reef Authority emphasized its lack of relevant "jurisdictional responsibility," and only briefly noted its potential role in advising other agencies about climate change mitigation.[77] Omitting climate mitigation caused public concern, especially given Queensland's fossil fuel sector.[78] Nevertheless, the impacts of climate change on the Reef were seen solely as a matter of adaptation.

9.4 REGULATORY MECHANISMS FOR INFORMATION AND THE REEF SEA

The mere fact that the Reef SEA provides information about the Reef's condition and threats does not break new ground. Rather, its function as an information mechanism is important because, together, the strategic assessment reports and program reports formalize nonstatutory information initiatives and expand them. Crucially, for cumulative environmental problems, they also bring information together and link it to intervention, incorporating design features that address challenges related to cost, sustainability, and legitimacy. These are key challenges for cumulative environmental problems generally.[79] After briefly reviewing historical arrangements for information about water quality and climate change, this section analyzes, in turn, how the strategic assessment reports and the program reports played an important information function in the context of impacts on the Reef as a cumulative environmental problem.

[75] Rebecca Nelson, "Regulating Hidden Risks to Conservation Lands in Resource Rich Areas" (2021) 40 *University of Queensland Law Journal* 491–530, 504–514.

[76] DSDIPQ, *GBR Coastal Zone Strategic Assessment Report*, 5-153.

[77] GBRMPA, *Reef Authority Strategic Assessment*, 8-15 to 8-16. Recent developments suggest the Reef Authority may act creatively on this front: see nn 168–172 and accompanying text.

[78] DSDIPQ, *Great Barrier Reef Coastal Zone Strategic Assessment Supplementary Report*, 144–145, 150–151.

[79] See Chapter 2.

Recall Chapter 5 (Information)

Key design features of regulatory mechanisms for information to address cumulative environmental problems include providing for gathering and sharing data and information from multiple government and nongovernment actors in a way that: **comprehensively** deals with conditions of the matter of concern (here, the Reef) over time and all important activities and impacts that contribute to the cumulative environmental problem; is **high quality**; is **easily shareable and interoperable; and manages cost**.

9.4.1 *A History of Regulating for Information*

Regulatory mechanisms for scientific expertise and information have long been central to Reef governance, beginning with the first Marine Park statute (1975) and intergovernmental agreement (1979),[80] the current version of which commits to coordinated monitoring of impacts on the Reef.[81] Since 2007, the Reef Authority has been required by statute to produce a five-yearly Reef "Outlook Report" that assesses the health and resilience of the Reef, risks to it, and measures to protect and manage it.[82] It expressly addresses indicators of water pollution and climate change threats.[83]

Numerous less formal, nonstatutory information programs have also arisen over time. Notably, since 2009, a nonstatutory annual Reef Report Card has tracked progress to water quality targets using a "Paddock to Reef" monitoring program.[84] The program assesses the adoption and effectiveness of management interventions, and both catchment and marine conditions.[85] It both

[80] Great Barrier Reef Marine Park Act 1975 (Australia) (as made) s 10(5); "Great Barrier Reef (Intergovernmental Agreement, Queensland and Commonwealth of Australia)" (1979) s 6 https://hdl.handle.net/11017/3367.

[81] "Great Barrier Reef (Intergovernmental Agreement, Commonwealth of Australia and Queensland)" (2009) 5, Sch D https://hdl.handle.net/11017/984.

[82] Great Barrier Reef Marine Park Act 1975 (Australia) s 54, introduced by Great Barrier Reef Marine Park Amendment Act 2007 (Australia) s 32.

[83] GBRMPA, *Great Barrier Reef Outlook Report 2019* (GBRMPA 2019) 161–167, 171–182, https://hdl.handle.net/11017/3474.

[84] DESQ, *WQIP*, 53; Department of Environment Science and Innovation (Queensland), "Reef Report Cards" (n.d.) www.reefplan.qld.gov.au/tracking-progress/reef-report-card, last accessed March 22, 2025, archived at https://perma.cc/69LA-NYA6.

[85] Jane Waterhouse, *Paddock to Reef Integrated Monitoring, Modelling and Reporting Program: Program Design 2018–2022* (Office of the Great Barrier Reef (Queensland) n.d.) 13–14, www.reefplan.qld.gov.au/__data/assets/pdf_file/0026/47249/paddock-to-reef-program-design .pdf, archived at https://perma.cc/6L9L-94ZM.

monitors and models pollution, since rivers have high flow variability and up to fifty-year time lags separate catchment interventions and monitorable changes to pollution.[86]

9.4.2 *The Reef SEA: Entrenching, Expanding, and Integrating Information Initiatives*

In line with their terms of reference, the strategic assessment reports used these existing and other sources to gather and assess information about the impacts on the Reef of climate change,[87] catchment-sourced sediment pollution,[88] other impacts, and cumulative impacts.[89] The cumulative impact assessment produced "cumulative exposure" maps showing how different areas of the Reef are exposed to multiple water quality impacts (sediment and other pollutants) and multiple key impacts (e.g., elevated temperatures, freshwater inflow, etc).[90] These are conceptually similar to California's cumulative environmental justice maps, discussed in the previous case study. These maps aggregate multiple sources of demographic and environmental risk experienced by human populations, and are used in California to prioritize some regulatory interventions.[91] The strategic assessment reports also noted key knowledge gaps regarding cumulative impact assessment, including relationships between the Great Barrier Reef (GBR) catchments and coastal zone.[92]

The endorsed program reports committed to ongoing information initiatives and linked them to planning future management. This provided for enduring influence in relation to information, thus addressing a frequent criticism of SEA as often limited to a "point in time" assessment.[93] The endorsed programs entrench and expand existing water quality monitoring through an expanded Paddock to Reef program intended to inform adaptive management of water quality interventions,[94] and introduce regular reporting of climate change indicators.[95]

86 Ibid 9.
87 GBRMPA, *Reef Authority Strategic Assessment*, 5-4 to 5-8, 6-10 to 6-15.
88 Ibid 5-18 to 5-19 and 6-22.
89 Ibid 6-55 to 6-67.
90 Ibid 6-58 to 6-65.
91 See Table 6.5, row 1.
92 DSDIPQ, *GBR Coastal Zone Strategic Assessment Report*, 5-192.
93 See n 9 and accompanying text.
94 DESQ, *WQIP*, 52; Department of State Development Infrastructure and Planning (Queensland), *Great Barrier Reef Coastal Program Report*, 77.
95 GBRMPA, *Great Barrier Reef Region Strategic Assessment: Supplementary Report*, 129.

The program reports also commit to a new integrated platform that reflects a cumulative impacts mindset of aggregating interoperable information.[96] A consolidated "Reef 2050 Integrated Monitoring and Reporting Program" (RIMReP) aims to integrate Reef-related monitoring undertaken by governments and other organizations,[97] including data on catchments, water quality, and climate indicators.[98] The RIMReP aims to provide interoperable data to guide management actions, including to understand the cumulative impact of pressures and interventions.[99]

RIMReP generally aligns well with a cumulative impact approach, but an important omission relating to activity-level information about impacts mars its comprehensiveness. There is no apparent link to government- or proponent-sourced data on the project-level (as opposed to catchment-level) impacts of regulated activities, for example, from environmental impact statements and compliance programs. This mirrors long-running criticism that Australia's national environmental law does not support aggregating environmental data produced by project proponents.[100] A Cumulative Impacts Policy linked to the SEA simply advises decision-makers to hold information about "current and reasonably foreseeable projects" to "allow stakeholders to accurately assess other sources."[101] Relatedly, Reef information programs apparently do not integrate data on compliance and enforcement of relevant activities, which might have been linked to a requirement to adapt interventions or their implementation. These are striking omissions given a history of concern about widespread noncompliance and minimal enforcement of

96 See Sections 5.3.1 and 5.3.3.

97 Australian Government and Queensland Government, *Reef 2050 Long-Term Sustainability Plan*, 65–66.

98 James Udy, *Identifying Management Needs: Informing the Program Design of the Reef 2050 Integrated Monitoring and Reporting Program* (GBRMPA 2018) 11, 12, https://hdl.handle.net/11017/3426; GBRMPA, *Great Barrier Reef Region Strategic Assessment: Supplementary Report*, 129. Also see generally Australian Government and Queensland Government, *Reef 2050 Integrated Monitoring and Reporting Program Business Strategy 2020–25* (GBRMPA 2022) https://hdl.handle.net/11017/3918.

99 Udy, *Identifying Management Needs: Program Design of RIMREP*, 11, 12. Also see generally, Australian Government and Queensland Government, *RIMREP Business Strategy*.

100 House of Representatives Standing Committee on the Environment (Australia), *Streamlining Environmental Legislation: Inquiry into Streamlining Environmental Regulation, "Green Tape," and One Stop Shops* (2014) 79–81, www.aph.gov.au/Parliamentary_Business/Committees/House/Environment/Green_Tape/Report, archived at https://perma.cc/9SMM-UA2Z.

101 GBRMPA, *Reef 2050 Plan: Cumulative Impact Management Policy* (GBRMPA 2018) 35, https://hdl.handle.net/11017/3389.

agricultural water quality requirements,[102] and about the transparency of compliance and monitoring data for mining projects.[103]

Information aspects of the SEA also demonstrate design features that address challenges related to cost and legitimacy of information.[104] Information initiatives manage the costs of monitoring in a large and challenging environment by including technologically driven approaches such as remotely sensed data.[105] RIMReP both manages cost and buttresses its legitimacy by including data from nongovernment sources, including the preexisting citizen science "Eye on the Reef" programs for assessing Reef conditions.[106] Formally requiring an independent review of the Reef SEA[107] also supports legitimacy, and mirrors statutory requirements of the Outlook report[108] and previous use of independent scientific "consensus statements" on water pollution, which have driven new interventions.[109] Independent reviewers complimented the reports' technical accuracy, but criticized proposed management of water quality and climate change issues as unlikely to be effective.[110]

Without more, gathering and sharing data and information about cumulative impacts simply shines a brighter light on decline: It is the regulatory links between information and intervention that enable information to influence cumulative impacts. The Reef SEA shows several types of these regulatory links in a way that seems relatively uncommon. The Reef SEA itself was spurred by an international regulatory mechanism for informing the World Heritage Committee about a major project on the Reef.[111] The endorsed program committed to an overarching "outcomes-based framework"[112] – the *Reef 2050 Long-Term Sustainability Plan* ("Reef 2050 Plan") – for improving the Reef to meet targets that would be "monitored, reported and adapted over time," fed by the program's information

[102] Evan Hamman and others, "Regulating Land Use in the Catchment of the Great Barrier Reef" (2022) 115:106001 *Land Use Policy* 1–15, 9.

[103] Productivity Commission (Australia), *Resources Sector Regulation* (2020) 202–205, www.pc.gov.au/inquiries/completed/resources/report/resources.pdf, arhived at https://perma.cc/9Q7C-32YL.

[104] See Section 5.3.

[105] Udy, *Identifying Management Needs: Program Design of RIMREP*, 19–22.

[106] Cheal and Emslie, *Coral Monitoring Supplementary Report*, 22–23.

[107] GBRMPA, *Great Barrier Reef Region Strategic Assessment: Terms of Reference*, 4.

[108] Great Barrier Reef Marine Park Act 1975 (Australia) s 54(4).

[109] Hamman and others, "Regulating Land Use," 9.

[110] GBRMPA, *Great Barrier Reef Region Strategic Assessment: Supplementary Report*, 11.

[111] See notes 57 to 60 and accompanying text.

[112] DSDIPQ, *Reef Coastal Program Report*, 74.

initiatives and revised every five years. The Reef 2050 Plan planned to deliver these targets in part by influencing other laws and management arrangements, facilitated by a policy to guide decision-makers on how to consider the Plan in "relevant decision making", and an initiative to collect information *about* intervention using a register of management plans.[113] As already discussed, though, information from project-level assessments and compliance and enforcement were blind spots. Now, a decade on from these commitments and aspirations, we can assess how these pathways for informing intervention have turned information into regulatory action.

9.5 REGULATORY MECHANISMS FOR INTERVENTION AND THE REEF SEA

This section analyzes how the Reef SEA influenced rules for interventions to address cumulative impacts on the Reef of greenhouse and sediment pollution from coal mining and cattle grazing. It shows that the Reef SEA increased the comprehensiveness of the overall regulatory regime – an important regulatory design feature for cumulative environmental problems.[114] It influenced and adapted existing water quality interventions and also drove the introduction of new interventions related to water quality. The Reef SEA also enhanced the diversity of regulatory approaches and strategies used in interventions (see text box).[115] Greenhouse gas emissions, though, lay beyond its reach. Australian climate law has advanced significantly since the Reef SEA, but it remains disconnected from the Reef context, with just a hint that this may change. This shows the barriers to SEA connecting decision-making across regulatory silos, and between intersecting local and global cumulative environmental problems,[116] especially in an unfavorable political context.

[113] Australian Government and Queensland Government, *Reef 2050 Long-Term Sustainability Plan*, 53 (action GA7).

[114] See Section 6.5.2.

[115] A single intervention may pursue multiple approaches or strategies (e.g., a "stick" mandate to obtain an environmental approval, which may have conditions attached to both reduce and offset harm; or an extension program [sermon] that uses incentives [carrot] to increase participation). A legally binding mechanism is categorized as only harm-reducing unless there is specific mention of offsetting or adapting in legislation, regulation or associated policy.

[116] See Section 9.2.3.

Recall from Chapter 6: Intervention

Key design features of regulatory mechanisms for intervention to address cumulative environmental problems include connecting decision-making about impacts that accumulate, intervening comprehensively across impact types and activities, intervening adaptively, and using diverse *regulatory approaches* and *strategies*. Regarding **regulatory approaches**, *sticks* refer to mandates about the carrying out of an activity that causes harm; *carrots* influence an activity through incentives and disincentives that apply to an activity in the absence of a mandate (e.g., a monetary incentive or tax); *sermons* influence the activity using information; and *state rescue* involves the state directly addressing harm rather than trying to change the behavior of contributors to the harm. Regarding **regulatory strategies**, *harm reducing* means changing an activity so that it causes less harm; *harm offsetting* means undertaking a second beneficial activity to counteract the negative effects of a first activity; *restoring* means undertaking a beneficial activity to counteract legacy harms that may have been caused by others; and *coping* refers to facilitating the matter of concern (here, the Reef) adapting to impacts so that harm decreases, even if impacts do not.

Table 9.1 summarizes the influences of the Reef SEA on national- and state-level regulatory interventions dealing with coal mining and cattle grazing, and the regulatory approaches and strategies of those interventions. Sections 9.5.1 to 9.5.3 and the notes to the table discuss these in more detail. Table 9.1 shows only formal rules[117] that expressly relate to water pollution or greenhouse gas emissions (either on their own terms or as explained through formal policy documents). An intervention is classified as applying to coal mining or cattle grazing based on the language of the rule, and, where necessary, evidence about whether the rule applies in practice to that activity. "Not routinely used" indicates an intervention that is not routinely applied to coal mining or cattle grazing, but in theory could be to some degree. Shaded rows show how the Reef SEA produces and influences relevant mechanisms for regulatory intervention, with darker shading indicating the strongest influence, where the SEA provided for creating a mechanism that is new or

[117] This necessarily omits other forms of influence, including non-state initiatives and state policies that are not reflected in formal rules. Rules are current to March 2024. This does not include legislative proposals in relation to climate-related financial disclosures and "nature repair," for which bills had not been introduced at the time of writing.

TABLE 9.1 *Major Australian federal (A) and Queensland (Q) regulatory interventions to address Reef-impacting greenhouse gas emissions (GHG) and water-borne sediment pollution (H_2O) from coal mines and cattle grazing, showing influences of the Reef SEA*

		Regulatory approach				Regulatory strategy				GHG		H_2O	
Australia/ Queensland	Legal mechanism (mechanism contained in a law or a document or plan for which a law provides)	Stick	Carrot	Sermon	State rescue	Harm-reducing	Harm-offsetting	Restoring	Coping	Coal	Cattle	Coal	Cattle
	(a) Mechanisms focused on the Reef as the matter of concern												
A	SEA, including endorsed program[i]	*Not specified*				*Not specified*						✓	✓
	EIA, approvals for actions[ii]	✓				✓	✓		✓			✓	✓
	Marine Park pollution regulation[iii]	✓				✓				*Not routinely used*			
A & Q	Reef catchment restoration[iv]		✓					✓					✓
	Extension and education for land managers[v]		✓			✓		✓					✓
	Voluntary Reef Credit Scheme[vi]		✓			✓		✓					✓
Q	Human rights to life, culture, property, etc[vii]	✓				✓				*Not routinely used*			
	(b) Mechanisms focused on a specific impact (H_2O or GHG emissions)												
A	GHG reporting mandate[viii]			✓		✓				✓			
	Emissions reduction transparency initiative[ix]			✓		✓				*Not routinely used*			
	Cap on GHG emissions[x]	✓				✓	✓			✓			
	Carbon credit scheme[xi]		✓				✓	✓		✓	✓		
	Clean energy loans and grants[xii]		✓			✓		✓			✓		
Q	Minimum land management standards[xiii]	✓				✓		✓					✓
	Point source pollution approvals[xiv]	✓				✓	✓					✓	

TABLE 9.1 (*continued*)

Australia/ Queensland	Legal mechanism (mechanism contained in a law or a document or plan for which a law provides)	Regulatory approach: Stick	Carrot	Sermon	State rescue	Regulatory strategy: Harm-reducing	Harm-offsetting	Restoring	Coping	GHG: Coal	Cattle	H_2O: Coal	Cattle
	General environmental duty[xv]	✓				✓				*Not routinely used*			
	Vegetation clearing restrictions, approvals[xvi]	✓					✓						✓
	(c) Mechanisms focused on specific activities												
A	Regional development loans and grants[xvii]		✓			✓				*Not routinely used*			
Q	EIA for "coordinated projects"[xviii]	✓				✓	✓	✓		✓		✓	
	Land development assessment, approvals[xix]	✓				✓				*Not routinely used*			
	Mining lease conditions[xx]	✓				✓				*Not routinely used*			
	Pastoral lease conditions relating to conserving soil[xxi]	✓				✓				*Not routinely used*			

NB: EIA, environmental impact assessment; SEA, strategic environmental assessment.

Key	Mechanism proposed by Reef SEA - either new or substantially modified	Existing mechanism directly influenced by Reef SEA	Mechanism under law influenced by Reef 2050 Cumulative Impacts Management Policy

References and provisions re regulatory strategies and approaches and GHG/H_2O focus

i SEA, including endorsed program (applies to "matters of national environmental significance"): EPBC Act (Australia) s 146 (noting that provisions for approving actions taken in accordance with the endorsed program in ss 146A–146M, a regulatory stick, were not used in the case of the Reef SEA)

ii EIA, approvals for actions (requires assessment and approval with binding conditions, i.e., harm-reducing regulatory stick, for any action likely to have a significant impact on a "matter of national environmental significance", but with no legal requirement to consider greenhouse gas emissions): EPBC Act (Australia) pts 7–9; Department of the Environment (Australia), *Significant Impact Guidelines 1.1: Matters of National Environmental Significance* (2013) www.dcceew.gov.au/sites/default/files/documents/nes-guidelines_1.pdf, archived at https://perma.cc/P4NR-YHXE; Department of the Environment (Australia),

TABLE 9.1 (*continued*)

Significant Impact Guidelines 1.3: Coal Seam Gas and Large Coal Mining Developments – Impacts on Water Resources (2022) www.dcceew.gov.au/sites/default/files/documents/significant-impact-guidelines-1-3.pdf, archived at https://perma.cc/WUQ3-3KDZ; Department of Sustainability Environment Water Population and Communities (Australia), *Environment Protection and Biodiversity Conservation Act 1999 Environmental Offsets Policy* (2012) 9 (offsets applying via approval conditions, noting that "other compensatory measures" could include regulatory coping initiatives) www.dcceew.gov.au/sites/default/files/documents/offsets-policy_2.pdf, archived at https://perma.cc/EE73-7RZP; Wendy Craik, *Independent Review of Interactions between the EPBC Act and the Agriculture Sector: Independent Report Prepared for the Commonwealth Department of the Environment and Energy* (Aither 2018) www.dcceew.gov.au/sites/default/files/documents/review-interactions-epbc-act-agriculture-final-report.pdf, archived at https://perma.cc/4TNX-8V3C; Department of the Environment (Australia), *EPBC Act Referral Guidelines for the Outstanding Universal Value of the Great Barrier Reef World Heritage Area* (2014) www.dcceew.gov.au/sites/default/files/documents/referral-guidelines-great-barrier-reef_0.pdf, archived at https://perma.cc/Y5EV-9MH7.

iii Marine Park pollution regulation: Great Barrier Reef Marine Park Act 1975 (Australia) s 66(2)(e) ("regulating or prohibiting acts [whether in the Marine Park or elsewhere] that may pollute water in a manner harmful to animals and plants in the Marine Park")

iv Reef catchment restoration: Reef 2050 WQIP, 34, 36 (targeted catchment repair projects through incentives to landholders e.g., riparian revegetation, gully repair, streambank stabilization; carbon sequestration noted as an additional benefit, but this is noted only tangentially); not categorized as a state rescue approach since it lacks a clear focus on public land

v Extension and education for land managers: Reef 2050 WQIP, 31 ("Deliver extension and education targeted at adoption of improved practices . . . through the Reef Water Quality Program and Reef Trust projects, e.g., BMP extension and education, Project Pioneer – Innovation in Grazing Management, and Reef Alliance – Growing a Great Barrier Reef"); Project Pioneer, www.projectpioneer.com.au (n.d.).

vi Voluntary Reef Credit Scheme: Reef 2050 WQIP, 30, 44, EcoMarkets Australia, *Reef Credit Guide V. 2.1* (2024) https://eco-markets.org.au/rules-and-requirements, archived at https://perma.cc/5ZUL-FXK7. NB: both harm-offsetting and restoring projects seem theoretically permissible under this incentive scheme.

vii Human rights to life, culture, property, etc: Human Rights Act 2019 (Queensland) ss 8, 13, 15(2), 16, 24(2), 25(a), 26(2), 28, 58 (prohibition on unjustifiably limiting human rights, assumed generally to be harm-reducing); *Waratah Coal Pty Ltd v Youth Verdict Ltd* (No 6) [2022] QLC 21, [1297]–[1694].

viii GHG reporting mandate: National Greenhouse and Energy Reporting Act 2007 (Australia) s 7 and pts 3, 3H, National Greenhouse and Energy Reporting (Measurement) Determination 2008 (Australia) ch 3 (applies GHG reporting requirements to companies that exceed scope 1 or 2 GHG emissions thresholds, with presumed harm-reducing strategy through public pressure; agricultural activities excluded because reporting requirements only apply where the Minister has determined approved measurement approaches: methods apply to coal mine emissions, but not agriculture)

ix Corporate emissions reduction transparency initiative: Clean Energy Regulator (Australia), "Corporate Emissions Reduction Transparency (CERT) Report Guidelines FY2022–23 and CY2023, Version 1.2" (2024) https://cer.gov.au/markets/reports-and-data/corporate-emissions-reduction-transparency-report/participating-corporate, archived at https://perma.cc/8HNN-L7QA (opt-in standardized reporting scheme for broad climate-related commitments that covers entities that are covered by the statutory GHG reporting mandate, with presumed harm-reducing strategy through public pressure; formal guidelines apply to

TABLE 9.1 *(continued)*

participants). As at July 2024, no coal mining or pastoral grazing companies had submitted a relevant report under this initiative: Clean Energy Regulator (Australia), "Corporate Emissions Reduction Transparency Report 2023," https://cer.gov.au/markets/reports-and-data/corporate-emissions-reduction-transparency-report/corporate-emissions-0, archived at https://perma.cc/RW3N-UM5J.

x Cap on GHG emissions: National Greenhouse and Energy Reporting Act 2007 (Australia) pt 3H; National Greenhouse and Energy Reporting (Safeguard Mechanism) Rule 2015 (Australia) (requiring covered facilities to either reduce their emissions to meet a declining baseline or surrender credits to offset excess emissions). Some coal mines, but apparently no cattle grazing operations are presently covered: Clean Energy Regulator, "2022–23 Safeguard Facility Data" (2024) https://cer.gov.au/document/safeguard-facilities-data-2022-23-excel (listing data for 2022–2023), last accessed March 22, 2025, archived at https://perma.cc/5LD4-3J5Q.

xi Carbon credit scheme: Carbon Credits (Carbon Farming Initiative) Act 2011 (Australia); provides market incentives to engage in approved credit generation methods, including some that expressly target both the cattle and coal sectors, including flaring or converting methane from underground coal mines, managing beef cattle using specified practices and reducing methane by feeding nitrate to cattle (some now closed to new projects): Clean Energy Regulator (Australia), "ACCU Scheme Methods" (n.d.), https://cer.gov.au/schemes/australian-carbon-credit-unit-scheme/accu-scheme-methods, last accessed March 22, 2025, archived at https://perma.cc/M99E-GER6, Clean Energy Regulator (Australia), "Closed Methods" (n.d.), https://cer.gov.au/schemes/australian-carbon-credit-unit-scheme/accu-scheme-methods/closed-methods, last accessed March 22, 2025, archived at https://perma.cc/9ZAZ-TPWW.

xii Clean energy loans and grants: Clean Energy Finance Corporation Act 2012 (Australia) ss 58, 60; Clean Energy Finance Corporation (Australia), "Investment Priorities" (n.d.) www.cefc.com.au/about-us/who-we-are/investment-priorities/, last accessed March 22, 2025, archived at https://perma.cc/N4G6-FXHF (prioritizes investing in agricultural "natural capital" and carbon sequestration and technology to encourage emissions reductions, i.e. incentives to reduce harm or restore); Clean Energy Finance Corporation (Australia), "New Capital, New Ambition: Annual Report 2022–2023" (2024) 37, www.cefc.com.au/media/l4igzbpf/cefc_ar23_web_sml.pdf, archived at https://perma.cc/M4LR-JDQ2 (projects include "sustainable grazing" to generate carbon credits). No coal mine-related projects were noted in the 2022–2023 annual report, nor in the 2021–2022 annual report.

xiii Minimum land management standards: Environmental Protection Act 1994 (Queensland) ("EP Act") ss 18(a), 79(1) (cattle grazing in a Reef catchment is an agricultural "environmentally relevant activity" or "ERA"), 81 (binding agricultural ERA standards, i.e. regulatory stick), 426(2)(a) (environmental authority not required for agricultural ERA that is not a prescribed ERA); *Agricultural ERA Standard for Beef Cattle Grazing*, v2 (2022) www.des.qld.gov.au/policies?a=272936:policy_registry/pr-es-grazing.pdf, archived at https://perma.cc/8KEP-YV76, e.g., maintain land in good condition (SC1), implement measures to improve condition of land in poor condition (SC2), i.e. harm reducing and restoring.

xiv Point source pollution approvals ("environmental authorities"): EP Act ss 18 (resource activity is an ERA), 77 (environmental protection policy for reduced contaminant loads to Reef), 88 (Reef water quality offsets under *Environmental Offsets Act 2014* (Queensland)), 107 (mining activity is a resource activity), 209 (offset conditions), 426(1) (requirement for environmental authority for ERA), Environmental Protection Regulation 2019 (Queensland) ("EP Regulation") s 41AA(3) (prohibition on approving release of sediment to Reef without offset); Department of Environment and Science (Queensland), *Point Source Water Quality Offsets Policy* (2019) https://environment.des.qld.gov.au/__data/assets/pdf_file/0033/97845/point-source-wq-offsets-policy-2019.pdf, archived at https://perma.

TABLE 9.1 *(continued)*

cc/RXR7-JQNL; Department of Environment and Science (Queensland), *Guideline: Model Mining Conditions Version* 6.03 ESR/2016/1936 (2024) 16–30 (re water releases) www.des.qld.gov.au/policies?a=272936:policy_registry/rs-gl-model-mining-conditions.pdf, archived at https://perma.cc/D4SD-BQE7. NB: an environmental authority is not required for cattle grazing, because it is an agricultural ERA that is not a prescribed ERA (EP Act ss 19, 79(1)(a), 106, 426(2)(a), EP Regulation s 19(1), Sch. 2).

xv General environmental duty: EP Act s 319

xvi Vegetation clearing approvals: Vegetation clearing is classified as a kind of "development": Planning Act 2016 (Queensland) Sch 2 "development," "operational work." Clearing for extractive activities like mining will usually be exempt from a requirement for a permit under this regime: Planning Act 2016 (Queensland) s 107(c); Planning Regulation 2017 (Queensland) Sch 10 ss 4(1), 5; Sch 21 s 1(6). Clearing of regrowth vegetation on grazing land within 50 m of a watercourse located in specified Reef catchments (termed "category R areas") will usually be prohibited, as it is deemed not for a "relevant purpose": Vegetation Management Act 1999 (Queensland) ss 22A(2B)(b) (relevant purpose re grazing land and category R area), 22ANA (category R area). Note that offsets may be required for vegetation clearing under the Environmental Offsets Act 2014 (Queensland) Sch 1, but this relates to the biodiversity of the cleared vegetation, rather than carbon- or water quality-related aspects: Department of Environment and Science, *Queensland Environmental Offsets Policy Version 1.16* (State of Queensland 2024) www.des.qld.gov.au/policies?a=272936:policy_registry/envoff-offsets-policy.pdf, archived at https://perma.cc/TV3G-M8QJ.

xvii Regional development loans and grants, providing incentives, potentially indirectly targeted at harm reduction: Northern Australia Infrastructure Facility Act 2016 (Australia) (financial assistance for economic development); Northern Australia Infrastructure Facility, *Public Benefit Guideline* (2024) 7 (investment mandate requires considering positive and negative environmental impacts in these general terms) www.naif.gov.au/media/4lmhutf1/public-benefit-guideline-update-march-24.pdf, archived at https://perma.cc/66P9-7JPF; Northern Australia Infrastructure Facility, "Our Projects" (n.d.) www.naif.gov.au/our-projects, last accessed March 22, 2025 (projects include a coal mine, but no clear grazing project to date); Regional Investment Corporation Act 2018 (Cth) s 8(1)(a) (farm business loans); Regional Investment Corporation (Australia), *Annual Report* 2022/23 (2023) 11 www.ric.gov.au/sites/default/files/documents/2022-23%20Annual%20Report_Regional%20Investment%20Corporation%20cl.pdf, archived at https://perma.cc/F9GL-CK27 (developing environment, social and governance framework).

xviii Project EIA for "coordinated projects": State Development and Public Works Organisation Act 1971 (Queensland) Pts 4, 4A (declaration of coordinated project; considerations relevant to declaration; assessment; power of Coordinator-General to impose harm-reducing and offset conditions, and including, under s 54U(2)(b) re repairing or mitigating damage to the environment, whether or not the damage has been or will be caused by the project, but only if the proponent consents); Department of State Development Tourism and Innovation (Queensland), "Preparing an Environmental Impact Statement: Guideline for Proponents" (2024) 19–21, 27–28 (re water and climate, but with no direct link to the Reef) www.statedevelopment.qld.gov.au/__data/assets/pdf_file/0034/86884/c9a552d64dbc27e6ff2d8f9cfb489fdfe467b066.pdf, archived at https://perma.cc/364C-33CS. NB: coal mines are regularly declared to be "coordinated projects," but it appears this has never occurred for a grazing development: Coordinator-General (Queensland), "Completed Projects" (n.d.) www.statedevelopment.qld.gov.au/coordinator-general/assessments-and-approvals/coordinated-projects/completed-projects, last accessed March 22, 2025.

TABLE 9.1 (*continued*)

xix Land development assessment, approvals and potential for harm-reducing conditions: Planning Act 2016 (Queensland) chapter 3, noting that mines are exempt from the application of planning legislation due to the operation of s 4A, Mineral Resources Act 1989 (Queensland); in rural zones under local government planning schemes, cattle grazing is usually categorized as "accepted development" for which development approval is not required: Planning Act 2016 (Queensland) s 44; e.g. Burdekin Shire Planning Scheme (2022) table 3.4.9 ("animal husbandry").

xx Mining lease conditions: Mineral Resources Act 1989 (Queensland) s 276 (general conditions of mining lease with potential for harm-reducing conditions); neither the statute nor the guidelines for mining leases foresee any significant use of these conditions for environmental purposes: Department of Resources (Queensland), "Mining Lease Application Guide" (September 2024) www.resources.qld.gov.au/__data/assets/pdf_file/0003/217893/mining-lease-guide.pdf, archived at https://perma.cc/4TPY-9T49.

xxi Pastoral lease conditions: Land Act 1994 (Queensland) chapters 4 and 5 (binding conditions of leases relate to harm reduction including conserving soil and protecting riparian vegetation under s 199(2)(d)); appears to be rarely enforced, e.g., current "strategic compliance areas" for non-freehold tenure management do not refer to pastoral leases: Department of Resources (Queensland), "Strategic Compliance Focus Areas 2024–25," www.nrmmrrd.qld.gov.au/__data/assets/pdf_file/0007/1893202/strategic-compliance-focus-areas-2024-25.pdf, archived at https://perma.cc/P9WN-JK73.

substantially modified (see Key). Regulatory mechanisms are arranged according to their focus using the broad categories introduced in Chapter 3, as mainly directed to: protecting the matter of concern (the Reef, (a)); a specific type of environmental impact, (b); or specific types of activities, (c).[118]

Before examining these areas in detail, here are some preliminary observations. While this chapter cannot assess the likely effectiveness of this regulatory toolbox "on the ground," nor the administrative gusto or resources applied to each mechanism, it is at least clear that the toolbox is diverse. It uses most categories of regulatory approaches and strategies discussed in Chapter 6. That diversity aligns with theoretical recommendations for dealing with diverse activities that contribute to cumulative environmental problems in a way that responds to the varying motivations and circumstances of the diverse contributors.[119] As might be expected, more burdensome "sticks" apply more commonly to coal mining than cattle grazing, to which regulatory carrots, and, to a lesser extent, sermons, apply. This reflects an implicit position that diverse activities require diverse approaches, particularly where some actors tend to be large, highly profitable, and traditionally regulated (coal miners), and others smaller, financially more precarious, and traditionally unregulated (cattle graziers). Concerns remain, however, at the financial impacts of water quality controls on graziers.[120] The policy mix also includes significant use of mechanisms that reduce regulatory burdens but also reduce reliability of outcomes (carrots and harm-offsetting).[121] The fainter traces of regulatory possibilities also emerge – those options for which laws already provide, but which do not routinely apply to the greenhouse gas or water pollution of coal mines or cattle grazing. Strikingly, all of the mechanisms noted as "not routinely used" involve regulatory sticks. This is a comparatively burdensome and politically difficult approach, the nonuse of these mechanisms bearing out these difficulties. Yet some of these mechanisms present particular promise for regulating cumulative risks, notably the general environmental duty discussed earlier in Chapter 6.[122]

9.5.1 *Influencing Regulatory Interventions in General*

The SEA "workhorses" for influencing rules for intervention are the twenty-five-year endorsed programs, and the policies and plans to which they commit.

[118] This follows the schema in Chapter 3, which argues that many areas of law can address cumulative environmental problems.

[119] See the approach for navigating large systems of laws described in Section 3.4.

[120] Jane Waterhouse and others, *2017 Scientific Consensus Statement: Land Use Impacts on Great Barrier Reef Water Quality and Ecosystem Condition* (Queensland Government 2017) 13, https://nla.gov.au/nla.obj-630161592/view.

[121] See Section 6.3.2.

[122] See Table 6.3, Table 6.8.

These policies are framed as influencing regulatory interventions in general, since they are not limited to a particular type of environmental impact or activity.[123]

The promisingly named Cumulative Impacts Management Policy requires policymakers to consider cumulative impacts when formulating plans and programs that influence relevant "drivers and pressures"[124] and project approvals under laws that are listed in the Policy[125] (light shaded rows, Table 9.1). Its potential influence extends across diverse regulatory strategies for which those listed laws provide: harm-reducing, offsetting, and restoring. Restoring is important given the legacy impacts of sediment pollution.[126] The Policy's link to project approvals is significant because a requirement to consider cumulative impacts would not otherwise generally apply: Unlike most national EIA legislation around the world,[127] neither Commonwealth nor Queensland environmental law expressly mandates considering a project's cumulative impacts.[128]

The Policy's likely influence is weakened, though, by its ambiguous wording and the fact that it does not call out activities like coal mining and cattle grazing that contribute to recognized high-risk[129] "drivers" of major pressures on the Reef, such as climate change and water pollution. Decision-makers need not assess cumulative impacts "[w]here assessment and management of cumulative impacts is consistent with this policy and has been included in plans, governing arrangements or class assessments."[130] It is unclear which plans and arrangements fulfill this criterion, and, therefore, when decision-makers must independently consider cumulative impacts: Each decision-maker must therefore determine whether the Policy requires

[123] Commonwealth of Australia, *Reef 2050 Plan Policy Guideline for Decision Makers* (2016) https://hdl.handle.net/11017/3164; GBRMPA, *Reef 2050 Plan Good Practice Management for the Great Barrier Reef* (GBRMPA 2018) https://hdl.handle.net/11017/3390; GBRMPA, *Reef 2050 Plan Net Benefit Policy* (GBRMPA 2018) https://hdl.handle.net/11017/3388; GBRMPA, *Reef 2050 Plan: Cumulative Impact Management Policy*.

[124] GBRMPA, *Reef 2050 Plan: Cumulative Impact Management Policy*, 9, 12.

[125] Ibid 3, 13.

[126] See n 19.

[127] See generally, Rebecca Nelson and L. M. Shirley, "The Latent Potential of Cumulative Effects Concepts in National and International Environmental Impact Assessment Regimes" (2023) 12 *Transnational Environmental Law* 150–174.

[128] Note a narrow requirement in relation to some coal mines and coal seam gas projects at the national level: Nelson, "Breaking Backs," 1194–1200. Queensland policy for EIA of "coordinated projects" briefly encourages proponents to consider cumulative effects: Department of State Development Tourism and Innovation (Queensland), "Preparing an Environmental Impact Statement: Guideline for Proponents," 4, 16.

[129] GBRMPA, *Reef 2050 Plan: Cumulative Impact Management Policy*, 12, Att 1 and 2.

[130] Ibid 12.

them to do something extra. This introduces the potential that these connections are not made, and hampers accountability.

The Cumulative Impacts Policy recognizes that "new information, emerging issues and changing circumstances" require managing adaptively, including "if the condition of [Reef] values declines,"[131] but it provides no further detail, process, or principles for when or how to adapt. Intervening adaptively is vital for regulating cumulative impacts,[132] but requires further guidance given the uncertainties and time lags involved, for example, between land practice changes and observed reductions in sediment pollution.

9.5.2 *Influencing Interventions Concerning Water Quality*

The Reef SEA endorsed program led to significant changes in existing regulatory interventions and new regulatory interventions aimed at water quality (rows with shaded cells in last two columns, Table 9.1). The *Reef 2050 Water Quality Improvement Plan* sets multiscale targets for sediment load reduction,[133] and for land cover and management practices on grazing lands in "priority areas" to reduce sediment.[134] These targets influence how existing laws operate, such as point-source water pollution approvals for coal mines, which Queensland's program report repeatedly insisted it would "rigorously condition."[135]

New interventions also pursue these water quality targets (Table 9.1, dark shaded rows). These new mechanisms include mandatory minimum land management standards for graziers, which apply requirements to maintain ground cover – Queensland's first generally applicable regulatory stick applied to grazing practices.[136] A new A$3.7 billion (since inception) Commonwealth Reef Trust[137] delivers incentive-based ("carrot") and information-based ("sermon") interventions:[138] extension and education programs for land

[131] Ibid 35.

[132] See Section 2.2.3.3 (need for adapting) and Section 6.5.4 (approaches to adapting).

[133] DESQ, *WQIP*, 16, 19.

[134] Ibid 27.

[135] DSDIPQ, *Reef Coastal Program Report*, 29–30, 64, 79, 82, 83. See n. xiv to Table 9.1.

[136] Note an earlier geographically restricted mandate: Great Barrier Reef Protection Amendment Act 2009 (Queensland) s 6, introducing chapter 4A to Environmental Protection Act 1994 (Queensland).

[137] PGPA Act (Reef Trust Special Account 2014) Determination 01 2023 (Australia).

[138] DESQ, *WQIP*, 26–36. See generally Alluvium Consulting Australia, *Final Report: Part A. An Evaluation of the Australian Government Reef Trust Water Quality Investments* (2023) especially 7–11, appendix A (list of projects), www.dcceew.gov.au/sites/default/files/documents/alluvium-part-a-evaluation-report.pdf, archived at https://perma.cc/KXU5-TPBB.

managers about best management practices;[139] funded catchment restoration activities such as revegetation and gully repair to control soil erosion;[140] and a government-supported, voluntary Reef Credit scheme to facilitate landholders selling water quality credits to government, industry, and nonprofit buyers.[141] These mechanisms focus on both harm-reducing and restoring strategies (Table 9.1), providing important incentives to address legacy harms that continue to cause impacts. The sheer number of available mechanisms – of which Table 9.1 presents a simplified view – itself presents an implementation challenge, however. That there are so many possible options for landholders itself creates complexity and cost, and is seen to require more extension work to explain.[142] Distrust of government and scientists further impedes take-up of these options.[143]

These influences are significant from a cumulative impacts perspective. While similar voluntary initiatives existed previously, the Reef Trust provided a "large, overarching initiative" with robust reporting arrangements for increased accountability.[144] More generally, the Reef SEA has diversified the policy mix through the first generally applicable regulatory "stick" applied to graziers to reduce sediment pollution, potentially influencing contributors who were not responsive to incentives.

In a missed opportunity to adopt a stronger cumulative impacts mindset, though, the Plan's spatial prioritization for implementing these initiatives is based on the ecosystem's risk of exposure to pollutants[145] rather than cumulative exposure to multiple stressors. An alternative would have been to investigate building on the SEA's cumulative exposure mapping[146] to target water quality reduction efforts to areas suffering from greatest cumulative stress.

Given how deforestation for pasture contributes to sediment pollution,[147] Queensland's vegetation clearing laws deserve special mention. Before the

[139] DESQ, *WQIP*, 31.

[140] Ibid 34, 36.

[141] Ibid 30, 44.

[142] Hugh Possingham and others, *Native Vegetation Expert Panel Report* (Queensland Government 2023) 32, https://environment.desi.qld.gov.au/__data/assets/pdf_file/0025/324574/expert-panel-report.pdf, archived at https://perma.cc/37EE-2GGR.

[143] J. Waterhouse and others, *2022 Scientific Consensus Statement Summary: Land-Based Impacts on Great Barrier Reef Water Quality and Ecosystem Condition* (Government of Australia and Queensland Government 2024) 83, https://reefwqconsensus.com.au/wp-content/uploads/2024/06/2022-Scientific-Consensus-Statement-Summary_FINAL.pdf, archived at https://perma.cc/TKU4-AF9Z.

[144] Australian National Audit Office, *Reef Trust – Design and Implementation*, 26–27.

[145] DESQ, *WQIP*, 19.

[146] See n 90 and accompanying text.

[147] See above nn 36 to 38 and accompanying text.

Reef SEA, a prohibition on clearing riparian vegetation in certain Reef catchments was introduced in 2009,[148] and has since been expanded more generally to Reef catchments.[149] Amid intense conflict with farmers, land clearing laws later alternated between phases of greater and lesser robustness.[150] The Reef SEA conspicuously made no clear commitments on this front, and its progeny, the Reef 2050 Water Quality Improvement Plan, merely promised vaguely to strengthen and enforce the laws.[151] However, rates of land clearing – under both significant exemptions from regulation, and illegal land clearing – remain high, and the most significant concern related to sediment pollution of the Reef.[152]

9.5.3 *Influencing Interventions Concerning Climate Change*

Given its scoping, it is unsurprising that the Reef SEA had little influence on climate-directed mechanisms (shaded rows in third and fourth columns from the right, Table 9.1). Its influence was circuitous at best, highlighting the importance of water quality on the basis that climate impacts require "building resilience," for which water quality is "the most critical issue."[153] The endorsed programs and policies did not directly contemplate new or existing measures to reduce greenhouse gas emissions, and only briefly mention Australia's international mitigation commitments.[154] An implementation policy for Queensland's EIA laws (which are expressed to be subject to the Cumulative Impacts Management Policy) only briefly mentions considering climate.[155] The Commonwealth EIA law contains no requirement for a decision-maker to consider greenhouse gas emissions, which has spurred several unsuccessful lawsuits using the Reef to argue for an implicit requirement to consider climate.[156] This is a significant gap in comprehensiveness of

148 Vegetation Management (Regrowth Clearing Moratorium) Act 2009 (Queensland) ss 3(1)(b), 5(1)(b).

149 See note xvi to Table 9.1.

150 Philippa England, "Between Regulation and Markets: Ironies and Anomalies in the Regulatory Governance of Biodiversity Conservation in Australia" (2016) 3 *Australian Journal of Environmental Law* 44–66, 48–51.

151 DESQ, *WQIP* 29.

152 Possingham and others, *Native Vegetation Expert Panel Report*, 12; Waterhouse and others, 2022 *Scientific Consensus Statement*, 38–40.

153 DSDIPQ, *Reef Coastal Program Report*, 77.

154 E.g., Commonwealth of Australia, *Reef 2050 Plan Policy Guideline for Decision Makers*, 12.

155 See n xviii to Table 9.1.

156 See generally, Jacqueline Peel, *Legal Opinion – Gaps in the Environment Protection and Biodiversity Conservation Act and Other Federal Laws for Protection of the Climate: Report for the Climate Council* (2023) www.climatecouncil.org.au/resources/expert-opinion-our-national-environment-law-is-fundamentally-flawed/.

the Reef SEA's coverage of important impact types (a key regulatory design feature for cumulative environmental problems), especially for a jurisdiction that prominently produces and exports emissions-intensive products.

Although the Reef Authority's strategic assessment report committed to continue implementing its climate adaptation plan,[157] by 2019, staffing changes had removed its climate unit and the plan was defunded.[158] According to independent reviewers, this shifted the Reef Authority from "being a 'consequence maker' advocating for effective climate mitigation to being a 'consequence taker' responding to climate change impacts with actions to improve Reef resilience as part of an adaptation strategy."[159]

This situation is now changing. The Reef Trust now invests significantly in a Reef Restoration and Adaptation Program – said to be "the world's largest effort to help an ecosystem survive climate change"[160] – which is cofunded by nongovernment organizations. Its research and development programs investigate Reef cooling through marine cloud brightening and climate-resilient coral larvae seeding (a coping intervention strategy) and restoring carbon-storing coastal and marine ecosystems (a restoring intervention strategy).[161] Implementing the strategy, however, would require regulatory reform.[162] Despite this shift in attention, these changes are disconnected from interventions related to water quality, raising the question of how interventions dealing with climate change, and the Reef, respectively, might better connect decision-making, and deal with the most threatened areas in terms of cumulative stress.

9.5.4 *Connecting across Problems and Impacts: Possibilities and Prospects*

The earlier analysis shows that the Reef SEA did not effectively connect decision-making across the regulatory silos that correspond to two separately conceived cumulative environmental problems: first climate change, focusing on the climate in general as the matter of concern; and second, conceiving of the Reef as the matter of concern, affected by both climate change and other

[157] GBRMPA, *Great Barrier Reef Region Strategic Assessment: Supplementary Report*, 143–144.

[158] GBRMPA, *Great Barrier Reef Outlook Report* 2019, 208.

[159] Ibid.

[160] DCCEEW, "Reef Restoration and Adaptation" (n.d.) www.dcceew.gov.au/parks-heritage/great-barrier-reef/protecting/case-studies/helping-the-gbr-adapt-changing-climate, last accessed March 22, 2025, archived at https://perma.cc/BXT9-LYF8.

[161] Ibid; L. K. Bay and others, *Reef Restoration and Adaptation Program: Intervention Technical Summary* (Australian Institute of Marine Science 2019) https://gbrrestoration.org/wp-content/uploads/2020/09/T3-Intervention-Technical-Summary-FINAL3.pdf, archived at https://perma.cc/WBR9-J4ST.

[162] See generally, Fidelman and others, "Regulatory Implications of Coral Reef Restoration."

impacts such as water pollution. The Reef SEA worked like a camera taking a zoomed-in photo of the Reef while missing the larger panorama of activities contributing to climate change that threatens the Reef. An alternative approach would connect decision-making across Australia's regulatory silos for climate mitigation and Reef impacts.

The most obvious and ambitious way to connect decision-making about protecting the climate and protecting the Reef would be to design climate-protecting interventions in a way that considers the Reef's climate-related vulnerability. Assessment and approval requirements for coal mines could follow an emerging approach to recognize all downstream emissions in the EIA context,[163] and compare these emissions to a cumulative threshold of global emissions informed by the Reef's vulnerability to determine the project's significance. Such an approach would implement that urged in multiple largely unsuccessful lawsuits under Australia's environmental laws.[164]

A less ambitious form of regulatory link-making between climate change and water pollution impacts on the Reef could recognize the nontarget effects of offset and credit regimes. These regimes apply to both water pollution and greenhouse gas emissions (Table 9.1(b)). Cattle graziers currently may generate carbon credits by sequestering carbon in soil, but this mechanism does not consider benefits for sediment pollution;[165] conversely, planned savanna burning that generates carbon credits does not consider impacts on sediment production.[166] Making these links would better harness synergies and avoid mutual undermining between interventions directed at overlapping problems.

[163] E.g., see generally, Benoit Mayer and Mateusz Slowik, "A Duty to Assess an Oil Project's Downstream Greenhouse Gas Emissions: The UK Supreme Court in *Finch*" (2025) 34 *Review of European, Comparative and International Environmental Law* 288–294 (advance).

[164] See generally, Peel, *Legal Opinion* esp. 13, 21–23.

[165] Carbon Credits (Carbon Farming Initiative – Estimating Sequestration of Carbon in Soil Using Default Values) Methodology Determination 2015 (Australia); Clean Energy Regulator (Australia), Participating in the Emissions Reduction Fund: A Guide to the Estimating Sequestration of Carbon in Soil Using Default Values Method (2015), https://cer.gov.au/document/guide-to-estimating-sequestration-carbon-soil-using-default-values-method, archived at https://perma.cc/9TWF-2BEH; DCCEEW, "Improving Soil Carbon Storage and Measurement" (n.d.) (recognizing benefits for water quality), www.dcceew.gov.au/climate-change/emissions-reduction/agricultural-land-sectors/soil-carbon-storage-measurement, archived at https://perma.cc/ALG2-HH29.

[166] Carbon Credits (Carbon Farming Initiative – Savanna Fire Management – Sequestration and Emissions Avoidance) Methodology Determination 2018 (Australia); Department of the Environment and Energy (Australia), "Understanding Savanna Fire Management Methods in the Emissions Reduction Fund: Frequently Asked Questions" (2019) www.dcceew.gov.au/sites/default/files/documents/understanding-savanna-fire-management-methods-in-the-emissions-reduction-fund-faqs.pdf, archived at https://perma.cc/B729-SUC5

A further alternative would be to better link interventions from an adaptation perspective. This could involve designing water quality interventions to prioritize areas of the Reef most at risk from climate change using cumulative exposure mapping, supported by further research on the interactions between these impacts, if necessary. Enforcement of interventions could equally be prioritized on this basis.

With wider terms of reference, the Reef SEA could also have generated insights from comparing across types of impacts and activities to reveal inconsistencies and gaps. Such insights could help assess issues of fairness, or inform revisions to interventions to increase comprehensiveness – a key design feature for regulating cumulative environmental problems. Unlike coal mines, cattle graziers need not report their greenhouse gas emissions nor comply with an emissions cap, but they benefit from being able to produce carbon credits and access grants for emissions-reducing activities in the same way as coal mines (Table 9.1(a) and (b)). Cattle graziers need no approval for activities that produce sediment in a diffuse way, while coal mines do in relation to point sources (Table 9.1(b)).

Similar comparisons could also reveal possibilities for change by identifying regulatory mechanisms that apply only in respect of one impact type, but theoretically might be suitable for another. Minimum land management standards and extension-based approaches to encourage good land management practices apply to cattle grazing to control sediment, but not yet to limit greenhouse gas emissions, which instead attracts carbon credits (Table 9.1(b)). Different forms of mandatory and voluntary disclosures (regulatory sermons) apply in the carbon context, but not yet in relation to water pollution. Carbon offset systems exist to soften burdens of regulatory sticks related to greenhouse gas emissions and mining point source pollution, but appear not to have been explored for grazing. Subsidized loans are available for greenhouse gas–reducing investments but not the equivalent for water pollution.

International concern about cumulative impacts on the Reef remains strong, and in 2022, UNESCO formally urged Australia to accelerate progress meeting water quality targets and revise the Reef 2050 Plan to incorporate greenhouse gas emissions mitigation.[167] Relevant regulatory revisions were yet to be made at the time of writing. However, after a change in national government, there are early signs of regulatory change to strengthen Reef-related intervention in relation to climate change mitigation. In the wake of

[167] Commonwealth of Australia, *Great Barrier Reef Progress Report to UNESCO World Heritage Centre* (2024) 9, 22, www.dcceew.gov.au/sites/default/files/documents/great-barrier-reef-progress-report-2024.pdf, archived at https://perma.cc/8MAY-4SCJ.

major coral bleaching in early 2024, and in parallel with Australia's formal response to UNESCO, the Reef Authority released a new climate plan. The plan continues an adaptation focus, but complements it with "new programs" for climate mitigation through influencing activities *both within and outside* its geographic jurisdiction.[168] These include advising government about climate change impacts on the Reef "and the need to urgently reduce CO_2 emissions,"[169] encouraging "transformative actions," "speak[ing] for the Reef and advocat[ing] for stronger global action" in international fora, and engaging with the Australian Government's emission reduction strategies and carbon sequestration initiatives.[170] Just as notably, the Reef Authority committed to "use its statutory powers or other management tools" to reduce carbon emissions from Reef users such as tourism vessels[171] – a symbolically important step.

These statements and commitments lie within the Reef Authority's existing statutory advisory purposes and functions,[172] and they are objectively modest, but in the context of the Reef SEA and its previous approach, they are extraordinary. They propose to use information to make links across regulatory silos: feeding information about climate change impacts on the Reef into government structures that have the capacity to influence interventions for greenhouse gas mitigation. At the very least, the proposal to regulate tourism vessels draws attention to other, more substantial contributors to climate change, such as coal mining. Controls over coal mines lie within the jurisdictions of the Queensland and Commonwealth governments that might receive relevant advice from the Reef Authority, perhaps informed by the Cumulative Impacts Management Policy that would seem capable of applying to greenhouse gas emissions.

9.6 CONCLUSION

SEA has long been considered well-suited to dealing with cumulative impacts, enabling proactive, larger scale assessment of multiple sources of impact. Ideally, SEA connects information and regulatory by influencing decisions about individual projects, and perhaps land use plans. The Reef SEA suggests this view underestimates the power of SEA to influence cumulative impacts

[168] GBRMPA, "Great Barrier Reef Blueprint for Climate Resilience and Adaptation" (2024) 9, https://hdl.handle.net/11017/4035.
[169] Ibid 16.
[170] Ibid 21.
[171] Ibid.
[172] Great Barrier Reef Marine Park Act 1975 (Australia) s 7(1)(ca), (cd).

from the perspective of regulatory intervention and information. In fact, SEA can be structured not only to influence project approvals but also to entrench and expand ongoing monitoring programs (information), and influence other, impact-focused laws, and thereby rules that influence activities that are cumulatively significant but do not trigger EIA, like cattle grazing.

In relation to water quality, the Reef SEA influenced existing regulatory interventions that provide for reducing and offsetting harm and restoring, and facilitated new interventions that diversified the regulatory mix, important for cumulative environmental problems. However, the Reef SEA viewed climate change solely through the lens of adaptation, overlooking greenhouse pollution from the same activities as contribute to sediment pollution, where both impact types are "external" to the Reef, both involve legacy impacts, and both involve data challenges. This blinkered view largely persisted long after the SEA.

SEA offers great potential to connect interventions that deal with different impact types across cumulative environmental problems. The Reef SEA might have better connected water quality interventions and both climate adaptation and mitigation. SEA scoping likely played a key limiting role in relation to mitigation. The analysis here has suggested possibilities to better connect interventions with varying degrees of ambition. However, continued flows of information under international arrangements for protecting World Heritage are even now demonstrating the enduring and adapting characteristics of the Reef SEA and its policy progeny.

10

Biocultural Landscapes

Cumulative Impacts and Alpine Grasslands

10.1 INTRODUCTION

Barren pastures overcrowded with cattle – perhaps no environmental problem has a more classic status.[1] But its contemporary manifestation is more complex than just too many cattle eating grass. The deterioration of many of Europe's mountain grasslands stems from the cumulative effects of not just overuse, but nonuse – the abandonment of traditional grazing practices. These effects combine to threaten not only ecosystems but also the cultural bedrock of these "hotspots of biological and cultural diversity."[2]

Take the Autonomous Province of Bozen/Bolzano-South Tyrol ("South Tyrol"), Italy's northernmost province (see Figure 1.2). More than just an economic resource, its Alpine grassland landscapes are a core ingredient in the identity of German-speaking ethnic populations. They have grazed Alpine grasslands for centuries or millennia, creating habitat for what are now some of Europe's most threatened bird and butterfly species. Addressing cumulative threats to South Tyrol's grassland biocultural landscapes engages diverse regulatory interventions directed to both controlling development and maintaining traditional uses. This set of interventions, in turn, engages the need to coordinate a dizzying array of formal rules applied across multiple levels of government and usually siloed legal areas: nature, development, agriculture, landscape, and governance. This chapter analyzes how this mix of regulatory interventions and key "vertical" coordination mechanisms combine to

1 Garrett Hardin, "The Tragedy of the Commons" (1968) 162 *Science* 1243–1248, 1244.
2 Leonith Hinojosa and others, "Geographical Heterogeneity in Mountain Grasslands Dynamics in the Austrian-Italian Tyrol Region" (2019) 106 *Applied Geography* 50–59, 50.

address, apparently with relative success, the cumulative biocultural problem of grassland degradation. The chapter builds on existing regulatory research that focuses on cross-border coordination and examines single or a small number of instruments related to Alpine grasslands.[3]

Section 10.2 provides context, describing how development and abandonment threaten South Tyrol's Alpine grasslands, and setting out key challenges related to regulatory intervention and coordination in managing these cumulative impacts. Section 10.3 reviews key regulatory jurisdictions and their areas of legal competence. Section 10.4 combines analysis of two of this book's CIRCle Framework of four regulatory functions required to address cumulative environmental problems – regulatory intervention and coordination. It first examines how interventions across governance levels can comprehensively address different key threats to grasslands. It then analyzes their diverse regulatory strategies and approaches. This supports the argument in Chapter 6 that having a diverse mix of regulatory interventions helps to influence the activities of the diverse contributors to cumulative environmental problems.[4] Finally, it focuses on design features for coordination among governments and stakeholders through linked laws and arrangements for implementation, coordination institutions, and conflict resolution mechanisms. Section 10.5 summarizes key insights and draws out lessons for other contexts.

10.2 CONTEXT AND CHALLENGES

10.2.1 *Key Threats to Alpine Grasslands: Abandonment and Development*

Across Europe, the conservation status of grasslands is deteriorating, and grasslands that depend on traditional agriculture fare worse than natural grasslands.[5] This deterioration most impacts pollinator species, butterflies,

[3] E.g., Maria Carla Lostrangio and Marie Clotteau, "A Review of Policy Frameworks Supporting Mountain Grasslands in Europe" (2021) 51 *Palaearctic Grasslands* 17–22; Anne Katrin Heinrichs, Yann Kohler and Aurelia Ullrich, *Implementing a Pan-Alpine Ecological Network: A Compilation of Major Approaches, Tools and Activities* (Federal Agency for Nature Conservation, Germany 2010) www.cipra.org/en/publications/4447, archived at https://perma.cc/T9NQ-WNZC; CIPRA, *Relevant Instruments in the Field of Ecological Networks in the Alpine Region: A Background Report* (CIPRA 2010) www.cipra.org/en/publications/2553, archived at https://perma.cc/ZW6D-738M.

[4] See Section 6.4.2.

[5] European Environment Agency, *State of Nature in the EU: Results from Reporting under the Nature Directives 2013–2018 (EEA Report No 10/2020)* (2020) 41, 53, 129–130, www.eea.europa.eu/en/analysis/publications/state-of-nature-in-the-eu-2020/state-of-nature-in-the-eu-2020/@@download/file, archived at https://perma.cc/8UGN-6TCB.

and farmland birds.[6] It also impairs cultural heritage and cultural ecosystem services.[7] This is salient for South Tyrol's German-speaking minority, and in the context of Italy's long-established focus on culture and aesthetics in protected conservation areas.[8]

Key threats to these grasslands come in two forms. The first is development, notably agricultural intensification, including intensive grazing and application of fertilizers.[9] Other development pressures arise from transport infrastructure, tourism accommodation and infrastructure, renewable energy projects, and urban expansion competing for flat land.[10] In contrast to past decades, small- rather than large-scale development is most concerning for its "subtle," "continuous," and cumulatively serious negative impacts on biodiversity and landscape.[11]

The second key threat is farmers abandoning summer pasturing and hay cutting in meadows[12] due to the high costs of traditional practices, and the older farming generation not being replaced.[13] Naturally spreading forests then replace grasslands, reducing biodiversity.[14] Abandonment has been the primary driver of Italy losing almost half its grasslands since the 1860s.[15] Measures to

6 Ibid 70, 131, 133.

7 Hinojosa and others, "Geographical Heterogeneity in Mountain Grasslands Dynamics," 51, 56.

8 Francesca Ferranti, Raoul Beunen and Maria Speranza, "Natura 2000 Network: A Comparison of the Italian and Dutch Implementation Experiences" (2010) 12 *Journal of Environmental Policy and Planning* 293–314, 301.

9 Guy Pe'Er and others, "How Can the European Common Agricultural Policy Help Halt Biodiversity Loss? Recommendations by over 300 Experts" (2022) 15:e12901 *Conservation Letters* 1–12, 7.

10 Academy for Territorial Development in the Leibniz Association, *Safeguarding Open Spaces in the Alpine Region* (2022) 4, www.arl-net.de/system/files/media-shop/pdf/pospapier/pospapier_133.pdf, archived at https://perma.cc/N45W-FAVH.

11 Marco Onida, "The Protection of Biodiversity and Ecological Connectivity in the Alpine Convention" in Mariachiara Alberton (ed), *Toward the Protection of Biodiversity and Ecological Connectivity in Multi-Layered Systems* (Nomos 2013) 57–79, 58.

12 European Environment Agency, *State of Nature in the EU*, 72–74, 131. See generally, Lubos Halada and others, "Which Habitats of European Importance Depend on Agricultural Practices?" (2011) 20 *Biodiversity and Conservation* 2365–2378.

13 Thomas Streifeneder, Clare Giuliani and Christian Hoffmann, "A Transnational Analysis of the Policies for Alpine Pasture Farming" in Tobias Chilla and Franziska Sielker (eds), *Cross-Border Spatial Development in Bavaria: Dynamics in Cooperation – Potentials of Integration* (Academy for Territorial Development in the Leibniz Association 2022) 44–54, 53, www.arl-net.de/system/files/media-shop/pdf/ab/ab_034/ab_034_gesamt.pdf.

14 Hinojosa and others, "Geographical Heterogeneity in Mountain Grasslands Dynamics," 50–51.

15 Csaba Centeri and others, "Wooded Grasslands as Part of the European Agricultural Heritage," in Mauro Agnoletti and Francesca Emanueli (eds), *Biocultural Diversity in Europe* (Springer 2016) 75–103, 89.

address these threats include avoiding converting grasslands for construction and infrastructure; continuing or reinstating extensive grazing or adapted mowing and grazing activities, and measures to "slow, stop, or reverse" natural afforestation.[16] In the language of the regulatory strategies introduced in Chapter 6, this equates to "reducing harm" and "restoring."[17]

Among European countries, Italy now reports the highest share of conservation improvements in grasslands.[18] Around two-thirds of South Tyrol's agricultural areas are grasslands,[19] and farm numbers have declined little. Commentators point to a strong tourism sector, good off-farm employment, and relatively high farm incomes as deterring abandonment,[20] and European Union ("EU") subsidies under the Common Agricultural Policy ("CAP") enabling Alpine grassland restoration.[21] This chapter analyzes how a broad, complex mix of regulatory mechanisms combines to support addressing these threats in South Tyrol.

10.2.2 *Challenges: Intervention and Coordination*

As a cumulative environmental problem, protecting Alpine grasslands looks different from many others, and its differences pose challenges for regulatory intervention using traditional Western environmental law. Land abandonment challenges a typical legal focus on prohibiting or restricting activities to prevent environmental harm rather than encouraging or compelling action. But restrictions alone cannot preserve the rural landscape.[22] Combating natural forest spread requires continuous action rather than "single, short-time efforts."[23] Interventions must be diverse to deal with both development and farm abandonment, as well as farmers with diverse characteristics: almost 2,200 agricultural companies of diverse farm sizes, from less

16 European Environment Agency, *State of Nature in the EU*, 92–94.

17 Section 6.2.1.

18 European Environment Agency, State of Nature in the EU, 63–64. For up-to-date reporting on the conservation status of Alpine grasslands in Italy, see European Environment Information and Observation Network, "Article 17 Web Tool" (n.d.) (for the period 2013–2018) https://nature-art17.eionet.europa.eu/article17/habitat/report/?period=5&group=Grasslands&country=IT&region=ALP, last accessed March 22, 2025.

19 Matteo Anderle and others, "The Contribution of Landscape Features, Climate and Topography in Shaping Taxonomical and Functional Diversity of Avian Communities in a Heterogeneous Alpine Region" (2022) 199 *Oecologia* 499–512, 500.

20 Streifeneder, Giuliani and Hoffmann, "A Transnational Analysis of the Policies for Alpine Pasture Farming," 64–65; Concetta Cardillo and Orlando Cimino, "Small Farms in Italy: What Is Their Impact on the Sustainability of Rural Areas?" (2022) 11:2142 *Land* 1–25, 13, 14.

21 Anderle and others, "Contribution of Landscape Features," 509.

22 Mauro Agnoletti and Antonio Santoro, "The Italian National Register of Historical Rural Landscapes" in Józef Hernik and others (eds), *Cultural Heritage – Possibilities for Land-Centered Societal Development* (Springer 2022) 15–34, 18.

23 Centeri and others, "Wooded Grasslands," 98.

than 1 to 30 hectares,[24] undertake farming in South Tyrol's EU-recognized Natura 2000 sites, a significant portion of which cover grasslands.[25] Finally, the significant historical loss of grasslands raises the question of restoration,[26] a less common but increasingly important task for environmental laws.[27]

Coordination between governments and across laws[28] arises as a prominent issue in addressing grassland loss because interventions engage several legal areas – laws for nature; development and impact assessment; agriculture; landscape; and governance arrangements in general. Each of these areas comprises multiple laws among the international, EU, national, provincial, district, and municipal levels. Since the Italian Parliament lacks a Senate that represents territorial subunits, it relies on a system of intergovernmental bodies that link not just the regions and autonomous provinces with the central State, but also municipalities, alongside a constitutional principle of "loyal cooperation" (*leale collaborazione*).[29]

Legislative powers related to the environment are interlocking, with blurred boundaries between the responsibilities of the State and regions/autonomous provinces.[30] This demands negotiation and dispute resolution for implementation. Though Italian scholars point to challenges with multilevel coordination,[31] globally, Italian approaches to coordinating and achieving coherence among multiple levels of government and with civil society and nongovernmental organizations (NGOs) in the broad area of sustainable development are held up as instructive examples of good practice.[32]

24 Luigi Servadei and others, *La Politica di Sviluppo Rurale per la Biodiversità, Natura 2000 e le Aree Protette*, vol. 1 (Rete Rurale Nazionale 2018) 159, 164, www.reterurale.it/RapportoNatura2000.

25 Ibid 153, 154, 159, 163 (using the SAT indicator), 170 (grasslands in Alpine Natura 2000 sites, though not disaggregated to the province level). For a discussion of Natura 2000, see Section 10.4.2.3.

26 European Environment Agency, *State of Nature in the EU*, 101.

27 See generally, Afshin Akhtar-Khavari and Benjamin J. Richardson (eds), *Ecological Restoration Law: Concepts and Case Studies* (Routledge 2019).

28 Coordination among governments and stakeholders lies outside the scope of this chapter, but note that the provincial agricultural association is relevant to grassland grazing, and is popular and powerful: Giovanni Poggeschi, "South Tyrol's Special Status in Private Law: The 'Entailed Farm' and the '*Grundbuch*' Systems" in Jens Woelk, Joseph Marko and Francesco Palermo (eds), *Tolerance through Law: Self Governance and Group Rights in South Tyrol* (Brill Nijhoff 2007) 201–300, 294.

29 See further Section 10.4.2.3.

30 See further Section 10.3.2.

31 See nn 164 and 165 and accompanying text.

32 OECD, *Unleashing Policy Coherence to Achieve the SDGs: An Assessment of Governance Mechanisms* (OECD Publishing 2024) 15, 19, 20, www.oecd.org/content/dam/oecd/en/publications/reports/2024/07/unleashing-policy-coherence-to-achieve-the-sdgs_c996cdoc/a1c8dbf8-en.pdf.

By contrast, the two other regulatory functions under the CIRCle Framework – conceptualization and information – are relatively less problematic in the context of South Tyrol's grasslands. An outside observer might assume that protecting Alpine grasslands is a niche or an obscure issue. Yet, Italian laws frequently conceptualize it as an important matter of concern. We see this across government levels, from national law that recognizes farmers as "environmental guardians" who protect mountain landscapes and combat biodiversity loss,[33] to municipal law that praises the beauty, ecology, and history of threatened mountain grasslands.[34] In other words, Alpine grasslands are an intentional legislative target, conceptualized as spanning ecological, agricultural, and cultural values, and therefore engaging these different areas of law. This attention also manifests as a focus on information. While criticism of grassland biodiversity monitoring under some EU instruments remains,[35] South Tyrol has a dedicated biodiversity monitoring program that emphasizes grasslands.[36] In relation to information, it likely also helps that grasslands are relatively small and sociopolitically salient in South Tyrol, reflected and reinforced by the multiple levels of laws discussed next.

10.3 FOUNDATIONS FOR COORDINATION: THE MULTILEVEL REGULATORY LANDSCAPE

Cumulative threats to South Tyrol's grasslands involve economic sectors and areas of regulation that engage many levels of government across traditional legal silos. This section sets the scene for analyzing regulatory mechanisms for intervention and coordination related to Alpine grasslands. It explains how responsibility for relevant matters is distributed and sometimes shared between government levels. This also begins a discussion about coordination, integration, and overlap to which Section 10.4 returns.

33 Legge 28 febbraio 2024, n. 24, Disposizioni per il riconoscimento della figura dell'agricoltore custode dell'ambiente e del territorio e per l'istituzione della Giornata nazionale dell'agricoltura [Law on provisions for the recognition of the figure of the farmer as custodian of the environment and the territory and for the establishment of the National Agriculture Day] (Italy) ("Italian Agricultural Recognition Law"), art. 1(1), 2(1).

34 *Piano Paesaggistico del Comune di Senales: Relazione Illustrativa* (Autonomous Province of South Tyrol 2011) 7, 8.

35 Ivon Cuadros-Casanova and others, "Opportunities and Challenges for Common Agricultural Policy Reform to Support the European Green Deal" (2023) 37:e14052 *Conservation Biology* 1–13, 4, 5 (citations omitted).

36 See generally, Andreas Hilpold and others, *Handbook Biodiversity Monitoring South Tyrol* (Eurac Research 2023) https://works.eurac.edu/Handbook-Biodiversity-Monitoring-South-Tyrol-2023.pdf.

10.3.1 *International and Supranational*

It is, perhaps, counterintuitive for a discussion about regulating small grasslands in a northern Italian province to start with international law. Yet, there is a lot of it, addressing cumulative harm to Alpine grasslands through five legal areas – nature, impact assessment, agriculture, landscape, and governance – in a way that Italian national and subnational law mirrors. Italy is bound by several relevant international biodiversity treaties and EU instruments on biodiversity, impact assessment, agriculture, and product labeling.[37] The EU shares competence in environmental policy with member states.[38] Its directives provide for protecting habitats and birds (Habitats and Birds Directives, together the "Nature Directives"),[39] and its impact assessment directives apply environmental impact assessment ("EIA") and strategic environmental assessment ("SEA") requirements to development projects and plans. The EU Common Agricultural Policy directly addresses the agriculture–environment interface, which also arises indirectly in EU product labeling rules. Finally, the broader idea of "landscape" is the focus of the European Landscape Convention[40] and a special multilateral environmental agreement for the Alps, the Alpine Convention, a key driver of which was addressing the cumulative impacts of small- and medium-scale developments.[41] (For completeness, grasslands are indirectly protected by listings under international heritage treaties for sites in the Dolomites,[42] which span South Tyrol and neighboring provinces; and the practice of transhumance, i.e., seasonal

[37] For discussion of these, see Section 10.4.

[38] See Josephine van Zeben, "Subsidiarity in European Environmental Law: A Competence Allocation Approach" (2014) 38 *Harvard Environmental Law Review* 414–464, 424–430.

[39] Council Directive 92/43/EEC of May 21, 1992 on the conservation of natural habitats and of wild fauna and flora [1992] OJ L206/7 (as amended) ("Habitats Directive"); Directive 2009/147/EC of the European Parliament and of the Council of November 30, 2009, conservation of wild birds [2010] OJ L20/7, as amended ("Birds Directive").

[40] Council of Europe Landscape Convention, adopted October 20, 2000, in force March 1, 2004 [2000] E.T.S. 176 ("European Landscape Convention").

[41] Convention on the Protection of the Alps, Salzburg, adopted November 7, 1991, in force March 6, 1995, [1996] OJ L61/32 ("Alpine Convention"); Onida, "The Protection of Biodiversity and Ecological Connectivity," 58.

[42] The Dolomites is inscribed with reference to natural values of "exceptional natural beauty" and geomorphic importance: World Heritage Committee, Report of Decisions, WHC-09/33.COM/20, July 20, 2009, 33 COM 8B.6. Its management plan makes only passing reference to meadows: Marcella Morandini and others, *The Dolomites: Overall Management Strategy [+ Tourism Strategy]* (Fondazione Dolomiti Dolomiten Dolomites Dolomitis UNESCO, 2015) 46, https://whc.unesco.org/document/207280.

droving of livestock.)[43] These international and supranational instruments rely on laws at the national and subnational levels for implementation,[44] discussed next.

10.3.2 *Italian Multilevel Government, Environment, Landscape, and Culture*

Multilevel governance in Italy involves multiple subnational governments (20 regions, 110 provinces, including 2 autonomous provinces that assume the substantive powers of a region, 15 "metropolitan cities" and 7,960 municipalities).[45] Multilevel governance in Italy is asymmetric – different units at the same level have varying degrees of autonomy – with the autonomous province of South Tyrol having, and exercising, a high degree of autonomy[46] within a "shell" region that lacks significant power. Autonomy arrangements are central to distributing legislative competency relevant to grasslands, and appreciating the context of South Tyrol's "consociational" governance[47] based on ethnic power-sharing.

Alpine grasslands, conceived as biocultural landscapes, cross the exclusive and shared competencies of the Italian State and the regions/provinces. Under the Constitution, the Italian State generally has exclusive competence over protection of the environment, ecosystems, and cultural heritage. Meanwhile, the regions have concurrent powers (subject to fundamental principles set by the State) over land use planning, enhancement of cultural and environmental properties, and matters not specified.[48] However, the Constitution expressly allows the regions and autonomous provinces to implement EU arrangements

43 Intergovernmental Committee for the Safeguarding of the Intangible Cultural Heritage ("ICSICH"), LHE/23/18.COM/Decisions, January 5, 2024, DECISION 18.COM 8.b.14; ICSICH, LHE/19/14.COM/Decisions, January 29, 2020, DECISION 14.COM 10.b.2.

44 The two inscriptions under the World Heritage Convention and Intangible Cultural Heritage Convention are implemented by Legge Provinciale 18 luglio 2023, n. 13, Gestione coordinata dei siti ed elementi oggetto di riconoscimenti UNESCO in provincia di Bolzano [Provincial law on coordinated management of UNESCO-recognized sites and elements in the province of Bolzano] (South Tyrol). This is not discussed further.

45 "Division of Powers: Italy – Systems of Multilevel Governance" (n.d.) https://portal.cor.europa.eu/divisionpowers/Pages/Italy-Systems-of-multilevel-governance.aspx, last accessed March 22, 2025, archived at https://perma.cc/M874-BV4K.

46 See generally, Elisabeth Alber and Carolin Zwilling, *A Primer on the Autonomy of South Tyrol: History, Law, Politics* (Autonomy Arrangements in the World, 2nd edn, Eurac Research 2022) www.world-autonomies.info/territorial-autonomies/south-tyrol.

47 Ibid 16–17.

48 Costituzione della Repubblica Italiana [Constitution of the Italian Republic] 1947, as amended, arts. 117(2)(s) and third paragraph.

and special arrangements increase the powers of the autonomous provinces.[49] Pursuant to a treaty between Italy and Austria, South Tyrol's autonomy statute supports self-determination through an ethnically divided governance system, which is aimed at protecting its German-speaking minority in the context of postwar fascist efforts to forcibly "Italianize" the population.[50]

The autonomy statute grants South Tyrol primary legislative competence over some important matters for Alpine grasslands. These include spatial planning, landscape protection, "closed farms" (also translated as "entailed farms," discussed further later), nature parks, agriculture, and EIA.[51] The autonomy arrangements are adjustable using a procedure of agreed "enactment decrees."[52]

Legislative responsibilities under this system are not always clear-cut, and many disputes have engaged Italy's Constitutional Court. The Court has established that the autonomy statute does not support a "general competence on environmental issues"; rather, the matters not expressly mentioned remain with the State, including minimum standards of environmental protection.[53] The matters specifically mentioned "are compressed to the minimum."[54] Accordingly, the task of environmental protection (broadly understood) is shared, and the legitimacy of provincial rules is evaluated "case-by-case."[55] Where an issue engages overlapping legislative competences, the "prevalent" power determines the level of government with power to legislate.[56] This engages the Constitutional Court's "extremely wide margin of interpretive freedom" and its centralizing tendencies.[57] The Court has, however, confirmed the autonomous provinces' power (under the autonomy statute) in

[49] Ibid, arts. 116(1) and 117(5).

[50] Alber and Zwilling, *Primer on the Autonomy of South Tyrol*, 5–8, 16–23.

[51] Decreto del Presidente della Repubblica 31 agosto 1972, n. 670, Approvazione del testo unico delle leggi costituzionali concernenti lo statuto speciale per il Trentino-Alto Adige [Presidential decree on the approval of the consolidated text of the constitutional laws concerning the special statute for Trentino-Alto Adige], as amended, art. 8(5), (6), (8), (16), (21), art. 13(1). Under art. 99, South Tyrol's laws are published in both German and Italian; I provide citations in Italian, as I used the Italian versions as the basis for research.

[52] Elisabeth Alber, "South Tyrol's Model of Conflict Resolution: Territorial Autonomy and Power-Sharing" in Soeren Keil and Allison McCulloch (eds), *Power-Sharing in Europe: Past Practice, Present Cases, and Future Directions* (Palgrave Macmillan 2021) 171–199, 179–180.

[53] Mariachiara Alberton, "The Swing of Intergovernmental Relations Concerning Environmental Matters through the (Un)Balanced Doctrines of the Constitutional Courts in Spain and in Italy" (2021) *Revista d'Estudis Autonòmics i Federals – Journal of Self-Government* 1–43, 28, 32.

[54] Ibid 37.

[55] Ibid 28, 36.

[56] Vittoria Barsotti and others, *Italian Constitutional Justice in Global Context* (OUP 2015) 194.

[57] Ibid.

relation to landscape and nature parks and their entitlement to implement the Nature Directives.[58] EIA is undertaken by both levels, with responsibility allocated depending on the nature of the project.[59] In intersecting areas, the constitutional principle of loyal cooperation and intergovernmental institutions provide for coordination, discussed further in Section 10.4.

The province also hosts multiple levels of government. South Tyrol has 118 mostly small municipalities (*comuni/Gemeinden*, averaging 4,500 inhabitants), many of which face challenges in resourcing the services that help to stem depopulation, especially in remote areas.[60] Seven mid-tier "district" governments (*Comunità comprensoriali/Bezirksgemeinschaften*) undertake tasks delegated by the province or the municipalities, which sometimes include environment-related activities,[61] though they appear only tangentially related to grasslands.

This complicated governance picture adds up to this: On each of the usually small, ecologically and culturally fragile Alpine grasslands of Italy's northernmost territory sits tremendous, multilayered governance machinery. Nature, impact assessment, agriculture, landscape, and governance laws sit at different and sometimes multiple layers: local, provincial, national, EU, and international. These are the foundations for regulatory interventions to address cumulative harm to the grasslands, to which we now turn.

58 Alberton, "Swing of Intergovernmental Relations," 33; Walter Obwexer and Esther Happacher, *Parere Legale: Sviluppi e Mutamenti dell'Autonomia dell'Alto Adige a Partire dalla Dichiarazione di Chiusura della Vertenza 1992* (in Italian and German) (University of Innsbruck 2015), 233–234, citing Constitutional Court judgment n. 226/2009, dealing with Decreto Legislativo 22 gennaio 2004, n. 42, Codice dei beni culturali e del paesaggio, ai sensi dell'articolo 10 della legge 6 luglio 2002, n. 137 [Legislative decree on cultural heritage and landscape code, pursuant to article 10 of Law n. 137 of July 6, 2002] (Italy) ("Italian Cultural Heritage and Landscape Code") www.osservatorioappalti.unitn.it/viewFile.do?id=1511601879728&dataId=9751&filename=Testo.pdf, archived at https://perma.cc/Z74W-BWK8.

59 "Projects Subject to Environmental Impact Assessment (EIA) or Verification of Eligibility (Screening) (in Italian)" (2017) https://ambiente.provincia.bz.it/it/valutazioni-ambientali/valutazione-impatto-ambientale-via, archived at https://perma.cc/HL6V-ZF4J.

60 Theresia Morandell and Karl Kössler, "Inter-Municipal Cooperation Based on a Model Agreement: A Top-Down Approach in South Tyrol" in Karl Kössler and Theresia Morandell (eds), *Local Government in Italy: Responses to Urban-Rural Challenges* (Institute for Comparative Federalism, Eurac Research 2021) 63–69, 63, www.logov-rise.eu/country-map/italy/.

61 Thomas Ohnewein, Elisabeth Parteli and Carmen Kollmann (eds), *Manuale dell'Alto Adige con lo Statuto di Autonomia* (Provincial Council of Bolzano 2024) 250 https://news.provincia.bz.it/it/pubblicazioni/manuale_dell_alto_adige_con_lo_statuto_di_autonomi, archived at https://perma.cc/H6BM-AXW3.

10.4 COORDINATED REGULATORY INTERVENTION TO PROTECT ALPINE GRASSLANDS

Amid the many laws relevant to South Tyrol's Alpine grasslands emerge design features that Chapters 6 and 7 on regulatory intervention and coordination advanced as important to addressing cumulative environmental problems. First, these laws make available a mix of regulatory interventions that combines diverse regulatory strategies and approaches to influence diverse contributors to a cumulative problem. Second, they span legal levels and areas to comprehensively address all important categories of impacts. And third, they do so in a consistent way, to avoid mutual undermining. Section 10.4.1 first analyzes comprehensiveness in the sense of addressing a full spectrum of types of harms and contributors to harm. It examines the degree to which interventions across multiple legal levels and areas target action at the three broad types of harm that accumulate to cause the problem: development, contemporary abandonment of traditional pastoral practices, and historical abandonment (i.e., providing for restoration). It also analyzes the regulatory strategies and approaches used to influence different contributors to impacts: farmers, consumers, would-be developers, and governments. Section 10.4.2 then points to the coordinating links associated with these interventions using Chapter 7's distinction between rules and institutions for coordination, including those for dispute resolution, using the example of Natura 2000.

Recall Chapter 6 (Intervention)

Key design features of regulatory mechanisms for intervention to address cumulative environmental problems include: intervening ***comprehensively*** across impact types and activities, and using a ***diverse toolbox*** of regulatory approaches and strategies. **Regulatory approaches** include ***sticks*** that mandate or prohibit the carrying out of an activity; ***carrots*** that apply to an activity in the absence of a mandate (e.g., a monetary incentive or tax); ***sermons***, which influence the activity using information; and ***state rescue***, involving direct government action to address the problem. **Regulatory strategies** are ***harm reducing***, meaning changing an activity so that it causes less harm; ***harm offsetting***, meaning undertaking a second beneficial activity to counteract the negative effects of a first activity; ***restoring***, meaning undertaking a beneficial activity to counteract legacy harms that may have been caused by others; and ***coping***, meaning facilitating the matter of concern (here, Alpine grasslands) adapting to impacts so that harm decreases.

10.4.1 *Regulatory Interventions: Comprehensiveness and Diversity*

Available regulatory interventions use diverse tools to address three important categories of harm to Alpine grasslands, which are used to structure this section (noting that comprehensive coverage *within* a category of threat is a separate issue).[62] First, laws address – directly and indirectly – "development" that would convert grasslands to another land use. Second, they encourage continuing, rather than abandoning, low-profit extensive grazing of grasslands. Third, they provide for restoring already abandoned grasslands. In doing so, they use varied regulatory strategies and approaches. Table 10.1 summarizes measures used in key laws relevant[63] to Alpine grasslands, using the broad categories of legal focus introduced in Chapter 3: the matter of concern (here, Alpine grasslands), impacts, activities, and indirect influences.[64]

Overall, each of the legal areas (Table 10.1(a) to (e)) includes multiple laws, and many laws include mechanisms that adopt different approaches, strategies, or both. It is relatively rare for a law to adopt a single approach, or a single strategy. The overall diversity aligns with the argument in Chapter 6 that cumulative environmental problems will typically need a mix of interventions to account for the many and diverse contributors to a cumulative problem, and the multiple types of impacts involved. Together, the interventions here span several distinct areas of law, influencing more actors than a narrower approach would allow. Laws dealing with nature, agriculture, impact assessment, and landscapes affect how farmers and landowners manage their land; agricultural product labeling and farmer recognition laws aim to influence consumers and the general public; and further governance laws bring in direct action by governments to protect grasslands.

[62] I describe these as "available" interventions because empirical analysis of implementation lies outside the present scope. For a discussion touching on comprehensiveness of intervention in relation to threats within a category, see nn. 128 to 131 and accompanying text.

[63] This table and the accompanying discussion exclude laws that restrict narrow kinds of development (as opposed to changes in land use in general), e.g., restrictions on tourism developments. They also exclude laws that provide for general governance arrangements (e.g., foundational EU treaties), EU sustainability disclosures in a large corporate context, like the EU "Taxonomy," which does not cover agriculture generally (see Saga Eriksson, "The Centrality of Law for EU Sustainable Finance Markets: Outlining a Research Agenda" (2024) 33 *Review of European, Comparative and International Environmental Law* 57–69); instruments that provide general economic support to local governments (but it includes economic supports directed expressly to Alpine grasslands); and that provide for general rules about local food products (but it includes specific rules related to mountain products).

[64] See Figure 3.1.

TABLE 10.1 *Regulatory interventions at international (INT), European (EU), Italian national (IT), and Autonomous Province of Bolzano-South Tyrol (ST) levels related to Alpine grasslands, and their regulatory approaches and strategies*

Level	Law and legal mechanisms	Regulatory approach				Regulatory strategy			
		Stick	Carrot	Sermon	State rescue	Harm-reducing	Harm-offsetting	Restoring	Coping
	(a) Nature laws (focus is on grasslands as the matter of concern)								
INT	Biodiversity Convention: general and in situ conservation, sustainable use of biodiversity, impact assessment, public awareness, incentive measures[i]	✓	✓	✓		✓		✓	
INT	Bern Wildlife Convention: conservation policies, habitat and species protections, education measures, reintroductions[ii]	✓		✓		✓		✓	
EU	Habitats Directive: conservation measures, impact assessment, compensatory measures, protected areas, protection measures[iii]	✓	✓			✓	✓	✓	
EU	Birds Directive: conservation measures, protected areas, protection measures[iv]	✓				✓		✓	
EU	Nature Restoration Law: restoration measures, targets, national plans[v]		✓			✓	✓	✓	✓
IT	Framework Law on Protected Areas: payments for conservation and restoration, activity restrictions, incentives for pastoralism and restoration[vi]	✓	✓	✓	✓	✓		✓	
ST	Nature Law: harm prohibition, protected areas, protection measures, impact assessment, compensatory measures, and awareness-raising measures[vii]	✓	✓	✓		✓	✓	✓	

TABLE 10.1 (*continued*)

Level	Law and legal mechanisms	Regulatory approach				Regulatory strategy			
		Stick	Carrot	Sermon	State rescue	Harm-reducing	Harm-offsetting	Restoring	Coping
	(b) Impact assessment laws, EIA, and SEA (focus is impacts)								
EU	EIA Directive: harm-reducing and -offsetting measures as conditions[viii]	✓				✓	✓		
EU	SEA Directive: harm-reducing and -offsetting measures[ix]		*Not specified*			✓	✓		
IT	Environment Code: SEA for plans and EIA for projects under IT jurisdiction, inc. harm-reducing and -offsetting measures[x]	✓				✓	✓		
ST	EIA and SEA law: SEA and EIA for projects under ST jurisdiction, including harm-reducing and -offsetting measures, provincial authorization [xi]	✓				✓	✓		
	(c) Agriculture laws (focus spans matter of concern and activities)								
EU	CAP Regulation: direct payments (eco-schemes enhanced conditionality), environment–rural development measures[xii]		✓	✓		✓		✓	✓
EU	Geographical Indications Regulation: mountain product labeling[xiii]		✓	✓			*Not specified*		
IT	Green Economy Law: ecosystem services payments[xiv]		✓			✓			
IT	Mountain Products Decree: mountain product labeling[xv]		✓	✓			*Not specified*		
IT	Agricultural Recognition Law: incentives and technical assistance, awareness-raising and merit awards for environmentally compatible farmers[xiv]		✓	✓		✓			
ST	Agricultural Incentive Law: incentives for landscape protection and environmental improvement[xvii]		✓	✓		✓		✓	
ST	Closed Farm Law: restricted disposal, subdivision and inheritance[xviii]	✓					*Not specified*		

TABLE 10.1 (*continued*)

Level	Law and legal mechanisms	Regulatory approach				Regulatory strategy			
		Stick	Carrot	Sermon	State rescue	Harm-reducing	Harm-offsetting	Restoring	Coping
	(d) Landscape laws (focus is matter of concern)								
INT	Alpine Convention: objectives to protect, conserve, and rehabilitate the environment[xix]	*Not specified*				✓		✓	
INT	↳ Mountain Farming Protocol: incentives to encourage mountain farming to conserve and maintain nature, conserve and restore pastures, training and technical assistance[xx]		✓	✓		✓		✓	
INT	↳ Nature Protection Protocol: landscape planning, agriculture incentives, protected areas, harm prohibition, offsetting unavoidable impairment, renaturalization, and reintroductions[xxi]	✓	✓			✓	✓	✓	
EU	European Landscape Convention: awareness raising, training and education, "instruments" for planning and management[xxii]			✓		✓		✓	
IT	Cultural Heritage and Landscape Code (applies to landscape in ST at the level of principles)[xxiii]	*Primary competency lies with ST*							
ST	Landscape Law: grassland protections; public interventions for conservation, restoration; contributions to landowners; Landscape Fund; public purchase for conservation; restrictions on land consumption; landscape alteration authorizations, including offsetting[xxiv]	✓	✓	✓	✓	✓	✓	✓	

TABLE 10.1 (*continued*)

Level	Law and legal mechanisms	Regulatory approach: Stick	Carrot	Sermon	State rescue	Regulatory strategy: Harm-reducing	Harm-offsetting	Restoring	Coping
	(e) Governance laws (focus is indirect influence)								
IT	Constitutional protection for ecosystems and landscapes[xxv]	*Not specified*				✓			
IT	Constitutional provision for mountains[xxvi]	*Not specified*				*Not specified*			
IT	Law for Small Municipalities: fund for public action, including to restore mountain pastures, acquire land to prevent biodiversity loss and restore environment on agricultural land[xxvii]				✓	✓		✓	
IT	Law for Mountain Development[xxviii]				✓	✓		✓	

NB: CAP, Common Agricultural Policy; EIA, environmental impact assessment; SEA, strategic environmental assessment.

References and provisions related to regulatory strategies and approaches

Parenthetical information gives information relevant to strategies and approaches given above, introduced in Chapter 6 and reviewed in the text box preceding Section 10.4.1. Note that references to "conservation" and "protection" are interpreted as a harm-reducing strategy, and references to prohibiting, regulating, authorizing, or licensing activities (or similar) are taken to amount to a regulatory stick. General words like 'policies' or 'measures' are not construed as a specific regulatory approach. Short names are used in references, will full references in the footnotes to the main body of the text either preceding or following this table.

i Biodiversity Convention arts. 6 (general measures for conservation), 8 (in situ conservation, including to promote recovery of species, i.e., restoration, and regulating activities), 10 (sustainable use of biodiversity, including remedial action, i.e., restoring), 11 (incentive measures), 13 (public awareness, i.e., a sermon), 14 (impact assessment, minimizing adverse impacts), 20 (financial incentives).

ii Bern Wildlife Convention arts. 3 (conservation policies and education, i.e., a sermon), 4 (conservation measures), 5 (measures to protect flora, harm prohibition), 6 (measures to protect fauna, harm prohibition), 11 (encouragement of reintroductions).

TABLE 10.1 (*continued*)

iii Habitats Directive arts. 6 (conservation measures, avoid deterioration, impact assessment, compensatory measures), 8 (EU co-financing of measures), 12 and 13 (harm prohibition), 14 (regulating access to property, regulating and licensing take of specimens), 16 (derogations, e.g., for imperative reasons of public interest), 22(a) (re-introducing species).

iv Birds Directive arts. 2 (conservation measures), 3 (protected areas and reestablishing biotopes), 4 (protected areas), 5 (harm prohibitions), 8 (prohibitions on nonselective capture).

v Nature Restoration Law art. 4 (member state habitat restoration measures to meet restoration targets, no significant deterioration requirement), 11 (restoration of agricultural ecosystems), 14–15 (national restoration plans, including promoting "the deployment of private or public support schemes," financing "support to stakeholders," and compensatory measures), ann. VII(9), (18), (20), (22) (examples of restoration measures including establishing meadows and pastures, reducing grazing intensity, stopping grassland plowing, assisting migration where needed due to climate change). Note that beyond brief reference to regulatory carrots, there is little discussion of the regulatory approach from the perspective of contributors to harm, most provisions being framed simply as "restoration measures."

vi Italian Framework Law on Protected Areas, e.g., for "national protected natural areas": arts. 1(3)(a), (b) (conservation and restoration objectives), 7 (payments to municipalities and provinces to undertake state rescue, and to individuals, to undertake environmental conservation and restoration), 11 (harm prohibition), 13 (authorizations), 14 (incentives to individuals; facilitating or promoting traditional pastoral activities and environmental restoration, or promoting local products i.e., carrot and sermon).

vii South Tyrol Nature Law arts. 7 (harm prohibition re plants); 9 (plants protected in protected areas); 14 (habitat protection and restoration); 20 (establishment of protected areas); 21 (compensatory measures); 26 (incentive and awareness-raising measures); 27 (contractual measures to services, including re meadows).

viii EIA Directive arts. 5(1)(c), 8a(1)(b)(4) and annex IV(7) (measures to prevent, reduce, offset adverse effects; development consent to incorporate such measures).

ix SEA Directive arts. 3, 5(1), annex I point (g), II (environmental report to be "taken into account" in decision-making about plan or program, i.e., not specifying a regulatory approach; relevant information includes measures to prevent, reduce and offset adverse effects).

x Italian Environment Code pt II and associated annexes (SEA and EIA for certain projects within Natura 2000 sites, includes measures to prevent, reduce, and offset adverse effects, including via authorization requirements): art. 26 (link to project authorization), pt II - ann. V point (g), ann. VII point 7).

xi South Tyrol EIA/SEA Law title II (SEA) (SEA to be "taken into account" in decision-making about plan, i.e., not specifying a regulatory approach) and III (EIA) (applies to annex A listed projects under the jurisdiction of South Tyrol; requires conditions to avoid or prevent negative impacts; measures to avoid, reduce, etc. and offset impacts; requirement for provincial authorization).

TABLE 10.1 (*continued*)

xii CAP Regulation arts. 6(d), (f) (objectives include climate change adaptation, i.e., coping, "halting and reversing biodiversity loss, enhance ecosystem services and preserve habitats and landscapes", i.e., harm-reducing and restoring); 12–13 (reducing harm through conditionality for direct payments re compliance with statutory management requirements (SMRs) and "good agricultural and environmental condition" (GAEC) standards); 15 (farm advisory services, i.e., a sermon); 31 (eco-schemes, including payments to protect biodiversity and restore habitats); 70 (payments for agri–environment–climate commitments that help achieve art. 6 objectives); 71 (payments for natural and area-specific constraints, including mountain areas); 72 (payments for area-specific disadvantages from mandatory requirements, including Natura 2000); 73 (support for investments in agricultural restoration and climate adaptation as an art. 6 objective); annex III (GAEC 1 re maintenance of permanent grassland, GAEC 9 re ban on plowing environmentally sensitive permanent grassland in Natura 2000 sites, SMR 3 re obligations under Birds Directive, SMR 4 re obligations under Habitats Directive). Note that prohibitions drawn from the Nature Directives are not classified as sticks here to avoid double counting.

xiii Geographical Indications Regulation art. 82 ("mountain product" as optional quality term). Note that this functions as a combined regulatory carrot and sermon – carrot from the perspective of the farmers who adopt the quality term, and sermon from the perspective of consumers. The instrument is silent as to regulatory strategy, since it requires merely a mountain location, and no specific environmental practices.

xiv Italian Green Economy Law art. 70(d), (f) (payment system for ecosystem services, including principles to safeguard biodiversity and landscape quality, i.e., harm reducing, and remunerating farmers to do so), 79 (applies in South Tyrol).

xv Italian Mountain Products Decree art. 2(2) (application of "mountain product quality" to animal products, including from transhumance pastures) (see also note xiii above for Geographical Indications Regulation).

xvi Italian Agricultural Recognition Law art. 2 (farmers who combat agricultural abandonment and biodiversity loss, i.e., harm reducing); 3 (projects, agreements and MoUs with farmers to combat abandonment and biodiversity loss and enhance the social role of farmers); 4 (preferential contracts for the promotion of agriculture that protects biodiversity and cultural heritage); 5 (list of farmers to be recognized); 6–10 (National Agriculture Day, award of merit for agriculturalists)

xvii South Tyrol Agricultural Incentive Law arts. 1 (purpose to promote agriculture in protecting cultural aspects of landscape, considering ecological aspects and with reference to mountain areas), 3, 4(1)(f), 5 (incentives and technical assistance for landscape protection and environmental improvement, i.e., harm reducing and restoring, either by the province alone, or jointly with the Italian State or the EU)

xviii South Tyrol Closed Farms Law art. 4–9 (limitations on disposal of registered closed farm); 5 (restrictions on detaching plots of land from the closed farm); 11 (farm indivisible in the context of inheritance, must be single heir); 14 (criteria for inheritance if multiple potential heirs, and they do not agree). Categorized as "not specified" in relation to regulatory strategy since there is no express reference to an environmental change, as opposed to an ownership change.

TABLE 10.1 *(continued)*

xix Alpine Convention art. 2 (preserving and protecting the Alps, conserving and rehabilitating natural habitats, preserving and promoting environmentally compatible farming).

xx Mountain Farming Protocol arts. 3 (encouraging environmentally compatible mountain farming; taking action against abandonment), 7 (providing compensation for mountain farming's contribution to conserving and maintaining nature and countryside), 8(3) (ensure conservation and restoration of traditional components of countryside, inc. Alpine pastures), 17–18 (training and technical assistance)

xxi Nature Protection Protocol arts. 8 (preserve species and habitats through landscape planning), 9 (offset unavoidable impairments), 10 (reduce impacts on nature and restore; use incentives to support agriculture), 11 (preserve, manage, extend protected areas and avoid and reduce impairments), 13 (preservation of biotopes, re-naturalization of impaired habitats, i.e., restoring), 14 (preserve species and habitats), 15 (prohibit harm), 16 (promote reintroductions).

xxii European Landscape Convention arts. 1(d), (e), (f) (conserve, maintain, restore landscape), 6(A) (awareness raising), (B) (training and education), (E) (instruments aimed at protecting, managing and/or planning the landscape), 11 (Landscape award of the Council of Europe).

xxiii Italian Cultural Heritage and Landscape Code. Note that under the Second Autonomy Statute, as modified by legislative decree, South Tyrol has responsibility for landscape-related laws, including landscape authorizations: Decreto Legislativo 26 settembre 2023, n. 143, Norme di attuazione dello Statuto speciale per la Regione Trentino-Alto Adige/Südtirol recanti modifiche al decreto del Presidente della Repubblica 22 marzo 1974, n. 381, in materia di urbanistica e di tutela del paesaggio [Legislative decree on implementation provisions of the Special Statute for the Trentino-Alto Adige/Südtirol Region containing amendments to the Presidential Decree of March 22, 1974, no. 381, on urban planning and landscape protection]. This Code applies at the level of principles.

xxiv South Tyrol Landscape Law arts. 14 (state interventions for conservation and restoration in place of owners/occupiers); 15, 16 (contributions to landowners and "Landscape Fund" for conserving and restoring natural and cultural landscapes, purchase of land by public bodies, awareness raising, i.e., a sermon), 17 (restrictions on land consumption by construction outside developed areas); 65 (landscape authorizations, may be subject to compensatory conditions).

xxv, xxvi Constitution of the Italian Republic, art. 9 (the Republic protects landscapes, the environment, biodiversity, ecosystems), 44 (the law makes provision for mountain areas).

xxvii Italian Small Municipalities Law arts. 3(3)(h), 5(1)(a) (fund for development, including for restoring mountain pastures and to combat land abandonment by acquiring properties to prevent biodiversity loss and to restore the environment on agricultural land).

xxviii Italian Mountain Development Law art. 9 (power to acquire, rent, or expropriate where necessary for the protection of the environment, abandoned mountain land for meadows and pastures).

10.4.1.1 Regulatory Mechanisms to Control Development

Laws that control development are perhaps the most familiar to environmental lawyers. Impact assessment laws apply the typical recipe. First, require the proponent of a plan or project to assess whether it would have a significant impact on the environment. Then, require a decision-maker to take account of that assessment in considering the plan or determining whether to allow the project, and the conditions to apply to it. EU Directives provide for EIA and SEA,[65] and are implemented by Italian national law or South Tyrol law,[66] depending on the kind of plan or project. They require cumulative impacts to be considered in SEA, at the project "screening" stage (determining whether EIA is required), and in the project EIA study itself.[67] Under these laws, environmental impacts include not just impacts on biodiversity but also impacts on "landscape."[68] They aim to reduce, avoid, and offset harm from these impacts using regulatory sticks, for example, by influencing whether a decision-maker issues a permit for development and its binding environmental conditions (Table 10.1(b)).

Nature laws (Table 10.1(a)) also use a familiar recipe of designating important areas, then limiting the activities that can happen inside them using regulatory sticks. The Convention on Biological Diversity and the Bern Convention both provide for this approach,[69] as do the EU "Nature

65 Directive 2011/92/EU of the European Parliament and of the Council of December 13, 2011, on the assessment of the effects of certain public and private projects on the environment [2012] OJ L26/1, as amended ("EIA Directive"); Directive 2001/42/EC of the European Parliament and of the Council of June 27, 2001, on the assessment of the effects of certain plans and programmes on the environment [2001] OJ L197/30, as amended ("SEA Directive").

66 Decreto Legislativo 3 aprile 2006, n. 152, Norme in materia ambientale [Legislative Decree on rules on environmental matters] (Italy) ("Italian Environment Code"); Legge Provinciale 13 ottobre 2017, n. 17, Valutazione ambientale per piani, programmi e progetti [Environmental assessment for plans, programs and projects] (South Tyrol) ("South Tyrol EIA/SEA Law").

67 E.g., EIA Directive arts. 4(3), 5(1), ann. III points 1(b), (3)(g); SEA Directive, arts. 3, 5(1), ann. I note i, ann. II point (2); Italian Environment Code, in relation to SEA: arts. 12, 13, pt II - ann. I point (2), ann. VI point (f), and in relation to EIA: arts. 19, 22, pt II - ann. V point (b), ann. VII point (5)(e); South Tyrol EIA/SEA Law, arts. 7(1), 10(3), 15, 17 (applying same criteria as corresponding national law).

68 EIA Directive arts. 1(2)(a), 3(1)(d), 4(2), 5(1), ann. II point 1(b), IV point (4); SEA Directive arts. 3, 5(1), ann. I point (f), ann. II point (2); Italian Environment Code pt II - ann. I point 2, ann. V point (2)(b), (c8), ann. VI point (f), ann. VII point (4), (5)(b), (d), (8); South Tyrol EIA/SEA Law, arts. 10(3), 17(1) (applying EU and national provisions).

69 Convention on Biological Diversity, June 5, 1992, Rio de Janeiro, in force December 29, 1993, 1760 U.N.T.S. 79, 143 ("Biodiversity Convention"), art. 8(c); Convention on the Conservation of European Wildlife and Natural Habitats, September 19, 1979, Bern, in force June 6, 1982, E.T.S. 104 ("Bern Wildlife Convention"), art. 4

Directives."[70] However, these sticks are carefully targeted: Italy's protected areas law expressly foresees that protected areas will allow and indeed value traditional pastoral activities and other activities that are characteristic of local community identity.[71] South Tyrol's law provides for Natura 2000 sites that protect grasslands and imposes accompanying special impact assessment requirements termed "appropriate assessments."[72] Restrictions do not apply to agricultural uses and laws expressly promote traditional, extensive agriculture.[73] While the EU CAP requires all farmers to comply with the Nature Directives,[74] farmers who receive direct payments must also observe a blanket ban on plowing or converting environmentally sensitive permanent grasslands in Natura 2000 sites and a broader 5 percent limit on the decrease in permanent grasslands compared to 2018 levels (termed "enhanced conditionality").[75]

Development-limiting landscape laws (Table 10.1(d)) in South Tyrol further protect Alpine grasslands, both directly and indirectly, using regulatory sticks. South Tyrol's Landscape Law requires a permit to alter the landscape in protected areas, in mountain areas over 1,600 m,[76] and in other areas set out in landscape plans (with exceptions for restoring degraded areas[77]). These include sites protected for ecological and agricultural reasons, including Alpine meadows and pastures.[78] Provincial and municipal planning instruments implement these provisions.[79] For example, a municipal plan for Schnalstal/Senales, a mountain municipality on the Austrian border, prohibits construction on Alpine grasslands, except for certain agricultural purposes, provided that conditions about minimum animal pasturage or hay cutting are met.[80]

70 Habitats Directive, art. 6(1), (2), 12, 13; Birds Directive, arts. 3, 4.

71 Legge 6 Dicembre 1991, n. 394, Legge quadro sulle aree protette [Framework law on protected areas], as amended (Italy) ("Italian Framework Law on Protected Areas"), arts. 11(2)(b), 2-bis, 12(2)(c) (all in relation to national parks).

72 E.g., Legge Provinciale 12 maggio 2010, n. 6, Legge di tutela della natura e altre disposizioni [Provincial law on nature conservation and other provisions], as amended (South Tyrol) ("South Tyrol Nature Law"), arts. 20, 22, ann. D.

73 E.g., ibid arts. 10, 21(8)(b).

74 Regulation 2021/2115 of the European Parliament and of the Council of December 2, 2021, on Common Agricultural Policy Strategic Plans [2021] OJ L435/1 (CAP Regulation), annex III (SMR 3, SMR 4).

75 Ibid annex III (GAEC 1, GAEC 9).

76 Legge provinciale 10 luglio 2018, n. 9, Territorio e paesaggio [Provincial law on territory and landscape] (South Tyrol) ("South Tyrol Landscape Law"), arts. 12, 14.

77 Ibid arts. 11, 13(2), 47(1)(f).

78 Ibid arts. 11(c)-(e), 13(2)(c), (d), 14(1).

79 Ibid art. 41.

80 *Piano Paesaggistico del Comune di Senales: Prescrizioni di Tutela e d'Uso* [Landscape Plan of the Municipality of Senales: Rules on Protection and Use] (Autonomous Province of South Tyrol 2011, as codified 2020), art. 13.

Indirect limits on developing Alpine grasslands have a unique vehicle: provincial inheritance law, which reflects centuries-old local norms related to agriculture (Table 10.1(c)). South Tyrol's Closed Farm Law imposes limitations on the owner of a registered "closed farm" selling or subdividing the farm, and makes it indivisible in the context of inheritance: Only one person may inherit the farm. In a contemporary twist that preserves the law's constitutionality,[81] the heir need not be the first-born son, but the person who demonstrates the highest capability to manage the farm, based on statutory criteria.[82] South Tyrol's Landscape Law applies even stricter limitations on construction ("land consumption") on closed farms than other farms.[83] Interestingly, South Tyrol's Closed Farm Law is the only one of numerous agriculture laws to provide for a regulatory stick, the others all use carrots and sermons (Table 10.1(c)) – a point to which we return later.

10.4.1.2 Regulatory Mechanisms to Promote Extensive Grazing

Laws also encourage traditional extensive grazing on Alpine grasslands using regulatory carrots and sermons aimed at farmers, community associations, and consumers. Agriculture laws are key here (Table 10.1(c)). The Province delivers direct to farmers under its own Agricultural Incentive Law[84] as well as the EU's CAP. CAP "eco-schemes" reward farmers who go beyond minimum environmental requirements,[85] and farmers in mountain areas and Natura 2000 sites are eligible for additional payments.[86] Strikingly, this is the only context in which we see coping mechanisms: Climate change adaptation is among the objectives of payments under eco-schemes and warrants extra payments for farmers in mountain areas and Natura 2000 sites.[87] Italy's national Green Economy law provides for further ecosystem services payments to farmers.[88]

81 Stefania Baroncelli, "A Fluid Implementation of the Special Statute of Autonomy of Trentino Alto Adige/South Tyrol? The Influence of the Court of Justice of the EU, the Council of Europe and the Italian Constitutional Court" (2022) 79 *Europa Ethnica* 69–80, 77–78.

82 Legge Provinciale 28 novembre 2001, n. 17, Legge sui masi chiusi [Provincial law on closed farms], as amended (South Tyrol) ("South Tyrol Closed Farm Law"), arts. 11, 14.

83 E.g., South Tyrol Landscape Law, art. 17(5), (5-bis).

84 Legge provinciale 14 dicembre 1998, n. 11, Disposizioni relative all'incentivazione in agricoltura [Provincial law relating to incentives in agriculture], as amended (South Tyrol) ("South Tyrol Agricultural Incentive Law").

85 CAP Regulation, art. 31.

86 Ibid arts. 71, 72.

87 Ibid arts. 6(1)(d), 70–72.

88 Legge 28 dicembre 2015, n. 221, Disposizioni in materia ambientale per promuovere misure di green economy e per il contenimento dell'uso eccessivo di risorse naturali [Law on

Funding is also available to local areas to support community-led initiatives and investments to preserve landscapes under the EU CAP.[89] South Tyrol's Nature Protection Law provides for subsidizing nature protection associations and paying landowners to conserve meadows.[90] These measures align with the Alpine Convention's Mountain Farming Protocol, which encourages mountain farming, compensating mountain farmers for conserving nature and not abandoning mountain pastures;[91] under its Nature Protection Protocol, parties agree to use incentives to support agriculture.[92]

Regulatory sermons aim to recognize and valorize traditional farmers, indirectly incentivizing them to continue traditional enterprises. The European Landscape Convention provides for awareness-raising measures about the value of landscapes, and training and education.[93] Italy's 2024 Agricultural Recognition Law provides for a list of agricultural–environmental guardians, a National Agriculture Day, merit awards, potentially lower provincial taxes, and other valorization activities for farmers.[94] EU and Italian laws support a labeling scheme for accredited "mountain products," which steers consumers toward supporting Alpine agriculture.[95]

environmental provisions to promote green economy measures and to contain the excessive use of natural resources] (Italy) ("Italian Green Economy Law"), art. 70(f).

89 CAP Regulation, art. 73.

90 South Tyrol Nature Law, arts. 26, 27.

91 Protocol on the Implementation of the 1991 Alpine Convention in the Field of Mountain Farming, December 20, 1994, Chambéry, in force December 18, 2002, [2006] OJ L 271/63, arts. 3, 7, 8.

92 Protocol on the Implementation of the Alpine Convention of 1991 Relating to Nature Protection and Landscape Conservation, December 20, 1994, Chambéry, in force December 18, 2002, art. 10.

93 European Landscape Convention, arts. 6(A), (B).

94 Italian Agricultural Recognition Law, arts. 3–10.

95 Regulation (EU) 1151/2012 of the European Parliament and of the Council of November 21, 2012 on quality schemes for agricultural products and foodstuffs [2012] OJ 343/1, now replaced by another regulation that continues the "mountain product" optional quality designation in art. 82: Regulation (EU) 2024/1143 of the European Parliament and of the Council of 11 April 2024 on geographical indications for wine, spirit drinks and agricultural products, as well as traditional specialities guaranteed and optional quality terms for agricultural products, amending Regulations (EU) No 1308/2013, (EU) 2019/787 and (EU) 2019/1753 and repealing Regulation (EU) No 1151/2012 [2024] OJ L 2024/1143 ("Geographical Indications Regulation"), art. 82; Decreto Ministeriale 26 luglio 2017, n. 57167, Disposizioni nazionali per l'attuazione del regolamento (UE) n. 1151/2012 e del regolamento delegato (UE) n. 665/2014 sulle condizioni di utilizzo dell'indicazione facoltativa di qualita' «prodotto di montagna» [Ministerial Decree 57167 on national provisions for the implementation of Regulation (EU) No. 1151/2012 and Delegated Regulation (EU) No. 665/2014 on the conditions of use of the optional quality indication "mountain product"] (Italy) ("Italian Mountain Products Decree"), as amended.

10.4.1.3 Regulatory Mechanisms to Support Restoring Grasslands

Regulatory measures for restoring degraded grasslands engage municipalities, community associations, and landowners using legal powers to undertake "state rescue" and offer incentives – strikingly, but not unsurprisingly, not applying regulatory sticks to reverse legacy harm. Relevant laws relate to nature, agriculture, landscape, and governance in general (Table 10.1(a), (c), (d), (e)). Italy's law for small municipalities provides for a fund and national plan for redeveloping small municipalities that includes restoring mountain pastures among its priorities.[96] National laws for both small and mountain municipalities empower them to acquire abandoned mountain grasslands to restore them and combat loss of biodiversity, and even to expropriate them where necessary for environmental protection.[97] The EU CAP and South Tyrol's Agricultural Incentive Law provide incentives for restoring mountain zones and grasslands.[98] South Tyrol's nature law expressly promotes restoring semi-natural habitats like grasslands and extensive agriculture and provides for grants to relevant associations and organizations and contracts with landowners to undertake relevant works.[99] Most recently, Europe's 2024 Nature Restoration Law requires member states to meet binding nature restoration targets, with specific mention of agricultural and grazing-dependent ecosystems.[100]

It is apparent, then, that not only are the available regulatory mechanisms comprehensive in terms of actors and impacts; the diversity of actors and rules makes for a complex, multilevel regulatory landscape. Each level has mechanisms in multiple areas. In this context, coordination is vital.

10.4.2 *Coordination*

Amid all the individual regulatory intervention pieces of the large puzzle described, it will already be evident that there are coordinating "rules" in

96 Legge 6 ottobre 2017, n. 158, Misure per il sostegno e la valorizzazione dei piccoli comuni, nonchè disposizioni per la riqualificazione e il recupero dei centri storici dei medesimi comuni [Law on measures for the support and enhancement of small municipalities, as well as provisions for the redevelopment and recovery of the historic centers of the same municipalities], as amended (Italy) ("Italian Small Municipalities Law"), art. 3(3)(h).

97 Legge 3 dicembre 1971, n. 1102, Nuove norme per lo sviluppo della montagna [Law on new rules for mountain development], as amended (Italy) ("Italian Mountain Development Law"), art. 9; Italian Small Municipalities Law, art. 5(1).

98 CAP Regulation, arts. 6(1)(f), 70(2), 71(1); South Tyrol Agricultural Incentive Law, art. 4(1)(f).

99 South Tyrol Nature Law, arts. 21(8)(b), (c), 26, 27.

100 Regulation (EU) 2024/1991 of the European Parliament and of the Council of June 24, 2024, on nature restoration and amending Regulation (EU) 2022/869, OJ L 2024/1991, arts. 4, 11, annex VII(18), (20).

the form of provisions in a law that connect it to another law in a different area. This section first observes how subsidiarity (as a high-level principle for coordination between levels) emerges in this complex regulatory mix, notably as increasingly restrictive interventions at lower levels of government. It then analyzes two forms of coordination introduced in Chapter 7 and depicted in Figure 10.1: rule-based links between laws, which reinforce regulatory interventions; and coordinating institutions and dispute resolution mechanisms as illustrated by Natura 2000 arrangements.

10.4.2.1 Multilevel Regulation, Regulatory Diversity, and Subsidiarity

At first glance, the fact that multiple levels of government operate in each area of law, often using the same regulatory approach (as shown in Table 10.1), seems to suggest problematic overlap and inefficiency. However, on closer analysis, overlap is reduced by differentiating regulatory tasks in a way that reflects subsidiarity – a principle of EU law and Italy's Constitution – that central authority should only perform tasks that a local level cannot adequately undertake.[101]

A nuanced view of subsidiarity differentiates between setting and implementing regulatory norms.[102] Here, we see differentiation between legal levels specifying regulatory strategies (approximating norms) versus approaches (approximating implementation). In the current context, treaties, EU Directives, and constitutional provisions in areas of shared competence usually set out norms and frameworks that lower-level laws implement.[103] Sometimes a treaty or EU directive specifies a regulatory strategy (i.e., the norm) and allows the party to the treaty or member state to determine the regulatory approach to deliver it, expressed as relevant "measures", "plans" or "instruments"[104] (i.e., implementation). This is also evidenced by the higher-level instruments that leave their regulatory approach unspecified (Table 10.1). The EU CAP Regulation offers member states less discretion

[101] Constitution of the Italian Republic, art. 118; Barsotti and others, *Italian Constitutional Justice*, 199–202; Erika Arban, "Re-Centralizing Subsidiarity: Interpretations by the Italian Constitutional Court" (2015) 25 *Regional and Federal Studies* 129–144, 134–137; van Zeben, "Subsidiarity," 417–419.

[102] van Zeben, "Subsidiarity," 416, 434–435.

[103] Ibid. See Section 10.2. Italy's constitutional amendment to include environmental protection as a fundamental principle (note Table 10.1, note xxv) prompted the appointment in late 2023 of a commission of experts to revise the national environment code, but no reforms had been introduced at the time of writing.

[104] Bern Wildlife Convention, art. 4(1); Biodiversity Convention, art. 8(f); European Landscape Convention, art. 6(E).

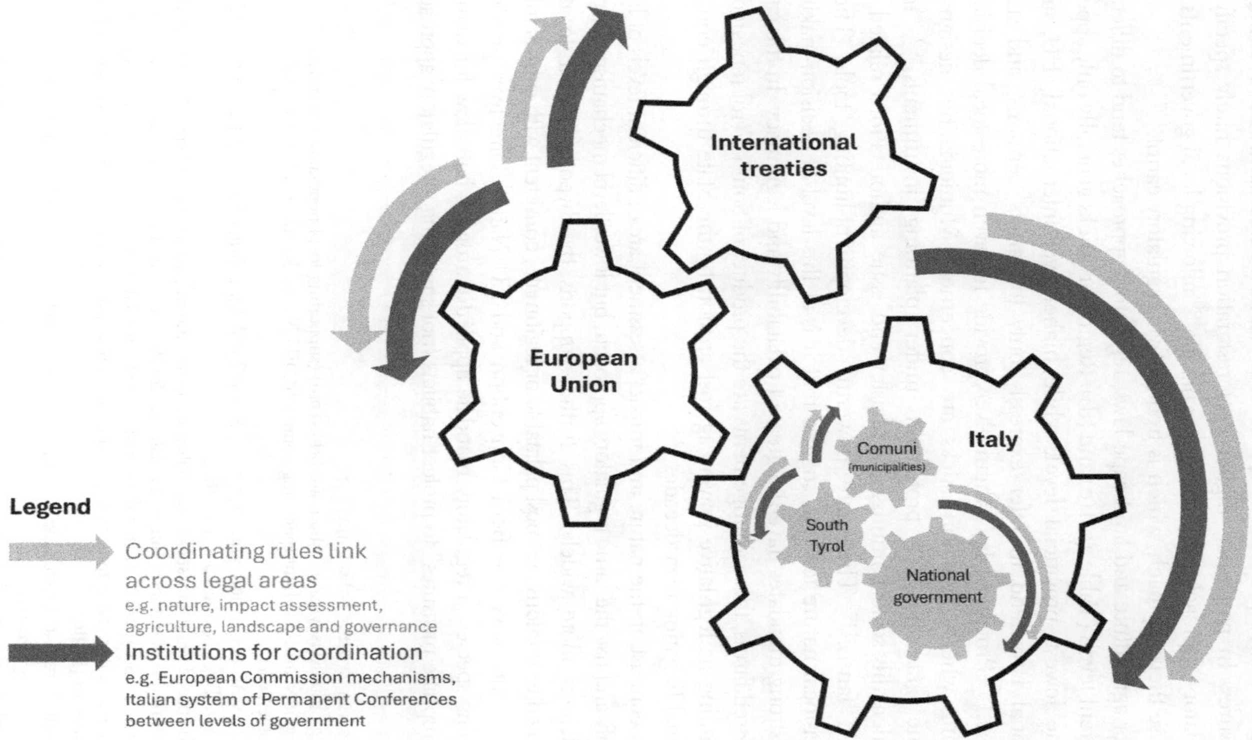

FIGURE 10.1 Coordination for protecting and restoring Alpine grasslands in South Tyrol: key government actors and mechanisms for interaction

compared to directives,[105] but still relies on member states implementing it using a strategic plan to set objectives, allocate resources, and select voluntary measures. In particular, higher-level restoration provisions rarely specify a regulatory approach, implicitly or explicitly[106] allowing local governments to choose their approach, which is frequently a regulatory carrot.[107]

For agriculture and landscape laws, regulatory approaches tend to differ at different levels (Table 10.1(c) and (d)). Regulatory sticks generally only appear at the lowest, provincial level, while higher-level international, EU, and national laws tend to refer expressly only to carrots, sermons, and state rescue.[108] Provincial laws themselves provide for even more local decision-making where regulatory sticks are concerned: Municipalities designate Alpine grasslands for protection under planning instruments,[109] and municipality-scale commissions register and issue authorizations related to closed farms.[110] These are powerful development-limiting tools. Their hyper-local nature tends to suggest that it is at this level of decision-making that strong mandates have the greatest palatability and legitimacy. In the case of closed farms, these arrangements are the product of South Tyrol repeatedly defending its legislative powers against erosion by the State through constitutional litigation over decades.[111]

By contrast, in the nature and impact assessment areas, different levels of law specify and use the same regulatory approach, but lower-level mechanisms apply restrictions more widely. This further supports the hypothesis that locally imposed restrictions are most palatable or legitimate, consistent with subsidiarity. Take nature laws: the Bern Convention and EU Nature Directives prohibit harming species (a regulatory mandate applied narrowly), but allow for vaguer "appropriate measures" to protect habitats (not specifying a regulatory approach

105 See van Zeben, "Subsidiarity," 425.

106 E.g., Biodiversity Convention, art. 8(f), 10(d) (supporting local populations to restore degraded areas, without specifying approach); EU Nature Restoration Law (see note v to Table 10.1).

107 E.g., CAP Regulation, arts. 31, 70, 71; South Tyrol Agricultural Incentive Law, art. 4(1)(f); South Tyrol Nature Law, arts. 26, 27.

108 The use of regulatory sticks (mandates) in nature and impact assessment laws does not greatly disturb this observation, since mandates under these laws are framed in narrow and often discretionary ways. Note that the mandate under the EU CAP replicates the requirements of the EU Nature Directives, rather than representing a new mandate: CAP Regulation, art. 12, annex III (SMRs).

109 South Tyrol Landscape Law, arts. 13(2), 14, 65 (protecting entails obtaining an authorization for certain activities).

110 South Tyrol Closed Farm Law, arts. 3(1) (e.g., to establish a closed farm), 7 (e.g. authorization and conditions for aggregating closed farms), 39, 42.

111 Poggeschi, "South Tyrol's Special Status in Private Law," 295–298.

for this wider subject matter).[112] On the other hand, South Tyrol's Nature Law, which implements the EU Nature Directives, prohibits harm to both species and natural habitats in Natura 2000 sites, and also imposes outright prohibitions on specific uses such as quarries and wind farms.[113] Accordingly, we see a nuanced version of subsidiarity at work across this complex network of interventions, despite the initial appearance of duplication.

10.4.2.2 Mutually Reinforcing Legal Links

Express regulatory links between areas of law reinforce grassland protection mechanisms and allow one area of law to "borrow" a regulatory approach used in another. Thus, impact assessment laws support the protection of habitats protected under nature and landscape laws.[114] Nature laws allow complementary agricultural activities in protected areas,[115] and expressly seek synergies between nature and agricultural law interventions.[116] Agriculture laws reward nature-promoting practices and compensate for nature-related restrictions that apply in protected areas.[117] At the EU level, the CAP expressly emphasizes the need for complementarity across CAP mechanisms, other EU interventions, and member states' other relevant instruments.[118]

Sometimes these reinforcing links correct a previous problem, where one law undermined another. This occurred in 2013, when, to address criticisms that the CAP had encouraged environmental damage,[119] a revised EU CAP first imposed a plowing ban and 5 percent limit on grassland loss for

[112] Bern Wildlife Convention, arts. 4(1), 5; Habitats Directive, arts. 6(1), 12, 13.

[113] South Tyrol Nature Law, art. 21(3), (4)(c), (d).

[114] E.g., EIA Directive, arts. 3(b), 4(3), ann. III(2)(c)(v), (viii).

[115] See 71 and 73.

[116] E.g., EU Nature Restoration Law, art. 14(10) (member state nature restoration plans "shall identify synergies with agriculture and forestry ... including CAP interventions, that contribute to the objectives of this Regulation"); 15(3)(c) (expressly drawing out measures intended for Natura 2000 sites in national restoration plans), 15(5) (national restoration plan to describe "the interplay between the measures included in the national restoration plan and the national CAP strategic plan").

[117] E.g., CAP Regulation, arts. 31, 70–72; Italian Agricultural Recognition Law, arts. 2–10; South Tyrol Agricultural Incentive Law, arts. 1, 4(1)(f).

[118] CAP Regulation arts. 118(2) (re approval of CAP Strategic Plan), 139(3)(b) (coherence with other instruments). See also preambular notes (101) and (102) in the CAP Regulation as originally passed.

[119] Cuadros-Casanova and others, "Opportunities and Challenges for Common Agricultural Policy Reform," 3, 7; European Environment Agency, *State of Nature in the EU*, 126 (EU 2020 Biodiversity Strategy target 3A), 132; Brian Jack, "Ecosystem Services: European Agricultural Law and Rural Development" in Massimo Monteduro and others (eds), *Law and Agroecology: A Transdisciplinary Dialogue* (Springer 2015) 127–150, 131, 137.

subsidized farmers.[120] Concerns remain, however, that few grasslands are deemed "sensitive" and attract protections[121] – that is (to use the language of Chapter 6), interventions are insufficiently comprehensive due to gaps by omission.[122]

These integrating links between laws in different areas reinforce or bring in more regulatory approaches to support nature objectives than nature laws alone provide. Carrots under agriculture laws support and reinforce the same approach under EU nature laws (Table 10.1(a), (c)). Funded state rescue powers under governance laws assist nature laws that generally lack this regulatory approach (Table 10.1(a), (e)). This borrowing of regulatory approaches between legal areas is only possible because, whether by luck or design, laws in different areas express coherent regulatory strategies: Nature laws and impact assessment laws focus on conserving, protecting, minimizing disturbing, and so on, nature, biodiversity, or grassland species and habitats;[123] so do agriculture laws[124] and governance and landscape laws.[125] It is important to note, though, that this picture of relative harmony does not account for other laws beyond the present scope that may incentivize developments and activities, such as tourism, with the potential for conflicting outcomes; nor does it compare the economic rewards of industrialized agriculture to subsidies for traditional grazing.

In some cases, regulatory approaches are duplicated across government levels, as has also been observed for some aspects of climate change policy in South Tyrol.[126] In this case, redundancy has usefully insured against regulatory changes at one level, promoting regulatory stability through a different government (here, the Province) acting as a "norm sustainer."[127]

[120] See n 75 and accompanying text.

[121] Cuadros-Casanova and others, "Opportunities and Challenges for Common Agricultural Policy Reform," 4 (citations omitted).

[122] See Section 6.5.2.1.

[123] E.g., Biodiversity Convention, arts. 6(a), 8(a), 14(1)(a); Bern Wildlife Convention, arts. 4(1), 5; Habitats Directive, art. 6(1), (2), annexes I ("semi-natural dry grasslands"), II; South Tyrol Nature Law, arts. 14, 21(3); SEA Directive, arts 3, 5(1), ann. I point (d), (f); South Tyrol EIA/SEA Law, arts. 10(3), 17(1) (drawing on EU and national laws).

[124] CAP Regulation, art. 6(1)(f); Italian Agricultural Recognition Law, art. 2(1)(a), (f); South Tyrol Agricultural Incentive Law, art. 4(1)(f) (environmental improvement generally). See also Table 7.3 and accompanying text.

[125] E.g., Alpine Convention, art. 2(2)(b), (f); Nature Protection Protocol, arts. 10(1), 11; Italian Small Municipalities Law, art. 3(3)(h), South Tyrol Landscape Law, arts. 13(2)(c), (d).

[126] Federica Cittadino and others, "Which Factors Influence Climate Policy Integration?" in Federica Cittadino and others (eds), *Climate Change Integration in the Multilevel Governance of Italy and Austria: Shaping Subnational Policies in the Transport, Energy, and Spatial Planning Sectors* (Brill Nijhoff 2023) 251–279, 260.

[127] See Section 2.2.4.1.

After months of farmers' protests, in April 2024, the European Parliament – with Italy's Prime Minister a key supporter – weakened environmental aspects of the EU CAP.[128] The amendments exempt farms of up to ten hectares from enhanced conditionality requirements, so that exempt farmers can receive payments even if they plow sensitive grasslands or breach the 5 percent loss limit.[129] This would exempt, at minimum, around 40 percent of South Tyrol's farms.[130] By any measure, this exemption significantly reduces the comprehensiveness of the CAP intervention by expanding "gaps by exemptions," a key risk for cumulative environmental problems.[131] Yet, South Tyrol's provincial incentives, municipally driven landscape laws and Closed Farm law remain, continuing to disincentivize and control grassland destruction.

10.4.2.3 Coordinating through Institutions and to Resolve Conflict: The Example of Natura 2000

Multilevel institutions that operate between the European and Italian levels and between the Italian State and the regions and autonomous provinces are also key to coordinating the implementation of regulatory mechanisms relevant to South Tyrol's grasslands. This is illustrated by the context of Natura 2000 sites, which are widely used in protecting Italy's Alpine grasslands.[132] Protected areas have been a prominent and somewhat fraught issue in the relationship between the Italian State and autonomous provinces, sitting in the "gray zone" of interlocking legislative powers.[133] The much-litigated Italian constitutional principle of loyal cooperation provides for the involvement of each level in the decision-making of the other "in order to prevent unilateral intervention into the sphere of competence of the other side, respectively."[134] As discussed further later, the *intesa* (multilevel coordinating

[128] See generally, Nikolina Šajn, "Regulation Amending CAP Strategic Plans Regulation and CAP Horizontal Regulation" (*European Parliament*, May 2024) www.europarl.europa.eu/legislative-train/theme-a-european-green-deal/file-targeted-amendments-of-cap-regulations, archived at https://perma.cc/5DUT-YHZE.

[129] Ibid.

[130] Servadei and others, *La Politica di Sviluppo Rurale*, 164.

[131] See Section 6.5.2.2.

[132] See n 25 and accompanying text.

[133] See Section 10.3.2.

[134] Constitution of the Republic of Italy, 1947, as amended, art. 120(2); Jens Woelk, "Loyal Cooperation: Systemic Principle of Italy's Regionalism?" in Erika Arban, Giuseppe Martinico and Francesco Palermo (eds), *Federalism and Constitutional Law: The Italian Contribution to Comparative Regionalism* (Routledge 2021) 170–188, 173.

agreement) and coordinating institutions are key ways of operationalizing the principle,[135] though the *intesa* appears to be used less where the primary legislative competence lies with the State (e.g., in environmental protection) than with the province (e.g., nature parks).[136]

Natura 2000 sites are discussed here using the example of a major grassland area in South Tyrol, the Texelgruppe Nature Park ("Texelgruppe"), which accounts for two of South Tyrol's forty-four Natura 2000 sites.[137] Texelgruppe supports ibex, golden eagles, pygmy owls, rare herbs, and some of the highest-altitude settlements in the Alps, and has been grazed for centuries.[138]

Texelgruppe's journey to becoming a Natura 2000 site illustrates the challenges of vertical coordination in Italy's implementation of the Habitats Directive. Problems arose early, when Italy's national protected area law failed to meet requirements to transpose the Habitats Directive. This triggered a European Commission warning and ultimately a new national transposing law.[139]

The designation, management, and assessment of proposed impacts on Natura 2000 sites also struck difficulties that coordination mechanisms have largely resolved. Under the Habitats Directive, member states designate Natura 2000 sites in a multistage process that involves interacting with the Commission and meeting regulatory deadlines.[140] In Italy, it also involves a multilevel exercise that varies by region. Italy's national protected areas law sets out principles and requires agreement with an autonomous province in relation to designating nationally and internationally important protected areas, while the province itself designates areas of regional and local

[135] Ibid 177, 181–182; for an overview of coordinating institutions (standing conferences, joint commissions), see: Niccolò Bertuzzi, Peter Bußjäger and Alice Meier, "Coordination and Leadership" in Federica Cittadino and others (eds), *Climate Change Integration in the Multilevel Governance of Italy and Austria: Shaping Subnational Policies in the Transport, Energy, and Spatial Planning Sectors* (Brill Nijhoff 2023) 165–192, 167–170.

[136] Obwexer and Happacher, *Parere Legale*, 239.

[137] Autonomous Province of South Tyrol, "Siti Natura 2000 in Alto Adige" (n.d.) https://natura-territorio.provincia.bz.it/it/siti-natura-2000-in-alto-adige, last accessed March 23, 2025, archived at https://perma.cc/SG64-VL6U.

[138] European Environment Agency, "Val di Fosse nel Parco Naturale Gruppo di Tessa: IT3110011" (March 12, 2024) https://natura2000.eea.europa.eu/Natura2000/SDF.aspx?site=IT3110011, archived at https://perma.cc/XZW9-RSLW.

[139] Decreto del Presidente della Repubblica 8 settembre 1997, n. 357, Regolamento recante attuazione della direttiva 92/43/CEE relativa alla conservazione degli habitat natuali e seminaturali, nonchè della flora e della fauna selvatiche [Presidential Decree on regulations implementing Directive 92/43/EEC on the conservation of natural and semi-natural habitats and of wild fauna and flora].

[140] Habitats Directive, art. 4.

interest.[141] The designation of the Texelgruppe sites was initiated by South Tyrol in 1995 after it entered an agreement with the Italian State to join an EU-funded and NGO-supported project to propose sites.[142] The designation process for Texelgruppe was only completed in 2016, after much delay.[143] In the meantime, in 2003, the province approved a municipality's request to alter the park's boundaries to exclude an area of proposed infrastructure for a ski area, snow-making system, and hydroelectric plant.[144] This boundary change effectively reconceptualized a core dimension of the matter of concern to avoid development constraints – a risk to which an earlier chapter adverted.[145]

Delay in fully designating sites produced two formal infringement proceedings against Italy, neither of which is fully resolved[146] (South Tyrol still has four incomplete designations). Nonetheless, these proceedings, and the larger enforcement policy that they advance, illustrate useful points from the perspective of intervention and coordination to address cumulative environmental problems. Formal infringement proceedings involve institutional coordination through escalating interactions between the Commission and a member state, which ultimately ends in the European Court of Justice.[147] In choosing when to bring proceedings, the Commission's strategic approach implicitly targets cumulative impacts of noncompliance: It focuses on the general interest, many individual "misapplications" and

141 Italian Framework Law on Protected Areas, art. 2(6), (8). See also n 51 and accompanying text.

142 Ferranti, Beunen and Speranza, "Natura 2000 Network," 302; Autonomous Province of South Tyrol, *Misure per la Conservazione e la Valorizzazione della Zona Speciale di Conservazione (ZSC) Val di Fosse nel Parco Naturale Gruppo di Tessa* (undated) 3–4, https://natur-raum.provinz.bz.it/it/siti-natura-2000-in-alto-adige, last accessed March 23, 2025, archived at https://perma.cc/PTJ6-SNAL.

143 European Environment Agency, "Val di Fosse nel Parco Naturale Gruppo di Tessa: IT3110011"; European Environment Agency, "Lacines – Catena del Monteneve nel Parco Naturale Gruppo di Tessa: IT3110012" (March 12, 2024) https://natura2000.eea.europa.eu/Natura2000/SDF.aspx?site=IT3110012, archived at https://perma.cc/V4PL-3KQV.

144 *Natura 2000 Piano di Gestione: Parco Naturale Gruppo di Tessa* (Provincia Autonoma di Bolzano – Alto Adige undated) 6, https://static.provinz.bz.it/natur-raum/managementplaene/Piano%20di%20gestione%20Parco%20naturale%20Gruppo%20di%20Tessa.pdf, archived at https://perma.cc/BXR2-NAHE.

145 See Section 4.3.2.

146 INFR(2015)2163 and INFR(2021)2028; status as of June 2024, available at European Commission, "Environmental Infringements Map and Dashboard" (n.d.) https://environment.ec.europa.eu/law-and-governance/environmental-implementation-review_en#environmental-infringements-map-and-dashboard (select search > country as "Italy," infringement status as "active," topic as "nature").

147 See European Commission, "Enforcement: Frequently Asked Questions" (November 28, 2022) https://ec.europa.eu/commission/presscorner/detail/en/MEMO_12_12, archived at https://perma.cc/9K8Q-8LLE.

"systemic shortcomings" rather than single instances of noncompliance or individual redress.[148]

Ongoing administration of designated Natura 2000 sites also involves coordination in relation to management and impact assessment. The management committee for Texelgruppe includes representatives of the province, municipalities, scientific experts, and farmers' associations.[149] National guidelines apply to ongoing site management,[150] but regions/provinces formulate conservation objectives and management plans for individual sites. South Tyrol's formal conservation objectives for Texelgruppe recognize intensive agriculture, farm abandonment, and sporting and recreational activities as key threats.[151] The management plan prescribes measures including incentives for extensive grazing, controlling forest spread, restoring abandoned meadows through resuming grazing or mowing, and measures for sustainable tourism,[152] addressing each of the key drivers of grassland degradation discussed earlier.

Assessing how proposed projects will affect Italy's Natura 2000 sites has also proven controversial, and illustrates rules and institutions for dispute resolution among the EU, Italian, and subnational levels.[153] Triggered by complaints from environmental NGOs that Italy used inappropriate impact assessment processes (or none at all), the Commission commenced a pre-infringement "Pilot" process in 2014.[154] This process involves the Commission and a member state informally interacting to resolve a complaint about inadequacies in implementing EU law.[155] In 2019, another informal

148 European Commission, Enforcing EU Law for a Europe That Delivers, COM(2022) 518 (2022) 20, https://eur-lex.europa.eu/legal-content/EN/TXT/?uri=celex:52022DC0518.

149 Autonomous Province of South Tyrol, "Parco naturale Gruppo di Tessa" (n. d.) https://parchi-naturali.provincia.bz.it/it/parco-naturale-gruppo-di-tessa, last accessed May 23, 2025, archived at https://perma.cc/5LQ8-8J3M.

150 Decreto Ministeriale (Ministro dell'Ambiente e della Tutela del Territorio) 3 settembre 2002, "Linee guida per la gestione dei siti Natura 2000" [Ministerial decree of the Ministry of the Environment and Protection of the Territory, Guidelines for the management of Natura 2000 sites], www.ecology.unibo.it/baiona/pg/Linee%20guida%20per%20la%20gestione%20dei%20siti%20Natura%202000.pdf, archived at https://perma.cc/5QX9-A69V.

151 Autonomous Province of South Tyrol, *Misure per la Conservazione … Val di Fosse*, 5.

152 Ibid 7–8.

153 Formal proceedings were also instituted in relation to Italy's designation of Natura 2000 sites: see note 146 and accompanying text.

154 Gruppo Intervento Giuridico, "La Commissione Europea Insiste nella sua Indagine sulla Cattiva Applicazione della Valutazione di Incidenza Ambientale in Italia" (May 17, 2015) https://gruppodinterventogiuridicoweb.com/2015/05/17/la-commissione-europea-insiste-nella-sua-indagine-sulla-cattiva-applicazione-della-valutazione-di-incidenza-ambientale-in-italia/, archived at https://perma.cc/WNY5-4V73.

155 See David Hadroušek, "Speeding up Infringement Procedures: Recent Developments Designed to Make Infringement Procedures More Effective" (2012) 9 *Journal for European Environmental and Planning Law* 235–256, 245–247, 251–252. The subject proceeding was EU PILOT 6730/14/ENVI.

arrangement – the Commission's biannual assessment of how effectively member states implement EU environmental laws – recommended that Italy prioritize adopting and implementing new national guidelines for assessing impacts on Natura 2000 sites.[156] Concerns about coordination influenced both the establishment of this assessment process in general[157] and the Commission's recommendations to Italy.[158]

These interactions ultimately led to new Italian implementation guidelines following a multilevel *intesa* process. This agreement between the Italian national and subnational governments was negotiated over thirteen meetings held over three years[159] under the auspices of Italy's peak intergovernmental coordination institution, the Standing Conference for the Relations between the State, the Regions, and the Autonomous Provinces of Trento and Bolzano ("Standing Conference").[160] In environmental matters, the Standing Conference is advised by multi-ministry, multilevel technical working groups, which also include NGOs.[161] The new guidelines consider cumulative impacts at multiple stages[162] and expressly recognize that assessing cumulative impacts requires coordination.[163]

Scholars lament the slowness and feebleness of the Standing Conference[164] and the weak incentives for environmental cooperation produced by the

156 Directorate-General for Environment (European Commission), The EU Environmental Implementation Review 2019 Country Report – Italy, SWD/2019/123 final/2 (Commission Staff Working Document) (2019) 14, https://eur-lex.europa.eu/legal-content/EN/TXT/?uri=celex:52019SC0123R(01).

157 European Commission, Communication from the Commission to the European Parliament, the Council, the European Economic and Social Committee, and the Committee of the Regions: Delivering the Benefits of EU Environmental Policies through a Regular Environmental Implementation Review, COM(2016) 316 (2016) 3, https://eur-lex.europa.eu/legal-content/EN/TXT/?uri=COM:2016:316:FIN.

158 Elisa Cardarelli and others, "Italy" in Graham Tucker (ed), *Nature Conservation in Europe: Approaches and Lessons* (CUP 2023) 415–433, 424.

159 Conferenza Permanente per i rapporti tra lo Stato, le Regioni e le Province Autonome di Trento e Bolzano [Standing Conference for the Relations between the State, the Regions and the Autonomous Provinces of Trento and Bolzano] ("Standing Conference"), Intesa 28 novembre 2019, Gazzetta Ufficiale n. 303 of December 28, 2019, 22–130 ("Agreement of November 28, 2019").

160 Ibid 24.

161 Cardarelli and others, *Italy*, 417–418.

162 Standing Conference, *Agreement of November 28, 2019*, 40, 43, 57, 59.

163 Ibid 21.

164 Cardarelli and others, *Italy*, 430; Eleonora Ceccherini, "Intergovernmental Relationships in Italy: A Feeble but Useful Model" in Erika Arban, Giuseppe Martinico and Francesco Palermo (eds), *Federalism and Constitutional Law: The Italian Contribution to Comparative Regionalism* (Routledge 2021) 65–81, 69–72, 76–80.

Constitutional Court's centralizing tendencies.[165] In this case, though, combined with informal EU nudges, the Standing Conference succeeded. And while the use of multilevel agreements may be cumbersome, it secures a good degree of transparency. Whether all regions will adopt the guidelines, as agreed,[166] and whether this improves assessments and outcomes for Natura 2000 sites, remains to be seen.

10.5 CONCLUSION

At the intersection of natural and cultural landscapes, many legal layers provide for diverse interventions to protect and restore South Tyrol's Alpine grasslands, across legal areas focused on nature, impact assessment, agriculture, landscape, and governance. Their intervention mechanisms adopt different regulatory approaches aimed at diverse contributors to the cumulative environmental problem: subsidizing farmers to maintain grasslands, restricting landowners and developers from converting grassland to other uses, restricting owners of "closed farms" from subdividing and modifying agricultural practices and farm structures, funding municipalities to restore grasslands, and enabling consumers to support mountain farmers.

There are substantial synergies among these multilevel regulations. They coherently point in the same direction: maintain grasslands. They do not do so with uniform strength, though. Compared to mechanisms that advance a harm-reducing strategy, those with a restoration focus rely on weaker voluntary regulatory approaches – though the implementation of the June 2024 EU Nature Restoration Law may change this in the future. However, express integrating links between areas of law bring in regulatory reinforcements and allow for "borrowing" of different regulatory approaches to pursue the same objectives. The practice of multilevel regulation results in lower-level laws being comparatively more restrictive than higher-level laws in the areas of agriculture and landscape. This perhaps reflects the greater political sensitivity of direct farm- and land use–related mandates, requiring local government acceptance.

A theme of coordination runs through these links between laws, and the multilevel institutions and enforcement processes they engage, illustrated by Natura 2000 arrangements. We see formal and informal multilevel dispute

[165] Alberton, "Swing of Intergovernmental Relations," 38.

[166] See generally, Mario Castorina and others, "La Valutazione di Incidenza Ambientale (VIncA) nella Normativa Regionale Italiana (Seconda Ricognizione)" (*Association of Environmental Analysts, LIPU, WWF*, October 17, 2022) www.analistiambientali.org/vinca-report-associazioni-normativa-regionale/, archived at https://perma.cc/9GRR-Y7EN.

resolution mechanisms, general and special-purpose ongoing committees and working groups, and a process of formal agreement-making, all against a backdrop of contestation and litigation about legal competences between the autonomous province and the Italian State. But it seems that it is exactly this contestation, produced by blurred constitutional boundaries, that has produced such a rich range of coordinating rules and institutions.

Emerging issues beyond the scope of this chapter further highlight the need for coordination to address potential conflicts that could pose problems of inconsistency between interventions. These include restoration efforts that may require modifying Italy's forestry laws, which generally protect all forests;[167] and rewilding initiatives to reintroduce large carnivores, which are perceived to disincentivize traditional grazing, despite provisions to mitigate livestock losses.[168]

South Tyrol's grasslands fare comparatively well, but the precise contribution of this supporting regulatory system to that outcome is uncertain. South Tyrol's unique circumstances – comparative wealth, autonomy and greater political power, and foundational cultural norms – likely support implementing these laws as well as providing capacity and independent motivation to protect grasslands. Nonetheless, the experience in South Tyrol offers insights to other areas that face challenges of deeply multilevel governance, a biocultural matter of concern (take New Mexico's acequias,[169] or traditional savanna burning by Australia's First Nations[170]), or one that requires active management or restoration to address a cumulative environmental problem. It also underscores the potential strategic benefits of addressing cumulative environmental problems through mechanisms that span natural and cultural spheres, harnessing a wider and more diverse range of intervention mechanisms.

[167] Mauro Agnoletti and others, "Monitoring Traditional Rural Landscapes: The Case of Italy" (2019) 11:6107 *Sustainability* 1–19, 3.

[168] Cristina Stuffer and Urban Perkmann, "Il Futuro dell'Alpicoltura in Alto Adige: Sfide e Opportunita dal Punto di Vista delle Aziende Alpicole" (*Camera di Commercio, Industria, Artigianato e Agricoltura di Bolzano*, 2023) 8, www.wifo.bz.it/it/temi/studi-e-analisi/155-il-futuro-dell-alpicoltura-in-alto-adige-sfide-e-opportunita-dal-punto-di-vista-delle-aziende-alpicole.html, archived at https://perma.cc/FBQ4-PS4J.

[169] See generally, Enrique R. Lamadrid and José A. Rivera (eds), *Water for the People: The Acequia Heritage of New Mexico in a Global Context* (University of New Mexico Press 2023).

[170] Peter J. Whitehead, *Indigenous Livelihoods: Background Paper* (NAILSMA Knowledge Series, North Australian Indigenous Land and Sea Management Alliance 2012) 57–59, https://nailsma.org.au/uploads/resources/KS-011-Indigenous-Livelihoods-background-paper-Whitehead.pdf, archived at https://perma.cc/9YSR-5Y9R.

11

Design for Regulating a Thousand Cuts

Summary Guidance and Concluding Reflections

This guidance presents the key insights about designing **formal rules to deal with cumulative environmental problems** from the ten substantive chapters of this book. It is aimed at readers who work with laws and regulations in government agencies or as consultants, community advocates, or researchers, and who are considering how to improve those laws to better deal with cumulative impacts.

11.1 CUMULATIVE ENVIRONMENTAL PROBLEMS AND THE IMPORTANCE OF FORMAL RULES

Cumulative environmental problems are those that are caused by **many diverse actors** undertaking **diverse activities**, engaging **multiple regulatory regimes** that often deal with single natural resources (such as biodiversity, or water pollution), and where the **effects aggregate relatively slowly** in **scientifically complex and sometimes unpredictable ways**. Cumulative environmental problems are the result of "a thousand cuts" (figuratively) to something we care about, inflicted by many, sometimes unknowingly.

The three case studies in this book (for more details, see Section 11.5) illustrate the diverse scales and natures of these problems:

- Long-term overpumping for farms and cities has caused groundwater levels to decline and wells to go dry for some populations that lack other sources of water in California's Central Valley (Chapter 8).
- The health of a large, biodiverse, and beautiful coral reef is declining due to diverse impacts caused by many actors, from water pollution to climate change, and legacy effects from land management long ago (Australia's Great Barrier Reef, Chapter 9).

- The ecological and cultural values of Alpine meadows are threatened by the abandonment of traditional grazing practices that have maintained them for thousands of years, combined with many small developments (South Tyrol, northern Italy, Chapter 10).

While these problems are diverse, they suffer common challenges because of their key characteristics: many and diverse actors and activities; relatively slow, scientifically complex, and potentially uncertain aggregation; and links to multiple regulatory regimes. Many environmental problems have these aspects to varying degrees; this book focuses on problems in which these aspects are especially pronounced.

What Are "Formal Rules"?

As discussed here, formal rules appear in laws, regulations, and some formal policies. Critically, they are not just rules that try to influence behavior. Formal rules can – and should – also facilitate defining what matters for protection or restoration; collecting, sharing, and analyzing data and information, and coordinating different actors.

A foundational premise of this book is that for cumulative environmental problems, **adequate management is unlikely to arise informally, without intentional design**. Multidisciplinary research reported in this book (Chapter 2) suggests that many factors act as barriers to effective management. Effective action requires clarifying several dimensions of what we care about, which engages value-rich, subjective issues and the potential for contestation and inadvertent changes through time. Political, commercial, and community concerns and costs disincentivize generating, sharing, and aggregating the information that is needed to understand and respond to the problem. Risk perception, a sense of futility, ethical ambiguity, path dependence, and short-termism stand in the way of intervention. And the number and diversity of relevant actors and government silos mean that cooperation is unlikely to arise organically or be sustained through time.

Regulatory systems can anticipate and be designed to surmount these barriers and promote the conditions for addressing these problems. Synthesizing these challenges produces a framework of key interlinking functions that rules can be designed to support to help address cumulative environmental problems: conceptualization, information, regulatory intervention, and coordination (the "CIRCle Framework"). But – a caution and a disclaimer. **Good design does not guarantee a cure**. Formal rules have a unique and important role to play, but they may not be the whole solution to cumulative environmental problems. Introducing, implementing, and enforcing formal rules is rarely straightforward and trouble free. Many important issues lie outside the realm of what rules can solve, such as insufficient resources, loss of institutional knowledge, or difficult relationships with stakeholders or other agencies. Conversely, without careful design, rules may be part of the problem.

11.2 USING THIS GUIDANCE

This guidance does not prescribe specific rules to support each CIRCle Framework function. This necessarily depends on local context. Rather, it prescribes questions and considerations. **Practitioners can use these questions to diagnose gaps and other problems to improve existing rules, or to plan new rules.**

A practitioner might use this guidance in different situations, including when a cumulative environmental problem is possible, predicted, manifest, or critical, or when a formal scheduled review of a law or regulation is required. In many cases, some form of regulation will already exist to influence the problem. In other cases, perhaps in jurisdictions that are at an early stage of developing their environment-related laws, responding to a problem will require considering whether to introduce entirely new laws.

This guidance draws attention to "red flags" () that suggest addressing certain issues is likely to be needed. It also highlights key challenges associated with each function, and types of regulatory mechanisms () that can support dealing with that challenge. The Framework function chapters of this book (Chapters 4–7) provide numerous illustrative examples of these mechanisms. The case studies (Chapters 8–10) illustrate and analyze how these mechanisms can come together in a legal regime. This guidance includes cross-references to these chapters for more information ().

This book deals with a broad variety of environment-related laws across many jurisdictions globally. Because practitioners in different contexts often use different words to describe similar broad concepts, this book adopts terminology that is intended to be context-neutral and applicable in diverse situations (see Glossary).

While the examples given in this book attempt to reflect geographic and jurisdictional diversity, and innovative approaches emerge from around the world, jurisdictions with larger economies are overrepresented. If you are considering this guidance in the context of a less industrialized or smaller jurisdiction, you may need to give more emphasis to issues such as resourcing and local capacity,[1] but you also may benefit from less entrenched legal silos and less sprawling government bureaucracies.

11.3 THE CIRCLE FRAMEWORK FOR ANALYZING RULES

There are many government frameworks of "best practice principles" for regulating public policy problems in general. **This book offers a more targeted framework of four "best practice functions" that a regulatory system should deliver** to best support action to address cumulative environmental problems: **conceptualization** of the thing that matters ("matter of concern") and the conditions that should be protected or restored; **information** about the matter of concern and threats to it; **intervention** to influence human activities and other factors that impact the matter of concern; and **coordination** between agencies and levels of government, and between government and nongovernment actors in relation to each of the other three functions. Each function is important, and its absence would pose a key risk to effectively addressing a cumulative environmental problem (Table 11.1). In addition, each function integrates with all the others, and these linkages are key (Figure 11.1), see integration notes ( ) in text that follows.

This Framework was developed deductively, based on cross-disciplinary research about challenges, and refined inductively by considering numerous real-world examples of rules, many of which are presented as illustrative examples in this book.

11.4 APPLYING THE CIRCLE FRAMEWORK

The CIRCle Framework provides a structure for evaluating gaps and weaknesses in legal regimes for dealing with cumulative environmental problems. It is not designed to provide "the answer" to filling gaps and strengthening weaknesses, though Chapters 4 to 7 provide many sources of relevant legal inspiration drawn from 73 jurisdictions across 55 countries around the world. The following steps are a guide to applying the Framework, and a basis for discussions among agencies and stakeholders.

[1] E.g., see generally, Caroline Morris (ed), *Making and Changing Law in Small Jurisdictions* (Springer 2024).

TABLE 11.1 *Definitions and risks of rules omitting a CIRCle Framework function*

Brief definition of best practice function	Key risks if function is absent
Conceptualization: Rules clearly and coherently define or provide a process for defining the matter of concern in terms of spatial extent, what elements of it are important, and what level of change is unacceptable, and therefore constitutes a cumulative environmental problem.	• No clear focus or goal to guide action to prevent unacceptable change; • Contestation about goals; and • Information collection, intervention and coordination are not focused on addressing the same thing.
Information: Rules provide for collecting, sharing, aggregating, and analyzing data and information about the condition of the matter of concern, impacts, predicted future conditions due to cumulative impacts, and interventions.	A legal regime is ineffective because its implementation: • overlooks the emergence of the cumulative environmental problem, or • misunderstands the severity or causes of the problem, or • falsely assumes enough is being done to address the problem.
Regulatory intervention: Rules provide for influencing the behavior of contributors to cumulative harm or otherwise addressing impacts or creating benefits, using diverse regulatory approaches and strategies to match the different circumstances of the problem and of contributors to harm.	Unacceptable cumulative harm does not trigger intervention, or adequate intervention, so: • impacts continue to grow, and • unacceptable impacts remain.
Coordination: Laws provide for interaction between and across levels of government and with nongovernment stakeholders in carrying out functions related to conceptualization, information and intervention.	A legal regime has gaps, antagonistic features, or inefficient duplication in relation to conceptualization, information or regulatory intervention, and lacks useful ways to resolve disputes.

Preliminary step: Identify your cumulative environmental problem and related rules and actors

First, identify, in broad terms, the thing that you are concerned to protect or restore, or perhaps create: your "matter of concern." This might be one or more of:

- A species or place, for example, an ibex, a sacred site, a national park, a river basin, or a mountain range;

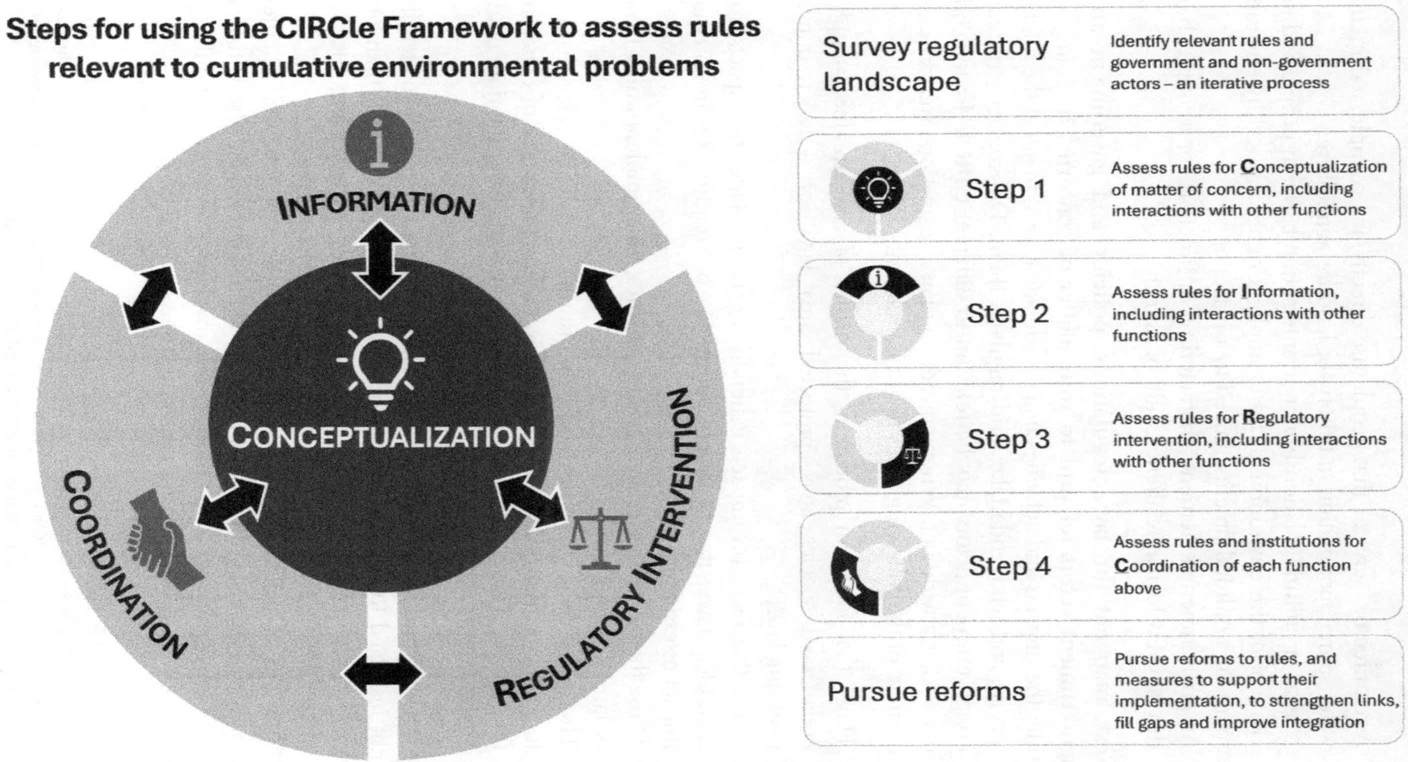

FIGURE 11.1 Applying the CIRCle Framework: integrated regulatory functions needed to address cumulative environmental problems

- A resource or "service" that people use directly, for example, a drinking water source, pollination, a fishery, or land for agriculture;
- A legal or cultural relationship or an interaction between people and an element of the environment, for example, a right to a healthy environment, or a cultural practice linked to a place; or
- An environmental element, characteristic or function, for example, biodiversity, ecological resilience, soil, or climate.

Next, map out the laws, regulations, policies, and government and nongovernment actors relevant to your matter of concern.[2] In doing so, consider the impacts and activities that are already known to affect the matter of concern, and who undertakes and regulates them. Different government and nongovernment actors may be relevant to different CIRCle Framework functions. Cast a wide net. When considering laws, regulations and policies, one or more of the following types might be relevant:

- Those that focus on protecting the matter of concern, for example, endangered species laws, protected area laws, or water resources planning laws;
- Those that focus on impacts generally, or specific kinds of impacts, for example, laws that control pollution, or require environmental impact assessment;
- Those that relate to specific kinds of activities, for example, mining laws, or land development laws; or
- Those that focus on governance or institutions that are relevant to a function, or that otherwise indirectly influence the matter of concern, for example, laws that provide for intergovernmental coordination, or an environmental data repository.

Look beyond narrow "regulation": Make sure that the rules you identify are not restricted to "regulation" in the narrow sense of rules that mandate changes in behavior. Relevant rules may also provide for collecting relevant data or coordinating between government actors, for example.

Sources of rules: As well as formal domestic law, consider whether customary, Indigenous, and international laws may be relevant. Also consider existing rules in which government is not involved – state rules should be designed not to undermine other effective rules.

[2] A complete review would also consider the laws, regulations, and policies that might *pose barriers* to dealing with the cumulative environmental problem or create drivers of activities that impact your matter of concern. This book and these guidelines focus on improving the support offered by regulation that is expressly aimed at the problem.

Rules in these different categories inherently may focus more or less on certain CIRCle Framework functions. Being alert to these possible differences can help prioritize functions for analysis, for example:

- laws focused on impacts prime contributors to expect *intervention*, but they may not provide for aggregating *information* across activities and impact types that affect the same matter of concern; this may require *coordination* across regulatory silos (e.g., in relation to water pollution and climate change impacts on the Great Barrier Reef: see Chapter 9); by contrast,
- laws focused on protecting a matter of concern may more clearly *conceptualize* what matters than other laws, but *interventions* may not apply comprehensively to activities that affect the matter of concern: addressing relevant activities comprehensively may require *coordination* and embracing more diverse approaches to intervention.

Jurisdictional boundaries: Responsibility for laws that affect a cumulative environmental problem probably lies with multiple agencies or levels of government. A regulatory designer dealing with one law may not be intimately familiar with others. However, it will not be possible to assess potential regulatory gaps and needs for coördination without looking at the "bigger picture," even if acting on this knowledge will require iterative regulatory change.

Sections 3.2 (Domestic Legal Landscape) and 3.3 (International Legal Landscape) elaborate on major categories of laws that often apply to cumulative environmental problems.

Step 1: Do laws clearly and coherently conceptualize the matter of concern, including elements of it that are important and "goal" conditions or thresholds of acceptable change for those elements?

Regulating a cumulative environmental problem requires clarity about the thing that matters and its important elements, such as its ecological and social elements and its spatial boundaries. This clarity is important so that rules for collecting *information* about it, including the activities and impacts that threaten it, and those that support it, and *intervening* and *coordinating* to address the problem, focus on the right thing, and do so in a coherent way.

Implementing a law to address a cumulative environmental problem may require trade-offs with other policy objectives and perhaps other environment-related matters of concern. **Clarity about what matters is important to ensure that trade-offs are made transparently, and not by arbitrarily or unintentionally**

reconceptualizing what matters if an element is hard to protect. Adjusting what matters in this way can create "shifting baselines," by changing conditions that are deemed acceptable. This can result in neglecting opportunities to use creative options for *intervention* to deal with the real problem.

Ensuring that different laws coherently conceive of what is important and thresholds of acceptable change helps to avoid conflicts and promote synergies in pursuing the same goal.

Clarity about matters of concern can be lacking in emerging areas of environment-related law (e.g., rights of nature), and in contexts that involve human relationships with aspects of the nonhuman environment (e.g., environmental justice; see Chapter 8).

The passage of time sometimes strengthens the value of what matters (e.g., biocultural value of seminatural Alpine grasslands; see Chapter 10); in other cases, values may change. Mechanisms for adapting a conceptualization may be warranted in that case, but watch for shifting baselines.

Key design features of regulatory mechanisms associated with conceptualization:

- Clearly specifying the important biophysical and social elements of the matter of concern, either by specifying them directly or by setting processes for establishing these elements where contestation is likely and debate and additional transparency are required, or where there is uncertainty that first needs to be resolved;
- Clearly specifying threshold conditions for these elements, beyond which any additional impact will be unacceptable and require intervention, or restoration goals for these elements; and
- Providing for adapting a conceptualization of a matter of concern, for example, in response to new information about it.

Integration with other functions (*see* Figure 4.2):

- Rules should provide for generating, sharing and analyzing data and *information* about the condition of important elements of the matter of concern, impacts on those elements, and interventions that deal with those impacts.
- Rules for *intervention* to address impacts on the matter of concern should support reaching the goals specified in rules for conceptualization; intervention may be triggered when conditions approach thresholds of unacceptable change specified in rules for conceptualization.
- *Coordination* between government actors and with nongovernment actors can support articulating what is important about the matter of

concern and reaching shared understanding, including, in settler states, between governments, and Indigenous governments and peoples.

Chapter 4 ("Conceptualization") sets out illustrative examples of legal mechanisms that include these design features, drawn from around the world. The *case study on California groundwater (Chapter 8)* shows how conceptualizing disadvantaged groundwater-dependent communities in different ways changes the interventions that are appropriate to deal with groundwater depletion, where information should be collected, and which agencies need to coordinate to deal with depletion (Chapter 8).

Step 2: Do laws provide for government or nongovernment entities to produce, share, aggregate, and analyze data and information about the matter of concern and threats to it?

Having information about the condition of what we care about, and a comprehensive view of the threats to it, lets us take action to address cumulative impacts to it (*regulatory intervention*). Laws can help build understanding of how impacts interact and aggregate through rules that make information "FAIR" (findable, accessible, interoperable, and reusable). This requires information sharing between public and private entities who hold it. Some contexts require integrating information produced outside Western science (e.g., Indigenous knowledge systems, local knowledge), with appropriate protections. Designing interventions also requires information about existing interventions and the circumstances and motivations of contributors to harms and benefits, as for policy problems in general.

It can be easy to overlook some kinds of threats and impacts. A comprehensive picture includes impacts of: (1) activities that are regulated and lawfully undertaken; (2) activities that are regulated but carried out unlawfully; (3) activities that are not subject to regulation; and (4) "background" factors that affect a matter of concern but are difficult to attribute to an individual actor or action, for example, climate change or the spread of invasive species. Information about each is necessary to address cumulative impacts.

Key design features of regulatory mechanisms associated with information:

- Providing for allocating and reducing costs associated with collecting, sharing, aggregating, and analyzing data and information;
- Guiding requirements for high-quality data and information and analysis;

- Providing for sharing privately held data relevant to a cumulative environmental problem; and
- Standardizing data to ensure interoperability.

Integration with other functions (*see* Figure 5.2):

- Rules for collecting data and information about the matter of concern should correspond to its important elements, aligned with rules for *conceptualization*.
- Rules for information should link that information to *intervention*, for example, triggering intervention when information reveals that the matter of concern is unacceptably declining or is predicted to do so, and facilitating decision-making with incomplete information to avoid "paralysis by analysis."
- *Coordination* between regulatory actors and stakeholders can support sharing information, and developing standard data collection and analysis methods to make sure that information can be aggregated to reveal cumulative impacts. It can also increase the legitimacy of the information.

Chapter 5 ("Information") sets out illustrative examples of legal mechanisms that include these design features, drawn from around the world. The *Great Barrier Reef case study (Chapter 9)* shows how a regulatory mechanism that focuses mostly on information – a strategic assessment – can influence intervention to address ecological decline in a multilevel government context that deals with diverse actors and impacts.

Step 3: Do laws provide for intervening to ensure cumulative impacts do not exceed acceptable levels? Do laws use diverse regulatory modes for intervention? Do they consider other intersecting problems?

Rules can influence behavior that causes harm in different ways. Major well-known approaches are "sticks," "carrots," and "sermons" (see Figure 11.2). In an environmental context, we can add the further option of "state rescue": where government acts directly to address harm instead of trying to change the behavior of the many actors that cause it. Each of these is here termed a "regulatory" approach in the sense that it can be supported by formal rules (e.g., a prohibition, a stewardship payment, a requirement to publish information, or a statutory power to undertake certain works).

But this is only half of the intervention story: **The other half of the intervention story is considering how the rule affects the harm.** It may

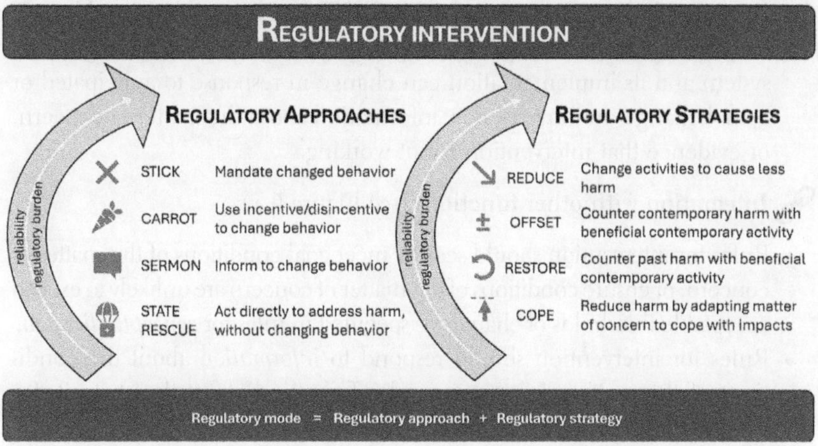

FIGURE 11.2 A "menu" of regulatory modes for intervening to address a cumulative environmental problem

directly reduce harm, offset harm, repair legacy harm, or help the matter of concern to cope, lessening the harm even though impacts stay the same (e.g., finding an alternative water supply for a town that has lost access to groundwater due to overpumping).

Combining regulatory approaches and strategies produces a menu of possible regulatory modes to "mix and match" for a given context (see Figure 11.2, and Chapter 6 for examples).

Since diverse actors and activities contribute to a cumulative environmental problem, and the nature of impacts can vary, using varied regulatory modes can help match these diverse circumstances. Combining different modes can also help balance different advantages and disadvantages. Some options may be less reliable in influencing behavior, but more palatable to governments and contributors to harms and benefits (e.g., regulatory carrots compared to sticks). Others may be more reliable but pose a greater regulatory burden (e.g., a strategy to reduce harm rather than offset it).

Key design features of regulatory mechanisms associated with regulatory intervention:

- Connecting decision-making so that individual activities or types of impact are not considered in isolation;
- Comprehensively addressing impacts, so that few or no actions, including small actions that could cause cumulatively significant impacts, are unaddressed (though different modes of intervention might be used for different types of actions);

- Keeping administrative costs associated with intervention manageable; and
- Intervening in an anticipatory and adaptive way, so that the regulatory system and its implementation can change in response to anticipated or actual changes in impacts, new information about the matter of concern, or evidence that intervention is not working.

Integration with other functions (*see* Figure 6.1):

- Rules for intervention should seek to meet goal conditions of the matter of concern, or ensure conditions of the matter of concern are unlikely to exceed acceptable thresholds of change, as specified in rules for *conceptualization*.
- Rules for intervention should respond to *information* about the conditions of the matter of concern, and information about threats to it, for which rules provide.
- Rules for *coordination* between key actors can help ensure interventions are connected (so that individual harms are not considered in isolation or in silos), comprehensive, not mutually undermining, and take account of intersecting environmental problems.

Chapter 6 ("Intervention") sets out illustrative examples of legal mechanisms that include these design features, drawn from around the world. *Two case studies (Chapters 9 and 10)* analyze how the respective legal regimes for dealing with cumulative environmental problems combine different regulatory modes for intervention.

Step 4: Do laws provide a framework for relevant government and nongovernment actors to coordinate in general, or in relation to conceptualization, information, or intervention?

Large-scale cumulative environmental problems can make it difficult for the numerous and diverse contributing actors to participate as individuals in problem-solving. Accordingly, the focus here is on rules that structure repeated interactions between and across levels of government and with nongovernmental actors, where those actors represent groups of individual contributing actors or other stakeholders. Rules for coordination to address a cumulative environmental problem support comprehensiveness, alignment in how different actors undertake key functions, and efficiency by providing repeated opportunities to reveal gaps, new approaches, lack of alignment, and unnecessary duplication.

The function of these rules is to bring relevant actors "to the table," and help create conditions for fruitful interactions. Other factors that are beyond the reach of rules, though, such as power dynamics, resources, and so on, will influence ultimate outcomes.

Coordination comes with its own challenges. Coordinating multiple actors can be expensive, time-consuming, complex, and challenging to maintain, especially in the face of policy "drift" and disagreement. Formalizing coordination through legal mechanisms can bring structure to navigate complexity and provide some stability.

Rules about preemption – where a decision or rule of one level of government prevails over another – do not remove the need for coordination to respond to cumulative environmental problems. These rules tend to apply to inconsistent regulatory *intervention*, rather than *conceptualization* or *information*. Coordination is required across all functions.

Key design features of regulatory mechanisms associated with coordination (*see* Figure 7.2):

- Rules for coordination tend to take two major approaches. One approach is establishing and using an institution as coordinator, often across multiple functions, for example, a general intergovernmental standing committee. Another approach is facilitating coordination through rules, such as a duty of one government actor to cooperate with or consult with another government or nongovernment actor in intervening to address a problem, or a duty to notify or share information with another. Both approaches can support dealing with cumulative environmental problems.
- Coordination mechanisms can expressly provide for dealing with policy "drift" and resolving disputes between regulatory actors where the cumulative environmental problem is regulated by multiple agencies or levels of government.

Integration with rules for other functions: The purpose of rules for coordination is to ensure that coordination among government actors and with nongovernment actors occurs in undertaking the other functions of the CIRCle Framework: conceptualization, information, and regulatory intervention.

Chapter 7 ("Coordination") sets out illustrative examples of legal mechanisms that include these design features, drawn from around the world. The *South Tyrol case study (Chapter 10)* analyzes coordination among regulatory mechanisms for intervention that are used across vertical levels of government, also involving nongovernment actors, to maintain and restore Alpine meadows as biocultural landscapes.

Next steps: Moving from analysis to implementing changes

While it is beyond the scope of this book to discuss implementation issues in any detail, and many others offer analysis that is likely to be as relevant for cumulative environmental problems as for other kinds of problems,[3] a brief word is warranted. Cumulative environmental problems can engage so many laws that **prioritizing reforms to address gaps and weaknesses emerges as a key issue**. Issues such as urgency; political viability; resource constraints; and legal, technical, and administrative barriers are all relevant to consider when prioritizing changes (as they always are). But the special characteristics of cumulative environmental problems point to some additional considerations in prioritizing change:

- Reforms confront the challenge of building consensus (or perhaps grudging acceptance) across many diverse actors. Approaches to building consensus about reforms can be the foundation for enduring **coordination mechanisms. Establishing these mechanisms is likely to be a priority**, since coordination is required across multiple regulatory functions. Formalizing coordination mechanisms may be a relatively easy starting point: They do not directly require anyone to change activities that contribute to the cumulative environmental problem though they may indirectly raise issues about regulatory "territory." Coordinating about information can be an easier entry point for relationship building than starting to talk about intervention or the fine details of conceptualization.
- If dramatic reform is required but is not feasible in the short term, **consider working from what you have**. This might mean collecting better information about compliance with existing rules using simple technology, prioritizing the enforcement of existing rules based on cumulative risk to the matter of concern,[4] or closing loopholes in existing rules.[5] Developing experience with voluntary interventions (carrots and sermons), or with sticks applied to smaller pilot areas, can pave the way for more generally applicable sticks where and if they are required.

3 See, e.g., Karoline S. Rogge and Kristin Reichardt, "Policy Mixes for Sustainability Transitions: An Extended Concept and Framework for Analysis" (2016) 45 *Research Policy* 1620–1635, 1625–1626 (re policy processes and policy implementation); Sebastian Sewerin, Benjamin Cashore and Michael Howlett, "New Pathways to Paradigm Change in Public Policy: Combining Insights from Policy Design, Mix and Feedback" (2022) 50 *Policy and Politics* 442–459 (re paradigmatic policy changes).

4 See, e.g., Table 6.5, row 1.

5 See, e.g., several approaches to this in Section 6.5.2.

- Since cumulative harm is often nonlinear, it can manifest as a step change in the conditions of a matter of concern. **A high-profile incident can be a window of opportunity for reform.** A massive coral bleaching event on the Great Barrier Reef allowed its Marine Park Authority to contemplate greenhouse gas regulation for the first time, albeit in a largely symbolic way, creatively reinterpreting its regulatory jurisdiction.[6] Severe drought, along with other factors, triggered California's inaugural and long-overdue general groundwater management law, which provided the first meaningful path to protect drinking water sources for some disadvantaged communities.[7]

11.5 GUIDE TO THE CASE STUDIES

The case studies in this book are illustrative rather than comparative. Diversity drove their selection. Each case study illustrates different parts of the CIRCle Framework and its application to diverse areas of law and legal mechanisms across diverse jurisdictions (California/United States, Queensland/Australia, South Tyrol/Italy/European Union (EU), see Figure 1.2) and environments (groundwater, the land–sea interface, and mountain grasslands). Each case study focuses on a central legal mechanism that is often advocated to manage cumulative environmental impacts (bold, Table 11.2).

You may find a case study useful to explore a particular regulatory function in more depth, especially if applying the CIRCle Framework through the above-mentioned steps suggests that that function needs special attention. You might also consider a case study if your situation has similar features in terms of a key element of the legal landscape or a similar matter of concern or type of impact (Table 11.2).

11.6 CONCLUDING CROSS-CASE REFLECTIONS

Though they are illustrative, rather than comparative case studies, when taken together, common themes recur and point to issues for further exploration.

11.6.1 *Taking a Panoramic View When Assessing Rules*

The case studies show that assessing rules for dealing with cumulative environmental problems benefits from a panoramic view of relevant laws,[8] rather than

6 See Section 9.5.4, especially n 171 and accompanying text.

7 See Section 8.4.1.

8 E.g., see Sections 8.3 and 8.4 (regulatory landscape relevant to managing groundwater for drinking water in California); Table 9.1 (laws relevant to intervening to address the impacts of coal mining and cattle grazing on the Great Barrier Reef); Table 10.1 (laws relevant to intervening to address grassland degradation in South Tyrol).

TABLE 11.2 *Key elements of case studies selected for diversity of legal mechanisms and environmental contexts*

Case study	Groundwater depletion and environmental justice in California's Central Valley, US	Biodiversity of the Great Barrier Reef, Australia	Alpine grasslands as biocultural landscapes, Italy
Legal landscape for addressing cumulative environmental problem (**major focus**)	**Water resources management plans**, safe drinking water, pollution, environmental impact assessment ("EIA"), land use law	EIA and **strategic assessment**; pollution law; land management standards; greenhouse gas emissions cap; carbon offsets; restoration subsidies	Constitutional protections for landscapes; landscape plans; EIA; protected species and **conservation areas**; farm subsidies; food product certification; farm inheritance law; public acquisition
Levels of governance	State and local laws	International convention, federal and state laws	International conventions, EU, national, provincial and local laws
Matter of concern and impacts in focus	Preventing aggregate withdrawal of water for farms and large cities reducing access to groundwater for vulnerable communities reliant on household or small community wells	Preventing decline in health of the World Heritage Great Barrier Reef due to polluted runoff from catchments and greenhouse gas emissions causing climate change, focusing on catchment grazing and coal mines	Maintaining and restoring biodiverse and culturally valuable Alpine grasslands, countering abandonment of traditional extensive grazing practices and small-scale development
CIRCle Framework functions in focus	Conceptualization and its links to the other CIRCle Framework functions	Information Regulatory intervention Links between intervention and information	Coordination Regulatory intervention Links between coordination and intervention

"tunnel vision" focusing on a single mechanism. This challenges the dominant focus of the scientific literature, at least, on rules for assessing cumulative environmental impacts in the context of environmental impact assessment. The case studies were chosen to explore key mechanisms that practitioners and scholars often advocate as being promising candidates for dealing with cumulative environmental problems. In practice, though, each case study reveals a much wider and sometimes unexpected landscape of laws that deals with the problem in important ways, from laws for groundwater monitoring in California, to minimum land management standards to benefit the Great Barrier Reef, to farm inheritance laws in South Tyrol.

11.6.2 *Local Influences and Vertical Coordination*

The case studies explore problems at very different scales – Alpine grasslands of a few hectares in South Tyrol, to the over five million hectares of the Central Valley in California, to the thirty-eight million hectares of catchments that drain to the equally large Great Barrier Reef. In each context, but in different ways, local factors matter, regardless of the scale of governance. In South Tyrol, local cultural identity links strongly to Alpine grassland landscapes as a matter of concern, producing modern interventions based on centuries-old local norms about inheritance. These norms flow from modern provincial law, administered locally, and operate alongside a complex web of provincially administered EU laws for biodiversity and many other relevant areas of law. In the Central Valley, local agencies set thresholds of acceptable groundwater level decline under state law, but some agencies have overlooked the reliance of disadvantaged local communities on groundwater for drinking water. In some areas, this oversight is escalating supervisory responsibility for interventions from local agencies to the state. Intervention to address the decline of the Great Barrier Reef in the face of climate change and catchment-sourced water pollution requires prioritizing actions at the local scale, such as targeting catchment repairs of highly eroding lands. But a key motivator for this action has been international attention through the Reef's World Heritage listing, which produced a large-scale mechanism for information, a strategic assessment.

In other words, large-scale problems can require legal functions tailored to the local scale, and small-scale problems can be influenced by laws at much higher levels. CIRCle Framework functions can connect these scales. For example, a regime of laws may seek to protect something because it is locally important; gather information about how impacts accumulate at a local scale; calibrate interventions with an eye to local factors that affect how effective those interventions will be; and coordinate stakeholders and agencies from the local to the international.

11.6.3 *Diverse Interventions, Unaddressed Tensions, and Agriculture*

Regulatory approaches have long diversified away from solely using regulatory sticks to change behavior. Carrots, sermons, and state rescue provide other options. Equally, the dominant focus of environment-related law has traditionally been protecting and conserving things (wilderness, species, etc.) by avoiding and reducing harm as the key regulatory strategy. But more recently, environmental legal scholarship has focused favorably on restoration, "rewilding," and repair,[9] more cautiously on offsetting harm through compensatory measures, and less overtly on coping.

Agriculture underscores the importance of taking a wide view of available regulatory approaches and strategies. Food production is a major use of habitable land,[10] and has produced a vast literature on sustainability and policy failures.[11] The analysis here points to the value of understanding the positive and negative environmental impacts of agriculture in a socially informed, place-based way in the context of a wider range of impacts that accumulate to affect specific matters of concern. Agriculture may be crucial to maintaining a matter of concern (traditional grazing that maintains bioculturally valuable grasslands in South Tyrol), produce a proximate cumulative impact on a matter of concern (irrigation that depletes groundwater in the Central Valley), or act as a distant but cumulatively significant influence on a matter of concern (grazing leading to polluted runoff from the Great Barrier Reef catchments). In all cases, *how* agriculture happens matters. This can be a challenge for formal rules based on sticks to reduce harm, given historically minimal intervention in agricultural operations, often supported by political factors and cultural resistance to interference. But the case studies present a combination of interventions that defy traditional lack of legal attention to agriculture, using diverse regulatory approaches and strategies.

Each case study involves laws that aim to both protect the matter of concern by reducing or avoiding harm to it, and by offsetting harm, as well as laws that facilitate restoration. Local agencies advance state rescue measures to help disadvantaged communities in the Central Valley cope with declining groundwater levels caused by pumping for irrigation. Regulatory carrots in the form of carbon credits, water quality credits, and funding for catchment

[9] See, e.g., Afshin Akhtar-Khavari and Benjamin J. Richardson (eds), *Ecological Restoration Law: Concepts and Case Studies* (Routledge 2019).

[10] Hannah Ritchie and Max Roser, "Land Use" (2019, revised 2024), https://ourworldindata.org/land-use.

[11] For a synthesis, see generally, FAO, *The State of Food and Agriculture 2023 – Revealing the True Cost of Food to Transform Agrifood Systems* (2023).

restoration address the impacts of grazing to the Great Barrier Reef, alongside efforts to breed heat-resistant coral that can better cope with climate change. In South Tyrol, international treaties, European, national, and provincial laws provide for restoring Alpine grasslands and maintaining traditional grazing using economic incentives, noneconomic sermons, and regulatory sticks that formalize local cultural norms.

These regulatory modes are adopted for reasons that are pragmatic (carrots are more palatable to government and regulated stakeholders than sticks) and necessary (restoration appropriately recognizes the ongoing effects of legacy impacts). But they raise questions about tensions with harm-reducing strategies, the comprehensiveness of interventions, and the difficulties of connected decision-making to address cumulative impacts. For example, to what extent are investments in restoration carrots reversed by allowing exemptions for activities that cause new harms of the same kind (e.g., governments paying to restore some Alpine grasslands while EU Common Agricultural Policy exemptions allow ongoing destruction) or a different kind (e.g., incentivizing catchment restoration to reduce water pollution to the Great Barrier Reef, while not intervening comprehensively to mitigate greenhouse gas emissions that also threaten the Reef)?

11.6.4 *Establishing and Integrating Functions and Mechanisms Takes Time*

None of the case studies is an unqualified success, but each has important design elements that integrate laws for CIRCle Framework functions to deal with diverse accumulating impacts to a matter of concern. In California's Central Valley, the vehicle for this integration is statutory groundwater planning. The key planning law deals with both the quality and quantity of groundwater in aquifers, but is yet to recognize a broader, cumulative view of environmental justice that has been prominent in environmental laws. In the Great Barrier Reef context, although laws dealing with water quality and greenhouse gas emissions are relatively unconnected, a strategic assessment provided a linking function between mechanisms for information and intervention. By contrast, more diverse laws relevant to South Tyrol's Alpine grasslands (which deal with nature, impact assessment, agriculture, and landscape) are well integrated through express and mutually supportive legislative links.

But in each case, integrating links have taken time to emerge. California's 2014 Sustainable Groundwater Management Act is the state's first comprehensive groundwater legislation, despite a long history of intensive groundwater usage. The first protections for the Great Barrier Reef were enacted half a century ago, but serious legal attention to catchment-sourced diffuse water pollution and greenhouse gas emissions has arisen only relatively recently. Laws for South Tyrol's grasslands build on centuries-old customary norms as well as decades-old treaties and agricultural incentives that have substantially changed in response to criticisms that they did little to address environmental destruction.

This observation about time is both cautionary and encouraging. Impacts accumulating to things that we care about mean that action is often needed urgently. Sometimes impacts are difficult or impossible to reverse. Where does that leave us, if assembling and linking the right tools is so time-consuming? I have argued that the CIRCle Framework functions of conceptualization, information, regulatory intervention, and coordination are all needed and must be integrated. We must look beyond law as a narrow tool to force behavior change (intervention in the form of sticks), to also recognize and use law as a tool to help us decide what matters, understand it, and take broader action to protect or restore it, together. Taking this wider view of law likely means some or even many elements of the toolbox are already in place. The journey has already begun.

Glossary

Term	Definition, as used in this book
CIRCle Framework	The framework of four functions – conceptualization, information, regulatory intervention, and coordination – that this book argues are necessary to address cumulative environmental problems, and which formal rules can support
Conceptualization	A clear understanding of the matter of concern, including elements of it that are important and "goal" conditions or thresholds of acceptable change for those elements; formal rules that relate to conceptualization
Coordination	Repeated interactions between government and nongovernment actors that relate to conceptualization, information, and intervention; formal rules that relate to coordination
Cumulative environmental problem	A situation in which many diverse contributing activities cause impacts (the "thousand cuts" in the title of this book) that aggregate in complex and unpredictable ways over relatively long periods of time, often extending across the boundaries of jurisdictions and legal regimes that deal with single natural resources; this aggregation exceeds acceptable thresholds of change or impact and is thus a problem
Cumulative threshold conditions	Conditions of a matter of concern, beyond which cumulative harm is unacceptable; this is a dimension of conceptualization that is distinct from the idea of ecological thresholds
Impact	The result of an activity or factor that changes the condition of a matter of concern, either in a negative or positive way

(*continued*)

(*continued*)

Term	Definition, as used in this book
Information	Knowledge about the matter of concern or threats to it, which may derive data produced using Western scientific methods and sources or other sources (e.g., traditional, local, and Indigenous knowledges), and rules to address it; formal rules that relate to information
Integrated regulatory functions	Mutually supportive links between functions in the CIRCle Framework – conceptualization, information, regulatory intervention, and coordination – within and between laws relevant to protecting a matter of concern from cumulative harm
Intervention (or regulatory intervention)	Action that aims to ensure that cumulative harm to a matter of concern does not exceed acceptable levels, or that restoration goals are achieved; formal rules that relate to intervention, which influence behavior of the state or those undertaking contributing activities
Law	Used in a wide sense to refer to formal government rules, including those in legislation adopted by a national or subnational parliament or congress or local government, regulations and other rules made by executive agencies
Legal mechanism	A provision or set of provisions in a law that deals with conceptualization, information, intervention, or coordination; used interchangeably with "regulatory mechanism"
Matter of concern	The thing that is affected by the accumulation of impacts; the focus of our concerns and the regulatory inquiry at the center of this book. It might be a nonhuman biophysical thing (e.g., a forest, body of water, or airshed) or a link between humans and an aspect of the nonhuman environment (e.g., a "healthy environment" for people, specific ecosystem services, or a culturally valued relationship between a community and a special place).

Index

Pages in italics indicate references to a table or figure.

Printed by Integrated Books International,
United States of America